MAN OF MANY FRONTIERS

THE DIARIES OF "BILLY THE BEAR" IAEGER

edited by
Dr. Allen Shepherd, Belvadine R. Lecher,
Lloy Chamberlin and Marguerite Radcliffe

Making History

Omaha, Nebraska
1994

MAN OF MANY FRONTIERS:
THE DIARIES OF "BILLY THE BEAR" IAEGER

Second Printing, 1994.
Page layout and typesetting by *Making History*.
Cover design by Shelly Bartek.

ISBN 0-9631699-3-9 25.00

For reproduction permissions or current ordering information, write or call *Making History*, 2415 N. 56th Street, Omaha, Nebraska 68104 (telephone 402-551-0747).

TABLE OF CONTENTS

Louis John Frederick Iaeger ("Billy the Bear")

Preface

It is said that history belongs to the intrepid, and Louis John Frederick Iaeger (also known as "Billy the Bear") was, without a doubt, bold and adventuresome. On sea and on land, he helped shape the character of the West in the late nineteenth and early twentieth centuries. Schooled as a navigator and eager to see the world, Iaeger sailed on the clipper *St. John* in 1874 with the same zest for adventure that had spurred Christopher Columbus and Vasco da Gama. On land, "Billy the Bear" tried his hand as a writer, actor, cowboy and gold miner before he finally settled in the raw frontier town of Chadron, Nebraska, in the 1880s. The detailed and colorful diaries that he kept throughout his adventures mirror the richness and turbulence of an America that was then coming of age.

Louis John Frederick Iaeger's diaries came to light in 1990 when Elizabeth Iaeger, widow of the author's youngest son Richard, moved to Chadron, Nebraska, and donated the diaries in her possession to the Dawes County Historical Society. She had five of them: One covered Iaeger's sea voyage of 1874; four chronicled his early Chadron years, from 1885 until 1890. We do not know whether he wrote others.

The five diaries presented here are broken and incomplete in nature, but we do not know if this stems from Iaeger's irregularity in keeping his journals or if it is a result of a loss over time of sections of the manuscript. Although Chapter I (the text of the sea diary) clearly indicates he recorded that one to send to his sister once he safely arrived in San Francisco, we do not know if he wrote the subsequent diaries with the same intent. Did he keep them simply as his own personal record of events? Did he mean to publish? We may never know the answer.

Shortly after the diaries were donated to the Dawes County Historical Society, Belvadine Lecher (then President of the Society) examined the recent acquisition and quickly saw the diaries for what they are—an extremely valuable primary source of information about various aspects of American history in the last quarter of the nineteenth century and the first quarter of the twentieth. Then the idea of publishing the diaries developed, so that the public, from scholars to general readers, could share these resources. Funding from the Nebraska Humanities Council, the C. A. Story Foundation and the Dawes County Historical Society ultimately made the publication possible.

Many people have played a role in bringing the diaries of "Billy the Bear" to print. Belvadine Lecher, Marguerite Radcliffe and Lloy Chamberlin devoted themselves to transcribing the original diaries. Lecher, the project coordinator, gathered information about the Iaeger family, and both Karen Schlais and Nina Plein contributed valuable family perspectives. Dr. Allen Shepherd, Professor of History at Chadron State College, researched periods for which no diaries are available and composed historical chapters chronicling Iaeger's life to connect the diary chapters. Several of Dr. Shepherd's colleagues at Chadron State College read his chapters and gave advice on style, content and interpretation.

Joanne Hulseman provided word-processing expertise. Dr. Martha Ellen Webb and her staff at Making History checked the transcription against the original, edited introductory and intermediate chapters, typeset, and directed the printing and binding.

Throughout, our editorial policy has been to invade Iaeger's diaries as little as possible. Like the famous explorer-journalists Meriwether Lewis (1774-1809) and William Clark (1752-1818), "Billy the Bear" was not the best speller. He often put down his ideas in tortured syntax. His penchant for incorrect capitalization would drive an English teacher to despair. Even so, we have left his diaries with all of their original linguistic blemishes—and with their historical richness. We might have edited seemingly endless repetitions out. His penchant for "weather reports" is at times mind-numbing. His jotting down of local minutia sometimes is distracting. His comments on race, gender, and party seem prejudicial in today's world. Agreed. Even so, we left the text in its original form. What appears here is "Billy the Bear's" story *as he wrote it.* We have retained his wording, spelling, grammar and capitalization. We removed nothing, but where meaning was unclear or where people, incidents or terms needed explanation, we have added bracketed clarification or footnotes. All illustrations included are the property of the Dawes County Historical Society, Inc., except that of the *St. John,* which is shown through the courtesy of the Mystic Seaport Museum, Inc., Mystic, Connecticut.

Louis John Frederick Iaeger's diaries, we are sure, will be a delight for both the professional historian and the general reader, for anyone who revels in the raw substance of history and wants to hear it first-hand, from an eye-witness. "Billy the Bear" will both educate *and* entertain you! Enjoy!

The Iaeger family coat of arms

Introduction
by Dr. Allen Shepherd

The life of Louis John Frederick ("Billy the Bear") Iaeger spanned the years from 1856 to 1930. His entry into American history came during the decade before the Civil War. It was a time fraught with the turmoil that accompanied the crucial issue of slavery in the United States. His life ended in a greatly changed America—one just entering "The Great Depression."

Iaeger was born in Berks County, Pennsylvania, on April 10, 1856. His ancestors were of German stock; his great grandfather reportedly was the spiritual advisor to Prussian Emperor Frederick the Great. "Billy the Bear's" grandfather, Rev. G. F. I. Iaeger, a Lutheran minister, helped settle Pennsylvania. Louis's father, Charles S. Iaeger, a carriagemaker in Hamburg, Pennsylvania, was killed in an accident when Louis was five. When his mother died two years later from injuries suffered in the same mishap, Louis, his three brothers and one sister were left without parents. After their parents' deaths, the children lived with relatives for several years.

At age ten, Louis was invited by a wealthy uncle to come to Arizona. "Don Diego," as uncle Louis John Frederick Iaeger was called by relatives of his Spanish wife, had left Pennsylvania in 1849, lured by the gold

1

rush in California. Reaching San Francisco, he worked as a carpenter before joining a company which organized a ferry at Yuma, Arizona, in 1850. "Billy the Bear's" uncle operated this ferry business until the coming of the Southern Pacific Railroad in 1877.

Young Louis travelled to live with his uncle in Yuma via the perilous Central American route. There he attended a Spanish school with his cousins and learned to navigate his uncle's ferry boats across the Colorado River.

Louis returned to Pennsylvania in 1870 and lived with his sister Lenora and her husband, John Vandersloot. At the age of sixteen, Louis passed the entrance exams for Annapolis Naval Academy, but due to an ear problem he was not admitted. Refusing to be denied a career at sea, he soon passed the New York Nautical Academy exam; two years later Iaeger also was awarded his navigator's certificate. Smitten with a spirit of adventure, the young man then signed on in New York as a sailor with the W. W. Grace Company which transported California grain between Liverpool, England, and San Francisco.

The ship "Billy the Bear" first was assigned to was the *St. John*. His adventure on this ship forms the content of the first part of his diary, Chapter I below. His writings call to mind John Masefield's hauntingly evocative poem, "Sea Fever."

> I must down to the seas again, to the lonely sea
>   and the sky,
> And all I ask is a tall ship and a star to steer her
>   by,
> And the wheel's kick and the wind's song and
>   the white sail's shaking,
> And a grey mist on the sea's face and a grey
>   dawn breaking.

I must down to the seas again, for the call of the
running tide
Is a wild call and a clear call that may not be
denied;
And all I ask is a windy day with the white
clouds flying,
And the flung spray and the blown spume, and
the sea-gulls crying.

I must down to the seas again to the vagrant
gypsy life,
To the gull's way and the whale's way where the
wind's like a whetted knife;
And all I ask is a merry yarn from a laughing
fellow-rover,
And quiet sleep and a sweet dream when the
long trick's over.[1]

The sea chapter, which is the first entry in the
diary of "Billy the Bear" Iaeger, covers May to October
1874. It has much of the same flavor that writers-of-the-
sea Richard Henry Dana, Jr., Herman Melville, Joseph
Conrad, Charles Bernhard Nordhoff and J.N. Hall
imparted in their works. Nautical terms such as "fore"
and "aft," "port" and "starboard," "quarterdeck" and
"forecastle" pepper their narratives. Iaeger succumbed
to the same lure of the sea; his characters are equally as
colorful; his shipboard experiences are as fascinating;
and he displayed the same penchant for adventure.

But, in the end, "Billy the Bear" yearned for
home, for land, for security, and consoled himself by
reading the *New Testament* and writing the first section
of his diary for his sister Lenora. If Iaeger in the end

---

[1]John Masefield, "Sea Fever," in *Salt-Water Ballads* (New
York: Macmillan Company, 1916), pp. 59-60.

was a land-lubber at heart and not cut out for the sea, it
in no way diminishes the worth of his sea account.

When Iaeger embarked on his sea journey in
1874, the United States was changing. Post-Civil-War
America provided a wealth of opportunity for adventure
on land and sea. Ferdinand de Lesseps's Suez Canal
recently had wrought major changes in world traffic
patterns, and the completion of the first transcontinental
railroad on May 10, 1869, at Promontory Point, Utah,
had eased land transit between the two seas. During his
lifetime, Iaeger saw the change from wooden to iron
ships, from sail to engine propulsion, from the horse to
the automobile. He saw the Wright brothers' invention
conquer the skies. He also witnessed the Westward
Movement, the demise of the Indians, and America's
shift from rural to urban life.

Yet "Billy the Bear" was not just an observer of
these changes. He participated in many of them.
Luckily for us, he recorded his perceptions, thoughts,
hopes and fears. We historians are indebted to people
like Iaeger, for without memoirs, diaries and personal
accounts, the pages of history would be drab indeed.
Their writings allow historians to more accurately
reconstruct bygone eras. The Roman Emperor Marcus
Aurelius's *Meditations,* Englishman Samuel Pepys's
diary, and Benjamin Franklin's *Autobiography* contain
material that adds invaluable dimension to our
understanding of the times in which they lived.

"Billy the Bear" Iaeger was no Marcus Aurelius.
Neither was he a Pepys nor a Franklin. He ruled no
Empire and was high in no political reign. He helped
found no Republic, only a small Nebraska town. Yet his
diaries, limited as we have them to two short periods of
his life, give us fresh insight into Gilded Age America.
In them we find the passions of "every man and every
woman," alongside local evidence of the forces shaping
American society from 1856 to 1930.

The **St. John** was a 1885-ton, record-setting sailing ship built in Bath, Maine.

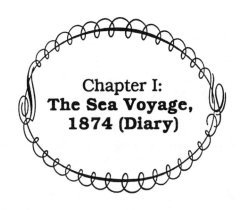

Chapter I:
The Sea Voyage, 1874 (Diary)

In The Dock, Stream And Ocean.
New York may 14th 1874
by L.J.F. Iaeger

May 14[.] Signed Ships papers at Sailor Exchange in company with the 2nd mate. Steward & Cook Stayed away till 6 came on board and Swept-decks, after that I cleaned my Self and went up to St. Nicholas to See J. J. Vandersloot of York my Bro in Law. after a final settlement he gave me $21.00[.] I went over to the Jersey Side with him to See him of[f]. He started 1/4 of 9 in the evening[.] I came home & Sleept at No. 9 east 9th St., N.Y. [I]n the morning of the 14 I stowed 21 Barrels potatoes for the Ships provisions.

[May] 15[.] I went and got a mattrass for $3.00[,] a Tin Basin[,] a plate[,] a fork[,] a knife[,] a Strap[,] a oil coat & hat[,] a flat iron[,] 2 lead pencil[,] 3 pairs gloves[,] Spoon[,] also my chest [and] had great trouble to get it. Came aboard and helped to Stow Stores[.] Felt tired but got good grub[.]

[May] 16[.] Cloudy and alternate rained[.] worked hard[,] got all wet[, and] helped to wash decks[.] 1, 2, & 3rd mates were drunk. worked hard all day but good grub.

[May] 17[,] Sunday[.] layed off[.] put thing[s] to rights in my chest[.] 1st mate Said our orders to us.

[May] 24[.] Never had time to post up[.] I am compelled to work hard all night and day only getting 8 hours sleep every other day out of 24. The grub is now very bad and only am allowed 1 1/3 pints of water per day. Am very Sea Sick and have been so for the past week. I have repented to You many a night Dear Sister for the wrongs done you and have prayed to God for forgiveness of the Same as well as for a Safe Journey[.] I find He is my only friend at Sea & on land. The Grub is <u>very</u> bad and I am as dirty as a pig because I have no Salt Water Soap[.] I feel as if I was now being reminded of what you always said to me, disobedience. O had I only obeyed You and Taken Your advice. a kind Sister like You can never be found[.] all this I am going to tell you to let you know the True Sentiments of my heart[.] I will now humble my Self and do as I am told when on land again for to Sea I will never in my life go again[,] as We are only 6 days out I have already learnt a lesson which I Shall never forget and feel as if I had been out 4 months[.] O that the lord may Spare my life till I again can See You to ask Your Forgiveness with my heart which is impossible for the pen to do[.] When We are not working, we are obliged to Walk around the Ship all the time for 8 hours at a time and then are allowed 4 hour[s] Sleep[.] I have already made up my mind not to go to Sea anymore but lea[r]n Something Else. I may go to Texas and go in the Cattle Business[.] I have as yet not decided altogether and it will be hard to do So till I get to "Frisco[.]" O had I only a pint of milk and Some peaches or a piece of pie or a good piece of Veal[,] all of which I made fun of while with you but would give my right arm now for the same. O dear Sister forgive me for what I have wronged You[,] for God Sake do[,] and know that it was not Sound Sense that done So. Advice is good but Experiance is better[.] I have not eaten any thing for 8 meals and feel weak[.] The Captain is a

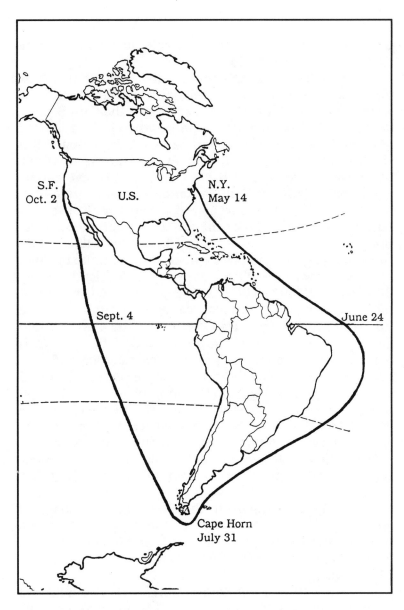

S.F.
Oct. 2

U.S.

N.Y.
May 14

Sept. 4

June 24

Cape Horn
July 31

*The route of the **St. John***

Gentliman but his Officers are Bruits and do any thing to put you to discomfitor[.]

May 27[.] Dear Sister it is my watch Below now for 4 hours and I will try to tell You everything I can the sligh[t]est chance I get[.] We are now in the Gulf Stream of the Bahamas' Islands. Fine weather but as usual I am Sea Sick and can eat but little. O Dear Sister this was the best thing could of happened to me as it will learn me a lesson to Obey. Could I only eat ashore again for instance at Aunt Amanda Bergers where I felt so much at home. I have cryed many a night over my Foolish folly and only for the love of god forgive me dear Sister which I hope You will do. I read my Bible but all the folks laugh at me but I will keep on in Spite of them all. I am now at the 2nd chapter of St Marks[,] having finished St. Matthew[.] I also find that god is a great relief to me in my Troubles. We will not Stop anyplace till we get to Frisco unless the rest of the Crew Should get Sick (of which there are now 2)[.] I have decided never again to go to Sea[,] to take Your advice and be a good and obedient Boy[.] I may Come home in about 1 or 2 years if I can get any money of my own in that time[.] please dont Worry about me. I wish I had a Water Mellon now or Some Strawberries. We are now again Tacking and I so must Stop, will write as soon as I can Slip another Such a fine chance[.] So Adew <u>Dearest</u> and <u>only</u> <u>Sister</u> and <u>forgive</u> Your <u>Bad</u> <u>Bro</u> <u>Louis</u>[.]

[May] 27[,] again in the Evening[.] fine day[.] I feel bad[.] The Capt. Spoke to me a little. We done much work today[.] I feel tired and wish I was in Frisco[.] I am anxious to get to texas where more of my money lies[.]

[May] 28[.] Dear Sister I have again leisure[.] We have not had much wind to day Thence making little progress. I was platting Manilla all day on deck. The Captain Caught a Fish to day, called A "Bueneto" But it only went into the Cabin. I thought I of course I could

not have any, but thought it no harm in getting around
the "Cook" (Which luckily is a good Chinaman) So I told
him that when ever He wanted Wood or Coal just to
come to me to which he Said all right and which put
him at once in a good humor[.] So when I went to the
Galley for my Supper What do you think I Saw on my
plate but a nice piece of Browned Fish with french fried
potatoes (cut in three side[s] and fried in lard like at 512
North 7th Phila.) all for me, and which my Chum (Boy
No. 2, I being No. 1) did not get any of[.] So I had the
first good Supper Since I left No. 9 East 9th Street N.Y.
where my meals were all put up in French Styles. I
dont expect to have another Fish Supper for a long time
unless the Captain Should Catch one again or Some
Sailor give me a hook, an article which I have not my
Self and for which the Mate wants $400 for one and
which price I will delay till in Frisco and do without
Fish[,] Though my chum has just now arrived with a
good Fishline but no hook[.] I will try again for a hook[.]
I have read 8 chapters in St. Mark to day[,] being now at
the 10 chapter[.] I love to read and I find the Bible
Consoles me much on the long Voyage[.] God is my
Strength and my Redeamer[.] fine weather[.] adew
good night and Forgive Your Bro Louis of his Wrongs to
his only Sister[.] kiss Bonny & Cassie for me.

[May] 29[,] 8.30 am[.] I just Turned in to Stay till
12 when my watch is out on deck again[.] it is fine
weather now and but little wind[.] I feel all well[.] I had
another piece of Fish for my Breakfast this morning
through the good graces of the Cook[,] as all [also] 3
boiled potatoes and some Bread. I feel dirty. I am now
at the Twelfth chapter of St Mark[.] Sister dont pay Mrs
Mayor the money as that Note is false it not being my
Correct Signitature.

[May 29,] 7 oclock [p]m. it is now my watch on
deck and I am just taking the time to write[.] I feel tired
and Sleepy. I had a good Supper (that is for a sea one)

but no more fish[.]   it is fine and very little wind blowing[.]

[May] 31[,] Sunday. Sister, I did not get time to post Yesterday as I was to busy. Suffice to Say that today is a fine day but we had to Clean Brass Work all this morning[.] I Jist got through with my dinner[.] I feel very dirty and mean and wish I were on Shore again but never mind[.] The end to this is Some place and we will find it yet at last. It is very warm and very little wind ablowing[.] I opened for the first time my Clothes from the Tailor[.] I Sewed a little this morning and Shaved my Self at dinner for the Second time. This is now the Second Sunday out and I only hope we will get around the Cape all Safe as that Seems now to be the Universal anxiety of the "Crew[.] "

June 1[.] Dear Sister I have not much time to write as the Bell now Strikes. Just think[,] 2 week[s] on Sea nearly[.]

[June 1,] 6.30 Pm[.] Just got done [with] my Supper[.]   I Still feel hungry[.]   We have now got Company (Sea Company)[,] the Ship Elisia McNeil from Baltimore having caught up with is [us] and came So close as to allow a continual Chat between the 2 Captains who know each other well[.]   We Still are together[,] with the St John a Ship length ahead[.] it is fine weather and I am compelled to cheer up as 4 months is a long time[.] I will now Read in my Bible again[.]

[June] 2[,] 8.45 am. We are now out 15 days[.] I Just got done reading the bible[.] I am in Luke now at chapter 3. Just finish my breakfast. I feel Sleepy but always like to post So that you may know what is going on. our Company Ship is Still in Sight[,] we being behind. [At] 12.30 P.M the Captain went on board of the other Ship and Stayed till 7 or 8 this evening[.] [At] 7.30 P.M. the Captain came on board of the St John[.] He had a package with him. He went and returned all Safe[.]

[June] 3[.] Sister I had a good long dream. In it I thought I was Standing on the North West Corner of Penn and Main Streets of York where I was consulting with Willie Miller and Johnny Berby about Phenias Palmer who I though[t] had removed to where the new Shoe factory is Situated[.] I also thought I Saw Amanda Laucks Standing in their door way Smileing but all at once I thought that you were again Stationed with Aunt Catherine as in 1867 and I thought I had left that house on account of the known trouble but had forgotten a Neck tie for which I went back[,] I thought[,] in the afternoon while Aunt C. was out and I thought you let me in and I at once proceeded in the hall on Uncle Louis'es floor and there I thought Stood a looking glass whence I proceeded to fasten my neck tie, but all this time dreading the arrival of Aunt C.[,] and all at once I thought She had come and was already coming up the front Stairs where She Saw me and called to me to Stay[,] that She would over look all past troubles. but it Seems there was no Stop in me, for having left my hat on the Rack down Stairs I thought I picked up a nice new one and ran through the house when I thought I went out by a large back door and also there was an Iron fence gateway[.] while I was running out, I thought Aunt C had Sent you after me to tell me to Come back, but I would not do it[.] And all at once Some fellow hollowed [hollered] 8 Bells in my ears which ment 12 oclock at night and go on watch till 4[.] This Music put a Stop on all further dreaming[.] [At] 10.45 the Captain of the Elizia McNeil came aboard and Stills [still] remains. We are having fine Weather. I Spent the Greater part of my watch out this morning aloft. I may yet make up my mind to keep on the Sea but not in this Vessel[.] I will now read my Bible as 3 Bells will Soon again take me on deck[.]

[June] 4[,] 8.50. a.m. Dear Sister last night we had a hard time of it as all hands were required to handle the Ship and in Consequence I got very little

Sleep[.] I feel Sleepy now but must yet mend Some articles before I can turn in[.] our "Companion" [h]as not left us yet. We are now having a moderate fair wind and Steering S.W.

June 5[.] We are 185 miles of[f] the Cost [coast] of Africa being obliged to go that far East to Strike the Trade Winds[.] I am now at the 6th Chapter of St Luke. Why did you not put my Slate in my chest[?]

[June] 5[,] 6.30. PM. Our Companion is now out of Sight on account of good winds. We are having a fine breeze. We tacked Ship once to day[.] I have done my days work and am retired till 8 when I have to go on deck till 12 again[.] I am glad Sunday is again near. I find God has Answered my prayers and I will do my best not to forsake him as I know he will not me[.] My arms are all blistered from the Sun and the Soules of my feet all Scorched and yet I must on.

"The Sailor Boy"
"Though the Strained mast Should"
quiver as a reed, and the rent Canvass
fluttering Strew the Gale,
still must I on

—Byron

[June] 6[,] 6.25 P.M. Just got my Supper. We Scoured Brass Work all afternoon. My feet pain me much. It rained a little this morning hence I washed my-self[.] We tacked Ship this morning at 5 oclock[.] O how I wish I were ashore[!] The Grub is not So good as it has been. Nevertheless my chum & I Succeeded in getting a piece of Sea pie but it tasted not like Grand-mother Slenkers. Tomorrow I expect to change some of my clothing, as many as I can Spare[.] I must now go as my watch is on deck waiting for me So goodnight. I am at the tenth chapter of St Luke now. adew and kiss Dear little Bonny for me also Cassie[.] also remember me to Abb Elliott[.]

June 7[.] Sunday has again come and with it the Work of cleaning the Brass Work around the Ship[,] a thing which is done every Sunday on board of this Ship[.] My Watch is below now till 8 oclock it being now 7.20 A.M. I will have breakfast at 7.30 and go to work at 8. where the port watch leaves off and finish all the work or work till 12.30, when the Starbord watch relieves us for one hour to get our dinner after which all hands must go to work till 5.30 P.M.[,] It being the rule not to have watch and watch in the afternoons[.] In fact it is a Sin and a Shame how a Sailor is made to work from morning till night and being Treated like a Brute at that[.] it is now time for breakfast So I will go[.]

[June 7,] 1.30 P.M. We got through Cleaning brass at 10 oclock after which I mended my Stockings and washed and dressed my Self. The weather is unusually Calm[.]

[June] 8[,] 9 AM[.] Dear Sister I am again in my room. I had my Breakfast after having Scoured the poops brass works but Alas just before our watch retired from deck the first Mate knocked down one of our men and kicked and tread on him to Such an extent as to cause a fright full looking face to look upon and hardly had this man got doctored up before a man in the port-watch took a fit which occupied 6 men to hold him for a Considerable time. It Seems that when-ever he is Struck that a little afterwards he is Subject to the fits and the Mate Struck him this morning also hence the fit[.] I will now turn to Sleep of which I am much in need of. I just read the 12 chapter of St Luke. I also have cleand my Teeth 2 times Since on the Ocean. It is useless for me to try and get Navigation as I find no one will take the time to learn me[.] the Captain refused me aid 2 time already[.]

June 8[,] 6[:]30[.] This Afternoon I was again Sent aloft at 2 oclock and remained out of Sight off the deck all afternoon[.] I feel very tired from having had to Sit on ropes So long[.] the Sailor I was aloft with was So carefull that I Should not fall that he tied a rope around my waist and made it fast to him Self Say[ing] that he would have to go before me. he never took his eyes from me all afternoon[.] He is a frenchman having been 14 years too Sea[,] hence experience[d.]

[June] 9[.] This morning all hands were aroused out of bed to tack Ship again which is a hard Job. I have made Sennet[2] all day almost. I feel Sick now again in my stomach. 4 of this crew are in bed. Sister you know not what kind of work is found for us men to do[.] there are things accomplished on board of this Ship which would almost Seem to puzzel Christ himself.

[June] 11[.] These last 3 days I have been very tired and busy So I had no time to post up[.] Suffice to Say that I am always thinking you would go crazy Should you know how I was Situated[.] I always thought Sea life was Splendid but I find it is horrid[.] Stay I cannot[,] at least not So far[.] I am crazy to get ashore again and when I get there I will take your advice. Sister I find you omitted a great many things of mine for the Chest which would now come handy but I do not believe you done it on purpose for I now come to See and am compelled to admitt that you done everything for my own good.

[June] 13[,] 6.20 P.M. You will See that I have not posted for the last day. The reason of which is we were too busy in fact I have made So much Sennet that my fingers are all Skin bear [bare,] the raw flesh being in Sight[.] I am hardly able too move them but nevertheless I am compelled to[.] I have now got the Master you always Spoke off—Just at this very moment the Cook calls me in the kitchen (after supper) and gives me 3 pieces of fine mush with molasses[,] also 2 fine pieces of Brown Bread[.] We are as yet not across the Equator. it is blowing a fine Breeze for sailing at present. We make about 10 to 10-1/2 knots an hour (1

---

[2]Sennet, a flat cordage used on ships, is made by plaiting strands of rope or other fiber together.

knot to a mile)[.] this ship is full of Cock Roaches. hence difficulty to keep anything. Sister You used to Say I cursed So hard[.] it is for that one reason why I Say you would go crazy Should you know how I was Situated[.] I always had an idea I could curse a little but I find I am a Saint too these officers on this ship. to morrow is Sunday again making 4 weeks on Sea. I feel well but Should like to be with you again[.] I think I could know how to appreciate Some of your and John's kindness. poor man how I did treat him[!] I only hope to God the man has and will forgive me as I have cryed and prayed many a night over that fatle [fatal] time[.] I intend writing to him on that Same Subject.

[June] 14[.] This morning as usual we Scoured the Brass work while the other Watch was below[.] after that we got breakfast, for which I managed to get an egg. after breakfast I cleaned up our room[,] washed and Shaved my self[,] put on a clean Shirt and pare of pants[,] changed my Stockings[,] combed my hair and actualy I hardly knew my Self any more. I have lent my razor to the mate, he having asked me to do So and for fear of him I complied[.] We are having a moderate wind, but O how I wish I was on Terra Ferma again but never the less everything has an end[.] My neck and hands would now remind you of a Mullatto Bro.

[June] 15[.] This morning we are having a fine wind[.] it is my watch on deck till 12.30 when I turn in till 1[:]30. I must now go[.]—1 p.m. I have just finished my Dinner which consisted of 2 Table Spoon fulls of Sour-crout and a piece of Salt Beef. I must however tell you my last nights dream. It seemed to me as if I were a General in the Roman Army[.] I thought I was higher in rank than Ceaser, and it Seemed to me that I had millions and millions of Soldiers under me and that I had come to take Little York but for the Sake of one thing I let it go. and that thing was this. it seemed to me that when I arrived at York I at once proceeded to Centre Square where I thought I told all the people my intention of taking their town, but at the Same Time I thought J. J. V. invited me to dine with him which invatation I accepted at the Same time remembering that my Sister was married to him. and I thought when I arrived at his house that I was told the Joy full news that You had been blessed with a New-born Child which proved to be a Son, and whose name was Thomas Vandersloot[.] having got So far my chim [chum] called 8 Bells in my ear which ended my dreams. any way for the Sake of this little Son I Saved York. The Steward gave me a half piece of Bread with Some butter which was the first butter I have had since I left N. Y.

June 16[,] 8[:]30 am. Our Course now is South East 1/2 East with Easterly winds we are going along moderatly[.] Strange to Say again last night I dreamed of you and the little Baby (Tom)[.] again Last night I thought I was holding it in my Arm and remarked that it looked just like "Bonny." O how I wish I could now See Dear little "Bonny." I am now in again till 12'30. I am at the 22nd Chapter of St. Luke[.]

[June] 17[,] 1.15 P.M. Just got through reading the 22nd Chapter of Luke, after a strong dinner. I have been busy oilyng the Walnut gratings on the main poop [deck]. what do you Suppose I am doing on board of this Ship in my leisure time[?] Why I am Teaching our Chinaman Cook how to read. dum is no name for him but after Several weeks of pain full Study I have Suceceded in getting him to remember the a.b.c as far as G where he makes a blank Stop. I don't know nor cur [care] how much he can read as long as he gives me good grub for my trouble[.] to tell the Truth good grub at Sea is an article at which I would turn up my nose on Shore. We are having a moderate wind Steering SE 1/2 E.

[June] 18[,] 10.30 AM. by rights I should be Sleeping. but alas there is no time, for early this morning at 2[:]45 all hands were called on deck to tack Ship[.] there was an awfull Storm, and raining at that[.]

it actually poured. Wet dont talk, for I had just given my oil Skin coat to be fixed when the morning after (this morning) it rained like fury. we were up in the rain from 2.45 am till 8. when the Starboard watch was relieved till 12.30 at which time we will again turn out. Just think I washed my own clothes This morning and[,] Such a wash as it is[,] You just aught to See my White flannel Shirt. The Streaks remind me of Grand Mothers Streaked Cow[.] I have as yet not used my new boots [or] one of the new pair of shoes, however I will be obliged to verry soon[.]

[June] 19[,] 1.30 P.M. On The Ocean in Lat 6°N[.] Today is the first time we have had Watch below on an afternoon[,] it being the rule for all hands to be out from 12 to 5 or 6, but this morning at 8 oclock just as our watch was turning out it actually poured down and oil skins were at once in demand. it continued to rain till 11 oclock so hard that we filled all the Water Casks on board and plenty was allowed to go waste however about 8.30 I found my oil Skins leaking So bad as to wet my clothes underneath So I took Every thing of[f] except my oil Skins and went bare footed. We worked till 12.30 at which time we got hash. I felt bad and cold[,] Shivering like a leaf all wet, however I now have on a dry undershirt and moist pants but I feel like a prince for the time[.] we will again turn out at 4 pm when I hope it will be done raining[.]

[June] 20[,] 9.30 AM. This morning we turned out at 4 again only to work in rain up to our knees till 8 when we went below all our watch to get hash. I have just got through giving myself a fine wash We now having plenty of rain water. I have now hanging over my head to dry one of the red flannel suits[,] two white flannel Shirts[,] 2 gray Shirts (I bought in N.Y.)[,] a pair of pants and coat[,] and 1 pair of pants I have on top of the house in the rain. I have on 1 red flannel suit[,] leaving 2 suits in my chest [and] 6 clean towels[.] my shoes as yet I have not touched[,] having a good pair of gum Boots[.] I feel like being ashore[.] if You wish to write to Irean Baeily I am not aware of their place of Boarding as I did not get time to See them before leaving N.Y. for which you will please apologize to them for me. I can however tell you where his Store is where You can as well direct. Edward Bailey[,] Cor [corner of] Court and State Sts[,] Brooklyn[,] Dealer in Carpets[.] please for god sakes write to her and give your kisses to her little Son Eddie. when you write to me please tell me Mrs Streets directions as She told me in her letter not to send them to 512 but some place else but I could not make it out. however she Said you knew where it was So please tell him[.] also please tell Abb Elliott that I am thinking of him now as also Mary V. My dream last night was all about a party given by Mrs. Lizzie Schald at which I figured among the prominent[.]

5 oclock p.m. a School of porpuses are around the ship[.] the 1st mate had already got his hook and harpoon ready[.] about 3 oclock this afternoon a large Shark came in Sight and actually was so bold as to come along-side of the ship. adew for today[.] thanks to god for a Safe journey So far and I hope he may Conduct us the Same way through the remainder.

[June] 21[.] Today is again Sunday and with it comes rest[.] the Mate did not Succeed in catching a Shark or porpus. last night it rained again making it very unpleasant to stay on deck. Today at dinner there will be a Serch made in the "Forecastle" (where the Sailors Stay) for that little sewing case Mrs Hewston gave me[.] it seems that I was useing it out side when I went in my room to get something and when I came out it was gone. We are having calm weather. I will now proceed to read the 2nd Chapter of St John[.]

[June] 22[,] 9[:]45 am. fine morning[.] a moderate Breeze but Still north of the Equator. You know not what a lesson this will be for me. I think every day what a fool I was. Still I feel comforted to know that my God is with me. I am getting to see my folly when once to late. I will now read a chapter or So in the Bible after which I will sleep. "Would I were with Thee Every day and hour." The cry of mutiny is now among the Sailors and we expect to have a Confusion every watch[,] the 3rd mate being the Objective party[.]

[June] 23[.] This morning the 3rd Mate was found to be missing at 4 oclock. He is supposed to have been thrown overboard. The crew insist that they are being used to[o] bad and will put Some more over the rail if the thing is not Soon Stoped[.] The fact is dear Sister we are treated badly[.]

6.25 p.m. The Melancholy news has just come from the "forecastle["] that 1 man is dead from Treatment received from the first Mate[,] He having been in bed only 24 hours. There are now 3 men sick leaving a surplus of 13 men to work the ship.

[June] 24[,] 9[:]15 AM[.] Today we crossed the Equator 9.15 am[.] This morning we buried the dead sailor after a small prayer and hymn. He was made to slide into the sea like a stone there to lay till "Judgement Day[.]" This occurrence seems not to have the least effect upon the officers as they are as bad as ever[.] I feel Sick and badly but must now serve my time. O what a fool I was. You know not how it worries me to think that I cannot stick to sailorism just on account of you[,] for I know you will worry your self to death to think that at nothing I will Stick[,] but believe me dear Sister, that on Sea is no place to lead a Godly life[.] There fore when I get to San Francisco I will leave the Sea[.]

[June] 25[.] a Strong Wind[.] We are now over the Equater[.] This morning an attempt was made to assasanate the 1st mate but with out Success, though in the Struggle, He was Severely wounded. The Captain Sees he can do nothing with his men[.] he lets them have a Shot guns contest once in a while[.] This morning when the crew tried to kill the Mate He came on deck with a shot-gun loaded with pistole [pistol] Balls and Shot into the crowd wounding 7 men badly[.] we are now 10 men short to work the ship with heavy Seas[.] My chum is also Sick[.] The Captain Says he will kill the first man that lifts a hand again and He has also given orders to the officers to use the men better[.] There is only one officer that is liked and that is the Boatswain and he himself Sides with the Crew[.] So do I[.]

[June] 26[,] 9.30 am[.] This Morning at 4 we tacked Ship[; again] at 6 [and] the Same again at 8. You may Know then how tired I am[.] The Mate Never the less has again knocked a man's two front teeth clear down his throat causing him to be out of his head[.] They now have him under the influence of Liquor[.] it is raining very hard and I am wet all through and through[.] last night I dreamed of John Reichart[.] I thought He was in 'Frisco and Said to me thus "Loui ain't you going to Say how do you do to me" upon which I shook his hand. Mutiny Still continues among us and I am afraid we will go into 'Frisco only to attend the Marine Court[.] We are now in Lat 2°.15" South Steering E by N1/2N.

4.30 p.m. it is raining hard[.] we just turned in again till 6[.] my two pair pants are wet—it is now I would like to get ahold of that York Tailor for not making my pants[.] I am writing this in my Bare feet and nothing on me but my underclothing knowing I must put on wet pants again when I turn out. We had our outer jib taken away in a gale[.] 11 men are now on the Sick List and unable to work leaving 17 hands to work Ship including the Captain[,] Steward[,] Cook[,] Carpenter and 3 Mates[,] 1 Boatswain and my chum and me[, thus] leaving only 7 men in the Forecastle, when there ought to be 16[.] but this is not one half what it will be arounding Cape Horn.

Think not Dear Sister that I never think of you for you are on my mind day and night for it troubles me to think of your advice[,] your kindness and C & C. Just to think 4 months more and my chest is all come apart from the heat and the wood is unseasoned[.] tell that carpenter that made it that I am coming to York again[.]

[June] 28[,] 10 am[.] This morning our Watch washed down decks and Scoured the Brass works after which all hands were free[.] I cleaned out our Room, washed and Shaved my self and again put a white shirt and a pair of linen pants on (which I bought in N. Y. to match my coat). it is a fine day[.] the waters as smooth as a looking glass[.] Not a Breath of wind[.] We are heading due South. I am on the outs with the Mate now[.] I will read my Bible after which I will go to Sleep. The reason I did not post yesterday was because I was to busy to[.] you must excuse me. I wish I could be home to go to Church again, but never mind, everything has an end[.] tell me if or not Nannie Ziegler is yet in York[.] you know her[,] the one that always was with Margie Scholl so much. You may tell Margie Scholl that I inquired of N. Ziegler and She will be sure to tell her[.] So adew for today unless something Serious occurs. kiss Bonny for me as also Cassie[.] Give my regards to J. J. V. and tell him I often think of him. I suppose it will be very hot this 4 of July but I expect to be in the middle of winter rounding Cape Horn. Have you yet a top on your Pheaton. Give my regards to Cassie & Sarah Connelles and Mary V and Pap and Mother also to Albert V[,] but under no circumstances to E. V. tell Jacob Scholl I was just reading my diary when I came across some of his writing which reminded me of him particularly. Though I wish you would tell Daniel Scholl that I think of their Family every meal I eat for I brought my tin quart cup of [from] Them and as I use it I am bound to think where I got it[.] have you heard anything about John Reichart[?] He again came to me last night in my dream[.]

June 29[,] 7[:]41 A.M. Just think Sister[,] This morning at 3.30 AM. a Steamer hove in Sight and imagine the feelings I then had when I wished my Self on board of her[.] She came So near to us that we could plainly See between her decks what was going on[.] She was a passenger boat[,] Very large and Commodious. We supposed her to be from Brazil heading for England[.] My Call bell now Striks So I must go[.]

12.30. Dear Sister I am again in my room and will let You know the Trouble between the Second Mate and I.   He had been Smoking a Strong Cigar and wanting to go forward where smoking was not allowed[.] he called me up and told me to keep the Cigar going till he came back which would be in 15 or 20 minits. I hereupon informed him that I could not smoke so he should get some one that Could[.] this he took for an insult and Slaped me over the mouth but I Said nothing though I could have killed him on the Spot. Since that time He is down on me in evry way[,] shap[e] or form[.]

[June] 29[,] Lat 6°55'South[.] it used to be that I was allowed to Sit down during the night watches a little but that is all done away with now[,] so I am obliged after a hard days work to walk the deck 8 hours 1 night and 4 the next[.] I have been working for the Captain all morning and will now do a Job for the Steward which is all now[.] 6.30 PM[.] You may know that I take a good deal of Sleep from my self just to keep the book agoing so You may see that I think of You always, for I write all this for You. my reason for writing at such a late hour as this is to let you know that The Captain this Afternoon Caught with the Graines[3] a Dolphin measuring 4 ft 6 inch which was cooked up for the Cabin only, but having worked for the Steward this Afternoon I again managed to get Some fish and being on good terms with the Cook I got two pieces[.]

[June] 30[.] To day is the last of June[.] o that I were with you again. But business now. last night the Second mate came and made a Sort of an Apoligy to me

---

[3]Harpoon.

which I accepted and there fore went aft and Setdown along Side of him again (having been forward with the men ever Since the fuss)[.] While setting aft the man at the Wheel got mixed up and Could not keep the Ship on her course[,] upon which the Captain Came on deck and The folling [following] words passed from the Captain to the man at the Wheel[:] ["](God dam your Soul to hell[;] get away from this[!] dam me if that Boy cant Steer better than you[)].["] knowing that I was able to Steer[,] I got to the wheel before the Captain could tell me and You may imagine his Surprise at finding that I actualy did know how to Steer. He was So Surprised that He asked me again if I was not an old Sailor in disguise, for many things have I done already while on board that puzzeled the Men. Among one of the most daring was, on a Stormy day the Lower Mizzen Top Sail brace got foul of the Main lower topsail Brace[,] upon which the Capt told one of the men to go aloft and fixe it[.] when he got aloft the Captain told him to go over on the brace and clear the block but this he failed to do[.] upon Seeing that the Captain Sang out to the rest on deck to ["]jump up there one of you and clear it["] and among the party I was the first to get to the ladder[.] The Captain told me to stay but I still went up[.] having got upon the Main top mast head[,] I left my self drop down a distance of 20 feet and landed right on the Brace and So cleared it before the other man. it was then again that the men thought I was an old Sailor[.] however the Captain has given me my title. I am to take the Starbord wheel this evening, We now being on a port tack[.]

[June 30,] 5.30 [p.m.] this being a fine day and a Ship being in Sight the Mate is in a good humor So he gave us Supper [a] little early. I Suppose You are just getting ready for a pheaton ride and little old York as gay as ever[,] while here the decks are Spread over & over with Sails[.] The 2nd mate was just in my room and had a Chat with me. Just think[,] the Captain allowed me to put the American flag to the mast head for the other ship as a Salute[.] I feel good to day for I got Some fish for Breakfast and Dinner[.]

July 1[,] Lat 9°17'South[.] The first 4 hours of this month I Spent at the wheel from 12 last night to 4 this morning. I feel Sick and mean[.] I dreamed last night of Bro's George, Thomas, Charlie and yourself[,] also J. B. Sprenkle. Geo I thought was go [gone] off to discover the head of Some great river while I was giving him directions how to go. J B S [Sprenkle] I thought had parasales [parasols] and canes which he would lay in the Gutter to see who would pick them up—alas the Bell rings—[.]

6.30 P.M. it rained this afternoon and the second Mate (Mr. Bension) threw a holy-stone[4] and [at] one of the men [and] knocked him down on deck[.] the Captain however was Setting at his supper and therefore saw the whole occurrance[.] he made a big row about it to the second mate in front of all the men[.] at the same time[,] after this Bension had threw the Stone he commenced kicking a man in the face So Badly as to cause the man to loose Several of his teeth[.] it was at this Juncture that the Crew began to fire up So the Captain[,] Seeing that He (to save mutny [mutiny]) at once went against the 2nd Mate thereby making his crew obedieant again[.] it is now raining and I will Stay below till 8 oclock when I go on deck till 12[.] I am writing this by the light of a miserable old lantern just so you can know what is going on as much as possible[.] the port Crew is now hauling taught [taut] the Braces as the wind has Shifted. tell Cassie Connelle that I am now thinking of her[.] please kiss Bonny and Cassie good night for me when you get this[.]

[July] 2[.] This morning a ship hove in sight but proved to be going the other way. evrything is going on

---

[4]Holy-stone is a soft sandstone used to scrub ships' decks.

Straight now. however last night I found out that evry man had his Dirk knife in his Sleeve ready for Action[.] The way things look now, I dont expect to see San Francisco with Some of the present officers[.] The 3rd mate was the first and the rest will I expect Soon follow him[.] it is a fine morning[,] a little wind[,] and steering SW 1/2W[.] I suppose the 4th of July you will have a fine time while I will be working. as far as health is concerned I am all right[.] You aught to see how fat I am now but it is the treatment and Authority According to law that I look therefore[.] unless the Captain changes all his officers in Frisco I will not go to Sea any more[.] I am now at the 14 chapter of St John[.]

[July] 3[,] 8.49 A.M. This is a fine morning[,] calm as anything[,] no wind of any account hence no distance made. I again dreamed I were in a big City and Still I am not. O how glad I will be when we get to Frisco[!] but to tell the Truth there is nothing more Grand than these moon light night[s] at Sea[.] You know I always used to say of a moon light on land[,] ["]oh what a fine night this must be at sea[!"] and now I have my hearts content of them[.] I suppose by this time it is as hot as blazes in York while here it is almost the same but we expect to be in the middle of Ice, Snow[,] Rain and hail in about 19 days[.] I hope you have persuade John to let you go to the Country this summer[;] by the way I just think of it when you get this book which I will send as Soon as I get on land[.] You will again be at "house cleaning" So it will not be difficult to remember me[.]

[July] 4[,] 8.30 am[.] Just think to day is the 4th of July, who thought last 4th that I would be Sitting on board of the Ship St John bound for "Frisco"[?] Darn I suppose You Folks are prepareing to go to a picnic, while I will be working like a Bloody Convict[.] it is now a fine morning, though not even the Flag of our Country is hoisted let alone us having a holliday[.] however as luck would have it[,] it is my watch below this morning so I will celebrate the 4th by sleeping at any rate[.] We are now on a port tack with one Sail in sight on the Starbord Side[,] steering SW by S 1/2W. with light easterly winds[.] I have as yet not touched my 2 suits of flannels as also my boots and one pair of Shoes all of which remain untouched[.] I will try and Save as much as possible So that I can get along when I get to Frisco[.] the days are getting Shorter and Shorter every day[,] it now getting dark at 5 oclock.

12.25 PM. the Bell just rings for me to go out but I want to tell you that while it is hot where you are it is getting cold where I am for it is necessary to put on an overcoat in the evenings[.] (I got an overcoat from one of the Sailors that was to Small for him So he gave it to me[.] it is torn under the Sleeves a little but I will try and mend it up for the "Horn[.)]"

5.35 P.M. I Suppose by this time little York is all in Blazes with fire works and as usual a large amount of fun going on while here we have just got through cleaning Brass work. it is very calm and no wind. how I have wished myself ashore this day but to no good[!]

July 5[.] Sunday has again reached us—Latitude unknown by me[.] it is now 11 oclock am and my watch on deck till 12.30 but as the men are all forward washing I thought I might as well post up my Diary. it is a very fine day with a very little winds (more So than we have had all week)[.] As I am Sitting on my chum's chest with this book laying on mine to write more easy I can imagine what is going on at home[.] John is just come home from church[,] goes up Stairs a while then comes down with Cassie or Mary on his back in the yard[.] then He goes down in the barn up on the Hay[,] Smelling around for Chickens and Eggs[.] this done[,] he Sees that Riely feeds the horse and perhaps tells him to dust the Pheaton of[f] as he wants to go out home After-Sunday School. I could say much more but as I must now go to the Wheel I will have to stop.

[July] 6[,] 9.20 A.M. This morning we are having a fine breeze which is hurring [hurrying] us to Frisco at the rate of 10 knots an hour. it commenced last night at 9 oclock and Still is So rather increasing[;] therefore you may know how glad I feel to know that so much time is made good[.] I have now got so far into Sailorism (finding that that is my only plan on this Ship) that I have been appointed as Cross Jack Brace Tender which was taken out of the hands of an old Sailor and given to me when I was found efficient to do the work. I only hope now that through the divine providence of God we may be blessed with good winds, an article for which I pray for every day almost[.] I wish Dear Sister that you would Remember me to Mr & Mrs Earney and tell them that on the 6th of July 1874 I was thinking about them[,] also the Same to Abb Elliott.

[July] 7[,] 7.45 A.M. On the Ocean Lat 20°37'South[.] This morning the wind is not so strong as it has been however these last 36 hours we have been steering due South there fore making every thing good on our course[.] last night it was a little Squaly but soon cleared up again this morning[.] I had a miserable breakfast offered me which consisted of 1 piece of Salt meet[,] So Salted that you would have to drink water to every mouthful[,] and Some hash that actually stunk[,] all of which I have returned with-out touching them though I feel as week as a cat in my Stomach but never mind "it wont last allways" as you used to say[.] I will now read my Bible after which I will hear 8 bells which is 8 oclock and makes me go to work.

[July] 8[,] 12.20 P.M. I just got through with my dinner after a hearty 2 hours Sleep, in a few minutes I expect to hear 1 Bell which is half past twelve and means go to work, but before going I shall try and tell you my last nights dream[.] I thought we were in a hurricane for about 10 minutes but during that time I thought all our Sails blew away, braces were braking and we were going So fast that we could hardly get our breath when the Captain I thought was crying like a child to think of losing his Ship but however we came out all safe. The bell now rings So I must go[.]

[July] 9[,] 7.25 am[.] Last night in my watch on deck between the hours of 12 and 4 I became very Sick at my stomach for which I took some of Hoffsadullers Paregoric which helped me very little however I feel a little better now though I am weak now[.] I can eat no breakfast as the grub is so bad[.] We changed 5 sails yesterday and will change the rest 9 today[.] it will be Seen by our Latitude that we are getting a little piece to the South of the line[,] also into Strong winds[.] So we must take down all our light wind Sails and put on heavier ones. The Captain was just in my room and looking at this book I am keeping making the remark that I would get Sick of it buy and buy. So I will for I expect to let you know nothing while rounding the cape[.] I have another dream to tell you—but 8 bells go.

12.20 P.M. I will now go on with my dream[.] I thought I was again overseer of Uncle Louis'es lands in California, and that you were living Some where near him and I thought Aunt Catharine wrote a letter to me demanding me to come back to her house again[,] that I had no business to go away, but I thought you made the expression "She got all the money from the rest that She brought up, but She Shant have what little we have got[.]" It seemed here that Father Vandersloot came in my mind and I thought his wife told me he was dead and buried long ago. poor soul He was Sick when I left and weather he is now dead or not I can not tell though I hope not. I feel very weak with my little dining though I am fat[.] I have as yet my 2 prs of underclothes new and my boots & shoes. Mothers Linen Sheets I have not used as I value them to much[.] it is getting to be cold. the bell now rings So I must go.

[July] 10[,] 9.10 A.M. yesterday afternoon about 4 oclock, I fell from the Gallant Fore-sail and Sprained my ankle badly[,] so much so that were I at home I should be in bed, while here I am compelled to work all the Same. My ankle is Swollen to Such an extent as to unable me to put on my Shoe though I hope it will be better by 12 oclock this afternoon as I am now below till than [then] and will bound [bind] it tight. I put on a Clean Pillow Case which now lets me with 1 clean on. I am now at the 5th Chapter of Acts. This morning we Sighted a "Sail" and the Captain at once ordered the ships helm in that direction[.] At last we came close enough for hailing when our Captain began thus "Ship Ahoy" Ans. ["]Where away.["] ["]Where are you from[?]" Ans. ["]Rio Janiero." ["]Where are you bound[?"] Ans. ["]Antwrept [Antwerp,] Europe["] ["]How many days are you out[?"] Ans ["]day before yesterday["]. ["]have you Seen any Vessels to the Southert[?"] Ans ["]No.["] ["]Report me please." Ans ["]Ay Ay Sir[."] Our Captain having now finished asking questions the other one commenced with ["]Whats your name[?"] to which we replied "St John." ["]Where bound[?"] "Frisco." ["]Where from[?"] "New York." ["]How many days out[?"] ["]52.["] ["]All well aboard[?"] ["]4 Sick.["] We now commenced to get apart Some distance So we dipped our colors and parted. The expression ["]dip["] may be Strange to you Sister but it means this. when 2 ships meet[,] the American Flag is hoisted to the mast heads[.] When they part it is hoisted and lowered 3 times which means adiew and is Commonly known as "dipping your Colors." The work of dipping was done by me as you will see in my fore going pages that the Captain has Appoined [appointed] me as "Ensign Boy[.]" I am working hard to become Boatswains first mate which I expect to Accomplish before we get to the horn.

12[:]30 P.M.[, Lat 25°31'South.] My foot is rather worse than better it is much Swollen[.]

6.25 P.M. My foot is decreasing a little and I can Stand on it with more Ease but it Still pains me[.]

July 11[,] 7.29. A.M. This morning my foot is better, I can again walk on it[.] The principal work done

on board now is Sail making. I gave my pantaloons to
one of the Sailors to be made up. I expect to get them
next week. We are having no wind now. So there is
little headway made. We are on a S.W. course, today we
will take the Mizzen Gallant Yard down for repairs. I
will now read my bible which is a thing I try and not
Neglect as much as possible though I do Some times[.]

    12.30 [p.m]. We just got done getting Sails out to
be repaired after having worked all morn at the Yard
aforesaid[—]it is all rotten So we must make a new one.
My dinner was very bad which consisted of horse meat
and bread but wait till I get ashore[,] than I can get a
deceant meal, though when I do get there I dont intend
to Spend all as I am now again going to try to paddle
across the river[.] in fact dear Sister I am so ashamed of
my Self that every time I look upon your work on my
clothes I almost cry blood. I must now go on deck[.]

    6[:]25 [p.m.]   This evening[,] as usual of a
Saturday[,] we were obliged to Clean that horrid Brass
Work again. We got the Spar all up again after having
Smashed one man's 2 fingers to a jelly, which again
deprives us of a good man. I will now go to give you the
Names of the Ships crew[.] Officers[:] Captain, D. S.
Scribner[;] 1st mate, Mr. Geary, alas [alias] Tullins. 2nd
mate[,] Mr Bennsion,[;] 3rd mate (lost overboard)[,] Mr
McCarthy.[;] Boat Swaine, E. H. Harrison[;] Carpenter, S.
B. Talkner, a Russian by berth [birth;] Boy No 1 Ensign,
and in charge of the pumps is Your Brother L. J. F.
Iaeger to which I hope Soon to add Boatswains 1s[t]
mate. Boy No 2 and in charge of the Buckets and axes
is My Chum George Ingraim of Maine.

    Steward is Ah Chan a Chinaman[.] The cook is
a Mr. Uo Cugn another bloody China man and who is
now laying in his room dead drunk. The crew is known
as the Starbord and port watches[—]half Sleep on one
Side of the ship and half on the other. My watch
(Starbord) consists of Charlie, Frenchie, Queebec,
Delmanic, Snyder, Scot, Peter, Jimmy the Boatswain[,]

2nd Mate and my self. all these men Sleep on the right hand Side of the Ship call[ed] Starbord Side hence the Name Starbord watch. The port watch Consists of John, Scott, Antonia, Sheets, Sam, Clark, Riess, Bricktop, Shanks, first mate[,] and my chum. This is the port watch and Sleeps on the left side of the ship known as the port Side, hence the name port watch[.]

[July] 12, 11. am[.] You may thank God that I am yet alive as well as this Ship is also afloat, for this morning it blew So hard as to rent in two of our 3 royals and break nearly all the Braces we had as well as Snapp of[f] our lower main Top Yard. I thought my time had come but I am yet alive. We did not get breakfast till 10 oclock[.] We worked So hard. The Captain almost was killed, he having been Struck by the Lee Wheel on the Shoulder[.] in fact this is nothing [to] what it will be off The "Cape[.]" There is also a ship in Sight but we cannot Speak [to] her[.] I feel very tired and Sleepy though I must again go on deck at 12.30 P.M. I will now imagine my-self in the German Reformed Church of York and will there fore read my Bible.

[July] 13[,] 12.15 P.M.[,] Lat 26°42'South[.] You have no Idea what kind of weather we had last night and Still have to the time of my writing[—]the Ship actualy rolls from one Side to the other[.] We lost 3 Sails last night[:] the inner, outer & flying Jibs. This morning part of the main Sail gave away. it is very bad weather though this is only one half to what it will be at the Cape. There is So much wind as only to allow us to carry 6 Sails out of 20[,] So you can imagine how things Stand yourself. by the by I almost forgot to tell you. last night we Sighted a Ship directly under our Bows[,] She being on the Same course as We[,] for we could See her Starboard light, but this Ship is a fast Sailer and in one hour we Caught[,] passed and lost her out of Sight[.] We came near enough to her to permit any one throwing a Stone aboard of her which I and Several others did only to receive the Curses of the other Crew.

The Captain did not Speak [to] her as the wind was to bad.

[July] 14, 9 A.M. Troubles are now commencing and will not ceace till on the otherside[.] it is getting very cold and I felt it to[o] this morning[.] We got Coffee for the first time at 4 oclock. There is a Sail in Sight but where and where from I do not know. My only friend now is God and his Word. You may be assured I wished my Self ashore this morning when I got my breakfast and found the Cook had on my plate 6 pancakes (the Size of a silver dollar) when immeaditly I thought of Shore again. I use the word ["]home["] to Signify Shore, for a home have I none untill in rest in Heaven with my Father & Mother. it is very rough and windy[.] We are now Steering West the wind coming from the South. Just think[,] 2 months out and only 4 hours Sleep at a time. M[a]y the blessing of God rest upon all Your Family dear Sister as I feel it is on me. His devine providence is to[o] great to be Spoken off [of]. I will now try and go to Sleep after Sharpning my knife and reading the 14 Chaper [Chapter] of Acts[.]

5.25 P.M.[,] Lat 29°34'S[.] We are now commencing to get watch below in the afternoons[,] at least we have been So far ever Since day before yesterday which gives us a little time to mend clothes[.] it is calm again with very little wind, but cold[.] We steer S.W. 1/2W. I miss many little things I laid aside for my chest but you failed to put them in[.] I have heard nothing of my Sewing case yet[.]

[July] 15[,] 7.50 a.m. I am now eating a Small piece of hard tack and salt beef. actually while I write this I almost cry to think of how good a person can have it on land but still goes to a worse place. I feel as faint as a cat just for the want of proper food to build me out[.] it is calm with very little wind[.] how we are heading or Steering I cannot tell you till I get to the wheel which will be from 10 to 12.30 this morning[.] oh, that I were ashore now. I have been thinking about

my not going to Sea any more, all my last nights watch
on deck, and have come to the Conclusion that Should
the Captain Change Some of his present Officers I will
Stay by the Ship and learn, and Should he not I will
Stay in Frisco for a Short time and try to get Work and
if I fail in doing that I will go to texas. I must now go on
deck as 8 bells have just gone[.] I will tell you my
nights dream about You and Bonny & Cassie this dinner
time[.]

July 16[,] 9.45. am.[,] Lat. 33°41'S[.] finding my
time to busy yesterday after dinner I will tell you my
dream now[.] I thought this Ship was a Steamer and
was laying in New York. I thought You and John,
Cassie and little Bonny came to See me and take
passage on board the ship. I thought as Soon as Bonny
Seen me she flew to my arms, it also Seemed to me as
if the Captain could never get done making extra
preperations for your Benefits and I thought He was So
glad to see you & me to See me [you] as well as himself
[the Captain.] but in the mean time I thought I [saw a]
man I know well in "Frisco" came to me and Confessed
a horrible murder he had committed and asked me to
get him out of it which I thought I did. here I was woke
up by the sound of 8 bell[s] in the night or 12 oclock.
We are now having a fine wind and are heading S.W.
1/2W[.] Since we are having watch and watch I am
begining to like the Sea better and better evry day and
Should I be of the Same opinion as to day I think I will
come back to New York in this Ship. I will now read my
bible after which I must Sleep a little. Remember me to
Daniel Schall and to Misses Conelleas[.] kiss little Bonny
and Cassie for me and let them know that they may yet
look for "lullue[.]"

[July] 17[,] 7.55. AM[.] We are having a fine wind
ever Since 6 oclock last evening and are going 13 knots
an hour which tells a good deal on our Course. It is
getting to be very cold but you are not allowed to come
on deck to work with a coat on. The officers claiming it

makes you to Stiff for work though they themselves have 3 or 4 shirts on at a time and care for nobody else but them Selves[;] however it will be only till I get to "Frisco" and Should I Still Stick to this Vessel I will prepare my Self in clothing as well a[s] Grub. You know not how it troubles me to think that I am again going to leave my place but believe me dear Sister the treatment is to harsh to put up with though I always talked Sea treatment and life up to you. You know well yourself that I had only Seen it as a passenger though I will go all according to your letters when I get to "Frisco" unless I find it to hard to put up with. I should like very much to come home to you as a well trained "sea man" which I know you Should be pleased to See.

1 P.M[.,] Lat 34°01'S[.] I just got through with my dinner[.] I am in hopes our watch will have 4 hours below this after noon though I doubt it a little. the weather is fine with a N.E. wind blowing which puts us on a SW 1/2 S course, at the rate of 11 knots an hour[.] We are lashing evrything down to their places now already as we have been for the last 3 day[—]Shipping a considerable amount of water on the decks which makes it very unpleasant[.] I will now proceed to read my bible[.]

[July] 18, 10 AM. last night it was very cold and we shiped [shipped] much water on decks[.] in fact the Sea was So heavy as to wash away things not lashed and also compelled me to have on my oil Skins all night in which I also Sleep. the weather this morning is very rough. I brought my fox Skin on deck this morning and all the Sailors did not know what to make of it[.] I have cut the tail and 2 front legs of [off] for ear muffs and a Scarf[.] I feel wet and tired as well as hungry, but this is not the worst yet. I will now read the 19 Chapter of Acts and then go to Sleep till 12. adew, kiss Bonny for me as I am always thinking of her.

4 oclock P.M. I am writing this while my watch is on deck yet expecting to be turned in but it looks

blue. I feel good again and am in brighter spirits[.] I only hope I will not be compelled to leave the Ship when I get to Frisco. I expect to get wages when we leave for Liverpool So that I can try and Shift[,] though if I do go I will get Uncle Louis to give me money to buy some provisions (which are not given me on board) so that I can live better. Now I am cozy for I can hear the foot-Steps of the Starboard watch going below So I am all right. Sister[,] you know not how many Sea Gulls are hovering around the Ship at present[.] in fact our Steward has broken the legs of about 1/2 doz. within the past 3 hours with only a Stick. I think of you every time I look at them and know how you would like to have their skins. They are as White as Snow[.] Just before our watch turned in we tryed to set the Fore.da. Gallant Sail but found a hole in it one fathom in length.

[July] 19[,] 10 am.[,] Lat 35°28'[.] Sunday again and calm as an old dying cow. Very little wind Stiring [stirring.] We are fixing the Fore da Gallant Sail. Just think on Sunday. This morning at 3 oclock while our watch on deck the Mate (2nd) was trying to harpoon porpuses but failed in the attempt. I gave myself a good Scrubbing down about 10 minutes ago and feel first rate now. there are 2 Sails in Sight now. by this time I suppose John is to church hearing the holy word of God which Seems to be forbidden on this Ship. I must now go to work on deck Signaling the 2 Sails.

6.30[.] I just got done with Signaling and you may depend that my arms feel tired for I hauled up 198 flags since 11 oclock this morning and I know I shall get through my Supper with ease, having Spoken till the wind got better I "dipped Colors" and parted[.] one Ship proves to be the John King Man of Baltimore and Bound for San Francisco, having been already 9 day out more than us, which would make her out 78 days out from Baltimore and we from N. Y. and only out 69 day. how do you like that kind of Sailing[?] the other was a Dutch vessel from Scotland bound for Monte Vedo [Montevideo]

Situated on the mouth of the Rio de la platt [Rio de la Plata.]

[July] 20, 9 A.M.[,] Lat 37°41'[.] Dear Sister[,] last night it again commenced with bad weather for it rained all night and was as cold as ice, though, we had to be in it all the time, while the officers Stood in dry quarters and could look on. You may imagine how I felt being wet through and through and almost froze, nor was this all[.] We had to go up the masts and furl the Fore Main and Mizzen Da Gallant Sails which was very tiresome indeed[.] I felt So cold and Stiff that I could hold no longer on the Sail with my fingers and Should have fallen down on deck or in the Sea had it not been for Scottie who caught me in his arms and took me from the Yard arm on the Top Mast, there to rest unobserved by the officers. I got down Safe, though I feel badly after it, though I am told by the Sailors that this is fine weather to what it will yet be when off the Cape. The bad treatment of the officers on the men is more than this pen or pencil can express, though no doubt it will be expressed when we get to Frisco and with a Tongue at that. I will now go for my Bible. May the Blessing of God rest upon us all for Christ's Sake, Amen[.]

[July] 21, 9 am.[,] Lat 38°00'S[.] last night we had an awfull Storm which last[ed] for 25 or 30 minutes only but in that Short Space of time done considerable damage, for things were breaking to such an extent that the life boats were already cut loose and things in general look a little Ship wreck but it Soon went away and left us with plenty of work on our hands. this morning we washed down decks again when actualy the water froze as fast as we could pour it down So you may imagine the intense cold we are having in July. it is rather calm with little wind. We are Steering a SW 1/2 W course. last night my fingers almost froze off from handling the cold Steel Spokes of the Wheel. I must now go to sleep as I feel tired[.]

[July] 23[,] 4 oclock[.] my reason for not writing yesterday is because I was to tired on account of 2 vessels being close by which you know kept me busy all day. one is an English Vessel and the other has as yet made no reply to our questions. it is very cold now and I can easy lay under cover of 3 blankets. I sold my goverment Blanket the other day for 7 dollars on an order on the Captain and I will Sell my Shawl if I can get 6 dollars for it[.] I must make money Some way So that I can do Something in Frisco[.] the heavy dews down this way are drenching to any one that is in its way[,] though the moon is great comfort and relief to ones troubles. last night I was Singing "Would I were with thee, over Land and Sea" and thought of you and Manda Laucks. oh that the days of labor on this Ship will Soon be over is my continual wish. Still I must Say this life brings me out as I always told you for my muscle is as big as a mans and yesterday morning I lifted a 200 pound weight right on my shoulder[.]

[July] 24[,] 9 AM. this morning is a beautiful morn for the climate we are in and for the first time I used a "Holy-Stone" to clean out my room with. we are also having a fine breeze which is propelling us along at a good rate and our Latitude is now 42°52'S, leaving 14°8' to make yet before Steering for 'Frisco, when we will steer a N.W. course[.] every-thing is now made Secure for the Cape and we only hope that this moon will See us around the Horn and with it come good winds[.] I thought I would write to Rev J O. Miller to let him know that he was not yet forgotten. I only hope I will be able to accompany this Ship to Liverpool and from there to New York when I will again come to You and See old times, that is if the 2nd Mate leaves in Frisco for I cannot bear him though I make great chums with him merely because I am afraid if I kick against him that he might Throw me over board and Say I droped over board, for I dont in my heart think him any to good to do Such a thing and besides all that He has told me Some awful crimes that He and his fellow Sailors used to do which if I were to tell ashore would criminate him for life and He even made a remark to me once that a cry from a boy like me would not be noticed in the water and that it was a common thing for Sailors to throw one another over board for malice[.]

[July] 25[.] We are now commencing our "Horn Life[.]" it is blowing head wind like forty and as I Sit at this book writing I am all wet through. I Still feel like Continuing this life though last night again I had a quarrel with Bennsion about Standing by the Main de Gallant halliards[5] which the Captain ordered me to do and also that if any one interfered with me to hit him over the head with a blain pin [belaying pin],[6] which I did to one of the men who was wanting to get the halliards him-Self and try-ing to make me believe the Captain was calling me but instead of me going to the Captain I hit him over the mouth which caused him to Scream and that brought Bennsion the 2nd Mate, who told me to get away but dared not come near me for I told him the Captain orders and also that He was no better than any of the rest.

12.30 P.M.[,] Lat 42°23'S. the Ship is rolling very hard and actually Some times Stands at an angle of 60 degrees and Shipping Seas fearfully[,] So much So that the coal buckets and other materials can swim around the kitchen[.] I was compelled to get another oil Coat from the Captain this morning as my first one leaks to bad. We are now under press of <u>very</u> <u>light</u> Sail having only the 6 Top Sails for Sail[:] Fore[,] Top Mast Stay Sel, Inner Jib, Main Top Mast Stay Sel and

---

[5]A halliard (or halyard) is a rope or tackle used on a ship to raise or lower sails, yards or flags.

[6]A belaying pin is a sturdy metal or wooden pin in a rail of a ship, around which ropes can be wound.

Spankers Sel at present, the rest all being furled[.] I must also make mention that while my foot is well[,] it only allows me to walk on it Straight as I cannot get on a boot nor can I take of[f] my Gum boots with[out] hurting it. The wind is blowing awfull hard[.] I will now try and Sleep a little, So kiss dear Bonnie and Cassie for me and Remember me to Mrs. Carney and all, adew, Louis[.]

P.S. I have accomplished my task now of Being Boatswain Mate. I must now go on deck as "about Ship" is the programme.

[July] 26[,] 9[:]15 a.m. all last night we Shiped heavy Seas and were under a Still lighter sail than during the day[.] it blew tremendously and hailed a little. I managed to keep dry till this morning while tacking Ship I got all wet. about 4 oclock this morning we pumped Ship which was very trouble some. Our cook gave me a cup of good Sea coffee this morning and allowed me to warm myself at the Stoves[.] it Seemed this morning as if it were going to be a fine Sunday but the way it looks now it will be as bad as the rest though the grub will be a little better but never the less God is with us in bad weather as well as in good and I only hope his hand will deliver us from the perils of the Horn. it is exceedingly cold as we are very near the Falkland Islands. I will now read my bible which I have neglected for a few days[,] only keep in mind that I think of you almost always[.] if I could wash my self now I would feel all right but I can get no water So adew dear Sister and pray for me.

[July] 27[,] 7.58 am., Lat 43°19'S[.] I expect the bell to call me evry minute[.] The Ship went last night 12[,] 12 1/2[,] 11 and 8 knots an hour on a SW 1/2 S course, with a fair wind but She is rolling fearfully now and again Shipping Seas[.] I Still feel my pain in my foot and it (the foot) is getting So bad as to make it very painfull for me to put on or take of[f] my rubber boots. Yesterday morning it Snowed a little, and this morning it is going to rain like forty and blow a reagular hurricane[.] I Suppose the Ship to be in Lat 48 or 49, but dont know for ceartain as I have not had time to work up the "days" Work of the Ship which will give you the exact Lat of the Ship. last night for the first time we were compelled to put 2 men to the wheel. alas the bell goes ringing for Sarah[,] So adew and know you then that we are very near Cape Horn.

3 P.M. this afternoon I made a table for my chest, So that my eatibles would not roll down for which I bored 4 Small holes in my chest lid to keep it Stationary. The wind is a little bit lighter though I hope it may yet come on So as we may go ahead fast[.] I am going to the Captain to See if he has any thing for my ankle as it pains me very much even now while I am doing nothing as it is my Watch below till 4 again[.]

[July] 29[,] 7[:]55 am[,] Lat 48°2'S[.] We were very busy yesterday and I felt to tired to write as I needed Sleep though I feel Sleepy yet as out of 36 hours I only get 8 hours Sleep and only 4 at a time so you know how I now feel. My foot is no better and the Captains Medicine is worth nothing, So I must lug along. I again dreamed of you last night and evry time I dream of you I commence to long to See land[.] We are in Longitude 62° West which you will See on the map comes just a few degrees north of the Falkland islands and puts us opposite Cape Blanco[.] We now have 4 men Sick which puts us back considerably especially when they are most needed but times tell all things and eventually we will be in Frisco. the bell now rings So I must go.

12.45. P.M. this morning while on deck we had a fine breeze of 8 and 9 knots, Steering due South[.] It is very cold [so] my fingers get perfectly stiff while plading [plaiting] Sennet. I managed to get a bit of butter from the steward but it is So Strong that I am afraind [afraid] if I eat it I will pull up the mast from its roots[;] however I will try Some this evening[.]

[July] 30[,] 9 a.m. We are Still having a fine breeze and I am in very good Spirits as I am thinking of Staying on the Sea, for how nice it will be when I come to See you in a blue Suit. when we get to Frisco I am agoing to leave the ship till She Sails again when I will join her[,] that is if the Captain is willing which I almost think he will[,] as He is getting very kind and good to me[.] in fact I am treated as an officer on board of her in stead of Boatswains Mate (which only allows me to repeat the Commands of the officers to the men[)].] last night I again dreamed of You and John[,] also Bro Thomas who I though[t] was Selling coats in Mexico Some place for a living. I thought you and John were collecting for a Sunday School and you got your School mates to give in and I thought Irean Clifford gave $50.00 and some one else the same. any way I thought you told me that your friends would give more than John's[.] I also Saw Geo Leber printing a Newspaper in one end of his ware house while at the other it very misterously turned into grain again, and last of all I Saw my Self coming into Uncle Louis'es Yard (in Arizonia) when his 2 Bull dogs almost tore me to pieces[.] her[e] I woke up and Still found the Skin on me[.] please give my kind regards to Mr Leber and Charles Shults as I Seen him Some place in my dream but cannot place him[.] I expect it will rain in half an hour So I must go on deck again hence I will Stop writing for the present.

[July] 31[,] Cape Horn. 12[:]30 P.M.[,] Lat 54°23'S[.] We are now hauled up for rounding Cape horn and the bad weather is again at our heels[.] it is very cold and our Watch has 8 hours out tonight which Still makes it worse for me but never the less I Still feel like going to Sea and am actually beginning to think of times to come when I will show myself in Phila[delphia] and York in a Blue suit and cap[,] rigged up as a Sailor. Still I See ma[n]y things here[—]you folks would never believe me. also a large amount of inhumanity is practiced on these large Ship[s] and you may be assured that a 2nd mate of one of these Ships is equal to a Captain of a Small Ship, as officers on these ship[s] must know something. In fact dear Sister I am all bruised up[,] my Thumb is cut[,] my neck is Sprained[,] as also my wrist and foot which worries me in my Sleep[,] and my back between the Shoulders Sometimes is So bad as to impead breathing[,] all on accou[n]t of the weather[.] We do not have rains down here but very heavy dews called "Chillian dews[.]"

6[:]30 P.M.[,] Lat 56°34'S[.] it now gets dark at 4 So by this time it is pitch dark, therefore it afords me no time to post up after 4 untill I get to the lamp and being as I have now 1 1/2 hours below yet[,] I will tell you my dream this afternoon from 2 to 4[.] I thought I was in Aunt Catherines house and Saw Uncle Samuel there all dressed up and acting as "private Secretary["] to Aunt C.[,] also that I was Sitting in the parlor and Aunt C. told me She pitied me very much and Said that if She knew the Audenrieds would not Say any thing She would take me up but afterwards Said for Sure that She would take me and asked me how I would like the Idea[,] where upon I replied that it would take a long time to Consider the matter over carefully. after that I thought Aunt Amanda Mayburry came to See Aunt C towards evening and when She came to go home She wanted me to escort her and Stay for Supper but Aunt C. Said I might go with her but to come home for Supper[,] that I might take Supper at mayburrys to morrow night[.] here dear Sister I woke up and found my Self as wet as a fish from persperation. Since my Philadelphia dream I have been thinking of you, and thought Should the Lord call you away what would I do[,] that then my best friend would be gone[.] I hope it may be the Lord's will to spare you[.] I hope you have enjoyed yourself during this month which is Something more than I can Say not only of this but of all the passage. nevertheless my Spirits are tempered yet and it will take a good deal to bring them away from the Sea.

could I but get a glimpse of you and your family to night it would Stir up my whole body. kiss Cassie and Bonny for me and Remember me to my friends all. So good night all while I go to the wheel[.]

August 1[,] Lat 56°34'S[.] Just think[,] august already. We are having fine weather for the place we are in as [and] also a good Easterly wind which allow us to head W by N and if the wind continues on we will be clear of the Horn in a few days. The Captain Stands on deck all night some times[,] being anxious I Suppose to clear this place as Soon as possible and indeed his Services are needed[,] for the 2nd Mate Actualy can not Trim Ship yet and claims to have been to Sea 18 years. I am Still thinking of returning in this Ship[.] There was a Ship in Sight yesterday afternoon but She can not be Seen now. We also passed Staten Land[7] yesterday afternoon while our watch was asleep but my Chum Says it was all covered with hills of Snow and on the whole made a beautifull Sight[.] He also Said that the Captain asked him how he would like to have a Farm on that place[.] The word ["]Farm["] reminds me of poor Grand mother Slenker who is not cared for at all, poor woman[.] I only hope I may Someday or another do her justice for just think how much She thinks of us and we to be to[o] proud to associate with her[.] let Geo instead of Marr[y]ing Support his Mothers Step Mother who was always kind to us and never believed the lies told her about us, and now She has no home[.] oh it is a perfect Sham[e] how we treat her.

[August] 4[,] 6.30 PM.[,] Lat 56°44'S[.] Dear Sister we are now a pretty good distance of[f] Cape Horn and it only took us 3 days in Clearing it. to day we buried another Victem to the Mates Tyranny though the Captain is under the impression that He died of Heart disease, though on his privates were Such bru[i]ses

---

[7]Staten Island lies off the southern tip of South America.

(which the mate gave him with a "Snatch Block["]⁸) as caused his immeadiate death. We now have only 24 Souls on board and God only knows who is the next one to go. indeed I have thought and thought over my case and find that I cannot stay by the ship in Frisco as the mate will be with her all the time. it is very Cold and Snowing to[o.] oh what a night, and to be out 10 hours in it yet after a hard days work during these past 3 days that I failed to post. You may be assured that I Saw life enough to put me against ever going to Sea again[.] evry bone in my body hurts and my foot is very bad in fact for weeks I have not had a dry foot, and the grub is very bad. I am entirely used up and I dont know where I am going to get money to doctor my Self up in Frisco but I will Sell my blankets and other things So that I may have enough to get along with[.] if I only was there[!] while I write this the Cook is looking over my shoulder trying to read. The Captain just now came to my room and asked for the book called "Ship wrecks and disasters at Sea[,]" a book that I took from Birty [Billy] Elliot. the ship is rolling very much[.] there is also a Ship in sight. I will now give the Cook his lesson after which I must again go on deck till 12 to night. today we holy[-]Stoned the poop and tomorrow we will do the main deck[.] kiss Bonny for me and Cassie[,] give my kindest wishes to John and accept my love for your self and remember me to all my friends[.] I am goin[']. Black Bro Lewis[.]

[August] 5[,] 9.28 A.M.[,] Lat 57[°]29['.] this morning is a fine morning So I had a good wash which consisted of my face and hands, which is the first time Since we left the River de la plata. There is now very little wind, the port-watch is HolyStoneing the main deck, which we will also commence at 12 this noon. it

---

⁸A snatch block is a block with an opening on one side that receives the loop of a rope.

rained a little this morning. My foot is as yet not better.
last night I had a dream about Schulls, how glad I am
feeling at the prospects of Soon again getting on land[.]
The ship that was in Sight yesterday afternoon is yet
not seen by the Captain who is keeping a hawks eye for
her. I must now turn in after reading the 9th Chapter
of 1 Corinthians So adew and give little Bonny another
kiss[.]

    [August] 7[,] 9 AM. it is blowing a hard head
wind and driving us back to the Cape again. We have
only enough Sail on her to keep her from taking charge
altogether[.] I am very tired and need Sleep[.] You
would not know me were you to See me now. good by[.]
kiss little Bonnie and Cassie—Lewis[.]

    August 9[,] Sunday Morning[,] 9 Am.[,] Lat.
64°23'S[.] My Dear Sister You Cannot imagine what I
have Seen in these last 48 hours Since I last posted. O
God knows that the pencil is unable to describe it[!]
Actually I have Seen enough in this Short Space of time
to last me till I die. on the morning of the 7th at 11
oclock the wind changed from a head wind to a fair one
which again allowed us to go on our course[,] but with
it Came Wind[,] Snow[,] hail[,] rain[,] break downs and
any thing a person Can think of to make one feel bad.
The water was So deep as to wash away any thing loose
4 feet from the Main deck[,] making it hazardous for one
to Cross it[.] Such a force has the water that a horse
would be knocked down in no time. The men are
Compelled to Stay on the poop aside of the Captain and
Officers for fear of being washed overboard and there is
not a man (with the exception of 3 sick) on board that
has been dry for the past 48 hours. the Boatswain is
Sick with the Eagie [ague?] and I being the right hand
man expected to be put up a Step instead of which the
Captain Sent me to the Wheel with a relief of 2 men and
there I have been lash[ed] (for fear of going overboard)
for 10 hours at a time without anything to eat and bare
footed with 1 pair drawers on and a Shirt[,] no pants on

nor Coat. there are only 8 men allowed at the wheel now of which the Carpenter is boss of the port side (4 men) and I of the Starboard (4 men)[.] my arms are nearly of[f] but the Captain cheered me this morning by giving the Carpenter and I a glass of good brandy and told me I was a brick to Steer and Said I aught to Stay to Sea as I could learn fast. He also Said when I told him that I was going to leave him that better times were Coming and He would give me Some wages. I must go to the wheel again at 12.30 PM to day and Stay till 8 to night[.] She Steers hard as [and] one of the Carpenters men is disabled for life[,] I Suppose he having got a knock from one of the Spokes in the abdoman[.] She kicks fearfully. You can See on the other page where It is rubbed out how wet my shirt is[.] I have got a cloth of the Cooks over the paper but Still it Soaks[.] I am writing this in the Gally or kitchen as my room has 1 foot of water in it this morning[.] the 2nd mate would have been washed over board had it not been for a Small piece of rope which He caught while going over the Side. The Sea was So heavy this morning as to outen the kitchen fires for Some time[.] the Cook is very good to me. in fact dear Sister I was wishing this morning at 4 oclock that God would pick you up out of your bed and hold you over the Ship where you might See me and all, then You <u>would</u> See Some thing that your eyes never could See[,] only here. the Ship is ice all around[,] not a rope dry[,] evry thing hanging with iceicles and blowing like the very old nick[.] We are Steering a NW 1/2 W Course and Vary Sometimes on the following courses[:] NW by W, NW 1/2 N, NW 1/2 W[,] NW by N, WNW, and WNW 1/2 N[.] the Cook is Just now throwing Salt beefe in the window from the Store room which is for the crew[.] things are not in danger of being handled to tenderly from the noise the beef mak[e]s Coming down on the bricks[.] if this wind keaps on we will be in better weather in a few day[s,] that is if it blows from the South as it does now. You Can tell

Cassie Connellee that while I Sleept from 12 to 2 last night I dreamed I Saw Michel Schull and his family and her getting in the Sleighs for a ride while I was holding the horses[.] I thought evry Sleigh had an Umbrella[.] I also dreamed about Aunt Mem Karg and John Gibbert[,] a boy Stoping with them. please tell J B Sprenkle to tell Aunt Mem. So I must no[w] stop as my arms pain me to much[.] Where is Aunt Catharines Magnetic Liniment now for I could use a hogsheads of it for my pain, especially for my back. in fact dear Sister I am thinking that when You read this you will not blame me for not going to Sea after getting to Frisco.

8.25 P.M. I just came from the wheel, and you cannot imagine how tired I am though I write this to let you know how often I think of you[.] the weather is bad and we are Shipping heavy Seas. I also had a good long talk with the Captain from 6 to half past 6 while I was relieved from the wheel. He said among other things that we would be in fine weather in 2 or 3 days if this breeze lasted[.]

[August] 10, 1 P.M.[,] S Pacific Ocean Lat 64°23'S[.] it is not so cold nor do we Ship Such a heavy Sea, but never-theless it is very disagreeable and my feet are begining to ache, especially my left foot which as yet is not well. I must hurry and write this as I have my bible to read yet after which I must get as much sleep a[s] possible[.] I every minute expect to get word from the port Forecastle that one of their men is dead as he is very poor. I am already getting glad at the prospects of Soon again Seeing my home "Frisco[.]"

[August] 11[,] 9'55 AM[,] S Pacific Ocean Lat 61°10'S[.] a fine day and good breeze but was very calm last night[.] the Sun is Shinning in my window like home again. Still it is a little cool as we are now getting into the Chillian dews. I just washed my face and Shaved my Self So I feel a little better and I also have my clothes dry again. So I may feel O.K. till 12 this noon when I expect to hear the dreadfull word

"Holy-Stone" again which is death on ones back. O how I wish I could See you all now at home. Evry one on board of the Ship is telling me that I am getting So fat, which makes me feel Still better. our Sick man in the Forecastle is a little bit better but very little[.] I am now relieved from the wheel duty again for a Short time as it is fine weather[.] in one of my foregoing pages I told you to write to Mrs Baily which I will repeat again So you Shall not forget it for I will do the Same to her Husband when to Frisco I get[.] I will now read my bible and a little of the Sermons of the Rev C. H. Spurgeon after which I will "dormear" [dormir] (Spanish)[.]

[August] 12[,] 1 P.M. We are now Steering North, being 5 points out of our course but still making a little headway[.] last night we were called to reef the Topsails which was a mean Job and made a person all wet[.] besides all that[,] when one turns in of a night-time he is not Sure how Soon he may be called out, therefore he must Just lay down as He comes from deck So that in a minutes notice he may have hold of a brace if required[.] I will however take of[f] my pantaloons this afternoon and risk it. I only have to look forward to the coming day when I can lay as long as I like and hear it rain Thunder and blow and know that there is no need of me going into it[.] Still I will remember my time at Sea when I used [to] wade into it up to my knees. The word "Holy Stone" is as yet not given out but I expect it daily. last night I was thinking of John's Chums coming into the Store of a winters night and detain me a little. how I used to growl when here we were all kept up for 6 hours last night over our time Just for letting the Fore upper Top Sail halliards unreave and get foul of the Fore Top Mast Stay Sell halliards which provoked the 1st Mate to Such and extent as to Cause the 6 hours overtime[.] So you may know how much Sleep I had within the past 36 hours (8). So I must try to Sleep a little this afternoon but however if I can work or Serve man 28 hours why not God 10 minutes[?] So I will first read my Bible, adew and give my respects to Mr Leber and tell him to write to me when I get to frisco as I am always thinking of him as an example of Goodness.

[August] 13[,] 8[:]45 A.M.[,] Lat 58°04'S[.] this morning it is very damp and misty which requires a Stationed <u>look</u> <u>out</u>[.] Wind is very Still[,] Sterring a W1/2S course on a Starboard Tack. I just got through mending my Second best Coat at the Sleeves (linning)[.] I dreamed last night that the Vessel was ashore and Going to Frisco by land beinging launched on runners and tearing everything down in her road. I thought I was packing my chest and getting dressed up for Shore duty when all at once I woke up and found my Self turning and twisting my blankets to Such an extent as to tear one of them almost in two[.] it seemed then to me as if we would never get ashore but patience endurith for ever. So adew[.] I Suppose this morning Riely is getting the horse and pheaton ready for a morning's ride. So go ahead and enjoy yourself that way while I take my Joy in a good old nap[.]

[August] 14[,] 1[:]30 PM.[,] Lat 57°01'S[.] this morning it was as usually very disagreeable but good winds ever Since last night at 5 oclock so we have gone Since that time from 7 to 9 and 9 1/2 knots an hour, and as we got the Sun we found ourselves to be in 43°71' South of the Equator. While I was making my bed 5 minutes ago I was looking at the blanket John Sent me (the Fancy one) and thought of how many times did I carry you in the Store from the pavement[,] little dreaming that you would ever cover me around Cape Horn, but it is a fact it is all So. This morning we washed up the lifeboats in all the rain and I am as wet as wet can be[;] however it is clearing up. I find that Boatswains mate has more work to look and do than a boy So I wish I was not able to be one but it is again done. our men with the exception of 1 in the Fore Castle are all out again which also aids in making things more pleasen.

[August] 15[,] 9 am.[,] S Pacific Ocean Lat
54°37'S[.] Could you only imagine how the Ship is
rolling now why I would feel Satisfied but I know you
Can have no idea how things are flying about this
morning[.] (only 20 minutes ago) while eating my
breakfast in the Galley I was Standing on the port Side
and talking with the Cook when all at once a roll found
us both to Leeward of the Ship on top of each other[,]
Scratching like a dog for a hold of Something. not only
did we fall[,] but my Grub came to the Conclusion to
follow its master while the Cooks Coffee pot was running
after him so we both had Company. also this morning
the After Cabin or Capts Parlor was filled with water[,]
it requiring the pump and hose to empty it[.] it is
blowing very hard, though we See the Sun which is the
first time for a good while (that is a good Sight of it)[.]
We are now under reefed Topsails[,] furled royals and
Gallants Sails. The Cross Jack is also Furled. The
Captain was in a bad humor again this morning, and He
did not know where to take it out of So He Commenced
with me and the man with me at the Wheel (for it was
my watch at the Wheel) and He is to this moment
Standing at the Wheel Cursing the Carpenter the Same
as He did Me and my Crowd[.] We are Steering NW by
N[.] I must now turn in as I have been to the Wheel 8
hours[.]

[August] 16[,] 10 AM[.] as it is Sunday we are
allowed a little rest and are having good weather, a
thing which we have not had for a good many
Sundays[.] We are having a fine breeze and if the Sun
Comes out I will try to get our latitude[.] in the mean-
time I will wash and dress my self as I feel and look to[o]
dirty for humanity[.] last night I had a dream in which
I thought that George Leber was Sole owner of the Grain
house and that He had Carpenters and brick layers to fix
up the SW Corner of the Warehouse, and I thought there
was a Conspiracy among the workmen to Rob him and
in order to do it they were building a private passage

along the wall of Said Corner (from the ground up) large enough for a man to pass through but which could not be noticed on the out Side. and I thought that I was Called upon to Join the robbers and done So but only with the intention of learning their whereabouts and Secrets So as to expose them. but before I could accomplish my object[,] I thought this Ship was running up to the dock in Frisco and I was So glad over it that I gave one Shout which woke me up when I found it near breakfast time. So my dreaming Stop[p]ed there. how I wish I were ashore now that I might eat a good Soft boiled egg and Some ham with good fried potatoes and onions and Some warm buscuts [biscuits] with butter and a good Cup of Chocolate[,] but alas I am condemned to wait till I get it and not demand[!] I think I will not go to church today as it is to[o] far[.]

3 P.M.[,] S Pacific Ocean Lat 47°,57'S[.] as I expected the Sun came out but with it came a Strong wind. however we have been making a very good run within the past 24 hours[,] as by observation we are found to have run 401 miles on 6°40'North of 54°37'. So the less Subtracted from the greater which is 47°57'S. you may think Strange of that little round ball and coma [comma] always after the figures but the round ball denotes degrees, and the coma miles. 60 miles to a degree and anything less is put down as minutes or miles[,] as 1 minute is equall to 1 mile but is Set down for minutes on account of working Chronometer time of the Ship[.]

7.45 PM.[,] S Pacific Ocean Lat 47°.57'S[.] in a few minutes I expect to go on deck again to Reef Topsails, the wind having turned into a perfect gale[.] it is raining and otherwise disagreeable[.]

[August] 17, 9.15 am[.] this morning at 4 oclock our watch turned out to unbend the reefs and Set Sails again which was all done till 8 bells or 8 oclock[.] the wind has Subsided considerably Since last night and the Sun now Shines in my window as it would of a March in

York. Still all this weather is pronounced fine [in comparison] to what we have had. Yesterday we Summed up the days (number of) we had our oil Skins on with putting them of[f] and found that for 3 1/2 weeks we had to have them on evry day. I have given up all the rest of my charge on this Ship with the exception of Boatswains mate which includes Ensign[,] boss of the watch at the wheel and orderly. My chum has taken the pumps and Cross Jack braces, He having been found efficient in yesterdays drilling for them. I am within five things of being able to be boatswain and Could learn them would I have a liking to this life, but when I get to Frisco, if I See a Chance to learn a trade (Carpenter) why I will take it. if not I expect to go to Galveston[,] Texas and from there to the Island of Jamaca [Jamaica,] West Indies unless Uncle Louis Should Send me to Yuma again. I must make a Strike Some place and fear now that if I am Compelled to Go to Jamaca I will be unable to celebrate the 100deth aneversary of America unless I Should make money enough to pay my passage home and back again[.] I am now to be kept awake again by that infernal turning machine of the Carpenters which is now in motion and will not Stop I Suppose till dinner time[.] So Adew to you all[.]

August 18[,] 2 P.M.[,] S Pacific Ocean Lat 41°,29'S[.] wind is again blowing hard and last night the Main Gallant Starbord Sheet gave away which caused another day's hard work. by observation of the Sun to day I found us to be in Latitude South 41°29' or having traveled 6°.28' to the Northest of 47° 57'[.] We are Shipping heavy Seas again[.] I am all wet, but all is well again when I get ashore[.] I have just been thinking of our poor Uncle Sam and then Comparing him with the 4th and 7th verses of I Corinthians 13 Chapter, where it say, "Charity Suffereth long, and is kind; Charity envieth not; Charity vaunteth not itself, is not puffed up." Again in the 7 it reads Thus "Beareth all things, believeth all things, hopeth all things, endureth all things.["] all these I think poor Uncle Samuel is possessed of and allwas [always] was but was Steped upon before he could Speak, but I hope god may yet look upon him with pity and aid him in his troubles[.] I must now go to Sleep[,] So adeu to you all and kiss little Bonny & Cassie for me.

[August] 19, 9 a.m. this morning is a windy one from the head. So we are not making much progress. ever Since 4 this morning we have been hard at work upon the Sails. the Captain has very likely Stoped our allowance of Coffee in the mornings as this morning he came on deck and gave orders to Set the Main Topsail when Just at that moment the watch were taking coffee, however he allowed them no time and Said that if that was the way we were going to obey his orders why he would Stop the Coffee So I dont expect to See any more Coffee in the 4 oclock watch. there has been a general fuss Since last night aboard and will very Soon terminate in either a fight or peace[,] but wait till Frisco is in Sight[,] then will be the time to See Some fighting as the Crew have already programmed the thing out[.]

August 20[,] 1[:]30 PM.[,] S Pacific Ocean Lat 36°41'S[.] This morning was a beautifull morning and Continues to be so all day at this rate. it is getting warm again and a person again feels him Self coming home. I have been lugging hard tack into the Cabin with my "Crowd" all morning. there is very little wind now[,] though I hope it may blow up towards night only not too hard. Just so as to get to Frisco on about the 25 of Sept. while going into the Cabin I Came across the California examiner which I never knew the Captain had till then and I will now make a raid on him for them[.]

[August] 21, 10.30 AM. I Just got done packing my Chest again and I hope the next packing it gets will be in "Frisco[.]" I had every thing out of it and Stowed them anew[.] I must hurry up or get no Sleep as I have yet my bible to read and Some news papers which the

Captain gave me[.] as reading news-papers makes me feel like being ashore I must not neglect it[.] yestterday by observation we were in Lat 36°.41'S. or having travell in 48 hours 288 miles or 4°48' to the nothest [northeast] of 41.29 hence decreesing[.] how I wish I were ashore. it is a fine day with wealing winds[.] We are Steering N.E.1/2 E[.] I expect all hands will be called on deck from Monday on till we get to Frisco[.] Adieu Dear Sister and know that I think of your [you] always[.]

5 P.M. this is a fine day[.] We Just got done Scraping the Main Gallant Mast which will be oiled to morrow. fine winds Steering NNE1/2E[.] I must now go to Supper. today, I gave the Steward a Glass Cutter which I bought in NY, Just so that he might keep giving me a little better Grub than is allowed us.

[August] 22[,] 7.50 AM[.] this is the first time for a good while that I post in the morning So early but I hurried up my breakfast in order to do So. It is a very pleasant morning and a moderate breeze[.] the Sun is Shinning in my room like home Sweet home again but still we get no more Sleep and will get less from Monday on and perhaps from to day[.] I expect to go to the wheel to day as my foot unables me very much in going up aloft. Just think we have now come down as low as week's when we come to talk of the time it will take her to get to Frisco: from 5 to 8 weeks rangs through the whole Ship as her time but I give her 5[,] my Chum 6. I am an[x]ious again to see "ground" as I am all buggard up from this life. We will Soon commence of Changing Sails but I must now go as 8 bell's have gone and it is my watch on deck.

6.30[,] S Pacific Ocean Lat 33°56'S[.] I have Just finished my Supper having been at the wheel 7 hours to day and you cannot imagine how tired my neck is from looking at the Mizzen Gallant Sail; We now being Compelled to Steer by the wind; I expect the next thing on the programme will be "About Ship" which will put us on a "Starboard Tack." today at noon I found us to be in Lat 33°56'S. which now puts us very near Valaporaso [Valparaiso.] I am writing this by lamplight while the Carpenter (who rooms with us) is Sitting on the water Cask with his Russian Finn book on my Chest reading away like a good fellow. he is a very good man and industerous. I must go on deck 8 hours tonight but I dont [dread] it as the weather is pleasant and besides all that tomorrow is Sunday and a gods blessing come[s] with it I hope as we all need it as [and] also rest. I expected to hear the Main brass work again this afternoon instead of which came the Holy Stoning again on the poop and Scraping the Cross Trees. I must Stop So good night dear Sister and kiss Bonny and Cassie for me. and remember me to Lizzie if you yet have her.

August 23[,] 9 AM[,] S Pacific Ocean, Lat unknown. this is a fine Sunday but we had to go to the brass work this morning which makes me Still feel bad to think of it[.] I only hope that in 4 or 5 weeks I will be clear of it. the Sundays here are not much regarded as a day of worship. indeed I have almost come to think that I never had relig[i]on were it not for my books which remind me of it.   Still we are having a fine breeze[.] Steering N1/2E, 5 knots[.] as I Set writing this I cannot See a clean Spot about me[,] the dog even having the impudence to come an[d] "Spew" on my bed (he being very sick)[,] not only that but a hog pen could not look worse than our floor[.] however I will try and clean it up a little which will at least take me till 4 bells or 10 oclock[.] when I Say 1 bell in the morning I mean half past 8 oclock, 2 bells 9 oclock[,] 3 bell half past 9, 4 bells 10, 5 bells half past 10[,] 6 bell 11[,] 7 bell half past 11[,] 8 bell 12[,] then it Starts in on one again the Same as before till 4 oclock when it Starts in new and so on for every 4 hours. last night I had Such a pain in my foot as to compell me to lay down on deck for awhile as I was not able to Stand on it any longer. I believe Something must be broke as I come down on it <u>very</u> hard when I hurt it[.]

[August] 24, 7.55 A.M. I will again try to post till 8 bells if I can get finished. last night about 10 oclock it commenced to blow a strong breeze of 12 and 11 knots an hour and Still Continues So which is making me feel happier every hour I know the wind is keeping on[.] besides all that we are Steering pretty near our course, she now heading NW by N3/4W[.] we have about 97 degrees to travel yet before we get to frisco on account of having to go to the westward as far as 122 and we are only in 92 or 93[.] So you may See for yourself it is a very fine morning but every once in a while we Ship and Spit a little water which makes us put on our oil-skins. I Sleept very little last night on account of my foot and back paining me So, but 8 bells now go So I must be on deck.

6[.]30. today was the first day for all hands on deck and will now be the universal rule.

[August] 25[,] 10. AM[,] S Pacific Ocean Lat 14°.02'S[.] this is a very [fine] morning and things look bright[.] We Just took our Sick man out in the air but there is little hope of him living longer[.] the Captain was in my room talking with me very pleasantly and acted like a good fellow[;] moreover yesterday He and I were doing nothing easle [else] but making fun of an old 60 year Sailer from 8 in the morn to 4 in the afternoon[.] I must now turn in as it is late. So adieu.

[August] 27, 9 AM. it was impossible for me to post yesterday as we have now commenced Scraping the Masts and Yards[,] Changing Sails and Holy Stoning [so] that I actualy find no time to write hardly[.] We are having a fair wind of from 10 to 13 knots and Steering NW by W as our course and are in Lat 14°02'S, according to yesterdays reckoning[.] our poor Sick man is very low[.] when he first took Sick He was a Stout and able man and now he looks as thin as a rail and must be Carried about. We dont expect him to live much longer and the Captain Seems much worried about him as there is a rumor afloat that He was not attended to properly[,] which if reported when on Coming ashore would Cause Considerable trouble with him and would very likly have his papers taken from him for a Con Siderable time.

[August] 28, 1[:]30 am. while I write this, there is a party watting [waiting] by the Side of our Sick man expecting him every minute to Breath his last, poor man. I know he goes to meet his God unprepared. this is a fine day and good winds[.] Still Steerings NW by W but our Lat [latitude] I cannot get as to be on deck now at 8 bell is almost impossible (which [I] must be to observe the Sun) Since there is So much work to be done[.] I only hope we will Soon be Across the line[.] as I am Just thinking of it lest I Should forget it again I will put it down. a few nights ago I dreamed and thought my Self again taken back by Aunt C. for training, but in a different way from my previous dreams. for I thought She caught my [me] by the neck and Commenced Choaking me and hitting me over the head at a terrible rate Saying that She would let me know Who She was, where upon I thought I Seized her but what I done I cannot remember any more. I must now Stop as 3 bell will again Soon go.

[August] 29, 8.30 AM[,] S Pacific Ocean Lat unkn[own.] this is a very fine morning again and hot but the hotter the better. but alas there is Something more sad to relate[:] last evening at 25 minutes past 8 our poor Sick man breathed his last. I am sorry to have Seen a man die So unprepared as he was. Still it Seemed that He knew he was to die, as Just half an hour before hand he asked what time it was and after being told, He Said we Should let him alone; and from his groan's it is very evident he dieid [died] a pain full death. His disease as yet unknown to you as I omitted telling was nothing but the Common Called Pox of which he was So effected as to be almost entirely rotten in his Stomach[.] in fact the Captain would allow no one to Sleep near him as the Stench was intollerable. After he died We took him out and tied his mouth Shut[,] his hand's and feet together, and as I had previously Sold my U. S. blanket to him on trust for [$]7.00 but which I will now loose. So We laid him on this blanket and put a large lump of Coal and two massive iron blain pins at his feet and thus he was Sewed up in his Sea Coffin. Next we took and laid him under the Gallant Forecastel till burial[,] which time no one knew. So last night at 11 oclock (while our watch was on deck) the Captain Came on deck[,] ordred the Ship to be hove to which Consisted of lowering the royals[,] hoisting the Mainsail and Cross Jack, and bracing up the Fore Yards[.]   having accomplished this He ordered the dead man to be brought forth, (who was now on a Sliding platform) which was done and one end of the platform being put on the rail So that when the other end was raised he would Slid down. this done the Captain asked the man at the wheel how he was heading and having got an answers he gave the order to launch him (the dead man) which was done without any Services being read ovr him as before and not even Calling all hands on deck to witness it. We are getting used to deaths it Seems on board here as now out of 27 man [men] only 23 live[.] this morning we holy Stoned the poop again. I am told by the Mate that our Lat is 15°S and 101'W which le[f]t us 72 degrees to make yet all together till we reach Frisco.

[August] 30, 9.30. AM[,] S Pacific Ocean Lat 15°.00'S[.] this morning is a fine day with fair wind Steering NW. last night it rained a very little Just enough to give a fellow a good Sundays wash. while I write this the Captain is Setting aside me Smoking a Cigar which now reminds me of home. He is having quite a conversation with us: Making free in every thing[.] He also has lent me one of Mark Twains books "Called Innocents abroad" which is very intresting[.] I have put my boots on for the first time Simply to Stretch them for Frisco.

1[:]30. P.M.[,] S Pacific Ocean Lat 10°.30'S[.] You will See by my todays latitude that evry day decreases our distance. the Capt Says that the place we are in now is the finest in the world for Steady winds for the time being and it is to be believed. but Still I cannot make up my mind to go to Sea. I would rather go to Church and Sunday School.

[August] 31, 8.45 AM[.] fine days I find are now again coming more regular as this is again one of them. things look pleasant now again and I feel happy. this morning we Cleaned the brass work, but I was Stationed up on the Fore truck or in other words went up as high as the mast head clear to the top and Sat there 3 hours watching for Ships but none were to be Seen. I expect the Captain to Come again to loaf here as usual. So I am prepared for him. I must now mend my pants and Cover a book after which I will go to Sleep[.] How I wish I had a plate of Strawberries now[,] but never mind, we wont be long from Frisco any more.

Sept 2[,] 8.45 AM. fine morning but much trouble again, as this morning the 2nd Mate again mutulated a man fearfully, which is getting the Crew up again. no doubt when we once get ashore this Bennsion will get the most fearfull beatings he ever had[.] We have been very busy these last 2 days, So I was unable to post. Yesterday we got up out of the hold the "port" Anchor Cable which is to be Scraped (80 fathoms) and Coal tared after which the "Starboard" one weill [will] be handled the Same. We are now pumice Stoning the masts and taring [tarring] the runing gear. Still there is 2 months work here all of which must be done before we get to Frisco. the Captain tells me that in 15 or 16 day from the Equator we aught to be in Frisco and according to that we aught to get there in 18 days or 19, as we are now Some place around 6 or 7 degrees South. a good plate of Strawberries and Ice cream would not go so bad Just now, but I am a little inclined to live on Salt horse meat a little while longer[.]

[September] 4[,] 9. AM, S Pacific Ocean Lat S. fine morning but very little wind[.] the Captain was talking with me all my watch below last night from 6 to 8 and Said that the line or equator would probably be crossed today. We have now the Main and Mizzen Masts pumicestoned and are beginning to work on the "Fore[.]" We have now the port Anchor Cable ready for use and will have the Starboard one the Same in a few days. things are beginning to look a little Showish but Still there are Some 14 or 18 day to be passed yet. how I do long to get ashore So as to get a decent meal and a nights Sleep which I cannot boast of hear.

[September] 6[,] 1.30 P.M. this is a beautifull Sunday, and I am looking Still more beautifull, for I have on my boots and Second best pants[,] white Shirt and a linen coat[,] So I feel a little Shoreish[.] I put on another dirty undershirt this morning but notwithstanding that it is cleaner than the one I had on. it is true I might put on my Suit of Clean under clothing but I must have Something for "Frisco[.]" the Captain now makes more Free with us then with his first Officer. He Says that for 19 years of his Sea life He never came across a man So hard on Sailors and So mean as this present first Officer, and He also Says that the first 3 days out Sickened him and had it not been for a bet on the trip that this Ship was to make He Says He would have gone back and put him ashore[;] however he Says He will allow it no longer than to Frisco[.] We Crossed the line [equator] on Friday evening at 6.48 PM[,] So you So [see] we are in the North Pacific Ocean[.] We are having a moderate breeze and Steering NW by N1/2N[.] yesterday my Chum and I cleaned out our room which Consisted of taking every loose thing out and Scrubbing the paint work with Canvas and Ashes (talk about house cleaning) and holystoning the Floor after which every thing was put in again and now it looks like a dollar[;] however in the Contest my chum went to Shake his blanket out and unexpectilly his pillow was in it but it was to[o] late to get it after once overboard. this morning I put on my last clean pillow case, which must now do me until we get to Frisco. the Steward caught a "bueneto" (fish) this morning of which I managed to get a piece. I now expect to get back my Sewing case again as the Captain is going to look it up[.] He Says we expect to get watch and watch the remainder of the trip which will not be quite So hard on us. this morning there was a general row again between the Captain and the 2nd officer Concerning my taking the wheel[.] the 2nd officer Said I could not steer in order to put one of his pets there and the Captain Called him a damn liar and Said He knew a little about Steering him-self[,] So much So that he did now [not] want a 2nd Mate to Come and tell him his business. I expect to See blows but however all passed of[f] well,[.] John as usual I Suppose is in Sunday School while you are laying on the lounge with Bonny by your Side and Cassie washing paint[,] the room darkened and evry thing upside down waiting for the coming of Papa[.] how I wish my Self back again but I Suppose Frisco is a finer place though there will be no kind Sisters advice to guide me there from the Snares of the devil but I hope the word of God may console me as much and even more[.]

[September] 10[,] 9.40 AM[,] N. Pacific Ocean Lat 2°.00'N. we have now lost the South East Trades [winds] and will fool around here till we get to 12 or 14 N. again afterwhich we will get the North East Trades again. it is a pleasant morning. we have been Scrubbing the paint work for painting[.] Last night I dreamed again a [of] Aunt C. in which I thought She (Aunt C) apologized to me for all wrongs done me by her and also took me to her again and gave me her gold watch. the Captain Says in about 19 days from now we aught to be in Frisco[.] I have been with him in his room for over an hour looking over Charts and He has been trying to teach me the use of a Chronometer, how it works and is wound[,] a thing very new to me. He is a very pleasant man and it Strikes me that many an order has come from his Officers, that he never knew any thing about. our Lat now is 120°West and 10°49'N, which lets us yet 26°39' to go yet or 1,599 miles to the Northeast and 15° west or 900 miles making a total of 2,499 miles to be made yet which be made very easy with a wind of 7 1/2 miles per hour which is very likely to be had[.]

[September] 12[,] 9 AM. Since the morning of the 10th we have been going one way and theen the other and So are not making any headway of any account what-ever untill this morning when Something like the N.E Trades presented its self which I hope will turn better by and by[.] during our Calms and fine weather every possible effort is made to bring the Ship into port in "Ship Shape Style." we are now Holy Stoning the Main Deck and Gallant Fore Castle, though they will have to be gone over Several times before Completed[.] about 5 oclock this morning a Ship "hove" in Sight Steering a SSE Course evidently bound around Cape Horn. She prowed [proved] to be an English man (or Lime Juicer[9] as a Sailor calls them[)], So we did not speak [to] her as it [is] uncustomary for american Ships to Speak [to] an English Man[.] last night it rained hard So I had a good wash any way to go to Frisco with. I must now turn in as I feel very tired and Sleepey. Kiss Bonny and Cassie for me and give my regards to Mrs Earney[.] also remember me to A W Elliot[.] as usual John is in the Store taking [talking] the life out of him Self trying to Sell a Silk or Alpaca dress about this time I Suppose[,] So He dont Just Care to hear about me at present[.] Adieu and I hope in 2 weeks I may be able to Stand on Terra Firma.

[September] 13[,] Sunday 9 a.m.[,] N. Pacific Ocean Lat 16°00'N. this is a fine morning and I am

---

[9]"Lime Juicer" is slang for a British sailor or ship.

Just expecting to wash my Self. I hope this will be the 2nd last Sunday aboard of this Ship[.] the Captain as usual has been in our room for a good long while. He is in hopes we will make it in 12 or 13 days though the wind is against us[,] for instead of Steering NW by 1/2N (our course) we are going N by E1/2E[,] So you See that is going against us Strongly but Still we are making headway[.] I have already made an Avowal that I would only eat on board this Ship 1 Sunday more which I hope may Come true.

[September] 14th[,] 9. AM. fine morning with light breeze[.] being as Holy Stoning is done now for a few days we are waiting for the NE Trades So as to go on the paint work. I feel clean Since we have been having these little "Showers" but Still I am and would be dirty in the eyes of a Shoresman. last night I had a dream about John V and my Self and Billy horse but exactly about what I cannot recollect any more[.] I must now turn my attention to business after which I shall leave for Sleep Town[.]

6.30 PM. Just think dear Sister We have had watch and watch given to us this afternoon <u>very</u> unexpectilly which is to last the remainder of the passage. it is very warm but no wind. Steering a N by E1/2E Course.

[September] 15[,] 2 PM[,] N. Pacific Ocean Lat 16°00N Long [1]19°00'W. being as watch and watch is now again in full Sway I will more regularly post up this book. I have been painting all morning at the Anchor Windlass[.] I expect to get done to day after which I Suppose I will be put on the poop. we are making very little headway as there is no wind but it is very hot[.] I have Sold my pillow for $1.40 and my fox skin for [$]1.00 making [$]2.40 and have [$]5.50 from my mattrass which is [$]7.90 pluss my money remaining from New York 875 [$8.75] which makes a total of [$]16.65 clear money without my wages, and I have now been 4 monthes employed by the Ship at [$]10.00 per

month [$]40.00 plus [$]16.65 which is [$]56.65 in
Greenbacks out of which comes [$]5.50 for articles
purchased on the trip makin [$]51.15 which when
changed into Gold is worth 4425 [$44.25] in Gold[.] Still
I have 3 Shirts and 2 blankets but I will Sell yet So as to
have as much as possible in Frisco[.]

[September] 16[,] 9 AM[.] Alas this morning I am
compelled to tell you bad news. Yesterday afternoon the
Captain and Mate had a long Quarrel about Some work
not having been done which resulted in the with drawal
of Watch and watch again, making it very unplesant for
us, however our hopes are that it will not be long So
anymore[.] The Captain never Could agree with the
Mate (first) and in plain words told him So yesterday[.]
ever since the Quarrel things look badly though it
Seems to have had an effect upon the wind for
immeadilly after the Occurrance the wind Shifted from
NW by W to SW by S which again allowed us to go our
Course though this morning it is a little Calm with
intermitante Showers[.] one pair of my Shoes are good
for nothing as they are to[o] tight around the instep. I
was in Arizona last night (dreaming) tending Uncle
Louises Ferry again but accidently I woke up on the St.
John to wash decks again[.]

[September] 17, 10.40 AM.[,] N. Pacific Ocean Lat
17°.10N. Long 117°55'W[.] you will see that I am a
little late this morning in posting up but Since the
Captain and 1st Mate have had the Quarrel they don't
eat nor work together and being as the 2nd Mate knows
nothing relating to Navigation which I do and therefore
am requested by The Captain every morning to work up
Chronometer time, which takes me Some time. We are
in company with an English Ship which proves to be
friendly in this kind of weather as She has hauled along
side and is within hailing distance but each Captain is
to[o] proud to either hoist his Country flag or Speak the
first word though I have no doubt if when once
commenced it would be kept up briskly. Such weather

I never heard tell of in my life of travels. it is nothing else with late than a 'Continual Course of Tuck's evry half hour. one minute we are Steering N next E next ESE Next W and So on all around the compass at a fear full rate. we are now in 18° 20' North which is 24 miles of being half way between Frisco and the Line[.] one of the Crew has asked me to make him a will of his property for his wife and child in England as he is afraid that he might die before getting home. I thought possibly he might have an old pair of Shoes for his wife and a Mathawaca knot for his child or a cat or dog or anything not wirth mentioning but He tells me he was heir to some 400 pounds Sterling and left a good trade (Carpenter) Just to go to See and Seeing his folly he wishes to make Sure of his wifes Safety[.] He Says that [h]is personal property amounts to 925 pounds or [$]4625 dollars in American Money. I told him to come to me on Sunday.

[September] 18, 9 AM[,] N Pacific Ocean Lat 18°20'N Long 118°.02'W[.] this is a fine morning but no wind as yet[.] our English Man is a little to the wind ward of us now but we will catch him Some Time to day. I feel like being ashore which I now hope will Soon be however I must turn in as I feel Sleepy. Kiss little Bonny for me[.] adieu[.]

[September] 20[,] Sunday, 7.30 AM[.] this morning we are not cleaning brass work on account of having everything around it painted thus one of these hateful trips is dispensed with[.] We are now getting a Slight touch of the N.E. Trades which cheers us up again after having been in Calm weather. the way things look now I Suppose there is as much work to be done as we can do till we get to Frisco. I am writing this while it is my watch on deck. I also washed my Self So now all I have to do is to make that Fellows will I spoke about after which I can turn in[.] today our Lat is 19°. 40'N and Longtitued is 118°08' west[.]

[September] 22[,] 9 AM[.] I am Sorry to have omitted 1 day but actually I found no time especially

when I had to be Second to a fight in the Fore castle
among the Sailors between the Starboard and Port
watches[.] It seems the Port watch Sailors have been
missing clothes (Small trifles) for Some Time past but
Said nothing untill last night at about 6 oclocks when
they thought they had the thief for certain. they
deliberatly went into our Fore castle and demanded an
explaination through one of their men who was the best
fighter among them[.] this man at once charged the
best man in our watch (Charles) of the theft[.] it took
but a little time for a fearfull fight. all this time,
however, I was Sitting with the Captain in his room, but
upon hearing a noise forward that Sounded like
Something falling (which afterwards proved to be these
2 fellows throwing one another on the decks) I
immeaditly Sprang out of the Cabin on deck while the
Captain was on my heels to know also what that noise
might be, whereupon our eyes beheld these 2 fellows
now on the deck going at each other with knives while
the whole Ships Company was Standing around and
very near all of them Sided against poor Charlie who
was now cut badly and bleeding hard[.] Seeing things
in this condution [condition] the Captain Said the
Starboard watch must thrash the port one and with his
pistole in hand came to See fair play while I ran in the
Cooks gally and took there from 2 large knives[.]
Swinging them around me I Soon cleared a circle for the
2 fellows to fight it out in[,] defying at the Same time the
port watch to fight our Side. So our Side hearing this at
once Set to work upon them and in 5 minutes they had
them all pened up between decks with the exception of
these 2 fellows fighting who had now relapsed, as one of
them was to[o] far gone from the loss of blood to Stand
up and is now feared wont live much longer[,] So
Charles came out all right with but a few cut on him
while his antagonist is very low at the present time of
writing. but in the Mean time the Captain and first
mate got at each other for Just So Soon as the mate

Seen his man getting the worst of it he undertook to go for Charlie but the Captain leveled his pistole at his head and kept it So till the fight was all over, and even now this morni[n]g we expected a renewal but it did not come. we are having a good wind and are now in hopes of getting up to Frisco in 8 or 9 days. Just think, 8 or 9 days to 18 weeks[.] I must now turn in[,] So kiss dear little Bonny for me and give my love to John[.]

[September] 24[,] 9 AM, N Pacific Ocean Lat 22°15'N Long 121°09'[.] Yesterday I again neglected posting but I am So much taken up with the winds now that I almost forget you[.] I am Sorry to say that instead of getting to Frisco in 8 or 9 day it is uncertain now when we will get there as the wind wont allow us to come up higher than WNW while we Should be going NNW for a good time[.] at this rate we will bring up at 139°00' Longtitude and 38 00° [38°00'] Latitude which will take us another week to run in from that point and we are only in 25°07' now[.] So there will be Some time yet till I can get to Frisco. I feel well and be assured that I look So too[.]

[September] 25[,] 7.45 A.M. Just finished my breakfast[.] It is a fine morning and I am in hopes the wind will change before much longer[.] the paint is progressing rapidly and will Soon be done for the Second coat[.] our Latitude yesterday was 27°20'N and Longtude 130°00'West So we are now pretty near the place where the winds generally change from the NE and W to NW. and W hence we are looking for it[.] the poor dog "Tip" is tied to my chest to keep him of[f] the fresh paint and you may be assured he makes quite a noise on the head of it[.] how I am longing to get ashore once again. oh how I hope the wind will change if it is Gods will[!]

Sept 26, 9 AM[,] N Pacific Ocean Lat 28°04' Long 131°09'W[.] fine morning and warm. We are now Completing painting very nearly. the Fore hold is thorely cleaned and the next is I Suppose to Holy Stone the deck and oil them once more before going in[.] this morning quite an excitment was created beween the Steward and Boatswaine which resulted in the lat[t]er Striking the former very Severely in the face for insulting him. however all is right again and things go on Smother [smoother] than I expected So near the discharge port. I must now turn in as I am very Sleepy[.] give my respect to the Connelles and A W Elliot. kiss little Bonny and Cassie for me[.] much love to You and John——Adieu[,] Louis[.]

[September] 27[,] 10 A.M. Sunday again and as usual always expecting it to be the last[.] this one I hope now will be the last as I am getting Sick of it, but I must go to bussines. The "Boatswaine" is now laying very Sick and in consequences thereof I am appointed in his Stead which desolves [devolves] another task on me but however I hope it will not be long[.] it is very warm now though we are having a good breeze and are now in Lat 30°00'N. and Long 130°02W which is to be hoped will Soon be completed[.]

[September] 28, 9 A.M. as Boatswaine I must now write like one. last night was my first night in Charge of the Crew though I Scarcely could comprehend it[.] Still, I was respected and looked up [to] as Such[.] I now have all the work to do that is requred [required] aloft[,] So you may imagine that I float pretty high Some times above the level of the Sea. The Captain told me last night that He thought of giving us watch and watch again which would give us 12 hours below out of 24 instead of 8. this is a beautifull morning but noe wind though this morning we had a breeze of 8 knots but it only lasted 3/4 of an hour. I must now turn in[,] So bid Bonny and Cassie a kiss for Lullie and remember me to Abb Elliot[.]

Sept 29[,] 1[:]30 P.M.[,] N Pacific Ocean Lat 32°19'N Long 127[°]47'SW[.] this is a fine day with good winds[.] We now expect to be in by Saturday if the winds keeps on but I doubt it. the deck will be finished

Holy-Stoning this evening[.] I just got through darning my Stockings[.] I must Soon get ready for Shore again[.] we will commence oiling down tomorrow at which time I expect to get Some for my chest[.]

[September] 30[,] 9. AM. Now over 4 months on board yet and Still not in Sight of Sand [land.] it Seems rough. last evening the wind changed from NNW to NNE which compelled us to Steer NW by W[,] hard braced up and making no headway towards Frisco but on the Contrary more towards the Cost [coast] of China[,] though[,] Should this wind last[,] in a few days we would again tacks for Standing in on Frisco[.] but it is to be hoped that it will Soon change. you will see from the Lat in yesterday that we were in a parrellel with "Fort Youma[.]" I will now explaine a Theif I have traced out from Liverpool when this Ship was there last[.] She had the Same Cook and 2nd Mate in her as now. this Cook while on a drunck last trip lost his watch and Knife (dirk) but knew know [no] one that Could be Suspected. while He and I were together a great deal He once commenced telling me about this watch and knife where upon I Just rememberd Seeing the 2nd Mate redeem the identical watch and knife as (identified by the Cook) from a pawnbrokers Shop and also Saw it while aboard. this led to a general Search for which purpose I put my Self up as a detective (to receive as a reward the knife if I gained the case)[.] So last night I watch my chance at 8 bells and went in the 2nd Mates room and ravished his things where upon I found this watch. having Showed it to the Cook He almost went crazy to think that his watch was again coming to him, but to avoid Suspieson [suspicion] I told him I would put it back again and in the morning He Should tell the Whaller (Captain) about it[.] So this morning he told the Captain who at once approved of my plan and told me to Get it for the Cook again and let him keep it while He would Settle it with the 2nd Mate[.] however I will leave now to demonstrate with him as I cannot altogether See through it fully[.]

Oct 2[,] 9 AM.[,] N Pacific Ocean Lat 35°20'N Long 125[°]00W[.] the watch affair is all over now as the 2nd Mate has not yet discovered its removal[.] We are now getting near Frisco and also into "Fogs;" the Correct distance from here now is 258 miles which Could be made easly in 2 days if we only had wind[;] however now there is hardly a breath of it again, though we have been having Splendid winds for the past 48 hours. I cannot tell just now wether or not I will remain on board of the Ship when She gets into port, though the Captain wants me badly to look after the "Cargo" while being discharged. if I Could get to go as "Super Cargo" on a ship I would willingly accept of it.

Nov. 5. I will Send this book to You to day as day after tomorrow I Shall leave for San Diego[.]

[This is the end of the voyage and its diary.]

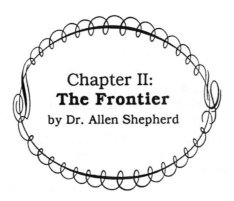

Chapter II:
The Frontier
by Dr. Allen Shepherd

Louis J. F. Iaeger's adventures did not end with his sea voyage from New York to San Francisco in the fall of 1874. Indeed, they had just begun. After completing that voyage on the *St. John*, he signed on with other ships. On one voyage he served as quartermaster aboard the Pacific Mail Steam Ship Company's *City of Pekin*, which plied a route from the Pacific to the Orient.

At some time between 1874 and 1876, Iaeger met a young English nobleman, who employed him as a companion and secretary to help write a book about a voyage around the world. While on board the *St. John* in 1874, "Billy the Bear" had borrowed a copy of Mark Twain's *The Innocents Abroad* from Capt. Scribner, and now his life would imitate art. He and his employer roamed across Europe, visiting many of its ports and large cities. In Paris, the pair probably visited Notre Dame cathedral and the Louvre, as Twain had; in Milan they likely saw the famous opera house, La Scala, and paid homage to Leonardo da Vinci's masterpiece, *The Last Supper*; in Constantinople, in all probability the travelers were awed by the beauty of the Hagia Sophia. The two eventually reached Australia, but after a time the restless Iaeger decided to return to the United States.

In his country's centennial year of 1876, Iaeger
landed a position with the Bancroft Publishing Company
in San Francisco and worked as a proofreader for Hubert
Howe Bancroft's Western America series. Bancroft had
come to California in 1852 as a book salesman. This
astute businessman then built the largest and most
diverse book store in the American West and gathered
the first Western Americana book collection. For the
Western America series, Bancroft hired over six hundred
men and women to extract the "facts" from his vast
library. He sent another staff of men out across the
West into the homes of the pioneers to extract their
reminiscences and copy their letters, records, and
diaries. Back in San Francisco, Iaeger and others
proofread the manuscripts.[1]

Soon Iaeger cast his eyes elsewhere. Early 1877
found him again in Australia, then back in California as
a member of an acting troupe. It was then that he
received his colorful nickname, "Billy the Bear." Iaeger
later explained it had been given to him by none other
than Col. William F. "Buffalo Bill" Cody:

> In the San Francisco grand opera house
> about 1877 I was cast in a fairy play called
> "Snowflake." I was a wicked bear and was
> supposed to drop dead at the touch of Cupid's
> wand. I fell directly under the heavy steel drop
> which started to descend on me. Simulating the
> dying spasms of a bear, as I imagined them, I
> worked myself to safety just in time to escape.
> My death quivers and agonies, combined with
> the situation, brought down the house. Colonel
> Cody, then an actor, was in the audience.

---

[1]Irving Stone, *Men To Match My Mountains* (New York:
Berkeley Books, 1983), p. 524. See also John Walton Caughey,
Hubert Howe Bancroft: Historian of the West (Berkeley,
California: University of California Press, 1946), pp. 99-117.

Portrait of "Buffalo Bill" Cody
which he gave to "Billy the Bear"

General McDowell asked who I was and Cody exclaimed: 'Why, that's Billy the Bear!' and it's been Billy the Bear ever since.[2]
The nickname followed Iaeger for the rest of his life.

Tiring of the stage, "Billy the Bear" Iaeger came to North Platte, Nebraska, as "Buffalo Bill's" private secretary and worked there at Cody's Scout's Rest Ranch until 1878. By that time, Cody had come a long way from his early days riding for the Pony Express and shooting bison for railroad workers. Although he had not yet organized his "Wild West Show," Cody was in the process of climbing to fame and fortune as a true American hero.[3]

Iaeger continued cowboying after he left "Buffalo Bill" and Scout's Rest in 1878. During the Cheyenne Indian uprising of 1878-1879, "Billy the Bear" escaped the fate of fellow cowboy James Williamson, who was killed by the Cheyenne on May 5, 1879, while working on the McCann Ranch near the Niobrara River in Cherry County, Nebraska. Iaeger, then a cowboy on the Sharpes Ranch east of Valentine, Nebraska, carved a red cedar marker for Williamson's grave in the Sand Hills. The original was returned to Iaeger around 1911 when a stone marker was placed on the grave, and he displayed it in his office for many years.[4] It was given

---

[2]The *Omaha World-Herald*, as quoted in Louis J. F. Iaeger obituary, *Chadron Chronicle*, March 13, 1930.

[3]For information on "Buffalo Bill" Cody, see his own *The Adventures of Buffalo Bill* (New York: Bonanza, 1904) or Don Russell's *The Lives and Legends of Buffalo Bill* (Norman, Oklahoma: University of Oklahoma Press, 1960).

[4]Memorandum from Jay Higgins (Forest Supervisor), Halsey, Nebraska, March 19, 1924, in E. Steve Cassells and Larry D. Agenbroad (comps.), *Cultural Resource Overview of*

to the Ft. Robinson Museum after "Billy the Bear's" death and now is in the Nebraska State Historical Society collections.

In the early 1880s, "Billy the Bear" Iaeger tried his hand at cattle ranching around Alliance, Nebraska, and in the newly-opened Niobrara River area. He purchased the Snake Creek Ranch in the Sand Hills, but he did not keep it long. Traveling to Texas, he purchased fifteen hundred horses, drove them to Kansas, and sold them for a profit. The early 1880s were still flush years for the open range: An expanding American beef appetite seemed insatiable; easy money was to be made;[5] and Iaeger took a small share of it.

During these years, Iaeger's wanderlust carried him to Denver, Colorado (where his brother Thomas lived), to Salt Lake City, Utah, and to Cheyenne, Wyoming. Then the lure of a new gold rush took him to Idaho. There, poor judgment cost "Billy the Bear" $45,000 in a gold-mining venture. Sluice boxes, assaying and Au were not Iaeger's strongest suit. Broke (or nearly so) after his Idaho experience, he took a job near Laramie, Wyoming, working for Sudduth & Montgomery as a rangehand. His pay was $75 a month.

Then "Billy the Bear" took advantage of "Buffalo Bill's" recommendation that he head the new "Yellowstone Cattle Co." being organized by eastern investors. During late 1882 and early 1883, Iaeger lived at the Bar M Ranch, north of Rock Creek, Wyoming, and bought cattle for the eastern market. As he rode to

---

the Nebraska National Forest (Longmont, Colorado: Plano Archaeological Consultants, 1981), pp. 121-124.

[5]The cattle kingdom is covered by Ernest Staples Osgood, The Day of the Cattleman (Chicago: University of Chicago Press, 1968); and Robert R. Dykstra, The Cattle Towns (New York: Atheneum, 1970).

"Billy the Bear" (at right)
with a cowboy friend
named McCall (ca. 1880)

Rock Creek to catch a train for Omaha, Nebraska, on January 31, 1883, Iaeger was caught unprepared in a four-day blizzard. He was so badly frozen when rescued that he subsequently lost both of his legs below the knees and all of his fingers, except for his thumbs.[6]

After Iaeger was released from the Laramie hospital, he went East to be fitted with two Kolbe artificial legs. It took "Billy the Bear" about two years to learn to balance himself on his new legs, to hold a writing utensil, and to hunt and peck on a typewriter keyboard with the short appendages his hands still retained. Thus equipped, Iaeger rejoined "Buffalo Bill" Cody as his personal secretary and bookkeeper.

"Billy the Bear" worked in Omaha for a year before settling in the brand-new Nebraska town of Chadron in October 1885. Iaeger's new home, a typical boom town of the Eighties, was a product of the extension of the Fremont, Elkhorn and Missouri Valley Railroad (later known as the Chicago and Northwestern) into the Nebraska Panhandle. The result of the competing metropolitan visions of Frances Brainard "Fannie" O'Linn (Chadron's first female attorney) and Edward E. Egan (the town's first newspaper publisher), Chadron was home to such notable personalities as James C. Dahlman (later long-time Omaha mayor).[7]

In Chadron, as readers will learn below, Iaeger's stints as Bancroft's proofreader and Cody's secretary/bookkeeper proved valuable experience as he searched for a new line of work. "Billy the Bear" also

---

[6]Louis J. F. Iaeger obituary, *Chadron Chronicle*, March 13, 1930.

[7]See Rolland Dewing, *et. al.*, *Chadron Centennial History: 1885-1985* (Chadron, Nebraska: Chadron Narrative History Project Committee, 1985), for more information on Chadron's history and famous residents.

*"Billy the Bear," posing with his "artificials"
and other handicapped friends*

quickly jumped into the hurly-burly of Chadron's local politics. Over the next four decades, the ex-sailor/actor/cowboy would serve four terms as Justice of the Peace (sometimes called "Police Magistrate" and "Police Judge"), eleven years as City Clerk, and several terms as Clerk of the Dawes County Court and Deputy Clerk of the U. S. District Court. Here in Chadron, Louis John Frederick Iaeger, alias "Billy the Bear," would play out the rest of his life.

Chapter III:
1885 (Diary)

Chadron[,] Neb[,] Oct 14th[,] 1885[.] arrived here and found every thing in a whirl[—]excitement[,] plenty of Cow-Boys in town and lots of gambling going. John Keys, Allen, Harvey and [name missing] are running the gambling in the Gold Bar Saloon which has just opened up and Shows Signs of doing a big business.

Oct 18th. Billy Carter and Tom Christan gave me the Hazzard Table in Carters Saloon, and I drew a good play from the Start[.]

Nov 2[.] Keys and Allen have quit the Gold Bar. McNutt has now got in as a partner.

Dec 15[.] Tom Christen leaves for the Hot Springs[.]

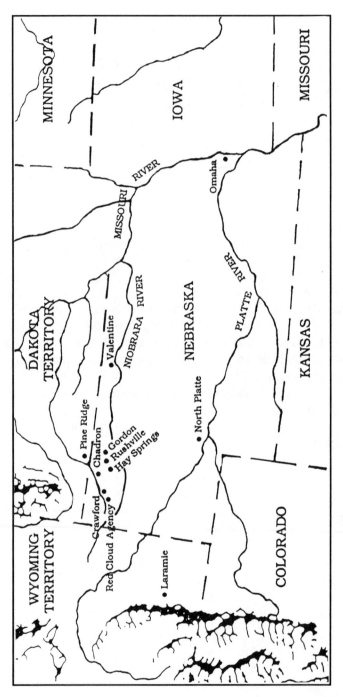

*Locations in the Northern Plains that
figured in "Billy the Bear's" life*

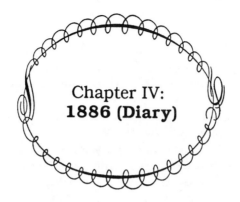

Chapter IV:
1886 (Diary)

Jan 1, 1886[.]   The Gold Bar Opera Co gave me a benefit at which I netted $56.00.

Jan 9th[,] 1886[.]   Hawks & West took a benefit at the Gold Bar, but did not make enough to pay expensis[.]

Jan 20.   Tom Christan got back from the Hot Springs[.]

Jan 24.   Tom Christan, Tony, Patsey and my self went down to Valentine in [to] take in the "soldiers[.]" Patsy and I had lots of fun on the train going down.

Jan 26.   all hand's (including Billy Carter [w]hom we met in Valentine) started back for [C]hadron.

Feb. 1st.   I Settled up by mutual agreement [w]ith Carter and Christensen and took the [g]ambling privelege at the "Gold Bar" where C A Burns is now as Receiver, The firm of [M]cNutt & McKie having appointed him.

March 14[.]   W. H. Tucker and Sam Roberts having made a bid for the Gambling priveleges [at] the Gold Bar and Suceeded in getting it, have compelled me to give away to them.   They [h]owever retained me as floor manager and gave me a 1/2 interest in the Hazzard Game.

83

Feb 26. Tucker and Roberts have thrown up the spongue [sponge] at the "Gold Bar" and McNutt & McKie again came to me and offered me the Saloon back. This I agreed to do if they would Sign a Contract for a certain length of time. And upon them failing to do so, I concluded to withdraw from the Sporting fraternity altogether. As I can now see where by good behavior, straigh[t] forwardness and honesty[,] I can in some way manage to make a little living whereby I may feel more comfortable and enjoy myself in many more ways, than

Advertisement in the **Chadron Citizen,** *February 23, 1893*

I could by prowling around a Saloon all night waiting for some sucker to show up which work, at its best, tends only to demoralize and degra[de] the most saintly man on Gods Earth. with this end in view I at once sent to Brother Thos for a Remington No. 2 Type writer stating to him my desire for wanting the same. This was forthcoming as soon as the mail and Express could carry it here from New York and on the 11th day of May 1886, I formally rented an office on Egan St from Boone & Myers at $15.00 per month, and Solicited Type writing from the Lawyers of the Chadron Bar. This however after a trial of 2 weeks proved unsuccessful as things commenced to develope themselves very plainly to myself that I had got into a Hot-bed of Republican Schemers and Cut-Throats, who[,] Jealous of my Ambition strove in many ways to make me trouble.

May 20. C. Dana Sayrs, a Gentleman and Lawyer from Girard[,] Crawford Co[.,] Ka. and with whom I had the honor of getting acquainted[,] I found was a man of undaunted courage and principal, bearing an honest looking countenance, and having as nice a family as any man could wish to have. with this man[,] I on the 21st of May formed an alliance of partnership so as in order that by the use of his law library I could in connection with an unlimited experience of himself benefit by the study of both. This at once drew the "Broad Side's" of the Republican Ring, which at this time was composed of Burr Shelton, A Bartow, G. W. Clark, N. P. Cook[,] J. A. Wilson, T. F. Powers and The Dawes County Journal[.] of these Powers made himself the most conspicuous, ably assisted by Cook and Wilson.

May 24th[.] The City Council appointed me Police Judge in place of J A Wilson who was elected and failed to qualify on account of having a Homestead. This appointment by the Council was about all that the "Ring" could stand without bursting. It caused a Stir among the prominent ones of that concern as was not caused Since the time of their first defeat in County politics, and the full force and tool of their venom kept things in Such an agitation untill on the 28 of July the Councill agreed to call an Special election for the Office of Police Judge.

Aug 10th. To day was special election day for Police Judge and it is needles[s] to say that I got elected by a majority of 103 votes.

Aug 12. now things are commencing to move on a little more regular and the "Brick Bank Gang" has not much to Say for themselves.

Sept. 11. To day was the time of Holding the Republican Primaries at the Court House. Bartow[,] Powers and Egan were the prime factors of the meeting but they and all their intentions and motions met with an overwhelming defeat, Contrary to the law of usurpers. the Pattison ticket was put through in this meeting, much to the disgust and mortification of the leaders of the Republican Gang of Bankers[,] Lawyers and Schemers.

Sept 18th[.] To day the Republican County Convention was held at the Court House and J. D. Pattison was not nominated by that body for County Commissioner[,] His principal Opponent being L. G. Sweat who in conjunction with his two Brothers-in[-]law defeated him. The principal cause of Pattison's defeat can only be attributed to the unavoidable absence of P. M. Dorrington whose influence in Pattisons favor was self evident to all.

In order to prevent the republican medlers of the M.A.A. (Mutual admiration Association) from seeing all[,] the Democratic Primaries were held on the Same day and hour of the Republican Convention. At this meeting the following parties were selected as delegates to the County Convention[:] T. H. Glover, C. D. Sayrs[,] Tim Morrisey, Tom Madden, Jim E. Owens, C. W. Allen, Joseph Maiden, C. V. Harris, J. W. OBrien, L. J. F. Iaeger, W. Morton[, and] Tom Moore.

after the meeting was over, The news that the Republican Convention in its meeting had not nominated J. D. Pattison for Commissioner Spread like wild fire among the local politicians of Daws Co. But the Brick Bank Gang, M[.]A.A. and "Journal" crew never were in a more jubulent State. Joy and Satisfaction reigned Supreame[—]the wild and Haggard countanance of the Editor of the "Journal[,]" as he with arms folded[,] was now changed to a Smile[,] indication of Such venomous words and noises as reminded a bystander of the famous "Devils Mills" in Persia.

Sept 19[.] To day I went to Dry Creek with Hank Simmons to look at some land.

Sept. 22. To day the Democratic County Convention met at the Court House[—]everything passed off quiet, [and] not a dissenting voice was heard from any of the delegates from abroad.

Sept 26. To day, J. D. Pattison, county commissioner and myself went over on Indian Creek to look at a School Section. We had a fine time but got caught in a wind Storm coming home when on Chadron Creek. after coming home, Sheriff Clark, J. W. OBrien and myself took a trip around Town to see if some clue to the disappearance of some money which was alleged to have been Stolen in One of the Sporting Houses from w. green [W. Green] could be found. We took in all the houses, but faild to come across anything that would even lead to suspicion. about 12 oclock while we were at Maud's we were joined by Dunlap and Alsop with their gang of cattle Shippers and then things commenced to fly high and wine began to flow freely. I however concluded that was a poor place for a Police Judge to be at the best. So I screwed my nut out the back door and went home where I belonged.

Sept. 27. Charley Nebo came to Town and I met him at Gottstien & Owens. He was just commencing to get full. I gave him a talk about it and then left.

Sept 28. Fred Danielson came back from Douglas, whence he fled 2 months ago to keep from being locked up. As I bound him over to keep the Peace and fined him $50.00 and costs for carrying concealed weapons[.]

Sept 29[.] Tommy Carter came back from Douglas whence he fled from here on the 6th inst. as a warrant had been issued for him. as soon as he landed on the platform[,] however[,] J. W. OBrien arrested him and he was arraigned henceforth. He plead not guilty but after all the evidence was in against him I fined him $5.00 and costs which he paid and went away kicking.

as soon as that was over OBrien arrested Chas Nebo for ridding on the Side walks. He plead guilty[—]$5.00 and costs. He had a lot of money on him, but I took it all away from him, and put it in the safe[.]

Sept 30. Charley Nebo was the first one who met my sight this morning. He was mounted and about 1/2 drunk. The Sheriff was watching him as a vulture only can when he awaits the death knell of a doomed beast, for it has leaked out that Charley has got a lot of money in his possession and that being the case, Clark would arrest him at the drop of the Hat. But his money is safe—Charley is one of my old time companions on the range and as long as I know anything he is not going to get the worst of anything. I finally persuaded him to come along with me to my Office where I got him to lay down and Sleep. Pete Nelson took his horse up to the Store or Stable[,] I do not know which[.]

Oct. [1 or 2.] Sayrs and myself left Chadron for Charley Neboes place down on Cottonwood. We first called on Dave Powers on Bordeaux and then took the road up the Canion [canyon]. Myers followed us and we had some beer. We got to Charlies place at 5.30 in the evening and were welcomed. Sayrs went down to the creek to fish and afterwards laid the fish line down on the ground with some bacon on the Hook and one of Charlies Cats got nipping at the bait and had a great time getting the Hook out of his mouth. Charlie's Wife was very sick with rheumatism.

Oct [2 or 3.] Sayrs and I left Charlie's for Chadron intending to call on A W Fowler but did not go on the right road. We came by McLaughlins place.

Oct 4[.] C W Allen[,] delegate to the Democratic State Convention from Dawes Co.[,] left Chadron for Hastings to be in attendance[.]

Oct 11[.] C. D. Sayrs, E S. Ricker, and A. J. Gillespie left for the Southern part of the county (Dawes[)] on an electioneering trip[.] the weather today was anything but inviting for such an undertaking, nevertheless after some sound turning over from myself they all concluded to Start out[.]

Oct 12[.] To day I put up my Office Stove which I bought from M. M. Harrah. The weather is still cold and disagreeable and I would not be surprised to see Sayrs and his gang come back. To day the Case of English vs West of Forcible entry and detainer Came up before me. A motion for continuanse was filed and granted for 8 days.

Oct 15[.] Fine weather again, and contrary to my expectation Sayrs and his gang of Democrats have not returned. I have just finished fixing up my winter Sleeping apartments and getting my wood Sawed for a while. To day the Case of Lullu Cassady vs. John P. Monnett came up before me on Forcible detention of Plffs [plaintiff's] property. A motion filed for a continuance and after much debate by Bartow I over ruled his objections and granted the motion for contionuance of 7 days[.] C. S. Goodrich's Salesman came to town to-day with his samples. I took him around and introduced him to the trade, endorsed his draft on his house, and treated him as a friend should.

Oct. 17. Nothing new. Sayrs and his gange are still unheard of and it may be surmised they are stumping the County in grand shape though I fear their trip was made to soon before the election as it gives the Other side a chance to follow up and undo all their work. There was quite a wreck on the road this morning near Hays springs, and in consequence the Passenger did not arrive here until 11 oclock am. 7 hours behind time. Concerning the coming election I can only see one thing of importance in it, and though it seems a secondary affair to a Democrat it nevertheless looms up apperantly in the front row, and that is the division of the County.[1]

Oct 18. Sayrs & his gang got back last eve at 8 oclock but did not show up at the Office till this morning. They report the feeling throughout the southern part of this County as rather more of a democratic nature than they expected to find and they feel jubulent over their trip. The day was put in by my self in writing to the State Dem. Central Committee in Omaha concerning the Democratic prospects in the County and requesting that some good speakers be sent up here before election. The Case of Fletcher vs C. A. Cooper came on for hearing today and upon agreement of both parties the case was continued Till Nov 10th 1886 at 10 oclock.

Oct 20. To day the celebrated case of James English vs Sanford C. West came on for hearing which was adjourned at 6 P.M. till tomorrow. There seems to be great anxiety on both Sides.

Oct 21. The English & West case was decided in favor of West after long and spirited arguments on both sides.

Oct 22. The case of Lullu Casady vs John P. Monnett for forcible detention of property came up and was decided in favor of Plaintiff. I wrote a letter to W. H. Webster to come up here and speak.

Oct 23. Case of Anderson Bros[.] vs. Calvin Lemmon came on to day and went by default[.]

Oct 24. Very dull Sunday. The main question at issue is County Democracy. Bennett Irwin came to Town and commenced getting things ready for the election. during the afternoon I stayed in my office and lectured on historical facts and in the evening made

---

[1]In 1886 the south half of Dawes County became Box Butte County.

researches in Johnsons Universal Cycloopaedia. Harry Young commenced rooming with me.

Oct 25[.] The weather has been fine all fall with the exception of a few rainy days[.] at present it is like spring. This morning I met Bennett Irwin[,] our candidate for representative from the 59th District[,] and introduced him to Mr Sayrs after which I wrote a letter to Sheriff Eubanks of Cheyenne Co contemplative of the support of B Irwin from that part of the district, also one to Bob Shuman at Sidney upon the Same subject.

Oct 31[.] The weather to day has been very fine. I Stayed in the Office nearly all day writing letters and getting out Subscribtion papers for Scrub Peelers benefit. Sampson woke me up this morning, during the afternoon Mr Sayrs Children and Glovers little girl came down to the Office. After Supper Sayrs came down Town and I met him at Carters Saloon. I gave him a great turning over about keeping full with in the past 2 weeks whereupon he struck out for home and promised me he would do better. during the evening Bob Lucas came over to my Office and we had a genial chat about travels over the world, after which Tom Madden joined us and we all repared to the Chadron House to see Mr Pattison (County Commissioner) as to designationg the voting place in the City, it being my object to have my office fixed upon in order to keep it from Egan St as there is all probability of a close contest and if we can keep Egan St in the dark there is Some Show of fair play. Yesterday All. C. Fowler was in from the Second Table Country and he reports the universal feeling among the people in his part of the Country as against division of the County. Notwithstanding which it is the hope of all democrats in Chadron precinct that it will be carried by a good round majority.

Nov 1st. Winter has at last set in, and Snow is once more on the ground. It rained nearly all day and towards evening turned into snow and Sleet. Tom Madden is flying around town feeling good over the prospect of bad weather for tomorrow as in that event there will be a great many republican voters stay at home, in consequence of which a democratic victory is almost assured. To day I got out the first issue of my political paper "The reporter[.]" Young Edgar, the Editor of the <u>Crawford</u> <u>Crescent</u>, came to Town this evening in Search of the Ballot Boxes for Crawford and also poll Books. Sayrs is keeping in good trim. I went to bed at 12 P.M.

No[v] 2[.] To day has been an eventfull one for the Second County and precinct election. I worked hard for the Democratic ticket. But by degrees things commenced to show up in favor of the Republican ticket. No attention was paid to the County ticket, the main issue being the State ticket. I however took a Snug position by the Ballot window and Succeeded in getting 2/3 of the Republican voters to Scratch in favor of myself. after the polls were closed and in order to prevent any miscounting by the clerks[,] one of whom was slower than the Second hinges of—[,] I made a tally list of my own and followed the counting business myself, and by 5 oclock in the morning we managed to get through which Showed a Republican majority of 66 in the Town. I beat my opponent for Justice by 85 Majority[.] Things look pretty gloomy for the rest of the Democratic gang and the Democratic Constable is beat right now by a Majority of 29. Rickers (Dem) chances over Spargur (rep) look good. But Sayrs and Gillespie look like the Hen pecked Husband.

Nov 5[.] The Election returns still keep the Town people astir and all reports go to confirm the sure election of Ricker for County Judge and Ballard for County Atty with Blanchard for Superintender of instruction. Thomas Carter and M Berry were sent to jail to day on a charge of vagrancy[.]

Nov 9[.] Mrs Joslyn has quit keeping boarding house and will go East in consequence of which I on Sunday last called on Mrs Hood to see about board, But have concluded to take up quarters at the Chapin House table. James OBrien and I had the riot act between us, and I gave him to understand just what I thought of his crooked work for the past 3 or 4 months, and let him know that he was not Shutting my eyes in any way. Jim is a good fellow and I shall always remember him but He has to[o] many of the "New York Boodle Politician" in him to ever succeed in getting any responsible office. Honesty is always at a premium and when a man is honest he can face the Devil with impunity[.] on the other hand[,] guilt will not let him sleep good. —The weather was again fine and fair, but towards evening it commenced to blow and cloud up as if it was getting ready to Snow.

Nov 12. To day has been a fine one again[,] Clear and warm with good Signs of it continuing so for Some time. last night Mr Howard Lander came up from Hays Springs having in custody Wm Summers who stole $10.00 from Tom Whites Saloon. I ordered him to be locked up but released him to day on account of Tom White not wanting to prosecute him properly. The Vagrants have all been pardoned out of Jail by the Mayor and are commencing to leave town as fast as they can. Tom Madden has come to Town to Stay and the next thing in progress will be a Young men's Democratic Club with Tom as our leader.

To day Sayrs and I got at the Chimney and had a nigger burn it out and fix it So as to keep it from Smoking. I also had all my wood cut up for both Stoves and had a great deal of fun with the darkey that cut it. As I am feeling in a pretty good mode [mood] I will devote my self to Politics for a little while[.] Now the Election is over, and the Democrats can ponder over and figur at the probable result of the next county election which will be next fall (1887) and then there will be no State ticket to give to those Republicans who only look at the word "Republican Ticket" and only vote for "Governor" or "Congressmen[.]" It is true enough that all elections have more or less both Republican and Democratic Tickets and it is also true that no matter whether it be a State ticket or a County ticket[,] there are always some who vote a Straight ticket no matter who may have his name thereon. But on the Other hand the Democrats has many claims of prominent distinction from the Republican voter in that he is more liberal in his views, he pays more attention for whom his honest and free vote is going to be cast, Thereby making more of a clean record for himself. Nevertheless there are always Republicans of that Same Stamp, but they are not as predominating as among the Democrats. Therefore in view of the fact that at this last election the Democratic ticket was over run in favor of a Democratic man for County Judge, and also that Chadron Precinct gave a majority for Justice of the Peace and Road over Seer[,] both Democratic men, while the popular vote of the County was Republican. This shows that there must have been some Scratching done in favor of Democratic men, also the Democratic County attorney only suffered defeat by 5 votes north of the proposed line of division of Dawes County and beat the Republican nomanee in every place that both candidates were known, which goes clearly to show that though a yellow dogs name had been on the Republican ticket he would have been elected and Simply because there are to many ignorant voters who vote for people they know nothing at all about. It is therefore to be hoped that at the next General County Election the voters may pay closer attention to the Candidates which of course will be the Case as there will then be no State ticket to deceive the voter, "who always wants to vote for President" and cares not what other name be on the ticket. Just so he votes his choice for president. This last dodge is of course taken advantage of in many cases by both parties. But while it is an historical fact that the Democrats of the "New York Boodle Gang" or "what are we here for" crowd knew not how to read and write and as the Republicans used to say[,] only voted the Democratic ticket in order to hold their Job. Such is nevertheless not So now in the days of refined and enlightened Democracy as the average raw Democrat having learned to read is able to see things for himself. But what do we find among the average raw Republicans[?] nothing but what the raw Democrat has lost can be noticed in Some of the would be wise Republicans who are ever ready to Show their gall as a Set of to what they Style Cheek in the Democrats.—

[November 13.] It is now 1.30 am. Nov 13th and as I am sitting here writing, there comes sounds and familiar noises which indicate to a well trained mind that there is just now a nice little "row" going on down in the Gold Bar Saloon—[.] Have Just returned from the Scene of the row and learned that George Spaulding and Joe Fielding have been having a Set to accompanied in all their manuvers by Maud Simpson who is on a glorious spree.

Nov 13. The day opened bright and Cheerful reminding one of the winter days of Honalulu. George Havens carried in my small wood and during the afternoon I took a ride out round Town and also made a trip to the artesian well, after I got back I mailed a lot of letters to "Pony Bill" at Cheyenne who is the traveling correspondent for the North Western Live Stock Journal. I also received a letter from Johnny Sims in Douglas. The day closes quiet and the Sun Sets for another bright one tomorrow[.]

Nov 14. Sunday and the weather is still fine but Showed Signs of Snow toward night[.] during the day Tom Madden and the rest of the Democratic Gang made their headquarters at my Office. Harry Young has come to Stay with me, he having been Sick with the Mountain fever. during the evening Charlie Morrisey came around. The main issue among the Democrats here now is Shall pattison be appointed as County Commissioner to fill the vacancy or Shall a democrat be put in[?] The argument in favor of Pattison is a good one in that that it will keep the Republicans at war with each other and thereby insure a complete victory for the Democrats next fall. Tom Madden is working hard for Pattison.—

Via last night after I had retired I was awakened by Sayrs, OBrien, Ben Tibbetts and Ed Hunter, who wanted to get out a warrant for a man in the South part of the County for having Shot one of Tibbetts horses. This caused a general Stir in my Office and after a long pow wow, the proper complaint was filed and the warrant will be issued as soon as they can send the proper name of the man whose name they are yet in ignorance of—[.]

Nov 15. It Snowed toward night to day. the Case of Fletcher vs C A Cooper came up and after a great many quarrels between Powers and Spargus the case was continued till nov 22[,] 1886. Hatch the barber came over and asked to sleep with me as he said he had had a quarrel with his land lord.

Nov 16. The day opened up Cold and some 3 inches of Snow on the ground. I turned my bed around in the bedroom and moved the Stove. Edd Burns came and asked me to see to Tom Dixons house who had left it in his care. I went up with a party to look it over with a view of renting it to him, But we could not agree upon the price. after I got back to the Office I found Mr Richard Frewen awaiting me for the purpose of getting some writing done on the Type writer, whereupon I packed up the Machine and we went over to the Danielson in his private room. after supper I went to the Congregational Church Sociable and found many new acquaintances. came home about 10 oclock and found Mr Frewen waiting for me.

Nov 17. Clear and Cold all day. after breakfast I went up to Tom Dixon's house and got his Sewing machine and took it to Mollie Lindsey's house for Safe keeping. I also took all his clothes and blankets to my room in order to prevent anyone useing the house for lodging purposes. Mrs Ann Smith applied to me for aid from the County in which she asked for some fuel. I gave her some of the wood at Dixons house and will charge it to the County for him. Wright came up to me for $30.00 but I could not let him have it. Mr Frewen called on me again during the day and told me he had lost his case before Wilson. Business is very dull. H. T Willoghs had a Mortgage deed acknowledged before me today. County Commissioner Pattison came in to see me to day. after supper Mr Frewen again called on me to have a Social Chat and after he went away I proceeded to look after some of the Vags [vagrants] around town.

Nov 18. Clear and cold all day. Mr Frewen and Mr Coe of Coe & Custer called on me today, at 1.30 P.M. the case of S. Fletcher vs C. A. Cooper came up and the Plaintiff asked that the Case be dismissed without prejudice. G. W. Clark came and asked to have complaints made out against all Prostitutes which was cheerfully granted[.] After Supper Mr Frewen called and gave me $5.00 to Start a fund to get my self a new pair of legs. after He left I Steped over to the Danielson House and met a great many old time friends from Douglas. after traveling around town with Atty Hamplin in hunting up Justice Wilson and County Judge Byington, we finally got down to the Depot just as the Snow bound train got in from the East.

Nov 19th. The day opened up with Cold and clear weather. I received my certificate of election as Justice of the Peace from the County Clerk. Sampson Came in to see me and left again for Douglas. The City Counsel met at my Office to discuss the Fire protection Question at the Instance [insistence] of F. M. Dorrington who Seems to be very anxious to have the City purchase a hand Engine. They the Counsel however done nothing more than to instruct the City Clerk to advertise for bids for Sinking 2 wells to hold 350 bbs of water each, whereupon they adjourned. about 2.30 Oclock P.M. a man by the name of Walker was brought in from Merritts Saw Mill, who had the misfortune to have his hand caught in the buzz Saw just above the wrist. Dr Davidson was called to do the work and at my instance [insistence] the Dr Sent for Dr Miller to assist him. I volunteered my services to put him asleep and between the three of us we managed to make a successful Operation, and the patient is now doing well.

After getting through with the Sick list I proceeded to Commence a Suit before Justice Wilson against R. E. W. Spargar for $2.00 which I done Simply to show him that he could not bull rag me. after Supper I called on Dr Miller and had a long talk with himself and wife about Salt Lake & C & C. after leaving there I went up to Mr Fullers house.

Nov 21[.] I missed Saturday but cannot stop to go back. today I passed nearly all my time in the Office. in the evening I went to Church to hear Dr Powell preach to the young men which proved to be a very good Sermon. I think I learned some good advice and trust that it may do me good. The weather during the evening was very blistery and all indications go to point out a Storm.

Nov 22[.] As anticipated last night the Storm is here in great Shape and "King Blizzard" is at present in all his glory. like the old Soldier "it reminds me of old times[.]" Oh that I may never again see or feel those agonies I suffered when freezing on the Laramie Plains. today has been rather a quiet one outside of the Howling and blinding Snow Storm for it is raging fearfull with not a Sign of any relaxious [relaxing]. I got a new coal Scuttle and Shovel and by dint of some great Squeezing I managed to borrow a Scuttle of coal for my little stove in the bedroom[.] I also rented Tom Dixons house for one month at $10.00 per month to E. W. Peterman a married man.

After Supper I called on Mrs Joselyn and Daughter and spent a very pleasant evening with them.

It is now 9 oclock p.m. and the Storm is Still on it's heels and as things look now there is little hope of getting any mail into Chadron from any point for quite a while.

Nov 25[.]   Since last posting up I have been pushing around considerably[.] The Snow Storm has let up ever since the 23rd. on the 22 I rented Tom Dixons house and on the 23 I went up and invoiced everything in it. on the 24 I had a general cleaning up in my office. my stove needing cleaning very bad.

This morning the weather showed up fine and as it was Thanksgiving day I concluded to go up to Mrs Hoods for my dinner where I spent a very pleasant afternoon[.] about 3 oclock I came down to my office and remitted the fine of F. O. Messinger who was Sentenced yesterday by me to pay a fine of $5.00 and costs for draying without a lisence—via. I almost forget to note the continuance of my Suit against R. E. W. Spargar before Judge Wilson for $2.00 to the 15th day of December at 1 oclock p.m.

after having dispensed with my office work, I set out for the Metheodist Church supper at May and Foxes Store where the Thanksgiving Turkey was quartered and distributed to the Queens taste[,] after which I repaired to my office in Company with one of the City Counselmen to discuss the legality of some of the City Ordinances[,] after which I went upstairs to see Mr. Walker, whose arm I helped to cut off last Friday.

Nov 26[.] The weather has again turned off nice and the Snow melted of considerably today. this morning I went up and helped to dress Walkers arm which looked very well, though it pained him some what. Nothing of any importance has occured all day, and business Seems to be getting a little dull. This evening Geo Clark arrested a man from Crawford for carry[ing] a concealed weapon[.] I Sent him up till 9 oclock tomorrow, whereupon Von Harris and P. G. Cooper went his Security for appearance[.] the City

Council seem to be in a great deal of trouble about their ordinances. After supper, Mr Stephan called on me by special request to find out as to what could be done to Thos Blackburn for not turning over certain money which he (Blackburn) claimed to have collected around town for a poor old man[.] I told him I did not know anything about it, and did not know any legal proceeding to go into concerning the Same, whereupon he left.

W. G. Pardoe called on me this evening and reports everything doing well in Crawford. he is looking about the Same as ever. Doc Parham is also down from Crawford as well as Von Harris and Cooper from Whitney.

Nov 27[.] N. P. Cook came and replaced his safe. We had a great time about it. the weather is fine again but business is dull[.] in the evening I got Tony's safe.

Nov 28[.] fine day all day. Tom Madden was in my office nearly all day. Bob Lucas and Allen were also around. In the evening I called on Mr Sayrs and on my way up I nearly broke my neck in front of the School house by falling. When I came home, I met Mr Alexander and had a few games of Billiards.

Nov 29[.] Rainy weather almost all day. in the afternoon moved Tony's safe into my office. Mr. Sayrs looks well again.

Nov 30[.] got up pretty early this morning in order to attend court before J. A. Wilson in a case of N. P. Cooke vs L. J. F. Iaeger. I filed motion for continuance of 30 days which was granted. —The weather is like Spring weather which [with] occasional rain Showers. after dinner, I went to Dawes Co Journal and got Jim Davises land matter fixed for him. I also had a long chat with Albert Paxton about making up land abstracts. about 4 oclock in the afternoon it commenced to Snow and at the time 9 oclock p.m. it is still snowing[.] after Supper I went up to Buck's drug Store and spent quite a nice time with him. in the evening Doctor Davidson came down Stairs to see me. I also recd a telegram from Mrs Langworthy telling me to collect the rent of the Magic City Hotel at once from McNutt or put him out. I served a notice on McNutt right off to Quit the premises by Dec 3rd. It was very slippery going up to the house and I almost fell down. When I came back I met Mr Sayrs at the Gold Bar Saloon coming out of the door. I seen he was drinking again. God help his poor wife and children in 5 years from today. I answered Mrs Langworthy's letter late at night.

Dec lst[.] the weather is Still a little damp. I got up pretty early and went to the Post Office where I found a letter from Brady & Bro Geo. I called on Mrs OLinn and got some pointers about the early political record of Dawes Co. about 2 oclock I was called out to take depositions in a land case in the place of E. S. Ricker who was unable to attend. McNutt called on Dr Davidson to day to rent his 3 rooms up Stairs. Nothing definate yet has come of the new artesian well and it is now coming to a Stage of the game where almost evrybody is watching it. Another feature of the present time in this City is the many parties anxious to make a bid on the proposed fire Water-Wells to be erected by the City. in the evening I wrote a letter to Bill Cody about my artificials and also one to J. W. Thompson at Pittsburgh.

Dec 2. Cold and clear all day. I recd a letter from Mrs Langworthy about her house. Also got a letter from Johnny Simons at Douglas stating that he was going to Denver[.] during the day I made out my bill of particulars to commence Suit against Fall Spargar and Fisher to recover costs in the case of Fletcher vs Cooper and placed the same in the hands of Major Powers who has promised to give his services in the case for nothing. Geo Clark got back from Omaha this morning. last night Jim OBrien and the Boys got on a Small tute at Carters. This afternoon I bought a pair of Shoes from

Mr McLeod who gave me Some time on them. To day John Root came in the office and notified Mr Sayrs that he would have Steve Harrah arrested in 3 days for destroying his property on his claim[.] After supper I went around to Dr Harris to View his new Drug Store which seems to be a nice one.

Dec 3. Clear weather with about 1/2 of an inch of Snow on the Ground. I got 2 papers from the Wild West this morning in which was noted the first opening of the "Wild West"[2] in New York, Nov 24th[,] 1886, at the Madison Square Garden.

To-day E. S. Ricker handed me the Special appointment to take depositions in the Timber Culture Entry Contest at the United States Land Office[.] Geo Clark went out to Steve Harrahs place to arrest Steve for destroying the property of John Root.— The weather is turning cold again. To-day Mike Gottstein Fore closed a certain mortgage against Mr McNutt and in consequence took some of his furniture out of the Magic City Hotel. at 8 oclock the City Council met and had quite a debate on the plans of the proposed Cisterns and[,] after much debating on the part of the City Council and City Attorney (Cook) who was beastly drunk[,] it was decided to instruct a committee to draw up new plans and Specifications, Submitting them for one week more. after the meeting I went to the Gold Bar and played a few games of Billiards with Mr Mead. After which Pete Brean came home and slept with me (during the night the bed broke and then there was fits to play[)].

Dec 4[.] The day opened up clear and cold. towards noon it moderated somewhat[.] I got a letter from Eddie Clark in Wyoming, also one from John Keyes and Frank Brady, the latter is very hard up.

---

[2]This was "Buffalo Bill's" "Wild West Show."

Dec 5[.] The day opened up Splendidly with regular Spring weather. Everybody around town got mixed up about the change of time as adopted by the Rail Road (Mountain time) which is just 1 hour Slower. I took dinner at the Danielson['s.] in the afternoon I managed to spend the most of my time in the Democrat Office. After supper I called to See the Hood Folks and had a very pleasant time Singing Sacred Music.

During the afternoon Dr. C. A. Cooper came to me to get a Certified Statement about the Judgment in the case of S. Fletcher vs. C. A. Cooper, which I gave him.

Dec 6[.] The weather opened up fine this morning and by noon nearly all the Snow on the ground was thawed up[.] at 10 oclock a.m. the case of State of Nebraska vs S. R. Harrah came up for hearing before me and by consent of attorneys the Case was adjourned till 1 oclock P.M. today. Mr White of the "Britania reprint Co." called to see me and tried to get Mr Sayrs to purchase his book.

The case of State of Nebraska vs Stephen Harrah came on at 1 oclock and no Jury being called, it was tried on its merits before me and after much arguing of Counsel on both Sides I was unable to find the defendant guilty as charged and found accordingly.

After the finding in the case, and dismissal, A. C. Fowler came in to have his pension papers acknowledged, which constitutes all the legal transactions for the day[.] After supper I went up to the Court house to present my bill for printing Summons in the last District Court. Thos Madden came to me this evening and made quite a plea in behalf of Spargur, in that I ought not to Sue him for any money and that by creating any unpleasant feelings now, I would lose his vote next year, as well also as his political influence[.] I cannot imagine how a man like Tom Madden could like [look] at the present Situation as he Seems to be doing now[,] for anyone with half an eye to business can see that Spargur's influence does not amount to much, as the figures of the late election will show plainer than the words. And where I lose his personal vote, I will gain 5 votes from the Republican Ranks right here in Town, which I would <u>not</u> get were I to allow Spargur to run over me. It is very Self evident that any one Seeing things in that light realizes their own weakness, for how could So haughty a man as Spargur ever consent to belittle himself as to Condesend to offer his political Strength for the small Sum of 2 dollars. oh no it is too cheap and entirely beyond comprehension[!]

Dec 7[.] To day has been more like Summer than any day since last July. very little business to day with the exception of a Coal bill of Tom Moore wherein Coal seems to be going up instead of down[.] Milo. M. Harrah came in to have his pension papers acknowledged. Recd a letter to day from Uncle Thos, John C. Sims and Mrs M. E. Langworthy[.] the latter said she would be down in the evening train from Lusk to attend to her Magic City Hotel property. Tom Madden was in the Office quite a while this evening. Albert Paxton is again on a drunk. Dr Davidson raised quite a fuss about Bob Dorr having a dog (pup) in the house. The old Gentleman is Slowly but surely going crazy.

Dec 8[.] Today has been a fine one all day[.] Mrs Langworthy came down from Lusk last evening and to day she has been busy getting McNutt and his family out of her Magic City Hotel. after breakfast, I went over to Justice Wilson and got him to dismiss some cases of mine against Spargur. I recd a letter from Lambertson telling me all about the "Casey" trial. This afternoon I made arraingments with Mr Sayrs to move his Office out of mine as I do not want anymore Lawyers around me. it hurts my business very much. Mrs Davidson came in for the rent to day, but she failed to get it as I had no money. Tom Moore presented his Coal bill $5.25 and which I paid at once. There are a great many old gambling Stiffs coming into Town again!

Dec 9[.] Today, if anything, was more pleasant than yesterday. Sayrs and Bob Dorr moved their office on Second St. in the Democratic printing Office. I got a boy to help me clean up their office after they left. Charlie Nebo came to town yesterday and left for home this afternoon again. Old Dr Davidson took some chances in a race horse today from Mr Quigley.

Dec 10[.] This morning the weather was a little colder than usual for the past 4 or 5 days, and towards evening it looked very much like Snow. Ben Tibbitts came to town to day and had a warrant issued for a man who shot one of his horses. last night Bob Dorr had quite an experience with Rail Roade Joe, who tried to force him to go give up some stuff. Bob got into the Gold Bar and there McNutt almost beat the would be robber to death[.] This morning Jim OBrien had a fuss with his wife and wound the matter up by moving all his household goods into my Office. the fuss is occasioned by McNutt and his family having moved next door to them, and it is generally conceded that Mrs McNutt is a hard one to get along with. —Yesterday Dr Davidson rented his rooms up Stairs. I have had no business to Speak of today and times are very dull. I gave the warrant for Ben Tibbetts's man to J. W. OBrien.

Dec 11. last night it Snowed a little and in consequence OBrien did not get of[f] for his man. This evening the Council had a special meeting to make a contract for a water engine and Hose and Hose cart, all of which was at the instance [insistence] of F. M. Dorrington[,] Chief of the fire department, who is to be commended for his unsparing energy in getting the Council woke up to the fact that Chadron is in need of an efficient fire department.

Dec 12th[.] To day it was fine weather all day, not very cold nor yet very warm. After dinner I called on Mr Alexander and there Met a Mr Knickerbocker formerly from California with whom I had a very pleasant chat about the pacific Sloop. I Stay for dinner at Alexanders. In the evening I caled [called] at Mrs Hood's and remained till 9.20 P.M. after which on my way home I met Emmet Albright and got things fixed with him whereby he was to try and get certain abstract books.

Dec 13[.] fine weather to day again and the Snow is about all gone. This morning while up at the mayors office I met little Guy Alexander and brought him down to the Office with me. he Stayed with me until dinner time amusing himself at the Typewriter. nothing of importance has happened today and in the evening I went to the Opera House to see "Mikado" with the "Democratic printing Gang.["] the House was crowded and all seemed well pleased with the play.

Dec 14[.] Fine weather again and Summer seems to be on hand before winter has Set in. Jim OBrien got back from the lower part of the County whence he had gone to arrest a man charged with having killed a horse belonging to Ben Tibbitts. The prisoner was arraigned and bound over for hearing till Dec 17th[,] 1886.

Dec 15th[.] The weather to day has been very fine. This Morning Tom Madden commenced work on digging the City Cisterns (2). he Commenced on the cor[ner] of Main and Second, and Second and Egan St. I got my Shoulder Strap repaired. The Mayor told me today to make out some complaints against the prostitutes and G. W. Clark Said he would Serve Them. Judge Cook Said he would draw up an Ordinance regulating a Stipulated fine in those cases so as to enable the prostitutes to pay a fine of $5.00 every month. In the evening Gerry came in to See me about the Warrants being gotten out against the prostitutes. The Rail Road Brakemen have their anual Ball at the Skating rink this evening. Miss Maud Chapin and Mr Pahl are to be married this evening. little Guy Alexander came down to See me this morning and I took him to dinner with me, after which he went home with Mr Burke[.] Von Harris came down from Whitney this evening.

Dec 16th. The weather opened up fine again and by all appearance, Things got to indicate that Tom Madden is going to have good weather for digging his Cisterns. Johnny Lama came in Town this morning enroute from Omaha west. Hee is one of my old time Chums on the running water. Mrs Langworthy got me into her Hotel this morning and gave me quite a talk about her hotel. it seems that the "Magic City" has about gone up the spout, towards evening the weather turned very Suddenly to bad, and by 9 oclock P.M. it was Snowing and Sleeting, with a Strong wind prevailing. after having gotten the Democrat out, Bob Lucas, Von Harris & myself went around to Trumans for lunch, after which I went to bed.

Dec 17. The weather opened up clear and cold this morning. The Witnesses in the Case of State vs Hoffman appeared this morning at 9.30 am. and being instructed by me that their expenses would be paid by Mr T they again depart to make their reappearances tomorrow at 2 P.M. about 4 oclock P.M. while in the Democrat Office Bob Lucas got on a high horse and I read the riot act to him and left. when I came in the office again Bob was as nice as pie.

After Supper I went with Mr Burke to his drug Store and there met Messers[.] Glover[,] Senior and Junior. We had Some very nice instrumental music. I came home about 10 Oclock in company with Young Geo Havens. After I had gone to bed and fell asleep I was aroused by a man who wanted a Search warrant for Minnie Sloggy's House where he claimed to have lost $450.00. Hee made no hesitation in putting up the required amount of money to get out the necessary papers. So I forthwith issued them, directed to J. W. OBrien, the City Marshall. But while I am positive that the money was taken by the parties accused, and that too as I am told the Marshall having been in the house at the time, nothing of the money or pocketbook could be found, with the help of a Search warrant.

Dec 18[.] To day was a fine one all day, but toward evening it Snowed a little. This morning at 9 oclock Ben Tibbitts came in the Office to see about his case. at 2 P.M. the case of the State vs Henry Hoffman came on for hearing on a Charge of Horse Killing. after having heard all the evidence in the case I decided that the Jury would convict So I bound him over to the district Court and also required certain of the witnesses to enter into proper recognizance for ther Appearance[.] The trial closed about 6 oclock and after evrybody having given recognizance, I went to Supper and while there J W OBrien went to pounding Henry Hoffman over the head for trying to get away from him, Jim thinking he had not given bonds for his appearance[.] the Dutchman came around to me for a United States warrant for OBrien so I Sent him to Hunt up the Mayor. This he failed to do and came back again, when I told him to waite a little as I was busy in getting out a warrant for Lake and Hally. But Hee would not waite, but ran out of the Office: to go elsewhere for Justice. H. C. Fowler called on me afterward and got me to make out a deed of some property he had sold in Pittburgh Kansas.

Dec 19. Fine morning. Mr Sayrs came down early and cleaned up the Office so as to look half respectible when Mrs. Fowler came down to sign the deed. This having been done, I repaired to the Democrat Office and the remainder of the day was spent around Town.

Dec 20[.] It Snowed a little this morning and more or less all day. G. W. Clark made out Complaints against the Sporting women of the Town today, and 7 of them came up and paid their fines, leaving 6 more to come tomorrow.

Mrs McNutt and Lizzie got on a Spree tonight and made quite a noise on the Street. in the evening after

Supper I called on Mr Bellanger and had quite a long chat with his family[.] I also called around at Burkes Drug Store. The weather is getting pretty cold again and by the looks of things it will snow tonight.

Dec 21st[.] To day has been rather a dull one[,] nothing of any importance going on in the Police Court. I made a Social call on the mayor this morning. To day Keys and Soder Sold out their news Stand on Second St to Lou Greishelhumer and Paul. The cisterns are getting along splendidly and Tom Madden is certainly the right man in the right place. The weather has been medium warm to day but towards evening it turned a little cold. about 4 oclock this afternoon one of Mr Wm Browns men out at the Slaughter House fell into a well backwards, a distance of 15 feet, and cut his head very badly[.] Dr Miller done the Sewing up and made a nice job of it it assisted by Mr Burke and Archerd.

Dec 22. To day has been a fine one all day and Tom Madden is getting along fine with his cisterns. Von Harris and P. G. Cooper came down from Whitney to attend the meeting of the K of P.[3] To day I made out the Transcript in the case of the State of Nebraska vs Henry Hoffman and sent it to the District Court.

Dec 23[.] last night was a pretty cold one but today the weather has been pretty good, and Tom Madden is doing finely on his cisterns. This morning I purchased a little Top & Sword for Guy Alexander and a Scrap book a piece for Etta & Mamie Sayrs. I also Bought a nice goose for Christmas Dinner, and if I live till then I hope to enjoy <u>one</u> good meal in the past few years. last night I beleive I spent the worst 2 Hours in Thinking and meditating over my past life That I have experienced during my existence in this world[.] I hope I may never more be troubled the Same way.— Visions

---

[3]This was the Chadron chapter of the Knights of Pythias, a men's fraternal order.

appeared to me in reality that Shocked me to my utmost
capacity and like "Dante" I was brought to a realization
of the Subject matter of mans existence and his mission
in this world. I found after Some serious meditation
That ever since 1869 and 1866, I have been on the
wrong road—the road of Sin, Corruption, and Utter run
[ruin]. It is my earnest hope to make amends
forthwith[,] Cheer up, have more Courage in my
hereafter, and leave behind me the inevitable
despondency always so predominating in one of my
Sensibilities. during the afternoon Dr Miller called
around and I had quite a nice chat with him about
things in general. about 4 oclock the Chadron Band
played on the Street as an advertisement for their "Ball"
tonight. after Supper I went up to the skating rink to
See the good dancers but failed to get a glimpse as they
did not come on account of the Cold weather.

Dec 24th. This morning I recd a nice letter from
my niece Cassie Vandersloot[.] in it I see That she must
be getting along splendidly with her education. She
says Bro Charles has now got a boy in Oregon which
makes the first Iaeger Boy for a long time. Dr Koons
was very sick last night, and I called to see him this
morning. He seems to have a high fever. Dr Jackson is
attending to him. The weather to day is rather colder
than what it Should be to Suit Tom Madden in getting
his Cisterns done. late in the evening I made out Jim
OBrien and my own accts [accounts] out against the
County and City as Jim OBrien goes out the last of this
year giving place to J. T. Sampson. Mr Eckles also
came and wanted a transcript in the case of Sparks vs
Bonnsell which I got ready for him but he did not come
back after it.

Emmet Albright came in from the table this
evening and we both went to Supper after which I wrote
a letter to W. S. Morgan at Powhaton, Ark[.] relative to
some abstract business for Emmet. I also wrote out 2
notes[—] 1 for 6 months from Jan 1st[,] 1887, and one

for 9 months from Jan 1st[,] 1887 for $25.00 respectively which Emmet signed to be accepted by the Said Morgan in lieu of pay for a $75.00 Abstract book which business is to be carried on here in the City of Chadron[,] Neb[.] and in which I and Emmet are to be equal partners in the business. Hee to furnish the books and I to do the work. after 10.30 P.M. I went to Dr Harris Drug Store and got some good Casteel Soap[,] Tooth powder, and Sponge and Came home and had a nice Sponge bath, after which I felt like jumping over the moon.

Dec 25[.] a Merry Merry Christmas has been repeated by many loving ones this day and while I did not dine with any of my relations I can safely say that no where else could I have enjoyed my-self more than I had the pleasure of doing while being entertained by Mr and Mrs Sayrs and Family. The little Girls both gave me a very nice book of poems which I hope may ever prove a benefit to me in Some of my weary and lonely hours[.] I am however sorry to say that I did not go to Church to day, but if I live till tomorrow I trust to do better[.] as I Sit on my bed in my room in the rear of my office with a good nice warm fire to cheer me, and literature of all kinds strewn about me, I cannot help feeling how nice it would be if I only were married and had my mind made up to Stay in one place and at one kind of business.

Dec 26[.] To day it has been a cold one, and all indications point to a continued cold spell for some time to come. Fred Rood came down from Lusk last evening and I met him in the Democrat Office this morning. I got a letter from Billy McCloud in Wyoming[,] also one from Jim Burns in Deadwood. After dinner I made a Social call on Mr & Mrs Miller with whom I spent a very pleasant time in conversing about almost every thing in General[.] Mrs Miller seems to be a lady of rare combinations, Such as are only found in people well raised. The Dr is a perfect Gentleman which is the least I can say.

In the evening when I came home I found my Office in a great Shape owing to the Stove pipe in the Office having become Stopped up with Suit [soot], and making the Office all Smoky[,] So I anticipate a nice time tomorrow. Well I am sorry to Say that I did not go to Church today as I contemplated I would last night, but the will power existed to a certain extent and in that case I will hope to not get so much of a black mark on the all Seeing record—I am writing this just before going to bed and I feel happy to know that I can read and be contented all by my self with no one to bother me[.] But as I am yet writing this I am bothered by Fannie Powers coming to me for a warrant for Robert Harrison for carrying concealed weapons and disturbing the peace[.] I Soon got rid of her and at last Succeeded in getting to read my great Chancellors of England.

Dec 27th—[.] The weather today has been fine[,] sun shining all the time, and toward 2 oclock it commenced to thaw out a little, but not enough to let Tom Madden get to work on his Cisterns[.] The first thing I done this morning was to get a man to Clean out my Office Stove pipe and after that I went to the Post Office and Sent $25.00 to Mr. Morgan at Powhatan[,] Arkansas for an Abstract book. In the afternoon I went around to Dr Millers office to learn Mrs Miller how to use the Typewriter. I spent all afternoon learning her.

Dec 28th. To day has again been fine weather but very little thawing took place. This morning I went over in Mr. Sweats Office and done some Typewriting. in the evening after Supper I made a call on the Hood family and Spent a very nice time with them.

Dec 29. The weather this morning was rather cold, but towards the afternoon it got warm enough to enable Tom Madden to go to work on his cisterns[.] I got a postal from Hay Springs from Cooper concerning a transcript of the Case of Fletcher vs Cooper, also got a letter from Henry Drexel about a certain Stone quarry in Buffalo Gap[,] D. T.[1]

The County Commissioners met here to day.

Sleighing is very good allover the Country and the farmers are coming into town in all kinds of make-ups on the way for a Sleigh[.] In the evening I went up to Hoods for my Supper after which I went over to the Skating rink to attend the Knights of Phythas Ball. after I got over there they asked me to take charge of the Hat room which I done and cleared about $5.00 for myself. The Ball was a Masquerade one, and proved a Success in Every way. dancing was kept up till 2 o'clock when Homesweet home announced to the tarrying ones that it was time to be in bed.

County Commissioner Pattison came home and slept with me.

Dec 30th[.] To day has been rather a medium one so far as the weather is concerned[.] Tom Madden is working away on his well in good shape.

Robert Dorr got out a warrant for Lemuel Meanor for beating a Hotel man[;] also C. F. Ferabache got out replivin papers on the same party for a gold watch. in the evening I called on Mrs Miller to see how she was getting along with her Type writing. I found her busy making a ladys work box.

Dec 31. last night or I should say early this morning, Mrs McNutt and her husband had a round up. and they had the whole neighborhood in a flame of excitement. The weather to day has not been as nice as it was yesterday although Tom Madden covered the Main & 2 St. Cistern today and is now ready to go ahead with cementing it. no business of importance in the Office to day. after Supper I and George Havens went up to the Masque Skate at the rink, where we had quite

---

[1]D. T. stands for Dakota Territory.

a nice time, until a fight Sprung up and that kind of dampened the evening's pleasure.

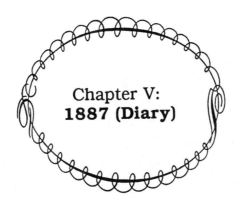

Chapter V:
1887 (Diary)

January 1st[,] 1887[.]   A Happy New Year is about all that can be said for to day, as it has snowed all day, and good Signs for a Continued Snow Storm exist at present. I managed to pass most of the day with Mr Burke at his drug Store[.]   I got a letter from Mrs Langworthy telling me to look out for her house and See to the things that are there now but I under Stand that the house has already been ransacked, and little if anything left.

I also got a letter from Tom Dixon in Chicago which I answered right away[.]

Jan 2[.]   To day has been a pretty fair one and the Sleigh-bells resounded merrily all day. I did not get up till late in the forenoon.   in fact just early enough to get to dinner, after which I repaired to the Democrat Office and helped Thompson make out a tabulated chart for the Skating Rink.

Jan 3.   To day I took an invoice of Mrs Langworthy House and afterward rented it to Mrs J. Wilson for [$]35.00 and made a lease out for 3 months. Mrs Wilson has not yet paid me the money.   I also mortgaged my Type writer for $25.00 to pay up the amount for Emmet Albright's Abstract book. and I now have his watch in Hock for the money.   after Supper I

Chadron, Nebraska, in 1887

went up to the Skating rink and seen the new class in dancing that has Started under Mrs Hawley's instruction. The weather to day has been very changeable and towards evening it turned very cold.

Jan 4. To day has been a fine one and everybody was busy in doing the work that required warm weather, busiest among who was Tom Madden with his cisterns work. after dinner I made a Sale of Dawes Co claim to M. A. Gottstein. after Supper I went to the Skating rink and for the first time in a long time I managed to fall down. after coming back from the Skating rink I met Tom Madden and Fred Dorrington in the post Office where we had quite a political discussion concerning Burr Shelton and the Brick Bank Gang. after which George Havens and myself came home to my Office, and George after Helping me to get coal in my room left for his own Home.

Jan 5th[.] The day opened up very stormy and cold and continued so all day. Notwithstanding the inclemency of the weather Tom Madden is Still working on his cistern, which he has now covered with boards, and is cementing over the brick. nothing of any importance happened to day. after Supper I went up to the Skating rink to witness the Magic Lantern Show of "War Scenes." the Rink was very cold and there was a very small audience in Consequence. after the Show Geo Havens came home with me, and got me some water and then went home himself.

Jan 6th[.] Very Cold all day and towards evening it blew fearfull. during the afternoon Tom Blackburn notified Clark and Obrien to the effect that Steve Harrah was out of his head, and was threatening to kill some one. Whereupon OBrien went and got Steve and after some parlaying they took him up to the "Magic City" [Hotel] and put him in care of 3 men and also had Dr Miller attend him. After Supper I made a call on Mr and Mrs Dr Miller and spent a very pleasant evening with them[.] Came home about 10 o'clock—.

before Calling on Mr & Mrs Miller I droped into the "Magic City" to see how Steve Harrah was getting along and I found him apperantly rational on every subject he touched upon (excepting his Pet one as to his Brother, Milo wanting to Kill him) which was not alluded to either my [by] Himself or me[.]

Jan 7th[.] very cold again, but clear weather[.] Report comes from the Magic City that Steve Harrahs is getting no better, Hee now having taken a fancy to religion[.] this evening the City Council met and during the meeting there was quite an animated discussion [that] took place relative to a letter handed in to the Council by Dr Davidson Concerning the payment of the rent of the Police Court. Mr Davidson surprised me very much by the course he took towards me as I always took him for a perfect gentleman, but find him to be a low lived Scoundrel without any principal whatever[.] I have no doubt in the world but that he was put up to the Course he persued by Robert Lucas of the Democrat. The Council however paid no heed to his prayer from the fact that he seems to have told some of the Council prior to the meeting that he had never recd a single dollar as rent for the Police Court from me, which when the question was submitted to the Council, I at once contradicted as false and untrue, and I further offered if necessary to produce the Drs receipts for the rent. This cornered him and upon the receipts being produced the Dr was forced to admit himself in the wrong and the Council acted accordingly.

Jan 8th[.] Today has been very cold, but clear. nothing of importance has happened to day more than I was pretty busy making out the Police Judge Reports, City Marshal and Marshall's Statement from May 31 to Dec 31, 1886. In the evening the City Council met and done nothing more than to allow a few bills & C & C. and Tom Maddens Cistern bill having been allowed finishes the amount of money allowed for the City of Chadron for the fiscal year of 86 + 87.

after Supper I called to See Steve Harrah again and found him pretty low, and Still crazy.

Jan 9th[.] To day has been a pretty nice one, not very cold, and clear[.]   I got up rather too late for breakfast and after dinner I called to See Steve Harrah again, who is now Hand Cuffed to the bed, He having played Havoc with the attendants early this morning and coming near killing Tom Blackburn[.]   To day the abstract book came. as soon as I got into the room He recognized me and wanted me to help him out of his trouble. I asked him if he would not eat with me. and upon my going out and getting eatables he did eat one mouth full of chicken, 2 bites of bread and a little coffee. He however imagined everything was poisoned and it required a great deal of pushing to get him to eat and drink. as soon as he got through I left the room, and have not been to See him since. about 2 P.M. I called on Mr and Mrs Sayrs, and Dr and Mrs Miller. at the latter place I met by introduction a Mr Berry traveling Salesman from a Chicago Grocery firm. after Supper I called on Mr & Mrs Milo Harrah and after a great deal of conversation concerning the future and present of Steve, it was decided that I should take Steve to Omaha to put him in a private Asylum[.]

[January] 10th[.] I got up very early as I did not rest very good last night. I went to see Milo Harrah after breakfast and found he had decided to send J W OBrien down to Omaha with his brother Steve[,] and So they Started to get the Board of Insanity to declare him insane. This was done at 2 P.M. and by 6 PM They got Steve ready for the train.

To day has been used by the "Water Wagon Gang" in filling up the cistern and Tom is busy at work on the one on Egan St. Recd [received] the abstract book to day. after supper I called on Tom Glover and T. M. Dorrington, after which I came down to the Democrat Office where Von Harris and P. G. Cooper, G. W. Clark, N. P. Cook, Bob Dorr, Lucas, and A. J. Gillespie were

discussing the celebrated "Casy" trial[.]   some lively
topics were touched which caused Clark to get pretty
hot[.]

Jan. 11th[,] 1887[.] Today has been a fine one
and as usual everybody is alive[.] I got my bond filed
before the Commissioners as a Justice to day. G. W.
Clark Commissioner from the lower end of the County
failed to get his official bond approved because he came
in with it to the County Judge too late. Tom Madden is
working hard on the Egan St Cistern which he proposes
to cover up before laying the brick in it. after supper I
called on Mrs Harrah and there met Mr Sayrs and his
family on their way to the Church to hear Blind Boone
give his Concerts. I went along with them and during
the performance there was quite a disturbance created
by a drunken man who had succeeded in getting in[.] I
finally had him put out and ordered him under arrest[.]
early in the evening Von Harris and Carley had a row.
J E Albright came home with me.

Jan 12th[.] To day has been a very fine one and
Tom Madden is getting in some good work on his
Cistern[.] I got my Benefit Tickets printed and got them
distributed around town[.] Van Horn is doing all he can
to help me in making it successfull. I wish to say right
here that at present there is quite a turmoil going on in
the Ranks of the Republican party of Chadron which
represents the Bolters of the Republican party over the
impossibility of getting their man to qualify for County
Commiss. in time as prescribed by law. So as to get
some of their enormous bills in on the County again[.]
What else their idea can have been is hard to construe
as the County of Dawes has been legally divided by a
vote of the people. the only material point at issue being
the none Compliance of the County Clerk to the Law in
sending the proper papers to the Secretary of the State
for the which there is plenty of time yet and all will
then be well.   After Supper I went up to Simon

Feldenheimer's Store and met quite a party of old timer[s]. Came home and went to bed at 10 Oclock.

Jan 13[.] To day has been a fine one again and another one like today will Send the Sleighs off the Streets. I recd a pair of Socks from Sister Lenora today. after supper I went to the skating Rink to see the Minstrel troup after which I came home and took a good cold water bath and also caught a nice cold[.]

Jan 14. This morning about 1 oclock I awoke with great pain in my stomach and at 6 oclock AM I sent Emmet Albright for some medicine which he brought me, but [it] did not do me any good[.] so about 10 oclock I sent for Dr Miller and he came about 12 oclock and gave me some medicine which did not relieve me and on account of my Stove pipes all being stopped up I was obliged to move up to the Magic City Hotel where I got good care from Mr. [name missing] who is a first rate nurse. I suffered a great deal all night and finally got asleep about 1 oclock Saturday morning.

Jan 15[.] Still no better and the Dr came to see me early this morning and along about 3 oclock this afternoon I got up and went down Town to see how the voting on the fire bond were getting along. But after being down Town a little while I found it impossible to stay up any longer as my bowels hurt me very much so after getting a can of Oysters I went to bed and rested easy all night[.]

Jan 16[.] To day has been not quite as nice as it has been for the past 3 or 4 days past. Still it is far from a wintery day[.] I am feeling very much better and would like to go out doors but the Dr is keeping me quarrintined so I must amuse myself with the Newspapers, "Biblical Litrature" and the "Chancellors of England[.]"

Jan 17th[.] To day the weather has been very fine throughout and I got out of my room early this morning and got to the Office where everything was in a turmoil. I got the Stove Pipes all cleaned out and the

Office Swept. had my nice Police Judge Sign hung up. Cleaned up my Type Writer and got my play cards out for my Benefit Ball. In fact for the first day out of the Sick room I feel about half exhausted, and more like laying down than anything else[.] James W. OBrien got back from Omaha[,] He having been obliged to take Steve Harrah clear to Lincoln to the State Asylum on account of the Omaha people not being able to take the proper care of him. Milo Harrah got back on Sunday Morning and called on me on Sunday evening while I was sick at the Magic City Hotel.

Guss the Carpenter made me a nice Bulletin Board today and made me a present of it too. He also helped me take my Type writer apart and adjust it[.] after supper I met F. E. Rood who just came down from Lusk[,] Wyo Terry [Wyoming Territory] enroute to New York on his propose[d] wedding tour[.] Fred gave some startling news to the Boys here about the Lusk Killing in which [name missing] Gunn met his death. I gave fred an introductory letter to Bill Cody in New York in order to be assured of his royal entertainment while sojourning in the Metropolis of the World.

We all went down to the train to see Fred off, and while there we met the smiling countenance of a long lost and old time Cow boy[,] none other than "Scrub Peeler" who was arrested here in November 1885 for killing some men in Montana. Scrub was pleased to get back among his old time friends and it is to be hoped that he may never more be in danger of "going through hell" as he termes it, but that he may now turn his attention to honorable persuits and endeavors always to govern a high Temper.

After coming from the Depot we all made a Social Call on W H McNutt who has again opened up a 5¢ beer bar and dance Hall. I am very sorry to be compelled to note such a performance from Such a man as McNutt[.] [He] has been trying to build himself up a Saloon Trade of a respectable character, but fate seems to be against him and most of all his wife is anything but a lady in about as short words as it is possible to tell it. after getting disgusted with human nature in general I left and went to bed.

Jan. 18th[.] To day the weather is very clear and mild. every thing is commencing to thaw out. during the afternoon I made out 13 warrants against Town people at the insistance of the City Marshall. after Supper I made a call on Dr Miller and spent a few moments with Myers & Boone. Came home early.

Jan 19[.] To day was a warm one throughout and reminded a person of spring weather, but towards 4 o'clock in the afternoon a severe wind Storm sprung up and things look[ed] for about an hour as if a cyclon was going to strike the Town.

I received a letter from Cousin Nora enclosing a $5.00 bill sent by Grandmother Iaeger as interest money from her estate, and which [interest] is annually divided among her many Children, Grand Children, Great Grand Children and Great Great Grand Children.

Mr Wright came in to see me about some money I owe him and asked me to assist his wife if she should get short for anything while he was away, which I of course consented to. early This morning about 4 oclock Mrs McNutt and Lillie St Clair had a grand Set-to and Hair pulling match, in which Mrs. McNutt came out Second best. She is now laying very ill from the effects of some injuries sustained in the affray, said to have been caused by the use of a "Billie" in the hands of Miss Lillie who at present is in a beastly state of intoxication in her Mansion of Vice. The whole fracas is reported by good authority to be a jealous play on the part of Mrs McNutt who[,] suspicioning that her better half was on too intimate terms with the Lady of vile Repute, opened up the Siege of Sebastopole, but unlike the [word illegible] she failed to carry her point and having no ships to go to the bottom of the waters she laid her self down on the hard and dirty floor (in obedience to the gentle annie taps of the said "Billie") there to remain in a State of vivid stupor untill the victor[,] thinking "lest there yet remain a spark of life[,]" She again applyed the leather bag and after raising another bump on the head of a once well respected Society damsel, concluded to measure her length on the floor herself, ably assisted in the effort by the Husband of the assalant. Time being now called[,] the fight was declared in favor of the vivacious and charming little equestrian of the 20 Century, who it is hoped may refrain from any similar occurance[.]

Jan 20. The day opened up bright and summer like and everybody is in fine spirits. Von Harris and P. G. Cooper are down from Whitney. G. W. Hatch is very hot at all the Officers in town for making fun of him about having been connected with the McNutt and St Clair fight[.] Mrs McNutt is recovering again and I understand that she anticipates having revenge as soon as her health will permit. Thus in all probability a fight may be looked for in a very short time. Today Tom Madden finished his Egan St Cistern and it will be ready for water in a few days. Four of the Courtesians paid their fines today.

after Supper I had Willie Mead carry my type writer up to Mr Harrahs where I spent a very pleasant evening at playing "Basique" after which I showed Mrs Harrah how to operate on the Type writer.

11 oclock P.M. the wind is blowing very strong and indicates bad weather for the morrow.

Jan 21st[.] Fine weather all day. after dinner I went to Harrahs and got my Type writer and done some writing for the K Of P. in the evening I met Mr Barlow from Lusk and Frank Aiken. we all went up to the "Dawes County Journal[.]" after supper I attended the meetings of the Council and found the Marshall and his deputy had been trying to Scheme against me again, but I finally got the best of them. I called on Mrs Kemmes to day.

Jan 22[.]   Fine weather all day.   Tom Madden asked me to write a letter for him to John A McShane the Democratic Representative from the 1st District in behalf of Cyrus Fair-Child for the Office of Register or Receiver of the New Land Office.   Blue Hall came in from the Saw mill and told me about the officers having tried to arrest "Bill Young" in Blackfoot[,] Idaho and he shot them both dead almost at the same time but a bystander jumping up behind "Bill" caught his arms and held him till they got him handcuffed.

Old Ben Arnold is also in Town. after Supper I went up to the Skating Rink where for a long time I have not seen as many people as were there[.]   all seemed to be enjoying themselves to the utmost, and most joy reigned in the ticket office where the ducats came in like old times again[.] after the Skating rink left out I came down to the Democrat Office where I met Eawel, Bross, Jim Patterson, Bob Dorr and Bob Lucas, who were playing "Casino[.]" This was soon changed into High Five which was kept up till 3 oclock in the morning when Doc Koons came in and got us some lunch, after which Jim Patterson came home with me.

Jan 23[.]   Fine weather all day. in the afternoon Mcgloughlin and I went buggy ridding, and took a trip out on Spring Creek to see some 10 or 15 Indians from Red Cloud [Agency] over on a hunting trip. While there we met Mr and Mrs Grady who had walked clean from Town. I offered Mrs Grady a seat in the Buggy but she did not wish to ride so Mack and I came Home.

after supper I called on the Hood Family and Had Supper with them. Came home and went to bed pretty early.

Jan 24th[.]   The weather opened up fine this morning but towards evening it commenced to show signs of a coming storm and a pretty high wind is at present prevailing (3 P.M.)[.]   I have been out all day trying to sell my Tickets for the Benefit[.] to day I got some muslin and got Bordman to paint it for my Benefit.

Jan 25th[.] Fine weather all day no business of anything going on at all. after supper I called on Harrahs and met Mr. A. C. Fowler there[.] during the evening we played "Bezique[.]" Mr Sayrs called while we were playing but did not stay very long[.] after leaving Harrahs I went up to the Skating rink and while there I laughed more than I have in a year at some new beginners.

Jan 26[.] Received a letter from Mrs Langworthy concerning her property. Dr Davidson gave me notice to quit his premises but gave no reasons why. to day I went up to Tom Dixons house and found things in a pretty bad shape as Petterman moved out without letting me know anything about it[.] after supper went up to the Rink to see the Dancing School.

Jan 27. Clear but pretty cold all day. I helped to get the Democrat out. Sayrs got back from Whitney but was unsuccessful in his trip. Beach and Bowers Minstrels are in Town and of course I will have to take them in too.

Jan 28th[.] The weather was a little cold today but clear. My left stump pained me so that I have been in the House all down and as usual have done very little business. Chas. W. Allen came over and got me to Copy a letter for him about the K & P Damascus Lodge. J. W. OBrien went out on Indian Creek to serve an execution on J. B. Gillespie. C. D. Sayrs commenced Civil proceedings against John & Mary Dombraske for Atty's fees before me, whereupon I deputized J. O. Hartzell as Special Constable[.] at present 5 oclock P.M. the wind has subsided and all is calm as calm can be. I recived another pair of woollen sock from Lenora, but cannot conceive why she never more writes to me. My servant for the day has been young Master Miller and I find him a very good, obedient boy. & after Supper I Sent him over to Bob Lucas to invited him over here this evening and spend the time with me which Bob graciously done and we passed a very pleasant time together reading

"Gems" from the Poets. Bob left for home about 10.20 PM and I retired forthwith to bed.

Jan 29th. To day I have spent all my time in bed being still confined with my Sore Stumps. Dr Miller came and seen me this morning. My boy has been attending to me very nicely all day. about 12 o'clock Schaub called on me and then Sayrs came to see me. J B Boyd also came and had some work for me to do on the Type writer, after which Mr Burk called to see me with whom I had a long talk about politics. after Supper Dr Miller called on me and as soon as he was gone Rev Dr Powell called so that I have been very well entertained in my "Prison House" all day, especially so by the last named Gentleman who I find extraordinary pleasant company.

Jan 30th[.] The day opened up pretty bright and I got up about 10 oclock but was in misery as soon as I tried to walk. I managed to get around and have the musicians go up to the Skating Rink and practice for the ball, after which I called on Mr and Mrs Harrah where I also met Mr Sayrs and Family. after Supper I called on little Guy Alexander and then went to hear Dr Davidson preach at the Methodist Church, after which I made a call on The Hood Family and from there went to bed, at which time it was snowing very hard and all indications go to point out bad weather for tomorrow.

Jan 31[.] Cold, Cold all day and at the present time it is getting colder (4 P.M.)[.] I have collected in my Tickets and find I am not going to have a big sale of them. after supper I went up to the Skating rink and got them to fire up. About 9 oclock P.M. the Band Boys came up and played Several pieces but it was useless to try and get people out such a cold night as this and consequently I only took in $48.00 cash which after paying 8.00 for the rink left me $40.00 clear. after dancing about 1/2 an hour, Everybody wanted to skate as there were not enough to make up a set. So all hands put on the skates and had fun to their hearts content.

After 11 oclock the rink was closed up and I came down Town and went to bed, not however before I learned there was a great fuss going on over at McNutts between Judd Brazil and some of the girls.

Feb lst[.] The weather is very cold and shows signs of getting colder[.] I was told this morning that Maud and Patsy had turned Geo Clark over in such grand shape last night in Carter's Saloon that in consequence he had given them till tonight to get out.

after supper I went over to Spargur & Fishers office and signed a petition to have Kincade appointed Judge of the 11th Judicial District, and while there Mr Westover from Gordon came in the office. after some introductions from Spargur we adjourned to the Sample Room of Gottstein & Owens. Jim Pattison came Home and slept with me.

Mr Sayrs did not get home till 2 oclock as he was very full.

Feb 2[.] I made arrangements to day whereby I am to rent the warehouse of Billy Carter for my Office. The weather is still very cold but clear throughout. after supper I went up to Simon Feidenhiemers and made a call on the New Management and while I was there Jim OBrien and Tony came for me to get out attachment papers against Maud Simpson in favor of W H Carter. This was very soon done, and of course Mauds trunks were Stoped at the depot.

Feb 3[.] To day has been clear and cold one and also one of stirring events. Early this morning I commenced to move my Office. The taking away of my petition from Dr Davidson caused a roar from Old Doc but to no purpose. I took the petition all the same. Some one seems to have instructed the old Doc about the law concerning articles as being Screwed or nailed to a building as he knew just what the law was but I got possession before he knew what I was about. Having once got the carpenters to work I kept them busy with the hammer till toward evening my New Office was nearly completed. Ace Johnson and Henry Miller helped me move[.] during the afternoon I got out new papers on Maud & attached trunks in favor of W H Carter again[—]it being claimed (as a technicality) by G W. Clark that the first papers[,] on account of having been served by J. W. OBrien whose term as Constable having expired last year but whom I as a Justice had appointed as a Special Constable to serve said attachment[,] was illegal[—]and in consequence thereof would let an opening for someone else. So in order to shut any possibility of a mistake off, I issued another attachment and delivered the same to J T Sampson who served them.

After supper I called on young Jake Nausbaum after which I came home and slept in the New Office.

Feb 4th[.] Today has been a little more mild than yesterday, and in consequence I got nearly all my work done in the New Office. Emmet Albright came in from the Table today. This evening the City Council met and again made a great mess of things. in not allowing Tom Maddens bill for the Cisterns it is very plain that the Brick Bank Gang has control of the City Council and nothing in an honest measure can be looked for until they shall have been eradicated at the next City election.

Emmet slept with me and before going to bed I gave him some instructions concerning the Justice Practice.

Feb 5th[.] To day the weather was a little more mild. I finished up moving today and gave the key to Dr Davidson. during the day Sampson was in the Office and had some conversation about Jim OBrien having authority to Serve papers. T. D. Blackburn came in about the same time and an argument on City Fire Cos was started and debated upon by all parties present[.]

after supper I called T M Dorrington to see about an Ordinance being introduced for consideration before the Council respecting compulsion of work upon the Hand Engine by Citizen in Case of a fire. I also made a call on Dalhman & Simmons[,] after which I went up to

Hoods where I played a game of chequers and spent an hour very pleasantly, after which I came down Town and met Harry Oelrichs, the English Dude Cow man.

At the present writing the weather is not quite as cold as it was this time last night. This morning I received a letter from J. W. Thompson offering me a reduction on my legs of $20.00 but am sorry to be obliged to record the fact that I am unable to purchase them even at that special offer as $40.00 is the most I was able to raise at my "Benefit" so I will have to be contented with my present ones notwithstanding they hurt me very much. Maud Simpson paid Billy Carter $45.00 on acct to day.

Feb 6th. To day has been a very pleasant one[.] This morning I attended the Congregational Church, and in the afternoon made a call on Dr & Mrs Miller[.] In the evening I attended the Methodist church where I heard Dr. Powell deliver a very nice sermon. Johny Stutter came up from Valentine. Thos Madden was in the office today as was also J. T. Sampson. In the evening I attended the Methodist Church[.]

Feb 7. To day has again been a very mild one[.] Al Fowler came in from the Table, and brought in his Daughter Minnie to spend a little time with Mrs Harrah.

Jake Lipson had 5 of the young blood of Town arrested for destroying his property one night last evening while they were out on a tear. They settled up the matter for $17.50.

This evening the Council allowed Tom Madden's bill for his cisterns and also my own bill against the City for various arrests.

Feb 8th[.] To day the weather was warm and pleasant all day[.] after dinner I moved my safe from the Old Office and now I feel about settled[.] Mr Dresser had a little business for me to do which was the first business of any importance that I have had in the new Office.

After supper I went up to Mr Harrah's house and found Miss Fowler and Mrs Harrah busy with the baby, it being a little sick. After a short stay I came home and met W. H. Carter with whom I made arrangements to commence purchasing approved County and City bills.

Feb 9[.] To day has been a very pleasant one. I learned this afternoon that Robt Lucas was going to leave the Editorial rooms of the Democrat and go back to Iowa.

Last night Mr. Turner and Miss Hollinback were married and the general rumor is that they are penniless which while it may be all right would look much better if at least they had a Sack of flour. nothing of importance has happened today[.] About 3 oclock the weather turned a little cold. The political cloud of the Republilican Party of Dawes County is already commencing to develope itself towards an anticipated head. Viz. Tucker for County Clerk and Clark and Sampson for Sheriff.

To day the appraisment of the McNutt property was gone through with and the only thing no[w] remaining to be done in order to complete the extinction of McNutt from the famous "Gold Bar" corner is a Sale of the Chattels which is now being brought to a finis under the supervision of Mike Gottstein.

Feb 10th[.] Today has been a very cold one, and winter is again on hand with everyone that you meet. I made a trade with the Chadron Publishing Co for 2 County approved bills 1 for $269.03 at 35% discount and 1 for $8.00 at 50% discount. About 4 o'clock P.M. a Case of Replevin was brought before me upon a change of venue from Justice J. A. Wilsons Court. I was busy in the afternoon helping to get the "Democrat" out. This evening Bob Lucas left for his home in Iowa, where he expects to practice law. Thos Madden, Judge Cook and myself went to the depot to see him off, after which I came to the office and made up my business of the day. Tony Barnard came in and Slept with me.

Feb 11th[.] Today the weather has been very nice, everybody thinks an early spring is on the programme which while it may be true, does nevertheless put aside the fact that by the 20th of March is time enough to [be] begining on the early spring business and that between now and that time there will yet be some cold cold days and nights.

Last night the Gang got on a grand hurrah and made quite a noise but towards 1 oclock things commenced to quiet down a little. At 10 oclock this morning the case of Aron vs Powers was called, and a jury being demanded the case was adjourned until after dinner[.] At 2 o'clock it was again called and [with] the Plaintiff failing to give security for costs[,] another adjournment was taken until tomorrow at 1 oclock P.M.

To day McNutts Saloon property was again Set up, and the Billiard Tables stored in W H Carters warehouse. The Gold Bar seems to have a varied Species of existence but it is still on the run, in Spite of all that Mike Gottstein can do to the contrary.

Feb 12th[.] To day the weather has been fine and nothing looks like winter anymore. At 1 oclock P.M. the case of Aron vs Powers was again called and the Plaintiff failing to give Security for costs asked to have the Case dismissed without prejudice to a future action. After supper The F. E. & M. V. [R.R.] Band got out on the Sidewalk and played a little while which attracted everybody to the Skating rink. on my way up I stoped in at Mr M. M. Harrahs and spent an hour playing a game of four handed "Bezique" after which I went up to the Skating Rink. About 11 oclock The Skating Rink closed and after everybody had gone we made up a committee of investigation to go and report on the "Masque Ball" at McNutts where upon our arrival there we found not only the usual frequenters of such places but also the most violent kickers against them enjoying themselves to their hearts content, looking on the festive gathering till their eyes watered with laughter. The

"Masque" was a grand Success and Mrs McNutt than whom no other sporting woman can be meaner was in the height of all her glory: and it caused an impression from a great many present that it seemed a pity she should have raised two small children before becoming convinced that nature had fitted her only for a Sporting Land lady of the lowest type.

Feb. 13th[.] Like yesterday, the weather is again summerlike and it being Sunday all hands are busy hunting livery rigs to go out ridding with. I have nearly omitted making any note whatever of a certain Artesian Well that has been under process of operation for the past 6 months more or less and principally less. Yesterday the Town was thrown into a vortex of excitement by the Sensational reports of a few of the "Gang" that there had been found a Strata of Coal at the 400 foot level of the well, which was Superior quality and which would yield a large sum of money to the Stock Holders. This had a little tendency to excite some few people and caused a momentary rise in the market of that Stock. There is at the present writing another Fulminating Scheme of Duplicity going the Rounds among the Councilmen composing and belonging to the party both heart and soul without any conciencious Scruple as to right or wrong, known as The "Brick Bank Republicans." It is beginning to dawn upon them who have been foremost in the Council about keeping Geo Clark as City Marshall at the enormous expenses of $780.00 per annum. That the people are going to stand no more Such work this spring at the City Election in that they will vote and be asked to vote (by a few honest democrats) for Councilmen who will not ever and anon have their own interests at heart[,] but take into consideration the wants of the Citizens whose servants they in reality are, and who will endeavor to spare their time more freely and at a much lower rate of charge not withstanding that no one came out here for his health, and "what are we here for" may be applicable to almost anyone[.]

The proposition as it is at present discussed among the aforesaid city dads is that The people are kicking against There being two men on the police force, namely Clark and OBrien. That it costs too much and that there are never any arrests made at the proper time and that they must cut down the payroll to please the people. This is their story so far. let us see into the facts of the case which stand thus[:] Geo W Clark is marshall getting $65.00 per month[;] J W OBrien is Night Policeman and gets $55.00. The latter is well liked by everybody, is an efficient Officer and has the good will of everybody he may meet. While the Former is unpopular both as a Sheriff of the County and Marshall of Chadron. Very few people like him either as an officer or citizen, and he carries the good will of very few, outside of his "Gang of Brick Bank Schemers" who while they may esteem him only do so from motives altogether beyond the reach of his comprehension[.] To be on the opposite side is always his motto and Duplicity is the largest tool he has been known to use upon those to whom he should show respect. The only excuse for him being his disbelief of any spiritual power which places him beyond the proper comprehension of an Oath and yet this man was sworn as the most important witness in the celebrated "Casey Case" where he fully demonstrated to the people both by his manner of speech and behavior[,] his incompetancy for filling so important an office as Sheriff of a County, claiming to be inhabited by people under a universal Government "of the people, for the people and by the people." If the Republican voters of Dawes County and especially such as vote a Straight ticket even though the name of a yellow dog be printed theron, I say if they were to take the requisite pains of a party worker and see the manner in which Geo Clark first got nominated for Sheriff They would never again be caught voting for anything he ever had any future dealings with.

I must not be to hard on him as man is never without faults and the words of Hamlet "To be an honest man now a days as this world goes, is to be one man picked out of Ten Thousand." I will therefor drop him for humanitys sake, but hope never the less he may never again be elected to a public office where the least speck of responsibility rests upon his shoulders.

Resuming however the Original thread of my Story for I have wandered toward the next County election, The "Gang" councilmen are trying to square themselves with the people before the City election in April next, and in doing so they want the appearance of economy to stand foremost, but in doing this instead of discharging the one receiving the most wages and being most unpopular, they are aiming to strike at the one receiving the least and doing the most good as an officer. What will eventually be done remains until next Wednesday evening to be heard. I trust and hope that if OBrien goes, Clark will also go, in which event the cause of Democracy will be much Strengthened thereby. I must however not go beyond the fact that while OBrien makes a good Officer it must not be omitted that he too has his faults, but his greatest are good in comparison to the least of Clarks. He drinks a little but that is all that can be said and no Sane man expects anything very good from another while under the influence of Liquor and to his credit can it be said that it is Seldom he ever does get intoxicated while on the other hand, to use a figurative sense of speech, Clark is <u>always</u> intoxicated in that he continually does what he can only persuade OBrien into doing when under the effects of liquor, which after it is once done he makes a business of going among OBriens Friends and telling them what a drunkard Jim is. and also among the "Brick Bank Click" for the which he need not repeat as it is an understood thing among them to use duplicity in all their transactions with and about confederates to their cause.

After supper I went over to the Democrat office from where by invitation of Chas W Allen in company with himself and Others Started out to attend the "Salvation Army" meeting which was being then conducted in a 24 x 36 tent on Bordeaux St[.] Upon our arrival there we found Seats but were just in time as in 10 minutes the house was crowded to its utmost and for fear of a Stampede occurring[,] Allen proposed that we go out which we done forthwith. After the meeting was out the Gang of Democratic usurpers of Republican rule adjourned to the Sanctum Sanctorium of the Democrat Office[.] when the General political outstanding of each and every party was discussed[,] the Roll having been first called showed an attendance of 6, 3 of whom were Republican (Radicals) whose names are, Spargur, Fisher and Pattison. The others were Thos. Madden, C. W. Allen and myself. Egan the Editor of the Dawes County Journal was the principal Subject of conversation, and it was decided to get the Radical Republicans to club together and Start a true principalled republican paper which I earnestly hope and trust they may do[,] which if it should be accomplished will clean out (or help at least) the venomous blood Sucking ["]Brick Bank Gang" who only hold up their tool and catspaw the "Journal" so they can beguile unsuspecting people from beleiving them to be anything but what they really are—[.]

It is now 3 o'clock AM and I have just returned from the Gold Bar whence I have been called to quell a row between Mr & Mrs McNutt. Mrs. McNutt was as usual on the tri-weekly drunk and proceeded to paint the town red. I deputized 2 men to take her to jail but she out flew them and persuit was impossible[.] She finally flew up into her room and there amused herself turning people over. She is certainly a curse to her husband and children.

Feb 14th[.] To day the weather has been exactly like yesterday. I did not get to bed this morning till 3.30 in consequence of the McNutt trouble, and when I did get to lay down my Stumps pained me so I could not get to Sleep. I got up and made a fire and went up to Jim Murrys Butcher Shop and took a nap on Louie Haters bed. nothing of importance occurred today more than I bought a load of wood from Belinger[.] after supper, Madden and OBrien spent some time in the office. E. Albright slept with me.

Feb 15th[.] The weather still continues fine but business is very dull. in the afternoon I took a Stroll up to the famous artesian well and of late the place where coal has been discovered "in good paying quantities" but I failed to see any indication of coal excepting the pieces picked up out of the dumpings which the "Salters" either left purposely or accidentally dropped. after remaining there until the drill was withdrawn and the cleaning process having gone through, I came down Town. in the evening Thos Madden and OBrien came in the office (I sent for Sayrs Encyclopedia).

Feb. 16. Weather continues fine. Thos Madden went to fixing the upper cistern. during the day about the only topic of importance to be heard upon the street was the proposed action of the City Council this evening upon the Marshall question. I borrowed Book "A" international Cyclopedia from Professor Blanchard. Tim Morrisey came into the office and wanted to see the map of the "Dawes County Boodle Gang" as portrayed by me, but I did not let him See it. After supper I attended the proposed regular meeting of the City Council but a quorum failing to be present I repaired home to my study where I found George Havens busy at his historical researches for his coming debate next Friday[.]

Feb 17. This morning the weather was not quite as nice as it has been for the past week or So. and about 2[:]30 PM after having fussed all day to get the temperature right it commenced to Snow as it [had] not

Snowed before and by 6 oclock fully 4 inches of "Beautiful Snow" covered "Mother earth." I went over to the Democrat office about 2.20 PM, and by 5.25 P.M. we had the paper run off, and all the work completed.

It now developes itself in the way of Dame rumor among the politicians of the local Government that the reason no quorum of the Councilmen being present at the meeting of the City Dads on the 16th inst. was that the "Brick Bank Gang" headed by Carley in this instance found prior to the said time of meeting that if they would undertake to get the Councilmen to force OBrien from the force that G. W. Clark the Pet of the Gang would have to go too, which being Strictly against and contrary to what they desired to accomplish, They very wisely concluded to absent themselves, accordingly there was nothing done and by consent and arrangement things will be allowed to take their natural course until the City Election comes off when the best man will certainly get there.

Feb 18[.] The weather commenced nice this AM and continued so all day although no trains ventured out from here last night. about 2 oclock PM quite an excitement occurred at the Gold Bar Saloon and in consequence I got up out of bed whence I had been confined with my left Stump, but upon seeing the fuss and excitement across the way where E S Ricker, J E Houghton, Tim Morrisey and Mr Miller were making a battering ram of a Saw log and finally broke in the back door to what is known as the Gold Bar Saloon where a Sale of Chattels was to be had, by virtue of a certain Chattel Mortgage of which J E Houghton was appointed assignee. The cause of the disturbance grew out of a complication of legal and Statuary proceedings in which J. E. Houghton claimed to have the right of possession by virtue of a Replevin Bond delivered by said J. E. Houghton to the Sheriff, who at that time was in lawful possession of the Chattels in controversy by virtue of said Chattels having[,] as the Sheriff claims[,] been

turned over to him by Spargur and Fisher, who finding
that a Replevin Bond had been given to the Sheriff by J
E Houghton, and that the Sheriff had given Houghton
peacefull possession of the same, proceeded and did
then and there in the City of Chadron aforesaid and
State of New Braska take the Said J. E. Houghton Esq.
and in a bone fida manner forcibly lay hold of his long
neck and eject him from the premises in a manner as to
denote a rapidity of locomotion on the part of aforesaid
Houghton Esq. whereupon the irate assignee blended
his Steps toward gathering a force with which to
repossess himself of his coveted goods. and soon the
army of the Philistines was arrayed in the rear of the
once famous resort of depravity and having a Battering
Ram at hand in the shape of a log of fire wood borrowed
from the owner of another Palace of Sin, The Said band
of Philistines and Mortgagors in the Style and ways of
the ancient "Salvation Army" proceeded to put the
Rams Head against the door of the said Dance Hall in a
manner which left no doubt that something must give
away. Entrance having been gained in[,] Tim Morrisey
headed in invading forces and in the Name of the
County of Dawes and the Mug waump Republicans took
charge of the Place of ill repute (Girls and All)[.] Now
must the force of imagination be brought to bear in
quick succession as the pen is unable to truly portray
the Spirit like evolutions of the Madame of this den of
reprobation, who seeing the usual horde of inquisitive
lookers on always at Such places and times proceeded
to amuse the assembly by Surnaming the assignee of
the sale "a toothless pimp" together with all manner of
She-devilment ever capable of having been inculcated in
So Small amount of humanity. and then[,] as if
determined that the curtain should not be ring down
without assurance of an hearty encore, [this]
Combination of Demi monde proceeded to water up the
hilarious crowd of Sightseers which water it was
rumored was not as it once came from the bowles

[bowels] of the earth, but it seemes that the climax was at last reached[,] for at this Juncture the Constable appointed about a dozen Citizens to assist him arrest the disturbers and in pursuiance of their mandate followed the formidable leader up a Small Stair way down which more ruin, degredation and depravity had come in one night than could be accounted for by Scores of Stud-Horse detectives in 3 months. The Sonorous tones of the Harlots were now changed to appeals for mercy and "I didn't do its[,]" ["]don't take me" & C & C intermingled with cries of little children[,] whose mother few worse women exist and whose action was now putting to shame everybody in the House. Mr McNutt having finally been collared by the Mob of Siegers promised obedience to the persual of the law in the case and the sale went on without further interruption[.] but while the Goods were being sold and being put out the back door and even the house being sold from over McNutts head, he was at that very time making arrangements to open up his Saloon in the front part of the Saloon. and even now while I am chronicleing the event, He is getting his bar fixtures ready to open up. and the only thing I can see of any importance as missing upon the occasion is a lot of printed Posters Strewn throughout the city calling attention to the passer by that There is to be a "Tree [Free?] Dance and Grand Opening intermixed with Swelled heads and black eyes, Cheap Ladies and fighting Whiskey at the Gold Bar Tonight." I say it is a Shame that the Council does not take some action in the matter and have this foul Stench hole of vice forever eradicated! during the afternoon I issued the warrant in the Larsen Case and J W OBrien arrested the man at once who failing to give bonds for his appearance tomorrow was committed to jail by me.

Feb 19[.] To day opened up with fine weather and the Snow that promised to lay so long and deep a few days ago is fast disappearing under the hot rays of the North coming Sun.

The case of State vs. Larsen was continued by me till 4 Oclock PM to day in order to give the County Atty time to appear and prosecute but upon his arrival from Whitney he asked for a continuance which was granted till 9 Oclock A.M. Feb 21st[,] 1887. The prisoner having procured good bonds I allowed him to be released forthwith. After supper I went up to the Skating Rink where I met the misses Fowler and Whitehall. The former of whom I introduced to Several young Gentlemen, with who she Skated and had a nice time. Capt Wright from [Ft.] Robinson was also there but did not Skate. Came home and went to bed pretty well tired out for rest.

Feb 20th[.] to day the weather started out to be fair but towards 3 oclock in the afternoon it commenced to grow cold and Snow a little and is still now (11.30 PM) Snowing.

after breakfast Jim Hartzell came and asked for the loan of my Type-writing machine and also that I should write a letter for him, which kept me busy till 2 P.M. after which I called on Mr and Mrs Sayrs and stayed till 5 Oclock when I went to Mrs Hoods for Supper, after which I called on Mrs Alexander and her Mother where I seen my little pet Master Guy Alexander. From there I accompanied Mrs Alexander's Mother to Church (Methodist) where I heard a very nice Sermon, and witnessed the first Sacramental service of that church in Chadron at which Dr Davidson was one of the officiating members. I am pained to think that I cannot be an active member of Some Church. what holds me I cannot tell, but Something Seems to whisper in my ear "it is no use[;] you are lost[.]" after Services I came down to the office and found Von Harris and Pattison waiting for me to see what I thought about having some of the Witnesses in the Case of State VS Larsh Larsen arrested and held[,] as it was told them that a certain one of them had been notified to leave Town, that they were dead on to him. after considerable talk and fussing it was finally decided to get G. W. Clark to arrest Jack the Italian fiddler and hold him upon which I called Jack out and Clark nailed him and took him up to the Jail[.] The Gang all appear to be on to the Racket, and all of them are on the look out. After the arrest Von Harris & Pattison left ostensably to go to bed and I also took my departure so as to be up early.

Feb 20[.] To day opened up pretty cool and throughout has been a pretty lively one[.] I adjourned my Court to the Court House where the case of State vs. Larsen was tried, and after a great deal of false Swearing on the part of the States witness, in which it was very apparent they were trying to fasten the guilt on an innocent man, the truth of the matter was finally concluded upon when Jack Cugno, one of the witnesses Squealed and told who realy stole the money, saying he himself had done it and after having been arrested according to his Statement and law he then made a written Confession in which he charged one James Davis with receiving some of the stolen money as hush money[,] whereupon motion I discharged the Defendant and dismissed the case. Court being now over and Supper having been got through with, Mr Ballard Sent for the Sheriff and had Jack Cugno Come down in my Office where he Swore out a complaint charging Jim Davis with being a party to the Theft. Issued warrant for Davis, and it was served by J. T. Sampson. I placed the bond for his appearance at $100.00 which was readily furnished with W. H. Carter as surety[.]

This being got through with G. W. Clark commenced pulling the delinquent Sporting women, which caused some excitement in the Police Court and as usual a great deal of hard feeling. I am Sorry to see and know that when ever the law is to be enforced someone is ever ready to make a kick and assume authority upon themselves altogether foreign to their Shoulders. It is now 1. Oclock AM and the wind is blowing fearful. while I was out of the Office it almost blew the window near my bed in, and did manage to break a pane of glass.

Feb 22. Fine weather all day and well do I remember 4 years ago today when Dr. Harris picked me up in his arms and carried me into the operating room at St. Josephs Hospital in Laramie City, Wyo. where after 2 hours and 35 minutes, I woke from the affects of chloroform and found my feet and fingers cut off—how can I ever forget that day!

New plots are at present springing into existance in regard to the case of State vs. James Davis and the longer the ball rolls the more dirt it Seems to gather on its course.

Feb 23[.] The day opened up fine and continued so all day. At 9 Oclock I again adjourned the Case of State vs J M Davis to the Court House for trial and it was not until 5 Oclock that the case was given to the Jury who remained out 3 hours and brought in a verdict of guilty as charged in the Complaint. This was the signal for every one to crowd towards the Court room to hear the Sentence which it puzzled me somewhat to bring my mind up to as I thought Correct and Just in case, but finally after weighing the matter careful, I fined the Defendant $75.00 and costs of the case taxed at $31.75 and in default to Stand committed to the County Jail[.] This caused some comment on the part of the Defendant but I think I have done my duty to the Citizens of Dawes County who placed enough confidence in me to elect me, and notwithstanding an offered bribe tendered me this morning by the Defendant J. M. Davis personally while on my way to the Court Room, but which I refused[.] I think I have shown my self worthy of their esteem and trust I may ever continue So!

The prosecuting Attorney seems to have it in for certain places of ill fame and his manner of Speech in the Court room today Suggested it from first to last. After having Sentenced the prisoner the Defendant gave notice of appeal whereupon I placed his bonds at

$500.00 and issued a Mittimus[1] forthwith and up to the present hour 2 A.M. Feb 24 he has not yet got the required Security. I have been around in all the Saloons and especially McNutts Dance Hall hoping to have some one offer to shoot me of which I had been appraised early last evening would Surely happen to me but no shoot occurred.

Feb 24[.] To day has been an eventful one and I have found out some Startling news about McNutt. James Davis paid his fine and costs in the afternoon after a great deal of fussing and kicking after which G. W. Clark arrested a prostitute whom I committed to Jail in default. M. M. Ballard is still raising hell with the boys and Girls and there is no telling where he will stop[.] The weather is not so very cold at present but the Barometor indicates bad weather. E. Albright came in from the Table[.] Sayrs was as full as a goat today again, making it embarrassing to any one having any business with him[.]

Feb 25th[.] To day opened up with the arrest of Mrs. McNutt by complaint of J W OBrien who is again on a spree. Mrs. McNutt plead not guilty and after examination I concluded the Same way and dismissed the charge[,] whereupon She informed Ballard that she wanted papers out against her husband in order to Compell him to keep the peace[,] but after having been out for about a half an hour and seeing her better half, she concluded to sign no Complaint against him[,] whereupon Mr. Ballard filed a complaint before me against them both for keeping and maintaining a house of public prostitution and upon their arrest forthwith and upon good grounds I adjourned the Case till 9 Oclock AM Feb 26th[,] 1887 requiring bonds for their appearance before me to the amount of One Hundred and Fifty Dollars a piece[.] Mr McNutt readily furnished

---

[1]A mittimus is a warrant committing a person to prison.

the bonds but Mrs McNutt being in default was committed as was also Josie Edwards who I held as a witness in the case[,] putting her bonds at One Hundred Dollars. At 11 Oclock PM M Gottstein came in the Office and went Mrs McNutts bond whereupon I ordered her release.

Feb 26th[.] 10 Oclock P.M. Fire[,] Hell and more off [of] it all day has been the go. This morning at about [number missing] Oclock a fire broke out in Waller & Lyman's Drug Store and in a few minutes the Danielson House, L Halls Grocery Store, Ricker & Houghton Law Office, E Sims Barber Shop, Lake and Haileys Bank, Fall Spargur and Fishers Office, G Eckles Office, W W Byingtons and Mrs OLinns office, Sayrs and Doors law Office, The "Chadron Democrat" office and Mr Joslyn's Candy Store were a total wreck and last but not least came poor babe Tuckers residence of one room. The citizens are to be commented for their zeal and energy in putting out the fire[,] and taking everything into consideration We are luck[y] as it is that no lives were lost and that we were enabled to stop the fiend of destruction right in the heart of town. after the fire was over, Mrs James W OBrien came in and laid a complaint against her Spouse for assault and Battery and he plead guilty whereupon I fined him $5.00 and costs which he did not pay[,] whereupon I issued a mittimus for him and after a great deal of mean doings he finally got Tom Coffey to go his Security which I approved[.] But Jim is fast losing his hold as an officer on account of his drinking during the day[.] it was made evident that the Case of Wm McNutt Et Al could not be tried today so I again adjourned it till Feb 28th[,] 1887 at 9 Oclock AM whereupon I released Josie Edwards from the jail, taking her personal recognizance for her appearance before me on Monday next. But no sooner had she got out than she employed her time in getting or at least trying to get Old Wilson to issue papers out against me for false imprisonment. This coming to my ears I went right off to Ballard and told him the case who forthwith went up to Wilsons with me and we there found out that although he had not issued any he would if he had jurisdiction in the matter. Then Mr. Ballard and I went to Supper together after which he filed a complaint against 3 prostitutes for whom I issued warrants, but the Sheriff failed to find one and brought 2 in Court[,] one of who filed the necessary bond for her appearance before me and the other got away from the sheriff. I then went to bed but being unable to sleep, I got up again and proceeded to fix up my Dockets[.] It was about 1 o'clock AM that W. D. Myers came in the office and asked to be released as surety on Josie Edwards bonds whereupon I forthwith ordered her arrest, which I done personally. Clark about the same time caught miss Jessie and took her up to the Jail. I met him on my way up to the Cooler with Josie Edwards. after having stored these vile wretches I came home and went to bed but could not Sleep well. I did not take off my artificials[.]

Feb 27th[,] 1887[.] This has been a fine day in every way and people have taken advantage of it by coming in from the Country to view the fire. Things about town are resuming themselves into proper shape again and the Gold Bar is fast becoming a remodeled Structure under the careful handling of Justice. This afternoon I made out about 20 subpoenas. in the evening I went to church[,] after which I came home and went to bed[.]

Feb 28. The weather opened up fine. the Case of State vs McNutts was tried today and it was not till 6 Oclock P.M. that I rendered a verdict of guilty against the defendants. I was compelled to go by evidence that I could not avoid as I believed. and according to the best of my judgment, I fined Mr McNutt $50.00 and costs, and sent Mrs McNutt to jail for 30 days[.] as soon as my judgment was rendered the Court room was emptied of its audience, and the general voice of the

people seemed to be that I had inflicted a bad Sentence.
If I have, I cannot help it as I followed the law to the best
of my ability. Spargur gave notice of an appeal before I
got the docket made up and I forthwith placed the
Bonds of each of the defendants at $1,000 a piece and
then Hell commenced to pop among the Lawyers
(Philadelphia) some claiming I had no right to call for
more than $100. bonds and others claiming I had a right
to call for what ever I wanted. Mike Gottstein called on
me right away and asked me not to take him[.] and
during the evening and up till 2 Oclock in the morning
every Lawyer in Town was in my Office trying to show
me that I had no right to put the bond at more than
$100.00 and that I should have done so and so[,] but all
to no purpose and I finally got to bed.

March 6. Since last posting up the book I have
had more trouble with the lawyers than can be recorded
verbatim in the same amount of time. They finally
persuaded [me] through my best friend Billy Carter to
let Mrs McNutt out of prison on her good behavior and
also to reduce McNutts fine to $25.00 which when the
point was once gained with them, They, Spargar, Fisher,
Cook and Sayrs proceeded to draw up articles of
impeachment against me and got Mr. Sperling to Sign
them, or at least tried to get him to sign them[.] But
Von Harris and Pattison getting wind of the matter soon
put a stop to their proceedings and some hot words
ensued over the Subject[.] while all this was going on I
was on a visit to the Country with Dr Miller to see a Sick
baby so it will be seen that they knowing of my absence
tried to Sting me unawares. and so much cannot be
forgotten wherein my friends took my part, gratitude is
a lasting debt and I hope I will never forget it[.]

James W. OBrien on the evening in question also
handed in his resignation as policeman. and I am sorry
to be compelled to record it that he was one of the
principal instigators as trying to have me impeached

after all that I had done for him. But such is the way of the world.

McNutt is once more running his Gold Bar Saloon ably assisted by his wife who never will lay low or quiet till she is incarcerated behind Some Steel bar[.] last Monday Feb 28th[,] 1887, McNutt came over and made application for assistance from the County in behalf of Miss Ollie, who was laying Sick and in want, and as an Overseer of the Poor, I went and made arrangements with Mrs. McNutt to keep her at the rate of $8.00 per week in County Script. But McNutt came in the office and objected this morning on account of the discount on Scrip which he claims he did not know when his wife made the bargain, but I have made no other arrangements with him than Von Harris and I made with Mrs McNutt.

This morning I got up and took a Spin around town. Arkansas John came down from Crawford. After dinner Davis (the jailor) hitched up his team and took Harvey, Scrub Peeler, Guy Alexander and myself out ridding towards the Bordeaux [Creek]. little Guy went to sleep. After we came Home I went to my Office to complete some Type-writing that L G Sweat asked me to do involving a contest on the present Site of Chadron. Today I took dinner and Supper at Mrs Hoods.

The weather has been splendid all day and I guess Spring has about set in for a certainty[.]

Mar 7th[.] Today has been fine all day. nothing of importance happened only that I finished up copying the famous Contest of Richard M. Stanton against the Western Town Lot Co for the land upon which Chadron now stands.

Miss Joslyn arrived from the East today. This afternoon The Chadron Gun Club had a Shooting match. D Y Mears measured the water in the Main St Cistern today. S. C. West came down from Crawford and asked for and got the fees of Mr Stewart as witness fees in the Case of English vs. S C West.

Mar 8th[.] To day has been fine as it could be and every body is getting ready to build before the new brick Ordinance becomes a law. I bought a bill of groceries at Tom Glovers for Miss Ollie and had them charged up to the County and took them to Tom Dixons House which I have concluded to let her have the use of till such time as the Dr shall discharge her.

This evening after train time I got Old Martin to take her up in his hack. after coming back from there I went to bed all tired out.

Mar 9th[.] Fine day again. This morning while at breakfast I met Lute North at the Chapin House and I could not have been more pleased if I had met a brother in fact not as much. I am glad to be enabled to record the fact that he is the Dep U S Internal Revenue Collector for this District and I feel convinced that he will make many new friends throughout this district and also be a good man for the business he is engaged in.

After dinner I took him out buggy riding Showing him the Town first after which we drove out to Chadron Creek, and while riding had a nice long chat about old times when we used to be on the Dismal River together in 1877 and 1878. upon my return to Town I found old Ben Arnold in a pretty good State of intoxication, and I forthwith had a buggy Sent around and took him down to the old Pet[e] Nelson place on Bordeaux to his home where I found his wife anxiously waiting for him. to her I gave $30.00 which I had succeeded in getting from Ben ere leaving Town, and I also made Ben pay the price of the Buggy for taking him home[.]

As soon as I got home I found an arrest had been made for disturbing the peace but upon inquiring into the facts of the case found it without any merits and ordered the prisoner to be turned loose. When this mess was off my hands I made a call on all the Sporting houses and read the riot act to them. principally consisting of that they are allowing themselves to be played by some of the Shyster Lawyers in Town who are willing to advise any and all things in order to procure red paint and colorization for their nasal extremities[.] I hope I may never get so low down myself. when a man once becomes a Slave to liquor he loses all taint of principal and morality and should only be considered as a brute in its proper place.

March 10th[,] 1887[.] The weather has been fine all day[.] last night about 12 Oclock the Ball of Fire commenced rolling by Mrs McNutt getting drunk and raising hell in the Streets again[.] Young Myers got bad and Shot off his pistol. After dinner I helped to get the Democrat out after which I went up to see Miss Ollie and find if she needed anything. I found she had no water and went and got her some[,] also 1 doz eggs. she seemed to be well contented with her lot. after supper I went up to the Skating rink to witness the masque skate, after which I came home and met and had quite a nice chat with Mr Yates[.] viz—before going to the Skating rink I called on Mr Alexander and Guy whom I found all alone, Mr and Mrs A. having gone to the Springs on a short visit[.]

Mar 11. Fine weather all day again! This morning Doc Middleton came up from Gordon, and being pretty tired laid down on the bed and slept until 3 Oclock P.M. After dinner I got Sloggys horse (Roxy) and done a good deal of business on him. Mr E. E. Bonnell came to Town for lumber. I tackled him for an allowed bill of his against the County for $28.50 in lieu of pay to W. H. Carter on a $16.90 bill. but he refused to comply.

Made arrangements with parties to loan them money on their land. Bought a County Claim from B F Helms for $18.20 for $10.50, paid too much. Carter kicked a little.

Went and Seen Ollie and had the water man go around to her. Clark filed a complaint against young Myers for discharging firearms, and I fined him $5.00 and costs. Fred Poll came down from Douglas to day. I did not know him anymore.

James M. Riley (alias "Doc" Middleton)

Mar 12. To day the weather was clear and nice with the exception of a little wind towards evening when it turned a little cold.

Sheriff Clark went up to Whitney today to bring down Wm. A. McMann and his wife who are accused of having stolen a cow. I understand that Billy Wilson went on their bonds. Clark also arrested, while on his way up to Whitney on the Cars, Some parties accused of Horse Stealing in DT. This evening a Mass Meeting of the citizens of Chadron was held in the Court House for the purpose of placing in nomination a Mayor, 4 Councilmen, City Clerk and Treasurer of the City. at 7.30 the Court House was packed. the meeting having been called to order by W. W. Byington, a motion was made to nominate Earnest Bross for Chairman which was Seconded, but before the motion could be put, Mr. T. Glover was also nominated for the position[.] this called some discussion but an amendment having finally been put to the first motion in which Glover was nominated and the vote on the Amendment having been Carried, Glover was elected Chairman with F Fuller as Secretary.

Motion was now made to adjourn to the Skating rink which was carried unanimously[.]

The meeting having been called to order again at the Skating Rink the balloting for Mayor commenced. It was now very plain to see that the influence of the Rail Road faction was in the ascendancy from the fact that Mike Gottstein had deserted his party colors and was now doing all in his power to aid the nomination of Hughes for Mayor[.] The ballots having been closed showed 108 votes for Hughes and 71 for Dahlman.

The next motion in order was for Treasurer. I nominated Ben Lowenthal. Some one nominated W L Casady, and Tom Moore was nominated. The ballots being counted the votes showed a good majority for Lowenthal who was declared nominated unanimously. The next motion was made to nominate Dorr for City

Clerk which was Seconded, and before the question was put W. L. Casady nominated F. J. Houghton. The ballots showed a good majority for Dorr. A motion was now made that each ward nominated their respective candidates for Councilman Separately[.] This was seconded right off and The crowd was Soon divided into 3 large bunches. The 1st was burdened with the selection of 2 candidates and upon the count of ballots there proved to be 3 nominations, two of which Stood tie. M. Carlton going in the vote on the tie after much work gave Mead a large majority. Fred Fuller received the nomination in the 2nd ward and Jas. C. Dahlman was renominated in the 3rd ward.

Mar. 13. To day has been a windy one through out. I got a letter from the Hog eye Kid. Pete Sweney came down from Douglas and Billy Haines also came in Town last evening. After dinner Billy Haines and Pete Von Harris & C, and myself all played High Five. After supper Billy Haines, Pete Sweney and myself started to go up to the Salvation Army, but upon arriving at their headquarters we found no one in, and were forced to come home without any religion[.]

High Five and Ben Tibbitts as Clown of the evening furnished fun and amusement enough to keep the Gang up till the "Wee Sma" hours of the morning[.]

March 14th[,] 1887. The weather opened up Splendid. I got up very early took a good walk up to Tom Dixons house to see if Ollie was Still there, and when I got to the house I found her Still in bed. So I Came away and let her alone.

This afternoon M Ballard Commenced his warfare against Prostitutes and in consequence thereof caused quite a Stir among business men who are now beginning to realize that Such people are to a great extent a necessary nuisance to the Community[.]

After Supper I went to the Methodist Church to hear Miss Day in her dramatic readings which was very good.

March 15th[.] fine weather again all day. about 10 Oclock A.M. The Indians commenced to pour into Town from Red Cloud Agency, and having been appraised of the presence of Ben Tibbitts in Town they at once proceeded to make medicine for him to Sober up on, but which I fear will not have the desired effect, as Ben has evidently come to Stay.

In the evening I went up and got Cora Carter to show her the Indians and She was wild with excitement as long as I kept her down town. After Supper I Started to go to Miss Days entertainment but like Richard III I was "interrupted in my expedition" by cries of "Fire!["] which upon investigation proved to be Mr Trumans House in the east part of Town. Now came the chance for the Fire Laddies to show their hand and to their credit can it be said that the fire suffered defeat in short order. I must however not forget to mention the presence of "Opportunity Hank" at the fire with his usual remarks and cracks at every one with in his reach, but he too was "interrupted" in his march by a Sound tap on the right chewer which laid him flat. This of course cooled his heated brow and the play went on.

I forgot to mention before saying anything about the Fire That early this morning the Fire engine came and was at once put into operation and proved a grand Success. After the fire I went back on my way to the entertainment for which I had Started in the first place, and having gotten through there I came down Town and met Mr Moffatt from Rapid City[,] D. T. after having talked with old time friends and taken a Social glass with them he came home with me.

Mar 16[.] To day the weather has been fine all day. at 10 AM I went up to the County Clerks Office where the commissioners were in Session, and there asked them to personally favor me in approving my my bill, which [word missing] done forthwith. after which I attended the preliminary examination before Justice Wilson in the State vs. John Doe for assault with a

Chadron Volunteer Fire Department

deadly weapon, with intent to kill. There was very little evidence introduced and the deft [defendant] was bound over to the District Court. The State vs. McMann was next on docket and the defendant was turned loose. McMann was however rearrested as soon as the judgment was rendered, upon a Warrant issued by the County Judge in pursuance of a complaint of G. W. Clark for resisting an officer. to this charge he plead not guilty and the Judge put his bond at $100.00 in accordance for his appearance on the 18th day of March.

About 3 o'clock PM the Fire Co got out the engine and again proceeded to test its qualities which after some improvements upon the method of working it proved a general Success. after which I got O. L. Sloggys horse "Roxy" and took a good horse back ride.

After supper I called on Mr and Mrs Miller whom I found enjoying good health. I did not Stay there long but at once made haste to attend the meeting of the City Council in Judge Cooks Office which was in session upon my arrival there[.] After some minor business having been disposed of an Ordinance pertaining to the regulations of Chadron Fire Department was read, and the rules having been Suspended it was passed as read. Then an ordinance was introduced to cut the Salaries of the City Officers down which met with some resistance from Van Horn only who seemed to be making the matter a personal affair but after some nice talking he was finally persuaded to vote in the affirmative and the rules having been suspended the Ordinance was passed and read. Therefore the Salaries of the incoming Council will be $50.00 for the Mayor, $1.00 each for the Councilmen (4) (2 holding over and who are entitled to their usual pay as from the first) $100.00 for City Atty. $200.00 for City Clerk, $100.00 for City Treasurer, $400.00 for City Marshall, $300.00 for night policeman and $4.00 per day for City Engineer. This was all that the Council could do and adjourn was the next thing in order. during the argument on the Salary Ordinance between some of the Council and Van Horn, the latter brought out some very forcible remarks. viz that he thought it strange that the Council could not see long ago that they were getting too much Salaries but could only tumble to that fact when nearly all the terms had expired. Mr Carly asserted that two wrongs did not make a right and it seems almost unpardonable that so great a Scheming Scoundrel should take advantage of a Saying and Maxum only intended for poor ignorant people!

March 17th—St. Patricks Day all day, and Irish as Billiard Cloth can make it. The dude element have come out with ther plug hats.

The Hose Cart came along today. business brisked up a little and in the afternoon Simon Krouse filed a complaint against Timothy Morrisey charging him with assault with a deadly weapon with intent to kill.

I issued a warrant for his arrest, and delivered the same to Geo Clark, and when he was brought into Court, he filed his motion for a change of venue to Justice Wilson. Atty for plff [plaintiff] objected to the Case going before Wilson for the reason of a Bias of Wilson toward Morrisey whereupon I ordered him to file an affidavit to that effect by tomorrow at 12 oclock M.

After Supper I went up to the Skating Rink where a Social dance was going on[.] Came home with Harry at 10. Oclock and went to bed.

Mar 18th[.] The weather opened up nice this morning and continued so all day.

Judge Cook came in the Office this Morning and notified me that he would not appear in the Case against Morrisey for the reason that he Could get no pay from the prosecuting witness, for his work. he said he would notify Mr. Bartow to that effect, and get him to withdraw his motion for a change of Venue and in consequence of no appearance being made on behalf of the prosecuting witness I should dismiss the Case at the complaining witnesse's cost, for the further reason also that Mr Ballard had expressed his opinion that there was nothing in the case and Mr Morrisey should not have been arrested in the first place. The Law says where a man is charged with a crime greater than a Misdemeanor, no Security need be given, and restricts no one from making such a Complaint. I fail to find anything in the Statute which says that a County Atty shall make a Grand Jury of himself, and that if any of his Friends do anything contrary to the law, That simply because he does not approve of the matter, that no process shall issue even though the person is Charged with felony. This cannot be the Spirit of the law, for were it so despots would have a grand field. After having Judge Cook, Morrisey came in the Office and asked where I was going to send the case to, and I replyed that in the absence of an affldavit from the Plff. as against the case going to Wilson, I would send it before Wilson as the hour to which I had given the Atty for Plff to Come in had passed. whereupon he paid $5.50 as all the costs in the case So far, but did not take the papers up to Wilson, he going out of Town on horseback and as I suppose home. In the afternoon I attended County Court where Wm A. McMann and Wife were on trial for resisting an Officer. The Jury took the case at 4 Oclock and rendered a verdict of guilty. They were Sentenced to pay a fine of $5.00 and Costs each, and an Appeal was of course taken. Mr Hill went to Valentine this eve. After Supper I attended the Fire Meeting at the Court House which lasted till 9 oclock, after which I came home and went to bed[.]

Mar 19. Fine day in the forenoon but a good deal of wind prevailed after dinner. At 9 A.M. Morrissey and Clark came and got the papers in the State vs Morrissey Case and took them to Justice Wilson's Court, after which I went to breakfast and on my way down I stopped at the Pacific House and handed Mr Henry

Stephan his money ($5.00) which he had left with me as Security for costs.

After Breakfast was over I met Mr Morrissey at the Post-Office in Company with Mr Turner, whereupon Morrissey said he had been instructed by his Atty to demand of me back all his money he had paid to take the change except the amount of the cost of the transcript, calling Mr Turner as a witness to that effect. I told him it was too late to commence kicking now that he had paid the money with out protest and that he and his Atty might keep on demanding the money till hell froze over and it would do no good.

In the afternoon Sayrs brought a Dutchman into the Office who wanted a warrant issued for the arrest of some mischeavous boys who he Claimed to have annoyed him and disturbed the peace of his family, but upon being informed that he would have to supply the Police Court Judge with a Ten dollar William as Security for costs in case he did not prove his complaint, he concluded that he did not want the lads arrested, and after a great deal of talking through his interpreter he left with assurance from me that in case of any further trouble I would see that the boys were hung. W. H. Carter went up to Crawford this morning.

After Supper there was an alarm of fire given which upon investigation proved to be in the rear of E. R. Sims barber Shop. Mr. L. M. Yates was the first to discover it. The Fire Co got out in good Shap and demonstrated the fact that hereafter the fire fiend will have to be a daisy with a good Start. I am sorry to have to note the fact that C. D. Sayrs is going to the dogs as fast as he possibly can get there with the aid of cheap whiskey and free beer, to use the expression of Mr Sweetzer "he is almost unable to keep his eyes open, on account of the extreme heat from his nose[.]" And for myself I think the time not distant when insurance companies will include him in their list of "dangerous and explosive articles" as against risks.

Last night while the Fire meeting was in Session Mr Thomas Blackburn gave notice of his intended departure from Chadron[.] Mr J. F. Sampson is at present in Omaha, where he will endeavor to have his "leg pulled" Straight. This morning Mr Edd Cameron came in my Office and hung up a very nice deer head which he leaves with me till he wants it again.

Mar 20th. Today has been a pretty fine one all day[.] I got up about 11 oclock and after dinner I went and got Fred Poll to fix my left leg which has been broken for the past month or so, this he willingly done and I of course bought a lot of beer on the strength of it. after Supper I got over to the "Gold Bar" where the Salvation army was having a meeting and having seen Ollie come in with Mrs McNutt in her company I concluded to repair up to her house and see about how much provisions she had left. This I done in Company with Harry and Herman and upon our return we all went to the Skating rink where we all met Oppertunity Hank, after a great deal of sport we all came home and I left the boys in Carters Saloon, while I came home to bed.

Mar 21[.] To day the weather was fine again and Billy Carter being up in Crawford, George Spaulding started on a little "Jambourie" ably assisted by W. H. McNutt. after dinner Jake Kass joined the Gang with O. L. Sloggy as his right bowe. The drunk racket was kept up till 5 oclock when they all dispersed to make way for Carter who came down from Crawford. I went down to the depot to meet the incoming train from Douglas and when it did come it was like the "Ship" loaded down with (not Chinamen) but toughs and gamblers, with here and there an honest John mixed in, but showing that the County Atty Scare had reached as far as Crawford. I took Supper for the first time Since my arrival in Chadron at the R. R. House[.] after supper I attended the "Salvation" Army in the rear of the "Gold Bar[.]" Harry Young came home very sick. Robert Dorr was in the Office this evening and we had a nice Social chat.

Mar 22[.] To day the weather was fine again but no business of any kind going on. Mrs McLynn called on me early this morning and gave me a turning over about Mr Sayrs.

Doc Middleton came up from Gordon and went back again this evening. John Larsh bought a fine Span of Mules and Started his Brother Frank out to his farm with them. I went up to see Ollie but she was not at home[.] After Supper the Fire Boys made an alarm in order to get help enough together to help raise the hose tower but it being too late they let it go till tomorrow. Tom Madden came in the Office and he and I talked politics till a late hour after which I went to bed.

Mar 23. The day opened up nice, but after dinner a heavy wind Storm Set in and made things disagreeable the remainder of the day.

I met Geo Clark at breakfast, and he told me of a Charles Parker having robbed the Paymaster of Ft. McKinney of $7,500 for which the Said Paymaster offered $1,000 reward, for the Capture of the robber. Billy Carter and Clark went out to Mrs OLinns right away, where it was reported the robber was in hidding but they returned without any game[.] I bought Burley C. Hills claim from the County for $16.00 for $9.00, after which I made a trip to the County Clerks Office on business, wrote letters to Bro Tom, John Christensen, and Sam Roberts.

The fire boys got up their Hose Tower and are at present building and [an] edifice for the accommodation of the Engine and Hose Cart.

I went to Glover's Store and ordered them to give Ollie no more goods, chargeable to the County, as I am now fully convinced that she is not entitled to anymore aid from charitable Sources as she cannot appreaciate a good turn. After supper the Hose Team had a meeting in my Office and among many other things they resolved to christen the Co. by the name of "The Dorrington Hose Team.["] This was a wise move on their part as Mr Dorrington is greatly entitled to all the praise of inaugurating the Fire department.

The nights have been rather cold for the past week and at present a fire would feel very good, but as it is getting quite late I will let go all holds and grasp King sleep for a few nights[.]

Mar 24. To day has been a pleasant one again, but no business going on. 1 Hose teame took a short run in the afternoon.

about 3 oclock I went over and helped to get the democrat out. Wm A. McMann came down from Whitney and gave him self up to the authorities as he said he understood there was a warrant out for him.

Billy Carter went down on his ranch on the East bound train[.] After supper I called on M. M. Harrah and Familey and Spent a pleasant evening with them.

Mar 25. fine day again but towards evening the weather commenced to cloud up and give good Signs of snow.

Business has been pretty lively in my office today. Harry Young commenced suit against Chester Ferbrache for a Silver watch. John Taylor commenced an action of Replevin against Geo W. Clark, and Dr O O Harris filed papers of Garnishment against V. H. Woolcott, which kept me busy all day. After Supper I made a short trip to Glovers Store and came home and went to bed.

Mar 26. The ground had on a nice white coat this morning and Snow is Still falling, although it has been Thawing as fast as it falls ever since 2 oclock P.M. and in consequence the Streets are muddy. M. M. Harrah commenced suit against D. E. Havens to recover $25 65/100 [$25.65][.] This afternoon I discharged Ollie from the care of the County as a pauper, she claiming to be well enough[.] also got T H Glover to render his bill of mdse [merchandise] furnished her, and Frank Ingersoll and Mr Bellanger, the same.

Mr Dresser came in the Office today and had me draw up a Warranty Deed from Himself to Marietta Hughes for Lots 35 & 36 in Block (17) in Chadron, Neb.

Jackson the Skating rink man came down from Whitney whence he had gone a few days ago to help Mr Bisbee get out the maiden sheet of the Whitney Times.

March 27. The weather opened up fine this morning and continued so all day. Harry Young and I went down to the Rail road house for dinner, where we were joined by the Simpson Bros[.,] Geo and Jakey. life seems short and sweet some times, but there was enough sweetness in connection with my dinner to day to do for 2 or 3 days to come. while at the Depot Hotel I met Mr Loui Cahn, formerly from North Platte, Neb. he seemed uncertain as to my identity, but recollected having seen me some where before. I was please to see him again, as his presence brought back pleasant recollections of the happy days I spent on the North Platte River in and around Sidney, Ogalalla, and North Platt City in 1877-78-79 & 80.

nothing of importance occurred during the day with the exception of the important event of my not having gone to church again to day. about 3 oclock P.M. Mr Alexander and I played a game of Cribbage, and Geo. W. Clark had no rest till we made a four handed game out of it, so as to enable him to show his dexterty at the game, but Alexander and I having been partners for 4 games showed Clark and his partner that Science and Bull headed luck, though sometimes running hand in hand, In this particular instance was not applicable as Science was out-winding luck in our favor[.] Bigotory [Bigotry] hates to be downed, and Clark soon allowed himself to go to sleep claiming to have been up a great deal of late at night, and in consequence was in no shape to play.

about 5 Oclock P.M. I took a stroll up to Burkes drug Store, and there met Bob Dickson, and had a nice long chat about old times on the Running Water, and Beef issues on the Indian Agencies in D. T.

After Supper in Company with Harry Young I set out to go to the Congregational Church, but meeting a pleasant crowd of boys at the post Office we all concluded to "about Ship" and Steer for the "Gold Bar Saloon" where it was reported the "Salvation Army" was holding forth. upon our arrival at that delapidated Castle of Sin, we found in the Supposed meeting room of the "army" nothing but Space and dreary darkness reigning supreme, while in the Bar room of this "College" were the usual hangers on of Sport and Orgies. Therefore with heavy hearts and down cast countenances Harry, Elmer and my self adjourned to my Office where after a few moments of our August presence, cheerfulness once more greeted us. A game of Cards was proposed, but being reproached for so unbecoming behavior upon the Sabbath, my 2 young friends soon devoted themselves with the literature of the day. Harry Young taking for his choice Wheel and Whistle, and Elmer, the Scribner Magazine. I am afraind that the "Wheel and Whistle" of Harry's is Something on the following order[:] "Through the vivid flashes of lightening could be seen the form of the undaunted Chieftan, as he closely followed the moccasin track of the dusky maiden of a once famous Tribe of Indians in the North western part of the hemisphere.["]

Mar 28th. This morning mother earth had on another mantle of innocience, but about 10 Oclock it commenced to thaw and by 3 Oclock the ground was again clear. I again had the luck to purchas another County Claim. Von Harris came down from Whitney to attend a famous trial wherein he is the complaining witness. August Kussel accompanied him and about 5 Oclock P.M. I had quite a chat with them about fees, in the Kussel Case of 1886. After Supper the Engine Co had a meeting in my Office. J W OBrien as foreman occupied the chairman place, and after having called the meeting to order, he got out of the Chair twice to make a speech without first having a chairman appointed pro-tem[.] Mr Sayrs made a great many amendments to motions made and put and finally Seeing that he was not in liking with the meeting got up and ["]skipped by the light of the moon[.]"

Nellie Aron and Maggie Glimes came up from Rushville this evening and I made a pleasant call on Fannie Powers where I found a grand Supper in preperation, which like a little man I proceeded to help devour. After I came home, Nellie and Maggie called on me to know what proceedings were going to be had in their particular case by the City Council, but I gave them no definate answer.

Mar 29. The weather has been wet and disagreeable all day, but it must not be overlooked that a certain amount of wet weather is essential to the interest of farming communities and consequently I consider the rainy Season now in vouge [vogue] a blessing, provided always it does not turn cold a[nd] freeze up.

The case of Taylor vs Clark was called up and the Defendant filed motion for change of Venue, which was granted. at 2 Oclock the case of Young vs Ferbrache was called and Plaintiff asked to have the case dismissed at his cost. M. Ballard the County Atty came down from Dawes [City][2] this evening. Von Harris came also. about 5 oclock Mr Sayrs came in with some parties, who wanted a warrant issued for a certain party for Assault and Battery, but before they left the Office they concluded to let the matter drop, but afterwards they

---

[2]This town no longer exists but was near Whitney, Nebraska.

changed their minds again and went before Justice Wilson, who got out a warrant forthwith.

After Supper I called on Fannie Powers and found out the particulars in the case of Wilson having ordered the "Sporting people" out of town. upon my arrival there, I found Geo. W. Clark and John Owens. I had quite an altercratio [altercation] with the former about some business matters. I came home and Seen Billy Wilson and McPheely in my Office.

March 30[.] The weather continues wet and disagreeable. I got a letter from Richard Frewen in London[,] Eng. also 1 from Buffalo Bill. I bought Mr Toomey's County Claim for [$]59.00 for which I gave him $32.50. Chadron has at last been gratified by the appointment of Receiver and Register of the New Land Office here. The expectations of all Schemers are however blasted, for no one was appointed from Dawes County. Therefore we must be contented with the matter and make the best of things.

The Dorrington Hose team met in the Office this evening.

There is at present a great deal of lawing going on. Von Harris recd a message from Whitney Stating that Wm. A. McMann had again run off with some of his cattle, He being at present time under bonds for his appearance before Justice James A. Wilson.

After Harry and I had started to go to bed, Doc Koons, Loui Grieshelhiemer and Jakey came into the office and asked accomodations for lodging, they having been locked out of their room by Loui having lost the key. after roaming around the office for an hour or so they left again, and finally succeeded in getting a bed.

Mar 31. About 9 Oclock Miss Mitchell rapped at my Office door before I was out of bed, and requested me to see about some business of Miss Powells'.

The weather was fine all day and the Ground certainly cannot be much finer for the Farmer than it is at present.

Very little business in my Court as Justice Wilson has the floor, and it seems as if all the lawyers in Town are trying to see how much business they possible can give him.

But they better give him all the trade they can while his term of Office lasts. For he never again will enjoy such a monopoly as the Republican Sheriff Clark is putting into his hands.

I have been in the County Clerks Office the greater part of the day, investigating things from the County Commissioners proceedings and am sorry to know of Such reckless management as they have been guilty of.

After 4 oclock I went over to the Democrat Office and helped get the town list out[.] After Supper I went up to Tom Dixons house. xxxx no never more!! about 9 Oclock I went up to G. W. Burkes Drug Store where I had quite a chat about old times on the Ocean while I was a Sailor and afterward when I was traveling for my "health" with another man['s] wealth, and in consequence of having had such a chat I feel very homesick to be in the sphere of life I used to be in, and have the same amount of sport I did, when it used to be all the same to me if I went to alaska or Denmark[.]

April 1st. To day the weather has been pretty fine but business has been very dull. I went out buggy ridding with Bob Dickson, in the evening I went to the M. E. Church Pink T party.

Billy Carter went up home to get ready to go west tomorrow.

April 2. Fine day again. at 8 A.M. some parties came to have a deed acknowledged. Young OLinn steped into the Office and wanted to purchase my type writer, but I Laughed at him. County Atty Ballard woke me up early this A.M. and wanted to know if there was a warrant against one Frank Conkling and upon being informed by me in the affirmative, replied that Conkling was at present in Town, and that he had just arrived from Valentine where he broke jail. Ballard said if the City Authorities did not deal with him that he would file a State complaint against him. On my road to breakfast I met Conkling, who informed me that he was in a bad fix both physically and financially, and that he was trying hard to collect money from the "Boys" here with which to persue his journey to the Hot Springs in Dakota. at 5 Oclock P.M. the Fire Dept had a Special call for the purpose of making a practice run. a fair Sized turn out demonstrated the fact that the Couplers had no time to lose in getting away from the nozzle before the water came rushing along. The Engine of the Dept. works perfect and is in liking with the citizens here. 2 Streams can be put on to a fire, capable of throwing water 125 fet [feet] each. One of the novel features of the Dept. is the possession by the Engine Co. of a Fireman whose chief duty is on the Wheel Horses and which bill can only be fulfilled by J. F. Tucker our Deputy County Clerk, for when he Snorts he causes tornadoes to run high and his tread is like unto the Trip hammer "Kiesar" used at essiene [Essen] in the manufacture of Kriepp [Krupp] guns. To day Timothy Morrisey started on a trip to the Running water to bring in a man for whom a warrant was Sworn out for assault with intent to murder. It seems as if whenever a case comes up in the county where an arrest is desired that may possibly cause some hard travel or perchance a lively tussel with Six shooters, the Brave and undaunted Chieftan of Liars[,] Geo. W. Clark, Dawes County Sheriff, always finds some excuse to hold himself in reserve for a Base ball game, or High Five outfit. Why should western people make fun of the Sportive nimrod and uninitiated youth from the East? when upon the thronged Thoroughfare of Chadron may at almost anytime be seen the native (as it were) dudes of the Typical New Yank Style, formost of who is Our polished sheriff, with his polished Rattan Cane, and Prince

Albert, finished up with a high heeled Shirt and bald face booties."

The Plug dicer, too has been hurled into permanet existance "and now instead of mounting barbed Steeds to fright the Souls of "fearful advesaries, They Caper nimbly" on the Chadron Side-walks, with their Black hats pluged.

Mr Short, one of the Editors of the "Crawford Cresent" came down from Crawford and in the evening called on me to see if I would act as their special Correspondent, to which I acceded and will endeavor to get up Chadron new[s] forthwith[.]

April 3[.] This morning the Streets were again covered with snow and dreariness reigned Supream throughout the day. I stayed in the Office all day in consequence of Having no washing from the Steam Laundry, which I cannot say that I regret, as I have in all events benefited myself by reading good litrature.

Harry Young was in the Office today and Signified his intention of leaving this place for a better field in the Laundry Business.

April 4th[.] This morning the temperature was a little low but soon the Sun Shone out and in a little while allway o.k. Depty [Deputy] Sheriff Sampson arrived home from Omaha.

The case of Harris vs. Woolcott was called up at 10 oclock A.M. and Deft asked for another continuance which I granted.

At 2 oclock P.M. the Case of M. M. Harrah vs D E Havens was called and defent [defendant] appeared and confessed Judgment.

Whereupon I rendered a Transcript to the Plff. for the purpose of filing the same in the District Court. Tommy Christen came up from Valentine this evening while we were playing high five in Carters.

To-night was to have been the regular meeting of the Engine Co, but no Quorum was present[.]

Mr Oppertunity Hank got the supreme life kicked out of him to-day and I am in hopes he may be quiet for a few days.

Mr and Mrs McNutt are having some trouble, but what it is I can not yet say, but in all events things will develope in a few days.

Apri[l] 5[.] To-day the weather has been fine and with all came the annual City election which I must say was a very tame affair, 52 Votes being cast in the 1st ward, [number missing] in the 2nd ward, and [number missing] in the 3rd ward and all this in a City Claiming a population of 1,000 inhabitants. There is however some excuse for this from the fact that there was only one ticket out, and parties not in concurrence with it did not vote. Judge Cook however managed to ring in for the usual amount of free Election drinks. Miss Maud Chapin was married to-day to L. A. Brower and now the Chapin Family is deserted altogether.

After Supper I went up Town to consult with some of the principal Citizens concerning the reported workings of M. Ballard. about 10 oclock I repaired to Stoggys and spent a pleasant time in Company with Doc Koons, Harry Young and Fred Poll.

Early this morning Dr Millers baby died[.]

Dr Koons leaves to morrow for Douglas to attend to his dental trade.

April 6[.] This morning the case of Harris vs. Woolcott was called and the deft. acknowledged the bill whereupon I ordered the Agent of the F. E. & M. R. R. Co. to pay the money into Court.

In the afternoon I attended the Meeting of the County Commissioners and got some bills allowed after which we adjourned to my Office and indulged in a political brawl about the standing of Dawes County. I also found out early this morning that the rumored report of the Marriage of L. A. Brower and Maud Chapin was erronious, in consequence of which I at once telegraphed the Editors of the <u>Crawford</u> <u>Cresent</u> to have its publication Supressed.

The City Council also met this evening and among other things refused to allow a warrant to be drawn for one of my bills. About 8 oclock I attended a Charity performance for the benefit of Mrs Gillette at the Skating Rink where "Red Riding Hood["] was enacted to the merriment of a well filled house.

James OBrien came down from Crawford this evening and reports business lively up there.

To-day the Fire Engine Company tested the engine and were not as well pleased with its working as might have been anticipated, on account of it not being in accordance to the Contract. Dr and Mrs Miller buried their baby today. Pete Cooper came down from Whitney. Geo Clark the Sheriff came down from Crawford with 6 people who are charged with arson and the time of examination Set for next Tuesday April 12th[.] Justice Wilsons Court has been very busy of late, in Straightening out the taxpayers of Dawes County[.]

April 7[.] This morning as I was getting up, I commenced spitting up blood again and Sent for Dr Miller who came accompanied by Dr Lewis. I got up but felt pretty bad during the fore part of the day.

The case of State vs McMann was tried on preliminary hearing before Justice Wilson who bound the Deft. over to the District Court.

This morning about 6 oclock, Henry Stephans Daughter died of Pheunomonia [pneumonia]. J. W. OBrien[,] O. S. Sloggy[,] Geo Minnick[,] headed by Geo Spaulding are again on a drunk in Carters.

I helped to get the <u>Democrat</u> out today. After Supper, Mrs McNutt came around and as usual Succeeded in Stirring up a fuss.

Pete Cooper, Frank Lambertson, and myself attended the Red Ridding Hood at the Skating rink again and every body seemed well pleased with the entertainment.

Johny Stutter came up from Valentine and meeting with him in the News stand[.] Doc Middleton and a friend of his came up from Gordon this eving [evening] and being unable to procure bed room at any of the Hotel's They came to me and I made them a good bed on the floor. I am now going to retire as my chest is causing a great deal of trouble.

April 8th[.] To day has been a pleasant one again and for the first time in a long time have I noticed the observance of "good Friday" and this in a Western Town too.

I have been Sick more or less all day with Bronchitis.

News reaches me that young Willie Mead and Miss Ollie were married in Hayes Springs last night. They having gone there from this place for that purpose. This will no doubt cause a great deal of trouble as young Mead came from a good Family and as usual marries a prostitute.

"Nut Shell" Billy from Deadwood is in the City enroute to Omaha to complete a Sale of Some mining property of which he is largly interested in. George Havens commenced sleeping with me in order to insure someone being near me in case of a hemorrhage. he is a good boy and good for anything he may be put at, except eating beans.

April 9. The day opened up bright but towards noon the usual spring shower came along, and no dowbt put many freckles on the faces of the Fair Chadron maiden.

I worked on L. G. Sweats, T. C. Contest till noon[.] when I started to go to dinner I was attacked with a small hemorrhage which made me pretty weak. I did but little eating on my dinner in consequence. Dr Harris ordered me to be more quiet.

To Day Mr Miller and De Forest Richards started for the Millar Ranche in Wyoming, It being the intention of De F. R. to go as far as Oelrichs [Dakota Territory.]

I called on A. Barton but he was not in.

The Republican Branch of Grand Army men of Chadron, together with the principal leaders in the Political world of the Dawes County Journal, and the Chadron Bank are all more or less abashed and nonplused by the nonconformity to their demanded desire of having Major T. F. Powers appointed to fill the Judgship of the New 12th Judicial District to which office the Ceasar [Caesar] of the Chadron Bar aspired. but now that he has fallen, his fall is so great, So demolishing that out of the ruined citadel of this once famous chancellor who might have put such men as "Coke" and "Moore" in oblivion, had he been so fortunate as to have lived in the times of those Expounders of Civil and Star Chamber Justice, nothing I say remains of this mighty and venturesome "Boston Ideal" but a wreck of an old crabbed man bedecked with a thread bare coat, minus (of late) the Rosco Conkling shirt fronts and Venetian Cuffs of the Van Wycke pattern, the wearing of which once before caused a Smart Young Editor of the <u>Omaha</u> <u>Bee</u> Staff, to be run out of this City of Chadronites.[3]

Well I guess I better let the old man alone, or he will perchance croak ere I get through, besides I am about half dead myself, with Bronchitis[.] This afternoon George Havens took his first lesson on the Typewriter.

April 10, 1887[.] My birthday[!] It was cloudy and cold[.] Dr Harris was in to see me at 4 oclock[.] Tom Madden was in in the afternoon. Harry Young was

---

[3]Sir Thomas More and Sir Edward Coke thwarted English monarchs in the sixteenth and seventeenth-centuries.
Conkling was a nineteenth-century senator from New York.

going from the office to Quigleys Livery B. he left his watch for fear he would get robbed. I had Easter Eggs[.] it rained some this evening[.]

April 11. To-day has been a lonesome one for me on account of having been confined to the room[.] I have not spit any blood for 8 hours now, and feel pretty good on account.

My Side partner Geo Havens has been to School all day but is at present studying hard at my table. W. G. Pardoe came down from Crawford to attend the Arson Case which will be tried before Judge Wilson Tomorrow. Tom Madden was in to see me today, as also Sayrs and Hickey (the famous boarding house man)[.] Dr Harris made his usual call about Supper time[.] Harry Young came in the Office and wanted attachment papers taken out against Keyes and Soder for $240.00 but I talked with him a little while about getting his money some other way and he finally concluded to let matters stand as they are for a little while. Rumor has it around Town that the County Atty Ballard is going to make another raid upon the Sporting fraternity. W. G. Pardoe is in Town.

April 12. I got up to day and went to breakfast, after which I made a trip to the Court House to hear the case of State vs Brose on charge of Felony[.] After dinner I came home and went to bed early[.] I was very tired and bled pretty bad during the afternoon.

Apri[l] 13. It rained all day. Geo Brought my meals to me again as I have concluded to stay indoors to day again. Sayrs and Madden were in to see me, and later on C. W. Allen and Bob Dorr, after which came the Rev A L Powell.

I managed to get up out of bed but did not feel well all day.

Apr 14th. This morning Snow was on the Ground with a moderate wind from the North. I however got up and have been out of the House all day. I feel as bright and fresh as a lark. in the afternoon I helped to get the "Democrat" out which did not go to press till 5 oclock.

Geo Havens is still with me. I have sent my weekly communication to the Crawford Crecent and when that paper comes out I better be in hiding somewhere.

Towards evening the weather stopped snowing and it has been thawing all day, consequently as night comes on it must be a little colder, but not much.

April 15. The weather to day has been very nice but owing to the Snow and rains during the past 3 days the streets are pretty muddy. while at breakfast at Sweetsers this morning I learned that yesterday Timothy Morrisey had Slapped Fannie Powers in her face while she was on trial before Justice Wilson, and for which Offense Justice Wilson wisely fined this brute [$]5.00 and costs which it is hoped may serve to teach him better in the future.

This afternoon at 2 o'clock a Black Bird Shooting Match came off at this place, between Mr Blakely, and James Boyd our 2nd St Gun Smith, the match being 18 yds rise, 50 Birds, for $25.00 a side. Score for the first 25 birds showed Boyd 21, Blakely 19—after which Boyd kept in the lead and Blakely seemed to be getting Careless and much worse[.] at the end of the match the Score Showed Boyd 43 out of a possible 50 and Blakely 34 out of a possible 50[.] Nothing else has happened all day with the exception that last night J. T. Sampson[,] Depty Sheriff[,] woke me up to ascertain the way of Serving a set of Attachment and Garnishment papers, connectedly.

Rumor also comes from Crawford to the effect that James W. OBrien is up there on a grand drunk and has quered himself with the Solid people up there as to getting any City position under the new government of Crawford. I am feeling very badly and my back is about broke. my lungs have bleed some to day but not as much as I thought they would.

April 16[.] To day has been a damp one throughout. the Crawford Cresent came by mail this morning and caused some comment from political circles about the article on Geo Clark. This evening the meeting of the Chadron Building and loan association held in the court house terminated without any benificial results whatever, from the fact that the election of Officers was claimed to be out of order untill Subscribers to Shares had been ascertained, thereby causing another delay in the election of the same of one week.

April 17th. The weather has been cloudy to a certain extent all day.

I stayed in the Office nearly all day and cleaned the type writer getting Tom Madden to help me.

This morning W. Christensen's baby died, and the first set of brick were made to day by the Chadron brick Co[.] Dr Koons came back from the west last evening, having had a pleasent and Successful trip.

April 18. To day the weather has been pretty good although the Sun might have Shone a little more. I amused my self drawing a map in the forenoon and after dinner, S. T. Hamm came in and got out a warrant for Mr & Mrs McNutt for disturbing the peace but upon being brought before me, Mr Hamm asked to have the case put off for a few days and see if they would not move away from the Side of his House. This I done gladly, as I do not Care to have to Send these parties to Jail again unless actually compelled to do So. I gave them till Wednesday april 20th to move their quarters.

Frank J. C. Tyler came into my Office and spoke to me about some abstract books, and after supper I called upon him at the Rail Road house where he showed me one of the most Complete set of Abstracts book that it has ever been my fortune to look at. afterwards we came up Town with a view of meeting Judge Byington, but not finding him in his Office we came to my place where we had quite a long chat together about Omaha, whereupon I found he was somewhat acquainted with W. F. Cody (Buffalo Bill) and this discovery served to make him all the more interesting to me. O. L. Sloggy, W. H. Carter[,] Bob Dickson and Mulcaghy are on a 3rd rate bender, but owing to the rain which has set in about an hower [hour] ago, they will probably Straighten up. Mike Gilmore (Frenchy) came in the Office about 11 Oclock P.M. and got me to write a letter for him to J. G. Mead in Buffalo Gap, D. T.

Apil 19th[.] The day opened up cloudy and very cold for this time of the year. towards 10 Oclock it commenced drizzling and kept it up till 3 oclock when a good rain Storm set in after which it cleared up again. J. D. Pattison came in the Office during the evening and told me about him self having been snow blind for the past 4 or 5 days. he is Still suffering intensley from the effects of the same.

Old Oppertunity Hank was a caller in the Office today. poor man he is to be pitied in some ways. W H McNutt also called on me to know if I would let him Stay longer than the stipulated time given him to remove from his present abode. Mike Gilmore came in during County Commissioner Pattisons presence and gave away some very interresting facts about the workings of Mrs McNutt, Ollie and Patsy. He seems to have fallen into a den of wolves, when on the contrary and by his own words he thought he was associating with very respectable people. Pattison and I had a great laugh over one of his remarks in which Mike said that Ollie and Dr Baker were married[.]

April 20. This morning Harry and I got up early. the weather has has been fine all day up to 7 Oclock this evening and at present a regular hurricane of wind is prevailing. no business occurred of any acct during the day till after supper. Tony came and got out attachment papers against Fannie Powers for [$]50.00. last night Billy Carter left for Valentine to attend Court. during the afternoon I made a call on Mr Hughes in quest of news concerning the proposed appointment of Tim Morrissy to the Marshalship of Chadron. while there I met Mrs Hughes. I failed to gather any thing positive from the mayor elect but from what he did say, I infer that Morrissy can not get the office although he may have the mayor at his back.

The government of Chadron has been tampered with about long enough and an honest Marshall is what is now wanted.

Curley the Saddler (formerly with D. Y. Mears[)] has sold his claim on the Beirdeaux and expects soon to leave for Washington D. C. with a view of trying to get a pension.

April 21. The weather this morning looked as if Summer was about to set in but towards 7 oclock P.M. anything to the contrary answered for weather. at present, 12.30 A.M. it is Raging high wind and Snow is falling heavy.

during the day Mr Dresser got out attachment papers against J. L. Howard and followed the same up with Garnishment against the M. V. R. R. Co.

Tim Morrissy's Brother came in the Office and wanted to know if I could do anything against his Bro Tim, in order to prevent him being appointed marshall by the new Council.

during the afternoon I helped to get the Chadron Democrat out. after Supper I went around to Tom Coffeys and had a very pleasent time playing billiards and pool. I won almost every game I went into and finally wound up the Gang by winning all their Checks against the Bar. Willie Mead Slept with me. Billy Carter came home from Valentine this morning. I got a letter from Frank Butterfield at Hot Springs asking about the probable prospective points of the B. & M. R. R. Co.

Wright and Jim Connolly arrived in Town today. Mrs Earnest and Harry Youngs wife came into Town also to day and Chadron is fast populating again.

April 22. Cold weather all day. Von Harris woke me up at 5 oclock this morning to get me to acknowledge a County Claim.

Tim Morrissy came in the Office to day, and I gave him a great turning over about having made a fool of himself in the eyes of Cautious Democrats. I very plainly informed him that I do not want him to be appointed Marshall and that made him pretty wild. I also told him that he could see what I thought of him by reading the Crawford Crescent of to-days issue. Ed. Cameron was also in the Office[.] Tim Morrissy seems to be sure of getting the Rail Road men in the Council to support him[.] Tom Madden was in the Office and most of all Burley B. Hill the Democratic Editor called on me for the first time since I have known him.

The "Dawes County Journal" Came out To-day and showed its filthy leper-like self in the usual Spotted way in commenting upon my article on "Our Own Major" or the "Caesar of the Chadron Bar (rooms)[."]

Geo Havens was in the Office to day learning to write on the Type-Writer[.] After Supper McPheely came in the Office to Swear to an account against P. Olsen for $29.24[.] as soon as he was gone Rev. Powell called by a special invitation[.] he and I had a long talk upon religious and moral Subjects[.] While we can not agree upon certain Subjects, I am glad to know that we will always be friends. I hope sincerely the day may come that and when I may be as good a religious man as Mr Powell. When he left the Hon[.] Mr Sperling and his Brother droped in with whom I had a few words about law and Order, whereupon they left and I think I will now go to bed after first going over to Coffeys to get a drink and mail a letter to Crawford.

April 23rd. the weather this morning opened very cold and continued so all day[.] C W Dresser came in the office early this morning and had some work done. The Rail Road Co came in and settled up the case of Garnishee of Harris vs Woolcott. a great deal of talk

has been going on about the Marshalship of the City. I
went to Supper at Smiths Hotel with Ed Cameron. After
Supper County Commissioners Harris & Pattison called
on me. This afternoon I made a raid on the County
Clerks Office for Blanks. about 8 Oclock P.M. I attended
the called meeting of the Chadron Building & Loan
Association at which we paid the initiation fee of 25 ct
[cents] per share. I signed for 5 Shares at $200.00 per
share which is about all I could stand[.]

April 24[.] To-day has been a moderate pleasant
day[.] Willie Mead and I got up rather late. I devoted
most of my time in the Office studying wether or not I
should make a reply to the Journal and after a great
deal of deliberation have concluded to treat him to Silent
Contempt, But such would not be the case if it were
nearer Election time.

I took Supper at the Sweetser House after which
I made a call on Mr and Mrs W. H. Carter whose little
Boy is very sick. after having spent a pleasant evening
with them I adjourned home and on my way stopped in
to tell Dr Harris to Call up and see the Baby. The night
feels chilly and no prospects of much warmer weather.

April 25. To-day has been a very hot one all day.
Anything to beat Tim Morrisey who has been in Town
all day working to be appointed City Marshall. toward
noon, thinking to play a little game on me, he gave it
out to dame rumor that he had withdrawn from the
race, in accordance with section 9, page 131 of the
Statutes, But I informed my Candidate Mr Cameron not
to believe it as it was only a dodge to throw me off. Geo
Clark has also his petition in and lives in great hopes,
But it developed itself that nothing in regard to the City
Council acting on the Marshall business would be done.
So we eased up a little not however without an avowal
that we would be on hand to see that nothing would be
done. This we done, and nothing more than Swearing
in the New Council was gone through with[.] I however
think after the meeting that Judge Cook Said something

about holding the next meeting of the Council with closed doors. After having conversed with nearly all the Councilmen I find that Morrissy has very little show, but I fear Clark has some weight with them.

To-day while going in Coffeys Saloon I met E. W. Baker who used to be on running water in 77-78-79 & 80. I Scarcely knew him.

This afternoon the Fire Engine was put to work pumping out the lower Cistern.

I made out a petition for D Burns as Overseer of Streets. I am given to understand there are several applicants for it, but I fear none will get there from the fact that the new Council will in all probability appoint the Marshall to that office[.] also W. D. Edgar of the Crescent arrived from Crawford.

After Supper I attended the special meeting of the City Council and witnessed the Swearing in of the new Board by the City Clerk, after which I came home, and before going to bed I played pin pool in Coffeys and won all the checks in the house. Willie Mead Slept with me.

April 26. Mrs Hickey Commenced a Garnishee against Costello before me early this morning. nothing new all day. towards evening Harry Faust, an old time Friend on the Running Water, came along and of course I put in some time giving my history for the past 9 years.

Edgar came in the Office and He and I had a long talk about politices [politics.] about 10 Oclock I adjourned to Coffeys Saloon and played pool and again won all the checks in the House. Willie Mead Slept with me.

April 27th. Got up late this morning[.] I met McNutt and gave him Orders to vacate his present abode at once. The School Bonds voting has been on the go all day and They have passed by 2/3 majority[.]

Quite an opposition to this was entertained by some of the property owners but after all I think it about as good a thing as could have happened. during the day I amused my self making price lists for J. Kass & Co.

In the evening I attended the Entertainment Supper and Ball given by the G.A.R. at the skating Rink and at which I enjoyed myself pretty well.

April 28. The weather opened up fine and all day long seemed like Summer again, but no business Seems to be Coming in and I guess the good people are boycotting me because I am common. Mike Gottstein got back from Douglass and reports that Bill Tucker got caught for a case of Gold Brick speculation in Colorado in 1879, thus murder will out.

It seems as if a great many of the citizens are displeased at the School Bonds having been passed and I doubt not but that there will be some kick before they pass through the Auditors Office in Lincoln[.] Today W. H. McNutt and his Harlots moved outside the City limits, and it now remains to be seen what County Atty Ballard will do with his moral ideas of easy virtue. This morning Ed Burns who came down from Crawford last evening bought the Bar Fixtures of Gottstein & Owens who are getting the "Gold Bar" Furniture out and will remodel their place on Main St. Mr Kellogg got back from Iowa this evening and Seems to have enjoyed himself very much. Tom Moore has Sold out his Flour and feed Store, and expects soon to give this Country the Grand shake. Willie Mead went out on Hollenbecks Claim yesterday and got back a few minutes ago. I guess I will go up Town and have a chat with Burke.

Just got back from Burkes and have made arrangments with Geo Birdsall to go along up the Bordeaux Creek to Merritts Saw Mill and bring in a Dead Man. So I guess I will go to bed.

April 29. Got up at 6 oclock a.m. fine weather. at 7.20 am. we left Town for Merritts Mills where we arrived at 10.20 A.M. having had funeral services and some lunch we proceeded to hitch up and while doing so and in trying to Crawl up in the Wagon I fell and Strained my knee bad, and at present I can Scarcely walk.

We left the mill for the School Section Burying Ground near Town at 11.15 and arrived at the Grave at

2.20. One of the Strangest features of the funeral was the deceased only had 1 relative in this Country (Mr Merritt) but this man could not find time time or compassion enough to go with this lone Deceased Cousin to his last resting place. it looked very hard even in the absence of any wrong intent on his part.

Mr and Mrs Brooks accompanied the remains and Seemed very much affected at the thought that this was the way we buried people in the West. She thought that "even the Cow-Boys had more respect for each other." Rough and wild as they were they would at least go to see their friends or relatives buried. I got home in the Office about 3.15 PM and called the case of Keyes vs Miller which was disposed off in Short order.

Geo Havens brought my Supper for me and will Sleep with me to-night[.] I learn by rumor that Bob Lucas is in Town but as yet I have not Seen him.

Major Powers, Geo Clark, Chas Allen, Tom Madden are working hard for the appointment of Lutz as Secretary of the Building and Loan Association which holds a meeting on the 2nd day of May and at which the perminent Officers for the Year will be installed.

April 30[.] To day has been a fine one all day, very hot. The Scrapers got to work on Ricker & Houghtons lots excavating for the New Brick Business House. I have been unable to put on my legs all day and consequently have been in the house all day. J Kass came in to get me to make out some price lists which I done.

2 Indians (Boys) were in the Office nearly all day admiring my artificial limbs. Bob Lucas has not yet been in to see me. Dr Miller came in to see me this evening about the McNutt Gas burner Stove. Tom Madden was in the Office to see if I would vote for Lutz. I told him if I did it would only be for his sake. About 3 Oclock P.M. Mrs McNutt came in and wanted an Order from me on the County for the burial of a poor Womans Child, but after investigating the matter I found Billy Wilson willing to Furnish her a Coffin at his own risk, providing I would see to the grave being dug, whereupon I sent for Mr Snell and

ordered him to have the grave opened. Geo Havens will sleep with me[.]

May lst[.] The weather opened up with rain[.] Geo and I did not wake till 10 Oclock A.M. Got up. Geo went home and I managed to get down to Sweetsers by 12 oclock, at which time the rain had turned into large flaked Snow. After dinner Geo came down to the Office and Stayed with me all day. He got my supper from Sweetsers. This afternoon I made out a report of the Police Court proceedings for the year ending May lst[,] 1887. Tim Morrissey's Bros. were in the Office today and Seemed pretty well worked up over the prospect of Tim getting appointed Marshall[,] in which event it seems to be understood that he will appoint his next oldest Brother Charley to be his deputy for the time during which Tim shall be engaged in the Capacity of Tax Collector. Their mission in my Office seems to be to get my assurance of not kicking against such a move in case Tim succeeds in getting the desired appointment upon which I assured Charley that I am not at all afraid of Tim getting the appointment. But He assured me the Lawyer Eckles had informed him that the mayor having canvassed the Town as to the desirability of Morrissy to the Citizens, and who seemed to be a majority in favor of Tim for Marshall, therefore as a Consequence, and notwithstanding that he is aware that the majority of the Council are against Morrissey[,] he will nominate him for Marshall, depending upon the Rail Road Support in the Council to uphold him and who dare not go against him, even though in the wrong, which they certain will be if they Support Morrissy for Marshall. I venture to assertion that of all the Citizen[s] Mr Hughes has consulted upon the Marshallship if they knew how Mr Morrissy had worked against the Police Court in the past and his open declarations as to his future course if he succeeds in getting the Marshall-ship. I say If they knew that he was going [to] try and hurt a cripple, who is utterly unable to do any labor and in doing all this use the protection of his Official Office, The Citizens would never ask to have such a man put in as Marshall.

May 2[.] The Ground was covered with 10 inches of snow this morning but it commenced thawing early and by 4 Oclock the street were again bare but muddy.

Tim Morrissey was in Town and rushed around quite lively looking after his future appointment of Marshall. I went out of the Office today to get breakfast but my leg hurt me very bad. after Supper I attend[ed] the Meeting of the Building & loan Association and after casting my vote for Directors, was compelled to come home on account of the severe pain in my knee. before coming away I gave my written proxie to Tom Madden[.] Geo Havens slept with me to night again[.]

May 3. The weather opene[d] up very fair and by 11 Oclock the Scrappers got to work on the Ricker & Houghton excavation, but owing to the dampness of the weather it was slow work with them[.] Geo Havens brought me my breakfast from Sweetsers[.] John Larsh came in and gave me the Sale of his City property[.] Van Horn came along and requested me to write him a petition to the Mayor for nomination to the Office of City Marshall. This I done, but not before I told him that I did not approve of the course nor would I countenance anything tending towards the defeat of Cameron.

John Owens from Lusk came to town today and looks as well as ever and reminds one of the first days of Chadron.

Billy Carter brought his little Girl "Cora" down Town, and she made quite a visit with me.

Business seems to be very dull and not a dollar Stirring any where, Neverthe less that must be over looked. I am about played out. Geo Havens has promised to come and stay with me to night but it is now 10 Oclock and as he has not yet come along I guess it is no use waiting any longer for him[.] I have just been in to Billy Carter to borrow $110.00 with which to get my new legs with but it is all to no use, and I guess I will soon be compelled to hustle some other way as the present ones are Slowly but surely wearing out.

May 4th.   The weather today has been splendid from beginning to end.   This morning at 10 Oclock, my pony from Ben Tibbitts came along, and it appears to be a daisy too.   all I need now is a Harness.   Geo Havens has had the Pony out ridding and when he came in I tried him and found he was favoring himself somewhere and upon an examination found he was Spavined in the right hind leg.   This will however all go away with a rest treatment and to that end Geo Havens and I hitched up after supper and took him out to Jim Tommys pasture and left him there for repaires[.]   after coming back we concluded to go down to the Chadron Brick yard where we found "Tip["] Morton Slick as a Whistle, Sizing up his anticipated proffits for this Summer in the brick business[.]   The Dorrington Hose team had a meeting in my Office this evening[.]

April [May] 5th[.]   The weather has been very nice and warm all day.   F. M. Dorrington came in to have some work done, which makes the Second time in 14 months that he has been in my Office.   After Dinner, I recd an invitation to go down on the Bordeaux to view the new Town Site laid out by G. D. Merryman and Miss Powell and Mitchell.   My candate [candid] opinion is not very good and I cannot bring my self to "write up" the place as high as I am wanted to.

Mrs Earnest and Tony Whitfields Lady came to Town today, but expect to leave again on the next train West.   Charley Weller came down from Lusk.   Bartlett Richards got back from Alabama and a Social Hop is being given at present in the Court House.

Tom Moore and Old Man Burns had a little set to early this evening but no blood was spilt.

My ride on the R. R. Engine today done my leg considerable good.   I am now almost able to walk.   Early this morning Charley Graham an old time Chum Cow-Boy of mine on the Niobrara came in the office to see me while I was yet in bed.   I did not know him until I caught sight of his arm being gone.

I reced [received] my book of my Sea Trip in '73 ['74] which is one of the most amusing things I have yet seen. I am anxious for the County Commissioners to meet so as to have them appoint a Constable, vice J. G. Sampson who has gone to Fremont.

After Supper I wrote out the bonds of the Treasurer and Secretary of the Chadron Loan and Building Association[.]

May 6. To-day has been a fine day again[.] work on the Ricker & Houghton excavation progressed fine.

Timothy Morrisey has been in Town and making his usual threats. This evening the Citizens held a called meeting at which was discussed the advisability of calling an Election for the voting on Court House bonds and after some discussion as to the proper amount to be fixed upon, the sum of $30,000 was declared as the sentiments of the majority of the assembly, and the Secty [secretary] was instructed to present the County Commrs [commissioners] with a copy of resolutions of the meeting and requesting a call for a special Election for the submission of the question to the people. After the Meeting I came home, and Geo Spaulding, Montt House and one of the "Journal Printers" (John) were getting pretty full and making a good deal of noise. Tommy Christian and his partner are staying up late to night to go to Crawford for pay day.

May 7. Fine weather all day[.] the graders have got down to Small Scrapers on the Ricker & Houghton lot. M. A. Gottstein bought out Loui Grashelhiemer's interest in the old Keys and Soder News Stand, and this promises now to be run in a business like manner. Mose is not without friends, and those too who will always patronize a Gentleman. He is a young, energetic and tenacious man whom success will not fail to crown. during the day the most important question agitating the minds of the Ring Masters of both City Gangs is who will the Council appoint Marshall at their meeting, which it is given out will be a private one, this evening?

A. G. Fisher borrowed my Typewriter on account of being to poor to pay to have his work done. I received a letter from F. E. Rood and answered it right off. W. H. Carter and Pat left for Carters Ranch. Mrs Carter called in my office today. Ed Cameron informed concerning Dr Waller's antipathy to Morrisey and added that Hughes and Waller were going on a little shooting jaunt this afternoon and if a flea could be put in Hughes ear about the unfitness of Morrisey for Marshall, that in all probability He never would nominate him, to which end I made a personal call on Dr Waller who was very much surprised at the Mayor being under the control of what he (the mayor) thought were first Class Attorneys and Citizens, but who in reality were Simply a lot of would be boodlers and out casts from the professional Ranks of respectable Lawyers. Dr. Waller needed very little persuasion to make him see the right way and I left him with his assurance of working any and all points against Morrisey. The Case of Hickey vs Costello came up upon answer of Garnishee this day and I ordered the Garnishee to pay $31.70 into Court. Also the case of Dresser vs Howard upon answer of Garnishee with an order to Garnishee to pay $28.19 into Court. After Supper and while I was at the Hotel listening to vocal and instrumental music, Mrs Dr E. P. Miller called for me to accompany her husband (Dr Miller) into the country 15 miles which of course I done forthwith, and thereby missed being present at the Council Meeting but in Lieu thereof I think I had as pleasant a time with the Dr as I have had in many a year. We got back at 3. A.M. May 8th.

May 8. To day has been clear and nice. Every body that could went out ridding[.] The first one to wake me from my peaceful Slumber was Tom Madden to tell me of the Delapidated features of Morrisey last night upon the failure of the Council to appoint him Marshall. It seems that he was nominated by the Mayor in Spite of all power brought to bear against so rash an act, and after speeches of Dahlman, Carley & Kass from which a Sane man must have been able to draw conclusions that such a nomination would only tend to disharmonize the Council as a body, the Mayor proceeded to put the Question to a vote, and of course it was lost by 4 to 2. Yeas Carlton, and Fuller, Nays Carley, Kass and Dahlman and Mead. This rebuke to the Debutantes in Municipal Society must seem as the unkindest cut of all. No other nominations were made for Marshall and the next nomination in order being for City Atty, for which place G. A. Eckles was voted upon unanimously.

In dwelling over the events of the past election once more, a person cannot fail to see the probability of an preconceived Scheme between the rail road people and Morrisey long before the first nominations for City Officers were made. this assertion[,] if made from no source at all, and if it had no circumstantial actions connected with it, would neverthe less be born out of itself by the remarks made by Morrisey to one of those whom he thought would be against him as for that Office of Marshall. and now that the first nominations for that office has been acted upon, and by which action Morrisey has been named[,] Dennis lets us see how the grand scheme was going to be worked, by which the pupil of Aristocracy and indolence and perchance New York Swell, or Sewer hand who claims to have been raised in Society, and, indulged in Luxury, and refinement to such extent as to have been spoiled, And who claims to be the best and most thorough political Schemer Dawes County, barring no one[,] was going to be installed into the combined Offices of City Marshall, Night Watchman, and Street Commissioner[.] C. C. Hughes a Railroad man was by the work of this Political Canard, Tim Morrisey[,] nominated for Mayor. a Rail road man and Subordinate to Hughes in his daily work, was selected in the 1st and 2nd ward for Councilman and of course everybody can see as is plain as the nose on his face that the last named Councilmen could never go against the inclinations of Mr. Hughes, else to their own detriment. This would very naturally leave only one man necessary to use any persuasion upon in order to make a dead lock in the Council, and in which case the Mayor would of course have the deciding vote, and by this means and no other was it and does it still seem is the purpose of the Mayor and his helpers to pass anything desirable to themselves.

This assertion, I say again is made from remarks of Morrisey, before the 1st. Meeting of the Council. for instance, he caused it generally to be talked about among the City Officers that "he would like to see the Color of 4 councilmens hair that would not vote for him!" again: "I have Hughes pledged." "Carlton is my solid man" and "Fuller has sworn to up hold me." and "I am sure of Mead for I spoke to him." also, "Hughes has promised me that if I am not confirmed, he will nominate no one else, and let Geo Clark hold over." also "I have it fixed that Hughes dare not bring up Camerons name for Marshall."

Now either C. C. Hughes or Tim Morrisey is a liar of the blackest dye, for on the 5th day May and before the meeting of the Council Ed Cameron says he approached Mr Hughes and told him he was a candidate for Marshall, that it would please him to get the appointment, but that he would not be disappointed if he failed of the mark, providing Morrisey did not get it. to which Mr Cameron Says, Hughes reply was that "I am going to bring up a certain party name and if he is not Confirmed I guess your chances are as good as anybody elses. You have been well recommended by some people to me for Marshall[."] but in the face of all this he goes into the Council, which is ordered with closed doors and proceeds to nominate Morrisey, and upon being rebuked by speeches of 3 Councilmen all of whom are as good and respectable as any Rail Road man and who are all interested in business in the City, he neverthe less put the nomination to a vote and upon it having been lost, he made no other nominations for Marshall.

What he intends doing at the next regular meeting remains to be seen, but at present his actions taken in connection with the remarks of Morrisey point strongly to the assumption on his part, that if he cannot have the kind of pie he wants he wont have any. It also remains to be seen whether he can bull rag the Councilmen as all Rail Road Men do their inferiors, as he is reported to be a man with a Strong Mind of his own, which if so, it will not bear him out in his assertion to me personally that Morrisey has been recommended to him by some of the oldest and most respected Citizens of Chadron. Supposing this to be so, I will guarantee that I have had as many Citizens express themselves against Morrisey, and some of them went to him and told him of Morriseys incapacity[,] to which he seems to have paid no heed, this showing conclusively that he was not willing to allow two sides to a question and using the advice of the "Oldest Citizens" as a blind to his preconceived plan, of putting Morrisey in as Marshall or die in the attempt.

Who per chance are these Oldest Citizens who recommended Morrisey so highly? What are they and what is the motive of the same, also who are the "leading attorneys" that have expressed themselves so fully on Mr Morrisey's Official Capacity?

To which the answer may be well written. I know Some of them, and their motive.

May 9th. The weather today has been very nice and warm all day. Nothing new turned up. Bob Dorr came in and wrote an Eulogy on Morrisey. Wm O Kiser commenced proceedings against A. H. Davis to recover $132.00. after supper I set around and read a while and went over to try to play a game of billiards but my leg played out. today a Swede came in and represented himself as having been confidenced out of some money, and wanted warrants got out for Mike Not, (McNutt) but I talked him out of the idea and finally he concluded he had made a mistake in the man, and upon finding out that he was liable for gambling himself, concluded to drop the matter. Pearsons Theatre Co is playing at the Rink to night but I never go to bad Theateracils [theatricals] so I stayed home and after 8 oclock made a call on Billy Burke. it is now 10:30 P.M. and the wind is raising higher and higher.

May 10. If I have not seen a wind storm in 5 years I certainly witnessed one today[.] the Office has been covered with dust and all efforts to keep it clean have proved futile. C. D. Sayrs came in the office about 6 oclock P.M. and got his books and eraiser and rumor has it now that he has doubled up with Judge Wilson, the man who he has hated from his first introduction into Chadron, but now that he sees himself beat and an out cast among his own party he turns tail and runs over to the Republicans, only to be used by them as a tool. I am sorry to see the man get down so low, but whiskey will always do its work, and is no respecter of persons, conforming some what to dame Nature in that respect. I am also sincerely sorry for Mrs Sayrs and her Children. May God have mercy on them as it seems her husband never will.

I had almost forgot to dwell upon an item of most important event to my self and all respecters of law and order, namely the selection of G. A. Eckles as City Atty in place of N. P. Cook. While it is in all probability a fact that Mr Eckles may not be a full fledged Atty, It is also a fact that by this appointment in the Place of Cook, the City is rid of one of the most Corrupt, incompetent and falsefying Atty's that it has ever, and it is hoped may never again, had anything to do with. The old saying is respect old age and gray hair but I do no [not] believe in respecting the Devil or any of his fiends, Just because He or they may be old and have the requisite white locks. But Cook endeavors to bear up under his defeat nobly by claiming to have never wanted the Office of City Atty. but such bosh will never work and he has good reasons for "not wanting" the attorney ship because it was utterly impossible to get it.

The City of Chadron wants an Atty that will at least see to its laws being enforced when called upon to prosecute in the Police Court, and does not want an Atty that will size up the prisoners purse and if Suitable defend him for a small fee, in the very Court that he is paid to prosecute in[!] of Such vile and unscrupulous practices has this old Gray haired venomed tongued wretch of an Atty Cook been [capable], deceptive to all and true to none. nor can he be blamed for bearing such impressions for if he will only recall the time when at Julesburg in 1865 & 66 when he was elected democratic Justice of the Peace (he is now a Republicn) where he is reported to have been one of the most corrupt men of the times.

Mr Clark from Omaha called on me. This evening after supper Tom Madden appraised me of the fact that J Kass and [had] been approached to see by Carlton who the Council wanted for Marshall, to which Kass replyed Ed Cameron whereupon Carlton assured Kass that it could be fixed with the Mayor so that Cameron's name would come up first at the next regular meeting. Ed Cameron was in the Office a little while to tell Madden, Dorr and My self about him having sent Morrisey 4 different bunches of hair with the Compliments of the Councilmen who voted against him.

I wrote a letter to Brother Tom. I met <u>Lawyer</u> Houghton in the Democrat Office today, and gave him a piece of my mind on the Morrisey appointment question, but he was very evasive upon the subject, and appeared worried and fretful, so I droped him in pity as he has enough of the Crow's foot on his face to mark him for life and consequently is in need of no more.

My right knee is still in a bad fix and I have had a hard time to day getting to and fro from my meals.

Jim Tommey came in the Office and reported that my poney was very lame, and not able to walk, so I gave him an order on the drug store for Medecine with instructions that I would be out in the morning myself.

May 11th. This morning the wind was considerably less than last night but still blowing some. After breakfast I went over to Birdsell's livery stable and got a team and took Dr Allen out to see my pony. We found upon our arrival at Tomeys that by some means or other he had cut his right hind leg very bad and the Dr after having the foot washed found exactly what was required to heal it, which I came to Town and got, and took it out with me.

Mr Stanton met me upon my return and paid me $5.70 for some Type-Writing a long time ago.

No business all day and money scarce.

After Supper I went to the Skating rink to see the Bittner Co play Inshavouge[,] an Irish Melo Drama.

About 10 oclock it commenced to rain very hard and this sudden turn in the weather will probably settle some of the dust.

May 12[.] The weather opened up fine but Towards the later part of the afternoon it commenced to cloud up and by 6 oclock a regular Hurricane Set in which lasted 2 hours followed by a rain Storm. just before dinner I met County Commis[.] Sperling and spoke to him about the appointment of a Constable in place of J. T. Sampson which Man is C. J. Davis a good Sober Steady man any place in the road. after dinner I took a petition around and got a lot of Signers on it and passed it in to the Commissioners, after which I took my departure for the Office where I found Cap Smith waiting for me to have a letter copied which took the rest of the afternoon.

Jim Tommey came in and wanted to know if I could put him on to where he could borrow $20.00, but the party I referred him to was no Good. Tommy Carter Came to Town again.

after Supper I went up to see the play of "Davy Crockett["] at the Rink which certainly was a good farce on the Original player (Mayo)[.] coming home I slipped and threw my right knee out of place again and Geo Birdsall and F. M. Van Horn had to help me home. it is now 10[:]47 and it is just pouring down so I guess I will go to bed and read about Secretary of War Edwin M. Stanton who so heroicaly braved the many perils and fault-finders during our civil Strife when to be a man of some will power of ones own, was essential for the good and benefit of all honest, free, and loyal American Citizen[s]. I take great pleasure in reading some of his whims and fancies, as I can almost See my own defects portrayed in this history, with the exception as to his brain ability which was at a point to which I shall never aspire.

May 13th. To day has been a rather slow one all around not very warm nor too cold, only Cold enough to make a little fire[.] during the day I went and got a petition circulated to have C. J. Davis appointed Constable vice J. F. Sampson, and after getting it circulated and Signed I presented it to the Board of Commrs who acted on it at once, and now I hope I have a Constable in the precinct who will be fair[.] Birdsall Bros put in a bill of $15.00 for livery hire in the Hoffman Case, but the Commrs did not allow the same, as they claimed to have already paid the bill.

I took Supper at the Chadron House with Commr Pattison, and while at Supper quite an excitment occurred across the Street in Sweetsers restraunt where Woodcock and Ike Brown got into words which lead to blows and wound up by neither one getting licked very badly. no arrests were made as no officers were in Sight.

To-day quite an interesting trial occurred before County Judg Ricker in which the Right to Sue at the time of the Cause of action was objected to by the Defts attorney, being backed up in his objections by the most conclusive and plain assertion contained in a Statute, but was overruled notwithstanding, after which Judgment was allowed to be entered against Defendant, whereupon an appeal was taken at once to the District Court for the Sept term. It is very evident that the County Judge and his Gang of rattle brained constituants are going to make things lively so long as they are in power.

After Supper I reced [received] a ticket from J. S. Cass for the Locomotive Engineers Ball at the Rink where fully 250 couples were assembled during the evening and had a fine time. The music on the Occasion being furnished by Professor Blums Orchastra, and commented upon by the dancers as the finest ever had in Chadron.

Early in the evening and just before the Ball, the Rush-ville Band arrived in Town and Serenaded the Boys of the F. E. & M. V. Band.

May 14[.] The weather has been nice and warm all day. Ricker & Houghton let a contract to have their excavation bailed out, it having been partly filled with rain water during the last rain storm[.] nothing of importance has happened all day.

The Case of Minnick Et al vs A. H. Davis was called this afternoon, and the Garnishee came in and answered, whereupon I ordered him to pay the money into Court.

There are at present quite a number of Rail Road men camped here which seems to liven up the Town. Mep Ballow & Casady have dissolved partnership and both will hereafter do business seperately[.]

Billy Carter arrived in the City from his ranch and reports every thing looking fine in the sand Hills. he goes back again Tomorrow.

John Henry the Black rascal from Texas came to town on the 13th and expect to remain here indefinately.

May 15[.] The weather has been pretty nice all day and every rig in Town was engaged. I intended going out to Jim Tommys place and break my pony to the Harness but failed to get a rig so I Stayed in the Office all day and read the newspapers. Geo Havens was with me the Greater part of the day.

Geo Clark and his Gang went out fishing but came home without any game. after Supper instead of going to church as a Christian should, I played pin pool in Coffeys and came out none the better for it, after which I witnessed a stiff poker hand in at Carters. towards 10 Oclock PM it rained very hard, and J. F. Houghton made himself busy ditching the gutter above the excavation in order to keep out the water.

May 16[.] To-day has not been the most pleasant one on earth but still it might have been much worse. C. W. Dresser came into Court and asked to have his Garnishment against J. L. Howard dismissed at his own cost. C. W. Allen and Tom Madden were in the Office to day.

In the evening P. G. Cooper, Dr Baker and Young Mr Narum came down from Whitney to see the elephant and after Supper we called on Miss Powers, and Mrs McNutt, after which we played pool at Coffey's[.]

Notice has been handed in that Mayor Hughes has gone away in which event a Marshall cannot be appointed this coming Wednesday and not June 1st.

May 17[.] Fine weather all day but business very dull. I rented Tom Dixons House for $10.00 per month with weekly payments of $2.50 in advance. Tommy Christian came up from Valentine yesterday and I have invited him to come and Stay with me.

Yesterday Geo Belden (Baldy the Check stacker) came back to Chadron and told about some hard times that he has experienced since his departure from here over a year ago. he tells about having gotten among the Farming element in the Eastern Part of this State and gone dead broke. had to dig post holes at a cent a piece with which to get a Stake to leave so good a country on.

To-day the B & M. R. R. filed their articles of incorporation in the County Clerks office which has a considerable meaning to it.

This evening at 8 Oclock County Commr Sperling made up his mind that batching was not quite the thing, and concluded to take back the rib which God deprived him of before Jumping out of Heaven into Dawes County. it will no doubt follow that he will take his newly made (my own Sweet dear) upon a wedding tour over Dawes Co to view the beautifull air (pudding) and Scenery (pie) the vast turning over of the Sod by the farmers of course, the delightfull $24.00 School lands, and $80.00 bridges[.] the wonder will only be how can he do all this viewing of these promised lands without a slight blush crawling from under his left ear.

John Stutter came up from Valentine.

May 18. The weather has been fine all day untill towards 9 Oclock P.M. when it began to blow a Hurricane. about 1 Oclock PM the Case called of the State vs J. B. White for assault with intent to rape[.] The Defendant plead not guilty and I set tomorrow at 1 P.M. as the time of Hearing.

in the afternoon I got a horse from Birdsalls and went out to Jim Tommeys and got my horse in. I left him with John Henry at Carters, where I also took Supper, and for once in my life I can say that I enjoyed myself at the Table.

when I came home I received a telegram from Harry Young telling me to attach the Steam Laundry Machinery but it is too late as I am told that it is already sold. I sent Arthur Carter down to C W Dresser to tell him to come up to my Office right off which he done, and it was he who told me of the Laundry.

Judge Cook left on this evenings train for rushville, where I hope he may not only get the Rush, but that he may be well cooked.

May 19. The weather has to all appearances set in for warm and clear. Geo Havens got the poney from Carters and Staked him out. Fred Meads team run away this forenoon with running gears of a wagon, they came to a stand still of their own accord after a short circle of the Town.

In the afternoon the case of State vs J. B. White was called at 1 P.M. and after hearing the evidence in the Case I discharged the defendant of the Complaint for assault with intent to rape and held him for indecent exposure of his person and upon trial of the Case I sentenced him to 5 days on bread and water and [$]5.00 and Costs taxed at $6.20 and stand Committed till paid[.] I helped to get out the Democrat in the afternoon.

One of the Land Officers came to Town this morning and County Judge Ricker has been lording him around all day. I done some work for County Atty Ballard with the Typewriter. W. D. Edgar came down from Crawford this evening and was in the Office after Supper. Tom Madden and I went into Coffeys. Reddy the Stud poker dealer came into Town this evening. Tommy Christensen and his Partner Mr Flood have started a Faro Game in Coffey[s].

John Bigelow came up from Valentine yesterday.

about 8 Oclock P.M. Billy Carter had a Set to with a Couple of wringgers on drinks. along about 9 Oclock it commenced to rain very hard and I came home to bed.

May 20th[.] The weather opened up fair and continued so till 4 Oclock when it rained till 6 after which it cleared up again.

There has been a great deal of Strategy accomplished to-day in the way of having the W. S. Land Office located. one of the Officers of the same, Mr Crites, being in Town. Mike Gottstein and Billy Carter aided by E. S. Ricker[,] Chas Allen[,] Tom Madden and myself were a little too much for the refined Clan on Egan St. and it is now a Settled fact that the Land office will be on Main St. both temporary and for all time to come.

Jerre the Bum and a flip Barber were in the Police Court today on Charges of Vagrancy. I gave them 5 minutes to make up their mind where to go to, and 12 hours to carry their conclusions into effect. I do not think they will appear in Chadron tomorrow.

Mr Crites left for Platsmouth this evening. he promised me before going that any and all work should be sent to me and if possible I should have a place in the Office[.]

C. D. Sayrs has now become a full fledged grainger[.] he lives 2 miles out of the way of anybody, and it is a Concluded fact by the Staunch Republicans that they will use him this fall as a Stumbling block and so long as Sayrs gets his Whiskey he will be all right with them.

Elmar Soder slept with me[.]

May 21[.] The weather has been changable all day, and at 7 Oclock this evening quite a hail Storm set in which lasted about half an hour. Early this morning Harry Young came up from Norfolk to see about getting his money from Keys & Soder and after Considerable Schemeing succeeded in getting Elmar Soder in giving him 2 notes of $100.00 a piece and a promise of $20.00 in Cash in a few days. Mr Merrell came in the Office to day and got me to do some work for the Band-boys. B. Richards also came with work and last of all came the saloon men to have their licenses printed, of which there were six and for which I Charged them 1 dollar a piece and took in 4 dollars.

I bought a sack of Oats for the pony, and paid G. D. Chapin $3.00. Elmar Soder slept with me[.]

May 22[.]   The weather opened up cold with drizzling rain. after breakfast I got Elmar to move my Type Writer over to Ballards Office where I proceeded to Copy a Post Office Book of L. G. Jenks for B. Richards and was interrupted by Mr Merrill coming in to have parts of the play pheonix written and who kept me busy the Greater part of the day.

Geo Havens had the pony out during the afternoon[.] after Supper I amused myself at Billiards in Coffeys[.] Elmar Slept with me.

May 23. To-day has been a pleasent on[e]. I have been busy most all day working on the Jenks Post Office book which I managed to get finished. Mr Melville the actor (bad) bothered me to death to have some parts written out for the benefit of the Band Boys. the F. E. & M. V. R. R. Co came in and paid the money as per order of the Court in the Hickey vs Castello Case. After Supper I went out ridding and then played pool at Coffeys where I found from news among the Gang that Some New Ladies have arrived in Town.

I wrote a letter to Tony Whitfield asking him for his Saddle[.] Elmar will again sleep with me.

May 24. To-day has been a pleasent one all along. not much business going on, but I managed to get in Some County Claims at 50 per cent. Von Harris sold me one and J. P. Glendening the other. J. D. Pattison was in Town today[.]   After Supper I took a horse back ride and afterwards came home in the Office.

Billy Carter and his Brother Arthur left on the passenger for Gordon this evening. Tony Barnard arrived back from Nonpariel. Dawes County School Lands were placed on sale by the County Treasurer to day.

May 25[.]   To day has been a grand one and business while it is Still slow shows signs of becoming better.

John Ormsby made complaint against his Son Patrick for assault with intent to Murder whereupon I issued papers and gave them to Davis who returned this evening with the prisoner[.]

Mrs Mears borrowed the pony and in Company with Mrs Simmons and Flanders went out to C. C. Sweats.

Charley Allen left on the evening passenger for Ainsworth to attend a family reunion. during his absence the editorial Chair will be filled by myself. about 10 Oclock in the evening Geo Spaulding, Harry Young, Elmar Soder, O. L. Sloggey, G. E. Myers, Bordman, Fred Danielson &c., got on a drunk and commenced to See which could howl the loudest, and upon going in and warning Touey about making Such noise, he succeeded in getting the crowd to go down to Sloggeys where they carried on to their hearts content.

May 26[.] To day has also been a nice one. the Case of the State of Neb vs Patrick Ormsby was called early this morning and upon which the evidence warranted the dismissal of the original Complaint and fining both the Complaining Witness and defendant for fighting which the Court done to the tune of [$]1.00 a piece & cost of Suit.

after dinner I helped get out the Democrat, and just as we got all the papers through press Ed Cameron came and invited us to his Ice Cream parlor which was fittened up neatly and yet Styleish.

after Supper I went out ridding and then attended the Hayes Minstrel Co. at the Rink which after I had witnessed the performance assured me of the fact that it is the best Show of its kind that has yet been in Chadron, the kind being also very good[.]

[May] 27. To day has again been pleasent but very little business going on[.] Politics are commencing to work up and the field of candidates will soon be too large for the Convention to make any kind of a Selection from. after dinner I took the pony and went down to the Chadron Brick Company Yard to see the full process of moulding the patent brick which is soon to replace building material in the erection of the many business houses and residences that Shall soon be under headway.

got back about 3 Oclock and went over to Birdsalls Stable to see the Sale of Bronchos by the Coffey Bros. who arrived here with a bunch, from Douglas a few days ago.

they are selling them off very fast and it is amusing to See a tender-foot work with a broncho.

Robt Dorr got back from the Box Butte Country this evening and while there he had the misfortune to lose his valuable hunting dog by having been poisoned accidently[.]

I made a call at the Shooting gallry and made one of the best records in Town by the use of a pistol[.]

after Supper I went up to the Rink to witness "out of bondage" by the Hayer Colored Minestrel Co. they had a very fair audience, but were not as much applauded as last night in "The Twin Sisters from Blackville[.]" After the performance I dropped in at W H Carters when Geo Clark and William Wilson were endeavori[n]g to Stuff Carter with political nonsense and feeling to See if he will be likely to put up any Stuff with them to induce people to vote County Bonds[.] Wm Wilson and Geo Clark are not workers or influential politicians, but when they see a Scheme like Court House Bonds looming up and aware that there are some rich men in Town who would like to see the bonds carried (which is already an assured fact) they would endeavor to make men, who are too busy with private affairs, believe that the Question of bonds being carried depends all upon themselves, and if per chance they had "Stuff" to work with they could assure anyone of a successful issue. Wilson is taking great pains to let those kind of unsuspecting people know and believe that he is the and a worker at the polls, and yet it is a true fact that this Same Democrat in Republican Harness voted a ticket pulled from a Sealed envelope at the last County Election.

May 28. To day has been a fine one again and while business has been rather dull, It has nevertheless been lively otherways. I took a ride early this morning and in the afternoon Tom Madden and I & Geo took the pony up to Davises and hitched him up[.] he went all ok. after which I went down to C W Dresser and got him to loan me his fancy Cart into which I Started to hitch him, but just then a horse race sprung up and I let everything rest and attended to that, which took up the rema[i]nder of the day, and made Suckers out of all the "Gang[.]"

Sam G came back to day. I got the Hayer Co to get off a Gag on Tim Morrissy wanting the Earth.

May 29. The weather opened up fine and continued so all day with the exception of a little wind coming up about 10 Oclock. this morning I hitched up "Dick" and drove him to Mr Dressers Cart[.] Harry at Kings, and Elmar Soder helped me, and by 12 Oclock I had him broke to drive right good. nothing of importance happened during the remainder of the day till after Supper, when I attended a concert given by the Hyer Minstrel Co, which was well attended.

[May] 30. "Decoration day" and with it also came a great deal of pleasure. The weather opened up fine and the Crowd that gathered at the depot to go to the "Grove" to attend the Decoration Services of the Lenington Post of the G.A.R. were to much to allow anyone to resist the temptation of joining the gang and having some fun too. So I got on board the train and soon 4 Coaches of excursionists were speeding on to glory in the direction of Butlers Grove on the little Bordeaux[—]then no better place can be found within the County for a Pic-nic.

I feel called upon to assert that in 10 years I have not had so pleasent a time. Every thing was harmonious from beginning to end and the ground affordes enough nooks for all lovers to kiss their Sweeties without being observed, and the Clear Cool and Swift stream that runs through the ground gave the Younger ones ample oppertunity of wading therein with their bare feet to their hearts content. too much praise cannot be bestowed upon this Grove as unlike most places of this kind it is perfectly for from that disagreeable and detestable weed, Poison Oak and Ivey which of itself bespeaks for it a good recommendation from all having children whom they may wish to enjoy themselves upon Such occasions. I earnestly hope that this place will receive a full share of Chadron's patronage in the future and especially so if it can be possible on the 4th of July next.

Upon the trip down, John, Luce Egan, John Willis and myself went through to Hays Springs and made a Stay of half an hour which we occupied by taking a stroll up one side of Main St. and making a Call on the Editor of the "Alert" of that place and coming down on the other side of the burg. The Town seemed to be rather lively but very few came up to the Grove with us as they seemed to be having a little hell of their own.

We arrived at the grounds at 11 Oclock and after some Singing exercises by professor Blanchards Choir and presentation of a Cake to the members of the Lenington post by Mr Wilson in behalf of the Family of Comrade Lenington, lately deceased and after whom the post has been named, the assembly were dismissed for dinner after which Speeches were made by [names missing.]

The march toward the grave was then commenced and there once more the beautiful and touching decoration ceremonies were gone through with which would seem should always be remembered by all.

The Homeward train left the ground[s] at 5.30 P.M. at 6 oclock the throng at Chadron Depot platform indicated the return of a well satisfied crowd.

During the decoration service the Fire-department paraded through the principal Streets which served to give that a pleasnt time and after Supper the Fire Laddies gave a Grand Ball which was enhanced by Professor Blums Superb Orchestra, and which made the affair just as neat and stylish as one could wish for.

May 31[.] To day the District Court commenced and as a consequence the City is flooded with Attys. nothing more than calling off the Docket and Organizing Court has been done to-day. I have been euchred out of some work by the Clever Scheme of the Deputy County Clerk, but I guess I can not have things my way all the time and must take crust with the pie. I failed to get my correspondence off for the Crawford Crescent but will do so tomorrow.

Jun 1[.] The weather to day has been fine up to 3 oclock P.M. when quite a hail Storm set in and last almost an hour. Charley Allen came in the Office and got some Typewriting done. I have been busy all day gathering news for the "Cresent" & Democrat. rumor now has it that the B & M. R R. is going to come into Chadron from the East Side of Town and north of the F. E & M. V. R. R.

Jack Cugno was placed on trial yesterday for Grand Larceny and plead guilty as charged. Judge Kinkaid set to day for the time to sentence him and about 12 oclock O. L. Sloggy came in and had me draw up a Petition to the Judge asking him to impose as light a Sentence as the case and the law will permit.

at 4 Oclock P.M. the Case of Simon Crouse Et al Charged with assault with intent to murder was taken up and at 9.25 P.M. the case went to the Jury who were given permission to go to their homes with the usual injunction to Juries in such cases and ordered to be in Court by nine oclock tomorrow morning[.]

Elmer Soder left for Nonpariel. broken nosed Curley came back to Chadron from Douglas & the West, also little smitty (sure thing) and Vince. nearly all the old time Gang are back again and things are commencing to loom up natural again.

I have made arrangements with Ricker & Houghton to rent Mr Kelloggs Office at $12.00 per month.

June 2nd. last night it rained some again but this morning everything loomed up clear & bright. The jury in the Case of State vs Eckellburger brought in a verdict of assault, where the deft had been tried for assault with intent to Murder. The case of State vs Cheney charged with Horse shooting was tried to day and a verdict of not guilty was returned. the first thing this morning was the arguing of motions to Quash to [the] inditements against Red Jacket.[1] I made arraingment with the Chadron Democrat to furnish enough local matter for an extra sheet at $5.00 per week on trial of a month to see how I would like it.

---

[1]Mary Woodward, alias "Red Jacket," was a notorious woman who was said to have murdered three men. She was jailed several times but never was convicted.

In the afternoon I put a man to work at my new Office cleaning up and filling in Dr Davidsons Yard.

at 3 Oclock I took a horse back ride and had some lively times with some of the boys ridding bro[n]choes.

The Chadron Democrat in consequence of their typo being on the jury did not come out this evening but will be all o.k. tomorrow[.] Just at Supper time I was called by the Sheriff to go and see a man who had been Shot and swear him to a Complaint and issue a warrant for the assalent which was done as Soon as possible and the accused having Given bonds in the sum of $500. for his appearance the Case was set for examination on June 4 at 10 Oclock P.M.

June 3. To day the weather has been very good and I moved over into my new Office on Main Street, not until however I had Mr Kellogg agree to have the premises put in better order as Mrs OBrien left her part of the House in a very bad fix[.] I got Mr Burns to help me move and paid my help $2[.]50 for Cleaning and Scrubbing the house out. Geo Havens came in the afternoon and helped Store the things[.] After supper I had a good rest and then Geo and I went to bed[.]

June 4. The weather opened up fine and continued so all day up till 5 Oclock when a regular Wind Storm set in and at present (11 oclock PM) it is blowing very hard.

the case of State vs Strickland was adjourned till Tuesday June 14[,] 1887, after which I loaned the poney to Tommy Christian[.] After dinner I took a Horse back ride and looked over the Town for News. I also went out and run a horse race with Kirmse and then came in and called on Mrs. Carter and asked her permission to use their buggy tomorrow to go out to Tom Maddens place[.] I then helped Charley Allen to get his cow & calf fixed and Homeward bound. After Supper I came home and Rose Cass showed me how the wind was tearing her house to pieces[.]

June 5[.] The weather opened up fine[.] I was too sleepy and instead of going out to Tom Maddens place with him I stayed in bed and left Tom to go for himself, which he did by taking my pony and he got back about 3 oclock.

This evening the wind has been tearing around pretty lively. W. G. Pardoe was in the office late this evening.

June 6. Fine weather again all day. Hank Simmons got his Collar bone broken while cutting out Cattle on the Bordeaux[.] I got young Lockett to get my pony and I took a Strole over Town to gather news.

at Noon time I went up to the District Court and copied the Criminal Docket for the Democrat.

Johny Owens, Depty Sheriff of Lusk[,] Wyo[ming] passed from above being on a hunting tour for Witnesses as in the Trumbell Murder Case. After supper I attended the MaGibbney Family entertainment which was very good.

June 7. Got up late. John Hoover got out warrant for John Green for Grand Larceny and afterwards took the papers from me and went before Wilson. got the pony shoed and got some rope from J. Kass. Copied the Court docket today again[.] Geo went out ridding[.] after supper I attended district Court and heard Sayrs and Powers argue the Madden and Turner Case to the Jury. Geo Clark arrested Jimmy Higgins this evening for fighting[.] Davis brought John Green in today.

I have been figuring on County Bonds considerably and am trying hard to understand the Question Thoroughly so as to stump the County on the matter in favor of Court House Bonds[.]

June 8. The weather opened up fine and continued so all day. Jim Higgins was arrigned before the Police Court this morning but no one appearing against him I accordingly turned him lose. The Case of Hoover vs Green came up today before Justice Wilson and was continued till the 16th inst. which was done in order of evading the present term of Court. I loaned the pony out to Mrs Alexander to day. also Mrs Joslyn had him before dinner[.]

June 9th. Fine day again. right after breakfast I got after Billy Carter to get around among the Citizens and gather up stuff with which to pay parties to Stump the Town which by 6 Oclock P.M. they succeeded in doing to the amount of $100. C. D. Sayrs[,] Judge Cook, E. S.

Ricker[,] F. M. Dorrington and Prof's Blanchard have been selected by the Committee to get over the County which leaves me out, but is Satisfactory[.] about 4 Oclock P.M. Eugene Spring was arrested and tried before the Police Court for Discharging Fire Arms and in default of paying his fine and Costs, he went to the "Freezer[.]" I bought a load of Hay to day for the Pony[.]

took supper with Hank Simmons and spent the evening with him and his wife.

June 10[.] The weather has been very nice all day. District Court was not in Session to day in order to give the Clerk time to make up the Journal. about 4 Oclock in afternoon a Horse Race was the feature for the time and Chadron took a temporary adjournment to the race track which while it was very interesting was also very much of a put up Job as against the winning horse.

After Supper all eyes and thought were upon the coming Ameteurial Debute of the Home Dramatic Co in the Play of "Lady Audley's Secret[.]" The Rink was well filled and most all the Company done well right through and were deserving of a much better house than they had.

The[y] must However feel proud of their effort as a dramatic Success even if not just exactly so in a financial sense[.] I took Miss Coeno Joslyn to the play and she enjoyed it very much.

Jack Cugno the Itallian felon was released from the County Jail after having been sentenced to 1 Year in the Pen. The County Atty took pity on him and got the Judge to release him by means of an affidavit setting forth that he had not proper Counsel or else he would never had plead guilty. This was probably the best way the thing could have been fixed up as any other way would have been at the Cost of this County, as she would have had to pay for prosecuting and defending him, and I do not remember exactly wether or not the Commissioners set aside any kind of a fund for that purpose or not? Geo Spaulding and McNutt had a row to-day but were stopped very efectually by Billy Carter the usual Jimmy good man in Such cases[.]

June 11. Fine weather again all day. Early this morning P B Danielson commenced tearing out the Store room back of Billy Carters, preparitory to getting ready to open up a restaraunt. I moved my sleeping room up in Henry Harrison's house on Bordeaux St. in the afternoon another horse race was sprung on the Boys but it did not go as they expected and Casadys Mare got the boodle in consequence[.] After the race and having returned from the track a free fight between J. E. Taylor and W. H. Tucker was the latest[,] but Tucker being the aggressor, I fined him $10.00 and Cost.

June 12. fine weather again. after dinner I went up to Hank Simmons and spent the afternoon there in Company with Mr and Mrs Mears and Mrs Dahlman. After Supper I attended the Children's exercises at the Congregational Church but not being able to get a seat I came home.

June 13. The weather has been fine again all day. Billy Carter discharged Geo. Spaulding. Mr. Dan is still hard at work getting his restaurant ready[.] S. R. Shinn came up from the Box Butte Co. to-day. Mr Patrick Ormsby came in and paid his fine and Costs for fighting as did also Mr. W. H. Tucker for last Saturdays performance[.]

In the afternoon I hitched Benny up to J. D. Pattisons Buckboard and had quite a ride. After supper I called on Guy Alexander.

June 14. To day the weather has been very warm with a Scorching wind in the afternoon.

Charles Allen and Egan got back from Pine Ridge where they have been for the past 3 days making arrangments to have the Indians come to Chadron this fourth of July.

at 1 oclock P.M. today the case of State vs. Frank M. Strickland charged with Shooting and wounding one Wm. N. Jones was Called and the Defendant plead not guilty[.] the evidence showed another state of facts however, and the Court (myself) held him in $500.00 for his appearance before the District Court, which bond was at once given, whereupon a complaint for carrying concealed weapons was filed against the said Strickland to which he plead not guilty, but the Court finding from the evidence that otherwise was the Case found him guilty and fined him $50.00 and costs taxed at $7.00 which was straightway appealed.

This afternoon the Democrat printing Co received a very fine new old Style Gordon printing press.

last night and up to 4 oclock this morning Geo Spaulding kept the town alive with his yells and drunken fights. No arrests were however made as poor Chadron is blessed at present with a Rail Road system of Government.

after Supper I called on Mr and Mrs Hank Simmons where I spent a very pleasant evening.

June 15. The weather opened up clear and warm. Mrs Joslyn and her son Bert went out to their claim to day. Mrs Joslyn rode Benny. they got back about 7.30 oclock.

Nothing of much importance happened during the day until evening when the City Council met and among other things they at last appointed a City Marshall[.] J Kass nominated Ed Cameron for that position and he was unanimously confirmed and now the trials and tribulations of the City Council may be said to be gone, and it remains for the new marshall to Show the Council his efficiency to fill the Marshals' Office.

during the meeting it rained and lightened very hard, on account of which Mayor Hughes retired from the Council Chamber and J Kass took his place as president Pro Tem. During the fore part of the Council proceedings the Citizens met in mass with them and urged upon them the necessity of making some kind of arrangements with parties for the introduction of water works into the city. After argument of which the citizens adjourned and left the council to proceed in their regular order of business.

After the meeting the main force of the Council went down to Ed Camerons Ice Cream parlor and eat him out of house and home on the Strength of his appointment.

June 16th. Nice weather again all day. Ross borrowed "Benny" a little this morning. I got out some papers for Mrs Leach against Daniel Coil and Ed. S. Casey. Judge Davis was in the Office a good deal to day. Atty. Bartow being unable to do much writing asked me to bring my typewriter over and help him which I did.

Charley Nebo came to town today. Rumor now has it that Old Judge Wilson is going to run for County Judge this fall on the Republican ticket.

Foot ball is getting to be quite a nuisance once in a while among our Town boys and soon the Authorities will have to interfere.

I helped to get the Democrat out today again.

R. E. W. Spargur left on the East bound train this evening and I am told he is bound for New York, but there must be some joke about it.

June 17. To day has been fine again and pretty hot. in the afternoon I went up to the Public School to witness the last days attendance.

after which I went to boyds and shot a match and beat one man out of 4. The Hose team got out this afternoon and filled the Hydrants again.

Last night the Town dudes painted the Town red again, but no arrests or complaints have yet been made[.]

E. N. Joslyn came in from White river[.]

Tony Whitfield came down from Douglas. he reports things pretty dull up that way.

June 18th[.] The weather opened up fine but not as pleasant to some as might be expect[ed], for again the supposed incindary [arsonist] is among us and no one is able to find out the party. last night after I had left the Office for home Someone undertook to burn the town up by setting fire to the Laundry building. the plot was detected in its infancy and another conflagration put to naught. the incindary has not yet been found and woe be tide him if he is[.]

This afternoon the Citizens held a special meeting at which certainly more harm was done than good, provided the posters offering $500.00 reward for any one caught Setting any building on fire. My sincere hope is that he may be caught.

June 22. Since last posting everything has been in a pell mell rush of excitement on the Election question for Court House bonds, which Election Came off yesterday and so far as Chadron is concerned the Bond issue is passed and a Court House will in all probability soon br under headway. 981 votes for it against 23 against Bonds was the tally of Chadrons poll books. rejoicing is going on all over the City. Dave Powers, W L Casady and W W Byington went to Whitney while Geo Clark and Bob Dickson went to Crawford, but they might as well have stayed at home for all the good accomplished[.] during the day in Chadron the Band played several pieces on the streets and livened up the Boys.

Issued warrant for John Lynch charged by David Hand with assault with intent to kill[.] gave the warrant to C. J. Davis to serve. Geo Havens and Dr Miller had a row this morning about the possession of the pony and consequently Geo refuses to take care of him any more[.]

June 23[.] C. J. Davis came in with John Lynch about 9 oclock this A.M. the Deft asked for a continuance for 3 days to get his witnesses which was granted and I issued the necessary subpoenas. The City Marshall woke me up early this morning and asked to have complaints made out for the Cream of Chadron's Jimmy toughs, comprising about all the youg dudes in town, but the Council Men got hold of it and endeavored and I think have succeeded in persuading the Marshal to not make any arrests. And thus the law goes on being broken, because some dear people while not too good to go raising hell around town are nevertheless too good to go to Jail[.]   it rained about 5 oclock.   the Chadron Democrat did not get out today owing to going to press too late.   Crites and Montgomery are in town[.]

June 24th[,] 1887[.]   The weather opened up fine today and everything went of[f] smoothly with the Ballots.   Mr Palmer and I took them to the County Clerk who gave us a receipt for them.

Yesterday I went up to B. F. Yates and acknowledged some papers for him.   I also broke my seal yesterday and had to send off for a new one from Hammond Bros. in Fremont[.]   To day Dr A. J. Gillespie came in from Dry Creek and talked some of putting in a prohibition paper here which if he does will be a great thing for Democracy.   After Supper I went up to the skating rink to witness the rehearsal of Ticket of Leave Man[.]

June 25[.]   To day has been one of "Continual round of pleasure[.]"   W. H. McNutt started the Ball rolling by getting out a warrant for Lovell Joy, charging him with disturbing the peace. He was found guilty and sentenced to pay $5.00 and costs after which Geo Clark wanted warrants for McNutt et al for Selling liquor without license and running a sporting house which I refused to issue whereupon he went straightway to Wilson who issued them.   After that was over with McNutt turned out and swore a warrant out against Geo spaulding for Carrying Concealed weapons of which, after a great deal of humbugging by Major Powers I found him guilty and sentenced him to pay [$]10.00 and costs taxed at $8.85 for default of which I issued a Mittimus and delivered the same to Ed Cameron, but he is not in Jail and the law seems to have no force what ever. after closing up Court and going down Town I met A. C. Kennedy formerly from Rock Creek, Albany Co Wyo., and next to the Heart out fit[.]   I was very much pleased to meet an old friend like Kennedy again but while indulging in my pleasure I was again called upon to issue a warrant for Jimmy Higgins for fighting which I complied in doing so, but the Night Police to whom I gave the warrant did not catch him on account of being a particular friend of his, and in about 1/2 an hour the same parties came to me and complained again that Jimmy had committed the same offense over again at which I proceeded to preambulate after the villian myself and failing to catch the bold desperado, I hastened to unlatch t[he] portals of the Marshall's sleeping apartment and appraised him of the defucualty, whereupon he got up and we proceeded to search the Town[.] not further and longer did we have to go than to the Gold Bar before we caught on to the Chap. Billy Carter went Security for his appearance. The wind has been blowing fearfully all day[,] in fact harder than I ever seen it blow for 10 years. . . .

June 26. The weather to day has been very nice all day. I went to Church in the morning and in the afternoon I took a ride in Company with Mort Morrisey out to Mr. sayrs place on spring Creek[.]

June 27. This morning early I tried Jimmy Higgins for fighting on Saturday evening last, and during progress of the trial I found the complaining witness guilty also and gave them $5.00 a piece and costs. Jimmy got away from the Marshall. I am afraid the new Marshall is not going to amount to much as he appears too easy with the boys.

after the morning trial Major powers came in the office and tendered me the legal fees for a transcript of the Case on my P. C. Docket, wherein the City of Chadron is Ptff and Geo Spaulding is Deft. I told him I would tend to the matter as soon as possible whereupon he proceeded to abuse me and caught hold of me by the neck[.] I asked him to unlose me, but not doing so I slaped the advocate of legal forms upon the softest side of his brazen face. this so enraged him that he Jumped on to me with all his force and pushed me off my balance so as to make me fall.

To say the least the affair was not a nice one as coming from so old a man and one who claims as high standing in legal professions as Powers[.] Geo Spaulding filed his bond for taking his Case up on error, giving Wm Clark as surety which the County Clerk approved.

towards night dame rumor had it that the gang were going to go down to McNutts and have a hell of a time breaking up things so Cameron and the New Night Watch Haddock[,] whom I swore in today, and myself got some arms and went down to lay in wait for them but they failed to do anything[.] on the contrary George Spaulding got on the 3 oclock train going East and departed from Chadron, so then we went home.

June 28.   The weather opened up nice but towards 7 oclock PM a wind started up which at present is ploughing along at hurricane speed. I have been busy a greater part of the day getting out the Democrat news, as Allen had to go out to the Sand Hills to write an article[.]

About 10 oclock I was subpoenaed to appear before Justice Wilson and testify in the House of prostitution Case[.] I was subpoened in order to prevent a change being taken but from some cause or other[,] shame sake I guess, the Case was dismissed.

June 29. To day the scheme of erecting the New Hotel was set in motion and if Carried out will prove beneficial to all[.]

about 11 oclock I went out to Tobe Driscoll's camp on spring Creek and had a regular old time Camp dinner with the Boys.

During the afternoon we had a Scrub trial race between S. A. Bryants pacer and Dr. Harris' New Horse in which Doc's Horse came in ahead[.] played billiards at Coffeys after supper.

June 30. This morning every thing opened up nice. Ballard came in the office to see the City Clerk's books. Mrs. Leach came in to See me about Dan Coil and Casey. Mr Harris from Laramie City was also in, then Mr. Yates came to have a paper acknowledged which made me go over to Kass & Co and put my seal together[.] in the afternoon I hitched up "Ben" to pattisons buckboard and went out to Sayrs house. Came home and went to the skating rink[.]

July 1[.] To day has been one of Continual rounds of pleasure. Frank Fruch came down from Hot springs with about 300 head of horses and at the same time Budd Driscoll left here with 50 odd head for his Ranch in Northern Wyoming, having been here 13 days with all broke saddle horses, but the Chadron horse market has been ruptured.

in the afternoon I had the blacksmith shoe Bens hind feet, after which the Black smith and I went out to look at Frank Fruch's Horses.

After Supper every body in Town almost attended the performance of Ticket of leave man by the Home Dramatic troupe and which was ordinarily well executed. I took Mrs and Miss Joslyn and we had a very pleasant time there. After the performance Opportunity Hank made 2 arrests and a great big name for himself as the parties he arrested were bad men and he had to use the Wah, Wah, a great deal.

July 2. Fine weather again. about noon the Indians who are to be here this 4th, Commenced to come from the agency and file into town. They demanded 10 head of beeves right off with which to feed the gang that are to be here on the fourth. their ideas of a white mans liberality is quite astonishing. of course they did not get it. After 6 oclock I saddled up and took a ride out to the Indian Camp on spring Creek whence every [one] was coming to and fro. after laying around their camp 2 or 3 hours I mounted my Bronc and took a ride through the foot hills. Came home and got supper at Mrs Joslyns and while eating[,] the same Cleona got on to Ben and took quite a ride with Ace Johnson as her guide and leader. I got my New Suit from the Tailor.

during the day I swore in Van Eution, O. F. Messenger as special Police for the fourth of July.

July 3rd. The weather opened up splendid and continued so all day. about 9 oclock the Indians commenced filing into Town. first came the Bucks on horseback then the Squaws and children in wagons and carriages and last the teppe pole outfit[.] fully 1500 are in Town and promise to make things lively tomorrow[.] about 12 oclock Nick Janis came in Town and reported the necessity of a strong police force in Town in order to hold down the half breds who he reports as having got considerable whiskey some where so the Marshall appointed a force of 10 Extras and I swore them in, after which I went out to see Red Cloud and read the riot act to the Half breeds.

in the evening the Richards Gang commenced to get pretty lively and by 11 oclock they made the Town howl. All day I have been busy getting the Indians fixed for water. I got Mr Plympton to loan me his water tank so as to have plenty of water on the ground tomorrow.

Oglala Lakota Chief Red Cloud and his son, Jack Red Cloud

during the evening the Police Caught two parties and arrested them on suspicion of having sold whiskey to the Indians.

July 4. I got up early and had the horse saddled so as to enable me to get around during the day. After breakfast I commenced getting the water barrels distributed in the most convenient places to allow the public access to them, after which I was instructed by Dorrington and Owens to go to the Indian Camp and get all the warriors ready for parade, which I done, and as soon as I rode among them giving the usual war Sign

*Fourth of July Indian parade
in Chadron, Nebraska (ca. 1887)*

you ought to have seen them flock around me. The parade started at 10.30 AM and got done at 12.15 P.M. then the speaking commenced but I went home to dinner and not being able to get in a hotel, I sat down on the side walk and took lunch with the graingers. After dinner every body proceeded to go to the races which came off at 2.30 P.M. afterwhich every thing devolved upon the Indian War Dance which through the Smartness of W. L. Casady was muddled up to a certain extent for some time, but finally everybody understood that the Dance was to be where the Indians were camped and thither they flocked like so many wild Geese. before the dance commenced the Indians insisted on being paid so I gave my hat to Jack Red Cloud and made him go around through the people and I went around the other way. Dorrington also took up a Collection and between the three we managed to collect Thirty four dollars. Now the dancing commenced and again the Indians made up their minds that more beef ought to be given them as a lunch after the dance, so we were again obliged to take up a Subscription to raise $30.00 to pay for a beef. Four times was I compelled to go the rounds and beg I did like a good fellow and finally succeeded in getting the full amount, and then the dance went on again all O.K. at 7.15 the dance broke up and all hands proceeded to witness the killing of the steer which by this time had been brought upon the scene of action. Red Cloud was invited by the Committee on arrangments to come down Town to see the performance of Hyers Colored Opera & Comedy Company and upon his arrival he reported to me and said one of his Indians had been struck by a man during the day, that he did not like it and it ought to be attended to, so I took the Indian that had been struck and went with him to find the Marshall[.] but it seems that a Rail Road Man done the striking and it was claimed to have been an accident and all this and that till however the gang of Rail Road men got together and fixed things up satisfactorily with the Indians. I felt very tired and got home to bed and went to sleep the moment I got laid down.

July 5. The Indians have all gone except Antoine Janis who is camped North of the R. R. Track and is very sick. everything has again quieted down to regular business. Jake Nausbaum left for Sioux City on account of being unable to run the Town to suit himself. during the afternoon a local Horse race came off between Claud

Glover's little mare and Frank Coffeys horse and an Indian Pony belonging to Charlie Janis in which the Coffey horse came out ahead.

July 6. To day I got Mr Burns to haul Mr Plimptons Water Tank home from the race track and found that some one had got away with one of the faucets to the same. Messrs Bisbee and Daly came down from Crawford and Whitney to contest the election and kick up general Hell about Court House bonds.

After Supper I went to the skating rink to see the New Malitia Company drill, but was called away on important business as Brother Bisbee and Daly wanted to know more about the election Contest. after I was at leisure again and just on my way from the Office to bed, I was stopped and requested to make out a warrant for a Chicken Thief, who Teddy Oneal had captured, but when Oneal was asked to sign a complaint he refused, so I dismissed the case, discharged the accused and went home to bed.

July 7[.] fine weather again till 6 oclock when it set in to raining and rained pretty much all night[.] The "Democrat" did not get out on account of the sickness of Thompson who is suffering from Mountain Fever.

during the afternoon Messrs Bisbee & Daly again called and argued the pros and cons relative to general laws and understandings about County Court House Bonds and about Judges of Election & C & C, but they failed to make fools of anyone except themselves, so they went away disgusted with everything, but in about an hour Mr Daly came back and informed me that if I would not do so and so he would have a mandamus issued and served upon me to compelle me to please him to which I informed him to go ahead. It rained pretty hard during the early part of the night, but I managed to get around on horse back pretty well in it, and keep sight of Bros Bisbee and Dalys transactions[.] I called on Bob Dickson in my rambles and found him in attendance upon his wife who was sick.

July 8. Fine day again[—]very hot. Bros Bisbee and Daly returned home early this morning, no doubt much in disgust over the bond issue. I helped the Chadron Democrat out again which is a day late this week. after that B. C. Hill told me that the managers of the Democrat had decided to make Allen do the reporting of the City so I laid off the rest and the Democrat has settled up with me.

July 9. To day has been a pleasant one again but rather warm. Tom Madden came down from Crawford today and reports things lively last thursday evening. Dick Lyman and M. Polly while out ridding had a team to run away and smash things up in general[.] Billy Carter and his wife left for their Gordon Ranch yesterday evening[.]

July 10[.] The weather opened up nice and continued so all day only it was rather hot. it now devolves that Judge Cook is taking a hand in the Contesting of Court House Bonds[.] I had dinner at Mrs Joslyn[.]

July ll[.] Earnest Bross is on a drunk again. I lent "Ben" to Mr Hawley[.] To day was fine again.

July 14. Fine weather till towards evening when it rained considerable. Early this morning at 1 oclock Geo Clark, Fred Danielson and others woke me up to have a warrant sworn out against one Jack Blade for disturbing the peace, which I done and the trial was postponed till 1 oclock P.M. at which time the parties appeared and the trial went on, at the completion of which I found the defendant guilty as charged. Sentenced him to One Hundred Dollars and Costs and stand Committed in default, but after having issued the mittimus, it was impossible to get the defendant incarcerated, he being in default, until as of last resource I had to threaten the Marshall with punishment for contempt and then he done his work in a very reluctant manner.

Since the 11th inst and up to the Evening of the 13th I have been very busy keeping eyes and ears open about the County Bond Election Contest. on the 13th in the afternoon about 4 oclock, the Rail Road Hotel caught on fire and for a while it seemed as if the whole house was gone[,] but by hard work of the Fire Department, ably assisted by the Rail Road employees, it was brought under control, and great damage averted.

W H McNutt was taken to Omaha on last evenings train and charged with having sold liquor without license.

July 15. Rain during the forenoon but cleared up towards dinner. O. C Waid of Cheyenne is here and has been here for the past 4 or 5 days. Earnest Bross is still on a drunk and aching to be put into jail[.]

Bob Thompson is still unable to be at his case in the "Democrat Office[.]"

Fannie Powers is all broke up about her dear Baby Jack being in jail and amuses herself by carrying ice cream, whiskey, opium and morphine to him. It rained in the evening pretty hard[.]

After Supper the Mayor came and spoke to me about the Circumstances connected with Jack Blades case, after which we both went up to the Jail to see him about [it], but nothing definate was done. I have telegraph[ed] all over Iowa concerning him and expect to hear some good reports from them by Monday. W D Edgar came down from Crawford this even[.]

July 16. The weather was a little Cool this morning owing to the heavy rain last night[.] "Ben" got back from his jaunt about 2 oclock P.M. Hee looked better than when he started. in the afternoon a horse race was indulged in and it was run right in the end of town.

Dave Powers coming out loser as usual.

Bob Thompson commenced work on the "Democrat" today. Yesterday O L Sloggy [sentence unfinished].

July 17. fine weather all day[.] Early this morning I got a Team from Birdsall's and by 9 oclock AM. Mrs Josselyn, Miss Josselyn, Rodiea and Little Guy Alexander and myself started for Josselyn's White River Ranch 15 miles distant, where we arrived 20 minutes before 12 M. We had a very nice time there and at 3.45 P.M. we hitched up again and started for home arriving there at 6.10 P.M. After Supper Fannie Powers came to see me about Jack Blade. W. H. McNutt arrived from Omaha from his Liquor trial. He is all togged out with a fine broad cloth suit and looked like a millionare. about 10 oclock P.M. a lot of half breds came in the City from Red Cloud Agency and commenced to get noisey and demonstrative in Carter's Saloon.

July 18. This morning bright and early trouble commenced among the saloons on account of the selling of Liquor to Indian half breds yesterday. C. D. Sayrs and old Ballard have put their heads together and are no doubt laughing to themselves at the fools they are going to make over the affair and figuring on their immense fees.

In the afternoon a horse race came off over at the track and between one of the races L. A Brower Started out for a 50 yds race, but his Saddle being lose[,] it turned and threw him to the ground with considerable force though without any injuries but his horse ran away with the Saddle and came in contact with a barb wire fence which cut the animal considerably. It was however soon caught before having done any serious damage to itself and may Mr Brower ever again refuse to run in a race.

July 19. Fine weather today with some rain during the afternoon. To day has been the fatal one to all those who have more or less been buying County Claims as all who have done so will come out at the little end of the horn.

Another horse race came off this afternoon which terminated very nicely, but I could not get to go to see it.

After Supper a foot race came off which created some excitement in front of the Skating rink, but the usual amount of backwardness in betting circles prevailed on account of being afraid of the prevailing tricks of runners[.]

after the race I went out horse back ridding with Mrs Alexander, Miss Powers and Dr Miller. We all had a very pleasant time. To day has been marked as an exodus for the liquor question in the County Court and rumor has it that the whole thing about which so much hub bub has been made is now quashed and C. D. Sayrs and Old Ballard are the victors of the spoils, one having been the prosecutor and the other defendant, but still the world continues to move.

July 20. Fine weather again.

July 23. to busy to post up since the 20th. The weather opened up this morning very nicely and continued so all day. Lute North came up from Columbus to day and called on me[.] he expects to go to Buffalo Gap on Monday after which he will return and remain here for some time. Since the 20th there has been great work going on concerning the Court House Bonds. Mr Handy from Whitney came down to copy the books but failed to accomplish the motive.

Jack Harrington came to Town on the 22 and is Still here. Billy Carter came up from his ranch yesterday and expects to go back again tomorrow.

July 24. Fine and warm weather again all day. I went to the Episcopal Church with Mrs and Miss Josselyn. took dinner at the "Hanlon" after which I made a call on Mr and Mrs Simmons. After supper a horse race being on the program I saddled up and took that in too, but it did not pan out as good as I thought it would.

July 25[.] Fine weather again but last night after having retired to bed a fearful wind Storm arose and at times I thought the house would surely go to pieces. I went out to Hollenbecks claim with O. L. Messinger.

July 26. Fine weather again all day. in the afternoon I hitched up "Ben" and Geo Havens and I went out to White river to See Kelloge about the Office rent. after we got back to Town which was about 5 oclock, Mrs Josselyn asked me to take her Daughter Cohena out to their ranch on White River so I got a buggy at Birdsalls and by Six Oclock P.M. we were on the way, but when we got to the White River it commenced to Cloud up and look like rain and after leaving the river it became too dark to hold the extreme dim tracks, and so we became lost and had to stay on the Prairie all night. Cohena took the situation very considerately and instead of crying and bawling as ladies generally do in such Cases, she helped me to unhitch the team and get things in readiness for a Rain Storm. Soon everything became dark as pitch and it looked as if one of the Severest Hail Storms of the season was going to come down upon us, but it all blew over and nothing but a hard gale of wind kept us busy trying to keep warm all night. At 3 oclock A.M. I again hitched up and by 5 P.M. [a.m.?] we got to the Ranch and left the word we wanted to leave and Started for Chadron again, where we arrived by 7 oclock A.M.

July 27. To day opened up a little Cloudy and Cold[.] at 9 Oclock AM the United Sunday Schools of Chadron Started for Butlers Grove on Little Bordeaux for a Picnic. I did not go as I was too tired from last nights trip, but Cohena went all the same. at 4 Oclock in the afternoon I went down on the train to meeting the Pic Nic party on their way home. They reported having had a Splendid time at the Grove and every thing passed of[f] smoothly.

After Supper I attended the Malitia Cos drill at the Skating rink. about 10 Oclock P.M. the F. E. & M. V. Band Serenaded the Masonic Lodge who gave a Banquet at the "Danielson."

July 28th. Fine weather all day. The Democrat did not come out on time today, but the Journal got out a day ahead of its regular time. in the evening Jim Owens and two other men hitched up a pair of iron gray Bronchos to Snyders heavy freight and dray wagon and when the outfit got in the East end of Town the Team ran away throwing Jim Owens from his high seat and hurting him to some slight extent. the most fun however that occurred was when Mike Gottstein wanted to send word out to the runaway and not being able to get his man started who was trying to go on a refractory Broncho, he concluded to go out himself[,] and a Single buggy, Mort Morriseys[,] being driven along the street at that time, Mike hailed Mort and asked him to take him out to where the runaway was, but what was Mikes great Surprise was that he had got into a buggy to which was hitched a balky broncho so he skipped out as quick as his Size would let him and off he started for the Scene of Action on foot. Geo Havens went home with me.

July 29. Fine day again. got up early and came down and helped to get out the "Democrat". After dinner I borrowed Mort Morriseys buggy and took Mr E N Josselyn out on White River to look at a piece of land. while out there we made a call on Mr Dell Ballard who invited us to Stay for Supper, but we declined the invitation. We got back to Chadron at 6.45 PM. after Supper Geo Havens and I attended a lecture on the Subject of "what is the Episcopal Church" given at the Episcopal Chapel by elder Chestnut. after lecture Geo and I had ice cream at Josselyns and then we returned home.

July 30[.] The weather opened up fine today and continued so all day. got up early and wrote a long letter to Brother Thomas[.] Dr A. J. Gillespie came in from Dry Creek and called on me. I informed him that I would be out to his place tomorrow with E. N. Josselyn to look at some land. Johny Green from Little Bordeaux came to Town today and offered his Farm for $1,000. After Supper E N Josselyn and I hitched up his team for a little drive to the Bordeaux to overhaul some of the Town boys, among whom was his son, Bert, who went off yesterday on an excursion tour, but we met them (six) coming home a little the other side of the Brick Yard and they were coming on the Jump. To day I bought a load of hay and moved my Pony "Ben" over in Sloggys Barn. Geo. Haven is now happy. after coming home from the Bordeaux trip I gave Josselyn some Hay for his team and Geo and I went up to attend a Temperance lecture but found it would not come off till tomorrow[.]

July 31. The weather opened up good and with the exception of a little shower in the afternoon, it continued so all day. Ed North and Lute North came up from Valentine this morning. Tom Madden came down from Crawford yesterday. This mornings mail brought the Joyfull news of Judge Kinkaids decision on the Court House Bond question in which he decided in favor of Chadron thereby causing the weeping and knashing of teeth among the Whitney people and Crawford spotters.

Just before Supper a horse race was gotten up between Claud Glover, Mont House and Jas Dahlman in which the later came out victorious he having been given 20 ft at the start. Ed North and his Friend Zackie returned to Valentine on the 10.30 P.M. Train.

Aug. 2nd. Yesterday I forgot to post up. The weather opened up fine this morning but towards evening the Table Country got quite a Shower about 2 Oclock P.M. Mr Josselyn and myself Started for the Dry Creek Country where we were hospitably entertained by Dr A J. Gillespie and his Family. the Dr showed us some as fine land as any in Dawes County and put us on to as good filing land as one could wish for at this Stage of the game. We stayed all night with the Dr.

Aug. 3rd. Fine weather again all day. Mr Josselyn and I having slept in our Buggy instead of going into the house, we got up with the sun. After breakfast the Dr took us over by the Sheridan Gate Valley and showed us a fine Stallion, after when we again returned to Dr [Gillespie's] Home where we were supplied with fresh Corn, Spring Chickens and Watermelons which were to be used at the Moonlight Pic Nic to be held at Butlers Park and where we are to meet the whole Josselyn Family who are to come from Chadron by the Passenger train.

Mr J and I took dinner at Mrs Lennington's after first having been up to the head of Little Bordeaux to see Johny Green but who was not at home. on our way to Lenningtons from Greens we overtook a number of Emigrants from Iowa in search of Nebraska land. we arrived at Butlers Grove at 2.30 to await the arrival of the Pic Nickers. at 10.45 the Passenger came along and brought a part of the Josselyn family and the rest arrived by horseback. Lunch being the next thing in order. Mr. Josselyn and I were given the preference at "all hands Grab" and of course my fingers being gone I could not grab very readily but managed to make Cohena think I had been eating. We Started for Chadron at 11.45 P.M., and with the exception of a little rude performance by some of Bordeaux's many Missouri Cow-Boys who were bent on making mischief for the first few miles[,] all passed off smoothly and the Moonlight Pic Nic and drive seemed to have been very much enjoyed by all, but I doubt very much if Mrs Josselyn enjoyed it although her assurance to the contrary. We arrived home at 3.10 A.M. and not being able to find Bob Dorr, I was obliged to take up lodging with O Patsey.

Aug 4. Ordinary weather with more or less clouds and wind. My new artificial limbs arrived from pittsburgh with a C.O.D. of $113.85 attached. M. Ballard arrived from the Dakota Hot Springs today.

Aug 5[.] I missed posting yesterday but nothing occurred of note beyond my going out to Old Mr Hartzells last evening in company with Lou Hartzell and Fred Danielson where I went to assure myself that one of Hartzells Boys had not been in the fracas at Butlers park as I have made up my mind to have the Gentlemen arrested and brought to trial. This morning the weather showed up fine and about 9 Oclock I got M Ballard to draw up the necessary complaint and Justice Wilson issued the warrants whereupon Constable Davis and I went out to get the parties. after a long drive we returned to Chadron with two of the Bad men who upon being taken before Judge Ricker were turned loose upon their own recognizance.

Aug 6. The Case against the Bad men has been continued till Tuesday August 9th at 9 oclock A.M. I had subpoena's issued for my witnesses. In the afternoon a horse race came off which I of course took in. after Supper I went over to see Billy Carter about County Warrants & C & C. Geo Havens went home with me[.]

Aug 7. The weather opened up very fine this morning but about 9 oclock it commenced to get very hot with a hot wind stirring. about 12 Oclock Ben Tibbitts and wife and daughter came through town enroute to their White River Horse Ranch. After dinner I made a call on Mr and Mrs Josselyn[.]

Aug 9. To day opened up pretty Cold. I got up early and after breakfast attended Court in the Case of State against John Jones Et-al. I demanded and got a Jury and at 1 Oclock sharp we commenced work. the case was given to the Jury at 5 oclock and at 5.30 they came in with a verdict of Guilty as against 2 of the parties and not guilty as against one[.] the Court passed sentence thereupon and fined the desperados 1 dollar a piece and costs—which amounted in all to $22.40 or $11.20 apiece which they did not pay but took up on

230

error. After Supper I went up to the Congregational Church[.]

Aug 17. I have omitted posting up my book for Some time for the reason that everything has been in a rush push and stew so that I have almost lost myself in the shuffle. I am however alive still with the hope of living many a long year to come yet. since last posting there have developed many changes that will show themselves at this coming fall Convention for County Offices. I have now my new Artificial limbs for which I paid $260.00 in hard cash, which almost tore me to pieces. The new limbs do not do as well as they might but I hope to be able to use them better by and by. Yesterday I loaned Cleona Josselyn "Ben" to ride out to the claim. She returned very tired. Nothing appears to be new in the Police Court and business in general seems to be on a Stand still. Major Powers, C. D. Sayrs, C. H. Lutz, J. A. Wilson, Geo. Clark, F. B. Carley and old Judge Cook still continue as they have done ever since I have been in office with the exception of Sayrs who turned against me some 6 months ago when I would not pay his office rent and tolerated his whiskey drinking no longer, to be my mortal enemy and no point of the swill barrel seems to be too low or filthy for them to get dirt from to fling at me.

Miss Bessie OLinn has been very sick for the past week with typhoid fever but is reported to be improving now. Mike Gottstein went to the Hills 2 days ago. Dr Jackson was in the Office this morning to see about getting "Curley" Bartletts "Girl" sent to the reform School as he claimed that he nor his wife are unable to do anything with the Child. Geo Havens asked for the use of "Ben" to go to Hemingford with, but I did not let him have Ben. Nigger John Henry got out of "Jail" last night.

Aug. 21. Fine weather today again. There have been some traveling ball players here and today every body is gone on ball playing. last week I let my watch fall on the floor in Sloggys Saloon and broke it all up. Kirmse has taken it to fix.

I attended the Episcopal Church this morning[,] and in the afternoon by invitation of Dr Miller, I took a drive into the Country to attend one of Drs patients.

Aug. 22. rained last night and opened up damp and cold this morning. Dr Miller & I got back from the Country (Mossmans) about 10 AM. Lake & Halley commenced throwing away dirt preparitory to erecting a New Bank on the corner of Main and 2nd st. Dr Waller refused to pay the money into Court as required to do in the Case of Bowman vs Steever as Garnishee. in the afternoon the weather looked more favorable. Quite a Sensation was created in front of Gottstein & Owens this morning by a Stranger putting on Sale on the Side Walk, a lot of Buffalo Horns. wrote a letter to A. C. Fowler for Money. Tom Madden was down from Crawford yesterday and gave me some great pointers about certain movements of the Democratic Candidates in the Western part of Dawes County. I wrote a letter to W. D. Edgar in response to an editorial of his relative to Candidates "ponying up" for the Securance of the Crescents influence in their respective behalf's.

Aug 24[.] I forgot to post again yesterday. The weather today opened up damp and disagreeable and continues so all day. I printed contracts for the School Board. Not much business today. had a great deal of fun with Truxes and his water melon. Today I shingled Tom Dixons House and went out to Newmans to see a herd of horses.

Aug 25th. I got shingle for Tom Dixons house and shingle nails. after dinner went over to Tim Morriseys with Charley Nebo[1] to get a horse for the mail carrier. Geo Havens & I took a ride out to Newmans Horse herd and while there one of the Boys gave us

[1]A cowboy on the Hunter Evans Ranch south of Chadron.

a Bridle Bit—Von Harris, Pattison & Sperling came to town. Ben Lowenthal commenced suit before me against John Haugh for $16.75. The weather is still cold and disagreeable.

Aug 26. Geo. got up early. I moved my sleeping out fit from Henry's House to my office today. Maher was in the Office a good bit

John G. Maher

today and after supper we had quite a conflab on short hand writing, he showed me a great many points about it.

Aug 27. Fine weather all day about 10 Oclock A.M. Sheriff Clark commenced selling out the "Ferbrache Jewelry Store" and things went remarkably cheap all day. The Jury in the Case of Chas Larsh vs John Larsh gave a verdict for $199.99 in favor of Chas Larsh. Frank Larsh promised to let me have the use of his mule tomorrow with which to go down on the Bordeaux to haul over a log house to E. N. Josselyns claim. I purchased the house from Pete Nelson to day for $30.00 in County Claims. Von Harris and Pattison have all been in Town today. Von was in the Office talking politics to me in great shape. W. D. Edgar is down from Crawford and the Sachems are now in convention in the Democratlic printing Office.

Aug 28. Fine weather again today. Frank Larsh and his man came in early this morning to go down on the Bordeaux to tear down the house, but when we arrived there which was about 10 Oclock A.M. I found the house too old and rotten to do or be any good so I concluded not to take it, whereupon we all proceeded to go up into the timber to look at some cut timber (house logs) and while there we were met by Mr. Ballard and Fredericks[.] we got back to Chadron by 3 oclock P.M.

Julis Halen, Dahlman & Simmons Butcher, received a very severe cut on his left hand while grinding a knife at the Slaughter house last week. unfortunately cutting an artery. on Sunday last the cauterization bursted and resulted in severe bleeding which was stopped by the timely arrival of Dr Harris who succeeded in fixing the man who for 14 years never cut a gut. Last night old Dr Richardson got run in for Drunk and disorderly conduct. after supper I went up to the rink to see the Malitia Co start to Lincoln. Mrs Josselyn[,] Mrs Wilcox, Cleona Josselyn and myself went to the depot to see them on the cars. about 9 oclock Mrs Botts shot two of Despoll's men who were trying to break into her house. There was quite a commotion over the affair. about 10[:]30 Rattlesnake Tom from Snake Creek commenced to paint the Town red and after firing off his pistol a couple of tim[e]s was taken in charge by the officers—[.]

Aug 29[.] Fine weather all day and more work in the Police Court than there has been for six months. Rattle snake Tom danced to the tune of $10.00 and costs after which Doc Richardson hoed down a [$]5.00 and Cost Jig, whereupon the spectators were anxious to see his snake-ship perform again, who gave a fine $10.00 and cost repeater reel. this brought down the gallery who were again thrown into mirth jolity by the performance of an ameteur horseman who was exhibiting his Skill in ridding on sidewalks. this gentleman gave a fine exhibition of an Irish shindig paying there for $7.50 which wound up the day. Mr Josselyn came in from the Ranch to day.

Aug 30th[.] Fine weather all day up till 10 oclock P.M. when a good wind started up[.] last night I got very sick after having gone to bed. about 9 oclock this AM G. E. Myers got out attachment papers against Miss E. M. Garrett who came into Court and paid the bill and costs[.] Lute North was in to see me—[.] The sale of Ferbraches Drug Store ended to-day. after supper Fred Fuller swore out warrants for two parties from Crawford for being drunk and disorderly. Politics are now in the pot and the water is commencing to boil and friends are getting few and far between with Cut-throat for a countersign.

Rose Kass is on the Sick list and people are commencing to think that diptheria is going to take the Town. I stopped my man from going into the timber to get out my house logs for a week or So.

Aug 31st. The prosecuting witness against John Doe (Tom Allen) and Nellie Ryan did not appear in Court this morning so the cases were dismissed[.] A. J. Johnson came in from the table to make a de[c]laritory stat[e]ment on pre-emption[.] My poison ivey is getting considerably better but it pains me a great deal yet. A. V. Harris is in from Whitney as is also Dick Lyman from Crawford. Old Joe Brown is here also and as usual he has been laying around drunk. John Bigaler purchased the little Bay race mare from Geo Birdsall for $125.00, and they expect to take her down to Valentine to get even with old Sigwert who has been beating the sports considerably in that part of the country.

Sept. 1st. last night I got very sick with my poison oak and got Judge Ricker to get Dr Miller to fix me, who gave me 1/2 grain of Morphine which settled me till this morning when I commenced to be very sick and I continued to vomit all day. Mrs Josselyn brought my meals. I stayed in bed all day. about 5 oclock it rained hard and made quite a lake back of the office.

Sept. 2. Fine weather again. I got up feeling splendidly. Bob Dorr bought a fine desk from Myers &

Boone[.]   Haddock filed complaints against all the prostitutes. We got out a warrant against Ollie.

Tony Bernard came up to see if I would let him have Ben to go down the Country on to see if he can catch a certain desperado for whom a large reward has been offered.

Tom Coffey commenced getting on a spree. Quite a number of graders and builders are in the town now.

Sept. 3rd—The weather opened up fine this AM[.] about 4 AM Mr. Fanning and Perry from Crawford woke me up to get out attachment papers against H F Clough which was very soon done.

Geo Havens went to Crawford with Bob Dorr. little Pete cleaned up the back yard for me. A. Haddock filed his complaint against Mr and Mrs Harris for vagrancy. both came up, Made a stormy fight, but I gave them a pretty good dose. Got my hay put in the Barn. a high wind set up[.]

Sep 4. fine weather today again. Geo Havens and Bob Dorr came back from Crawford.

Sept. 5 fine weather today again all day. Co. E. got back from Lincoln all o.k. and apperantly much pleased with their trip. the home band escorted them on their parade through town. News spredes now that C C Hughes has been promoted from train master to Division Superintendent taking the place of Halsey who is to assume the duties of Genl Supt. Howard Lander got me to make out a chattle mortgage for $35.00 in Favor of Miss Mary A. Powell. Geo Havens commenced work for Frank Ingersoll at $2.00 per week.

Sept. 6. fine weather all day. Von Harris and the rest of the Commissioners are in Town. Maher filed [failed] to come to the office this evening so I attended a meeting of the School Board who are meditating on discharging Prof. Foster. after listening to the pros and cons of the Board and Prof. I finally left, disgust[ed] with the action of the Board in the matter.

Sep. 7. Nice day but about 7 oclock a high wind started up and continues unabated. during the day I changed my Office furniture and got things ready for the Carpenter to commence putting in a partition but he failed to put in an apperance.

To-day has been a great day with local Contractors all of whom have been trying to get the work of erecting the $30,000.00 Court House, but luck seems to have been against them all, not withstanding that Jim Rothwell had bid $28,440.00 which was $60.00 lower than the next lowest bid of $28,500.00 by some Lincoln Parties who were finally awarded the job. It is useless to say that there will have to be some more bonds voted to complete the job. The City Council made an effort to have a meeting this evening, but it resulted in the usual manner of adjourning on account of no quorum.

Sept. 8. The weather opened up fine but the County Commissioners did not open up as fine, for every one seemed to be finding fault with them for having let the Lincoln party have the contract of building the Court House. It now however developes that the Bonds which were voted for the said Court house have been sent back from the State Auditors Office whence they had been sent for registration, with instructions from that official to have them corrected, and now that some of Chadron's prosperous business men are kicking so hard against the action of the Commissioners in letting the contract go to a good and responsible man. The Commissioners on their part now say that they will never make the requisite correction in which case there will be no Court House go up at all. I had a partition put in my office today.

Sep. 9. The weather opened up fine and so also did the prospects of the County Commissioners as to changing their minds about the bond business. they have to day rectified the error and now all goes on smoothly. I rented Henry Harrisons House taking as security for the rent W. Christensen for $6.00 fees month from today. I moved my stoves down to Harrisons saloon[.] Bob Harrison & Red came in from Sioux Co.

Sep 10th[.] Fine day again! T. J. Cook & Co. being plaintiff in a case with Schmoldt as Defendant. the case was brought on a Change of Venue from Wilson and set by me for trial on Monday next at 10 oclock AM. Herman Kermise came home this AM. Dr. Harris promenaded the streets this evening in a fine Speeding Sulky put up by Simpson of Omaha. James W. OBrien came to town this evening and rumor has it that he is on his way to Deadwood. Bob Dorr got back from Crawford. he was very tired.

Sept. 11th The weather opened up fine this morning. I went to the Episcopal Church in the morning. at dinner I met Bob Harrison[.] In the afternoon I whiled away a little time at Coffey's and during a few games of pool there sprang up some unpleasant words between Fred Poll and Jake Kass and Myself. Fred Finney came up from Hemingford he reports every thing lively down that way. it is now 9 oclock PM and the wind is tearing along terrifically[.] I am all alone in the Office and feel lonesome.

Sept. 12th. The weather opened out fine this morning but towards 2 oclock a heavy gale of wind set in and blew terrific for about 4 hours. at 10 AM. the case of J. P. Cook and Co. vs August Schmoldt was tried by a Jury before me. the verdict returned being in favor of the Plffs for one hundred Dollars and Costs. After supper I took a strole around town and about 10 oclock Nigger John Henry came to town.

Sep 13th[.] Bright and Early this morning Nigger John Henry and red Stewart were arrested by the City Marshall for fighting and being drunk and disorderly. I discharged Red and sent John Henry to the "Cooler" to serve out a $10.00 fine. After that was all over with, the "General" (Colored) at Gottsteins & Owens got on a Pony and rode up and down Main Street till his Saddle turned on him throwing him to the ground in a pretty rough manner. Politics is knocking around on every corner and C. D. Sayrs with Jimmy Cavanaugh goes ridding every day.

Sept 14th[.] to day I had my fire flue built and scrubed out the bed room. John Henry has been working on the streets.

Sept. 15th[.] The weather has been very disagreeable all day. a high wind has been going constantly and dust in abundance all day. This morning I fixed up the ceiling in the office, helped to get the Democrat out in the afternoon. after supper I went to see Pete Breen about seeing Counsoal the Contractor to have him office with me.

Tony Barnard came home from the B & M. Country. he reports his efforts to catch certain parties as having been unsuccessful.

I played a game of Billiards with P. B. Danielson & Patsy, the bar keeper, [and] after coming home to my Office Tony Barnard called on me and we had a nice quiet little chat about things in general. The Mayor remitted the fine and cost against John Henry.

Sep. 16th[.] The weather has been windy pretty much all day. Politics are being discussed on every corner and the cry against Pattison for County Commissioner goes up strong and regular from the "Dawes County Journal[.]" tomorrow is the day for the Republican Primaries and after which there will be wailing and gnashing of teeth from the defeated ones[.] I started to build myself a good bridle to day which I hope to get done soon. bought a load of hay yesterday and got the stable locked up[.] I worked till late.

Sep 17. Fine weather all day. The City has been full of Primary men and politicians fail description. C. W. Dresser filed a complaint against a Petty thief early this morning who was convicted before me. The gist of to-days doings has been centred upon the Republican

Primary[.] Eagan and the Brick Bank Gang are at work and anything went to beat Pattison men to day which they finally succeeded in doing and for once in a few years the Brick Bank has gained a point but only momentary, as Pattison will undoubtedly now know just what strings to pull in order to insure success in the convention.

Sep 18th[.] The weather opened fair but towards 2 o'clock P.M a wind came up[.] at this present time 8 PM, a perfect gale is going on outside. I stayed in the office all day and worked on a bridle. Tom Madden called and had a nice quiet little chat about politics. Tom Coffey has now announced himself as a candidate for County Commissioner. The "Dawes County Journal" and Brick Bank Gangs had all the fun they wanted with old Judge Cook last night. They made him plenty drunk and the poor old man wanted to be hauled home in a wheel-barrow. Geo. Havens rode "Ben" out today.

Sept 19. Fine day all day. The town is and has been full of Republicans all day.

I made out a mortgage for J. T. Wright to Billy Carter.

Lame Smitty and notorious smithy came down from Crawford[.] After supper all the prominent democrats held a meeting in the school House to discuss politics among the party. Van Harris seemed rather excited at this gathering and inferred that a Western man was being spoken of for County Clerk only to have him slaughtered.

Sept 20. fine weather and lots of would be leading Republicans and Democrats are on the streets[.] early this AM it seemed evident there was going to be a split in the Republican Convention, but by degrees every thing turned of smoothly, although nothing was accomplished untill 2 oclock P.M. when Lyman Brown received 39 votes against Dr. J M Davidson's 1 vote for Treasurer. after the convention was over a horse race was on the programe and all hands adjourned to see that[.] nothing but politics was the go in the evening.

Sept 21[.] Fine day again! Early this AM I recd a letter from Uncle Thos to draw on him for $50.00 which I did and that will serve to help me out of my Omaha Trouble.

I have been busy all day and cannot see what I have done either[.] every body seems to be crazy about politics and yet nothing will be definately settled untill the Democratic convention. it however appears that a greater portion of the Democratic Ticket is going to go through this fall[.]

Timothy Morrisey is trying his best to get up strife among the Democratic people but good sense seems to prevail wherever he turns his efforts to. Mike Haley came up from Hay Springs on the evening train to arrest a small sized petit larceny thief. it is now 2 oclock and I have been working on my bridle steady ever since 8 oclock this evening[.]

Via Last night a meeting of Chadron's Capatilists met in my office to get up a Hotel Co with a Capital of $10,000 and tonight they met again at Danielsons Restaurant.

Sept 22[.] To-day the fair of Dawes Co. commenced. it was cold[,] cloudy and misty all day but Farmers commenced coming in with their products all the same[.] I went out to the grounds with Tom Locket and helped him get his exhibit put in shape[.] he has a fine lot of vegetables[.] after supper Mike Ryan and I went over to Town together.

Sept 23. The weather opened up clear. I put in most of the day at the Fair Grounds getting items for the Democrat, and while I left my note book lay while engaged at something else the reporter of the Journal got hold of it and copied every thing.

after supper every body attended the performance of "Virginia Vetran" at the "rink["] by the G.A.R. it was very poorly rendered considering the amount of practice they had.

Sep 24. To day has been one of the eventful ones for Dawes Co. concerning Fair exhibition. Without any Question the Fair has been a grand success. the Farmers deserve great credit for the interest and enterprise shown in making the Fair go successful. I put in all day taking itemes for the Democrat and did not get to see much of the Horse racing which was one of the principal attractions during the day. at about 5[:]30 Quit [quite] a disgraceful affair was indulged in by the Marshall of the day Timothy Morrisey who, forgetting the duties of a peace officer engaged himself in a free fight with Joe Gillespie, but happily He got just what he deserved—for Joe drew blood on Irelands pet in the twinkling of an eye[.] Sheriff Clark interfered and Set things to rights after which all went as smooth again as hot cakes[.] in the evening the G.A.R. gave another performance of the "Virginia Vetran" which only served to draw a Slim audience to hear the discoursing of music by the F. E. and M. V. Band. did not go myself but stayed in the office and copied my notes off on the Type writer[.] John Magher (the land office Clerk) helped me a little while but he soon got tired and went home.

Sept. 25[.] To day I stayed in the Office all day and made out my reports about the fair. Nothing of Great importance happened during the day. Dr Harris has purchased the Cheyenne trotting horse. The Smilley Sorrel Race Horse was sold to Gordon Parties yesterday for $275.00.

County Atty Ballard called on me and gave notice that he would commence to prosecute all the Gamblers and Saloon men before me to morrow. This move is taken by the County Atty by Order of the Republican Ring and is not intended as a moral move but for the avowed purpose of killing two birds with one Stone,

(Namely the office of Democratic Sheriff and Democratic Justice of the Peace[)].

Sep 26. The weather was pretty cold last night, but it turned of[f] warm again by morning. Tom Lockett came in the office bright and early to have an affidavit made out for his "Golden Beauty Potatoes." Ballard and young Morrissey also were in the office to have papers got out against the Gamblers and Saloon men but I headed them off, and shortly afterwards old Ballard went to Whitney in answer to a summons to attend some Misdemeanor Case before the Justice Court. Nothing of importance happened during the day. After supper I went to Coffeys and played pool. Mr. H. N. Merritt was in the office to day to see about some work.

Sep 27. The weather opened up fine this A.M. Nothing new has turned up of much importance[.] I sent a little coat to Willie which was given to me. The County Commissioners held a meeting this afternoon. Dr. Miller called on me. I made arrangments to have little pete take care of the Pony and got some medicine put up for the horse. after supper I went up to the skating rink to witness a wrestling match, but no one coming by 8.45 I asked and got my money back and then came home and worked on a private letter of Mr Merritt, who seems to be in a great Family trouble caused by the lovemaking to his wife by a man named Dalrymple. Mr Merritt told me this evening just before I was going up to the rink that his wife had accidentally found out that he (Mr Merritt) was aware that she was getting correspondence in Box No. 151 in the Post Office whereupon Mrs Merritt said she would soon fix him that he never more would know who she was corresponding with. Mr Merritt seemed a little alarmed over the matter but upon longer consideration concluded to risk the idea of his wife drugging or poisoning him! Tommy Carter rode a Broncho today and got thrown.

Sept. 28th. The weather has been very pleasant all day. I done a great deal of writing for Merritt in the afternoon[.] Fenn Hartzell undertook to ride a bad broncho[.] at first the horse threw him off and got away, but the second time the horse was not so successful and his rider came out ahead.

Sam Hume has been tearing out his bath room department to day and contemplates using the room thus made for customers to sit while waiting to be called "Next Gent"[.] I left my measure for a suit of clothes today. Mrs Russell from Crawford is paying Chadron a visit. She is the guest of Mrs. E. N Josselyn.

In the Evening I invited Miss Cleona Josselyn, Mrs Josselyn, Mrs Bert Wilcox and Miss Brown for a Moonlight ride up the dead Horse. Mrs Josselyn having Company she was reluctantly obliged to decline so the rest of us all went and had a delightful trip. we got home at 2 oclock A.M.

Sept. 29, 1887. Today has been fine weather again. I fixed up some more business for Merritt in the afternoon—Miss Josselyn invited me to take a ride with her. after supper I took a letter out to Chas. Allen's place. Miss J. accompanied me. The Democrats are commencing to loom up, everybody seems to be on the look out and especially Tim Morrisey[.] After I came back from Allens, I copied some more letters for Merritt, who has informed me that he and his wife have made their trouble square again.

Sep 30[.] The weather opened up fine today. Charley Allen and Frank Van Horn started for Nonpariel this morning which is in utter contradiction of all political principal that the former may have entertained and the going to Nonpariel is also not in accord to the wishes of the Knights of Phythias of Nonpariel for they wrote up here in particular and the letter I took to Allen saying they could not now be ready and that their time was too much taken up with politics, but that was just what Allen did not want as he wanted to get away from Chadron before the Primaries and therefore in the face of having supported Madden for Sheriff and seeing that

there was going to be a little opposition and that if he
stayed here and made a fight for Madden he would
probably loose [lose] a little prestige and another reason
is that Dahlman belongs to a strong order of Knights of
pythias and Tom Madden is a poor Common Irish man.
again the Dahlman faction was run and controlled by
whiskey men who had plenty of money to spend, while
Tom Madden is a poor man. there seems to be a
combination among the wood be [would-be] rulers of the
Democratic party that some certain few shall name a
man for office, provided the Rulers can name a bunch
of delegates which all must Swallow in whole in order to
go to the Convention. There was a time when unison
seemed prevalent among our party but of a Sudden Tim
Morrisey undertook to run things a little in his own
interests and was sat down on accordingly, after which
Carter, Carlton, Kass, Poll and some of the principal
leaders of the "Brick Bank" republicans thought they
could see a dictorial opening in the party and they are
all going into the apparent opening with the Hope of
ruling and domineering over those Democrats who are
poor and afraid of them and their wealth. For these
usurpers are only dabbling in politics because they
think there is a big opening in the County for another
"Cook Co Court Hous" and they want their friends in
Office be they Democrats or Republicans and all this
they are going to do under the banner of Democracy.
No[,] Such politics does not eminate from the
Democratic party. The same old Democrats who voted
the[n] and worked for Democratic ticket first put up in
the County are still here and willing to work for
Democracy but[,] when a new set of men coming from
outside the county and knowing no partisians but these
"Would[-]be rulers[,]" I say when such men support a
Cause and interest utterly against the Democrats at
large through out the County, it is then time to stop and
(for the staunch Democrats) to say what they think
about such proceedings. I have printed tickets for

Madden for this afternoon[.] I got to the Racket of these would[-]be rulers having had their ticket printed in the Democrat office whereupon I immediately set out to see Madden, Clark, Larsh, Macomber, Rucker, Wilds & others.

Oct 1. fine weather all day. every democrat in Town seemed anxious for the work to commence. at 12 M. the primary Polls were opened with Joe Madden Clerk, J. W. Walz Chairman, and J Macomber and Mr Leonard as Judges. the "would[-]be rulers" were on the start in getting their forces organized and I posted myself by the ballot box and stayed there all day but notwithstanding that I challenged over 50 votes and had rejected some 10 votes, the money and whiskey of the "would[-]be voters" prevailed and a count of the ballots at 4 oclock, when the polls were close[d] showed the total number of votes cast to be 157 votes of which 91 were for the "would[-]be rulers" ticket and 30 for Tim Morrisey delegate and 36 for Tom Madden.

After the primaries every one of the "would[-]be rulers" commenced to get drunk and by 10 oclock PM they were howling so much so that one, Base brown, a voter who foreswore himself, went home and raised hell till his neighbors had him run into the cooler.

Oct 2[.] fine weather till towards evening when it commenced to clear off again and at present it is quite calm. I went to see Willie Bailey the printer who has been sick some time at the Magic City with Mountain fever.

Tom Madden and Tim Morrisey seem now to have consolidated and agreed to unite their strengths in favor of which everyone of them shall control the most delegates and it is also the intention of Madden and Morrisey to get Cooper from Whitney to go in with them and give their respective supports to either one of themselves who may seem to be the strongest with the Delegates the day before the Convention, and if this can be accomplished, all will be ruin to the would[-]be rulers.

Chas Allen and Van Horn got back from Nonpareil last evening and F Van Horn left again this evening for Smithwick to go to Chicago with Cattle. Bob Dorr leave[s] in the morning for Hermosia and Madden goes to Crawford but will come down with the delegates from there tomorrow evening.

Tim Morrisey and his Bro Charlie were in the Office and speculated considerably upon the prospects of beating the ring of "would[-]be rulers[.]" E S Ricker got back from Antelope precinct. Rumor is getting afloat that in all probability a Working men's Ticket will be put in the field.

Oct 3[.] The weather opened up fair and continued so all day. during the afternoon the delegates commenced to arrive from their various precincts and by night the city was crowded with democratic delegates, and all aspirants for Sheriff were busied getting around and seeing who were the strongest. If the Candidates can only manage to find out who is the strongest among them and then the rest withdraw which would beat any one Solid delegation, but right there is where the stick comes and the Cooper faction seem to insist that Cooper must get there for Sheriff—it will however all be solved by this time tomorrow[.] during the evening the Larsh Bros were arrested for being drunk and disorderly and fighting[.]

Oct 4th[.] The day opened up bright and fair for politics, but in the early dawn morning every finger of the delegates seemed to want to point towards Dahlman for sheriff although some dared not do so on acct having been solomnlly sworn not to do so untill told to so do by their leader. but towards dinner time and just before the Convention was called to order at 1 PM sharp, all the Candidates for Sheriff withdrew in favor of the Democratic favorite Jas Dahlman who was unanimously chosen as candidate, afterwhich every nomination on the ticket was gone through with in rapid succession until at 2.30 P.M. the entire nominations of the

Democratic Party in Dawes were completed and a more harmonious assembly of Republicans never existed. in the afternoon the Precinct ticket was attended too and there a load as large as a millstone seemed to roll off my back. The republicans seem now to be considerably worked up over the strength of the Democratic nominees and well they may be for it is safe to say that with the probable exception of County Treasurer, every Democrat on the ticket will get there. the Baptist Church gave a Small Festival in the Ferrebrach Drugstore[.] after supper I took Miss J. out horse back ridding. we went down on the Bordeaux and returned by the way of Waltzes Ice house. the wind raised a little towards 9 oclock.

Charley Nebo, Ben Tibbits, N Janis came to town today[.] they all look as natural as ever. Geo Haven slept with me last night[.]

Oct. 5th—Fine weather again all day. Breen was in the Office nearly all day paying of[f] some of the Stone Haulers. M. Patrick and E. Patrick were in Town enroute from their Wyoming Stock Ranches to Omaha.

N. Jamis was in town again. after Supper some of the City Council made an effort to get up a meeting of the City Dads, but it was impossible to get more than Kass, Carleton and Mead together[.] they knocked about till near nine O'clock when they adjourned after having been talked Silly by F. M. Dorrington who seems to forget that there will have to be another destructive fire before anything more towards the fire department can be accomplished[.] Ben Boyd & Mr Hughes came down from Crawford this evening. Ben looks healthy and natural as ever. he says he thinks Chadron has been grown [growing] right along ever since the first Palmy days when King Faro reigned Supreme.

Oct. 6. The weather Started in fair today but towards 9 Oclock a slight wind sprang up and by 12 M. a hurricane was the order of the day. Mr Maffett from Rapid City came in the Office and asked me to take a ride with him to see a Claim of his which I did but the wind was very strong and made the trip not so pleasant as it might otherwise have been. however notwithstanding all that he has a splendid Tree Claim and which he has put into my hands for sale at $500.00[.]

During the storm my saddle horse Ben got away by running on the picket rope and breaking the haulter. little Pete found him at C J Davises Livery stable.

In the afternoon I helped to get out the Democrat. Mr. B. C. Hill is to start for Valentine this evening[.] I have been on the trade for stoves during the afternoon. about 4 Oclock the wind storm slacked up and everything was again Calm and smooth. after supper the City Council held a meeting with Kass in the Chair. present, Kass, Carley, Carlton and Mead. they done a great deal of business in fact more has been accomplished that there has been done by the whole Council ever since their Election.

Oct. 7. To day the weather opened up a little cold and continued so all day. towards 6 oclock P.M. fine rain and mist commenced to fall and still continues to come down. I traided heating stoves with F. J. Cook, and made a sale to Mrs Josselyn. in the forenoon I got out the Democrat. in the afternoon I went up to the School House and seen the manner of Professor Dentons Teachings which after having seen and heard, seem to be well adapted with a view of bringing the Chadron youth to his senses. Messr J. P. Cook & Son commenced excavating for a business house on the Cor. of Second and Morehead St. The day has been taken up in the office by Breen and Cavanaugh[,] the latter being the most contrary man that I have ever seen.

Oct 8. Pretty cold and misty to commence with this morning bright and early. Breen and Cavanaugh commenced their business of settling up with the men engaged on the stone work by Cavanaugh and all day nothing could be heard but Jimmy Cavanaugh's arguing and fighting. I bought a bill of Native lumber from Mrs Powell and started a man to build a woodshed which got completed all except the outside door.

after supper I took the window blind over to Mrs Josselyn to have her lengthen it out. I also got some muslin to have sleeves made.

Geo Havens slept here last night. I will now get ready to take a bath.

Oct 9th[.] Fine weather all day. I went to the episcopal Church in the morning. This mornings mail brought me Photos of Brother Geo., Annie and Willie Street. After dinner I went out riding with W. Christensen's Brother. We went to P B Nelsons place on the Bordeaux at which place we attended Sunday School services all of which we enjoyed very much. Chas. W. Allen came to Town all dressed up in a new Suit[.] so much changed was he that scarcely anyone knew him. After supper I repaired to my Office where all the Democrats and irish were congregated and where I learned from their conversation that Chas Morrissey has been threatening to make trouble for Billy Carter and that Carter met the honorable Charlie this morning and read the riot act to him.

Oct. 10th[.] This morning the weather looked very much like snow, but it cleared off very nicely. I had the Carpenter finish up my wood shed and build a walk to the water closet, after which I got pete to scrap up the rubbish in the back yard and burned it all up. Ben Tibbits came to town yesterday and today he is putting in a grand drunk. Ben Arnold and Dom Pate came up to town. Ben got very drunk but not so much as to not be able to hitch up his Team.

Oct. 11. Fine weather again all day. nothing of much importance happened. Ben Tibbitts loaded up and went home. he had a fine Stallion with him. Miss Haddock came to the office early this morning to see about the whereabouts of her father. After supper Geo Havens and I stayed in my office. I tried [to] learn Geo the piece called Vale of Glencoe[.] Mrs Kass called on me about 9 P.M. and bid goodby prior to going to Chicago.

I have been in the House all day and I am as happy as happy can be for I am surrounded with good litreature and can read just what I want to.

Oct. 12. Fine day all day. I got a padlock for the water closet and loaned dick out to Mr Hawley. got up a lot of locals for the paper, after which I got in readiness to hear a trial in the County Court whereing [wherein] W H McKinney had Ike Brown arrested for assault and Battery. Dr Davidson has been quite ill for the past few days being confined to his bed with paralises of his left side and a general wearing out of the system.

Oct. 13. the weather was rather cold last night. I got up a little late and upon going over for breakfast at Mrs Josselyn[s], I found Cleona in readiness to go to their Ranch out home on Dry Creek. she went in Mr Christensens Cart[.] Shortly after she had gone, Mr Josselyn and Bert arrived having come another way, whereupon Mrs Josselyn sent Al Smith out on My pony to overtake Cleona. they returned at supper time.

I helped on the Democrat today again. B. C. Hill introduced me to his Mother, lately from Vermont. Hill recd a message this morning saying that Ricker had been nominated by the Democratic State Convention for Judge of the 12th Judicial District to run against M. P. Kinkaid on the Republican Side.

Mr Magher was in the Office a good deal today.

Bob Dorr and Ed Cameron started on a hunting trip this evening. A H Huddock got his warrant for extra pay as special police. Thomas Allen Caime applied to me for aid in the name of Charity from the City which I responded to giving him an order on the Hanlon House for his dinner and going to Mrs Leach and making arrangments for a weeks board for him.

Yesterday F B Carley brought some type writing work to me which I managed to finish this evening. about 6 Oclock P.M. today L G Sweat came in the office with an appeal case to be copied on [the] typewriter[.]

at present there is a high wind stirring but it is a warm one though may turn cold by morning[.]

Oct 14. The weather did not turn cold as I expected it would. I went to work on Sweets Contest case right after breakfast. in the afternoon I attended school. Ettie Sayrs told me her birth day was to day so I bought her a nice Sewing case which almost set her wild with joy. Just as I was going to supper I was called upon to issue attachment papers for G D Chapin against Earnest Bros. for $30.00[.]

A. C Fowler came to Town to day. News comes from the Depot to the effect that Bros left his watch with G D Chapin as security for his bill and upon Mr Chapin allowed the attached goods to go on their way[.]

Oct 15. The weather was a little bit chilly this morning. I got up a little late. after breakfast I made arrangments with Birdsall & Co for a team to go out to A J Gillespies with Tomorrow but I think the weather will not permit it. The Court House foundation was finished today and work on the brick wall will soon follow. the roof joists on the Lake & Halley building were put in yesterday and a temporary floor put on in case of bad weather. To day the arch way over the main door was put in.

The attachment suit of Chapin vs Bross was dismissed at Plaintiffs cost, and about 4 Oclock Mr William F. Hayward filed a complaint against Earnest Bross charging him with having sold mortgaged property. I issued a warrant for him.

I bought a load of cut wood for the Office for $2.50[,] the first this winter. A. J. Gillespie was in Town Today.

F. J. Houghton and his party of Friends got back from a dance in the Country and looking over land.

There was quite a crowd at the skating rink this evening[.] I went up and tried on the skates but found they would not work so I took them off and came home. this evening I worked on my bridle again.

Rumor has it now that the Danielson Hotel Company has fallen through. how true it is I cannot say but it appears that there is not much work going on anyway in that direction. Geo Havens quit working for Frank Ingersoll today. Charley Mann has been in the City all day looking after his progross [progress] and chances as to being elected for County commissioner. There is also a pretty good sized rumor aflot to the effect that Many Democrats are going to vote against James Dahlman because they think he will appoint Dave Powers as his Deputy if he is elected, and Dave seems to have a few enemies through out the County.

I seen Billy Carter about getting Dahlman to come out in the papers and say that such never has been nor never will be the Case or intention to putting Powers in as his deputy. Geo Clark sees that this is a weak point on the Democratic issue and is doing all he possibly can to tell people that Powers is going to be Dahlmans Deputy if he is elected.

James Toomey died this morning from Brights disease. Billy Carter, Fred Danielson[,] Dave Powers and [name missing] left for Carters Spring Lake Ranch to go on a hunting trip.

Oct 16. Geo & I got up at 9 oclock A.M. we both took a bath last night before going to bed. the weather started in very changable and continued so all day. Instead of going out to Gillespie as was my intention I remained and attended James Toomeys funeral. I went out to the house taking Pete Breen with me and going by Breens house. The funeral left Toomeys house 20 minutes to two P.M. and arrived at the Catholic Church at 2.10 P.M. having been met and preceeded by the G.A.R. after 30 minutes cervices at the church the procession started for the Cemetary.

I returned from there at 4.30 P.M. and took Miss Josselyn out ridding[.] we went out to where Sayrs lives. we came home at 5.50 P.M. after supper Miss Josselyn and I attended the Episcopal Church where we met Mrs Wilcox and her Sister[,] Miss Brown.

Breen and his Son called on me after church and we had a very nice talk on Catholicy[.]

Oct. 17. Pretty cold weather this morning. D. E. Havens appeared and confessed judgment in the case of Hood vs Havens. Biddy Doyle came to town yesterday[.] I met him in Coffeys Saloon this afternoon.

Cyrus Fairchild came down from Crow Butte. Chris Berger also came down from Crawford on Land Business[.]

Bisbee of the Whitney Times Sauntered into Town. Frank Van Horn came in from Chicago.

Oct 18[.] fine weather[.] Geo & I got up early. Though the Court House foundation was finished last Saturday, no news appears to be turning up about consoul. I put in today in doing a little of everything and not much of anything. I had a ride with "Ben[.]" I red [received] a letter from W. H. Disney in Rus[h]ville asking for a chance to go through with Cattle to Chicago. Mr Danielson received a verynice shipment of fresh game from W. H. Carters Ranch and which looks very tempting[.] Biddy Doyle is still in Town[.] Geo Havens is sitting at the table in Front of me doing his examples in arithmetic.

The Saul Bros commenced building their house next to D. E. Havens residence. Bartlett Richards returned from the East yesterday morning about 9 oclock. Tony Bernard came along and got out attachment papers on M. F. Coffey.

Oct 19[.] The weather started out fine this morning but towards 12 Oclock M. it commenced to blow and from 2 P.M. to 6 P.M. a perfect hurricane prevailed. Mrs Josselyn put in a large family table in her restaurant[.] after supper I attended the Episcopal

Church Sociable at the Rink which was very well patronized. some 200 persons were in attendance and seemed to enjoy themselves very much.

Tom Madden came down from Crawford to day. W. C. Brown hinted to me this morning that there was a Scheme on foot to change the Post Office from its present location to the Cor[ner] of Morehead and 2nd sts in the new building being erected by Messrs Cook and Carley, whereupon I proceeded to interview the Hon[.] A. W. Crites upon the subject, learning therefrom some interesting points in practical politics.

tonight there should have been a regular meeting of the City Council, but no one presented themselves. it is now 12.15 A.M. and I am as sleepy as I can be and tired too as I took down nearly all the names of persons in attendance at the Festival and Social gathering this evening[.]

Oct 20. after retiring to my bed I commenced to get sick and continued getting worse till finally I got up and went to Danielsons and had an Oyster stew, where I met a crowd of Boys from the Sociable. I took some pain Killer finally and came back to bed by 2 Oclock A.M. I did not get up till about 10 Oclock[.] Burley Hill brought me my breakfast as soon as I got up[.] C. D. Sayrs came and asked me to go out to his place and have his wife acknowledge a Warranty Deed to some Kansas property, which I done, we going out in a Single rig buggy of Quigleys and getting back by 11.30 A.M. The wind Started to blow this morning and has continued a perfect wind storm almost all day[.] Hill & I got out the Democrat on time today again.

Mr Fraley got married to day to Miss Fowler.

Kass & Co started putting in the cornice work on the Lake and Halley Bank.

I got a letter from J. M. Moffett about some land. C. D. Sayrs handed me a letter to answer for him to John Heatwale at Missouri Valley, Iowa[.]

Oct 21. Fine weather all day. Cleona Jossely went out to Gillespies to get one of the Girls to work for them but she was not at home. Cleona got back at 4 Oclock[.] I went up on top of the new Bank to take a look at the City.

James Connolly came back to day. Billy Carter, Fred Danielson & Powers returned from their hunt.

A New Barber shop will soon start up on Second st. All the County Commissioner[s] were in Town today[.] A New Shoe and Clothing store is being put in where Thompson used to have an Ice Cream parlor[.] Mrs Jossely has rented Mrs OLinns House on Main St[.] it is now raining[.]

Oct 22. rain this morning. Clared [cleared] up a little in the afternoon, and started to rain again about 4 oclock. Bob Dorr and Ed Cameron got back from their hunt. Ed gave me a duck. Peter Morgan came down and wanted a receipt for a Stove which I loaned him on condition of paying what rent he owed, but I did not give it to him, instead of which I went and took the stove away and put it in my back shed.

Jim Connolly left for the West again this morning. Geo Havens brought a little dog in the office and gave him to me. I have been working on shorthand all day. Charley Morrisey came in the office this evening while I was to Supper and wrote some letters.

Oct 23. last night about 9 oclock it commenced to snow and this morning the City was Clothed in a 3 inch thick Coat of Snow. I met a Mr Truax from Custer who claimed to be a great friend of Bob McKee. he finally promised to give me a young blooded colt tomorrow morning to take care of him at $1.50 per month. Charley Morrisey was in the Office nearly all day, so also was Geo Havens.

Bob Dorr took a bath in the office.

I had a duck for breakfast this morning.

I went and seen Jake Kass about getting Mr Caim out on a Stock train. I wrote a letter to Bob McKee.

after supper I came home in the office and studied shorthand. Geo Havens bought some apples and took some letters to the office for me.

Oct 24th. To day has been a pretty raw one all through. I got up early and went out on Spring Creek to see Mr Truax about the Colt and which he brought in about 4 oclock and gave it to me to keep. Ed Burnes, Geo Wm Hughes, C W Fairchild came down from Crawford this evening. I cleaned the type writer and put on a new tape[.] C W Allen got back from his trip. Van Horn worked in the barber shop to day.

Oct 25. To day has been a cold and raw one. I got the Colt into Birdsall['s] barn and fed and watered it, and had a halter made for it. in the afternoon I took it up to my stable.

Tom Madden came in the office before and after Supper. while I was at supper I recd a letter from Crawford asking me to write up the County Candidates[,] also that I procure some Dawes County Journal after July 4, 1888, whereupon I ordered out my horse and went out to Mrs OLinn's to get the files[.]

Oct 26. The weather to day opened up nice and continued so all day and with the exception of the Crossing being a little muddy, everybody seemed to be in good humor. I got back from Mrs OLinn's at 11.30 P.M. last night, and after I left the livery Stable, my legs got stiff and refused to work. F. M. Dorrington helped me down to Josselyns from where after getting a cup of coffey, I went home in Company with Van Horn[.] this morning I hammered around town. in the afternoon Atty Hayward brought an attachment suit for D. S. Hawley against the Pembroke Nursery Co. before me and in which C. J. Davis refused to serve the papers, whereupon I deputized a special constable.

To day the stone cutters commenced work on Ricker & Houghtons building. I answered a letter of John T. Green at Pine Ridge concerning a loan on his land[.] Mrs Josselyn was in the Office to day[.]

I seen L. G. Sweat about getting the Prohibition party to endorse me for Justice on their ticket to which he readily consented. Mr Josselyn came in from the ranch to day.

Atty Bartow received a hard fall from his horse to day in which he sprained his left wrist.

Oct. 27. Early this morning at 12.20 one Wm Waugh shot himself in front of Belanger Store. Fred Danielson and A. H. Haddock woke me up. I told them to take him up to the Engine House[.] at 9 AM. I held an inquest on the body owing to the absence of the Coroner and sheriff. the Jury rendered a verdict of death from a shot of a pistole in his own hands.

I removed him to Myers & Boon[e] and washed him myself after which I received a telegram to prepare the Body to ship to Virginia, that all expenses would be guarranteed at Blair. I thereupon looked around for an Embalmer as Myers & Boone had none, and after much fussing and Quarreling with Wm Wilson as to what was what, I finally had Wilsons men take Charge of the body again and had him embalmed in the proper manner, but about nine oclock P.M. after having put the Corpse in the Casket and taken it to the Depot, a message came to me Stating to hold the body till perry Haskins Could Come up from Blair after it and there upon we took it back to Wilsons again.

Geo Havens and I went to Mrs Josselyns about 11 P.M. and had Oysters.

Oct 28. Fine mild weather all day again. The Carpenters commenced work on the Ricker & Houghton building[.] I rented Tom Dixons House again to McKinzie and his partner[—]two stone cutters. their rent commenced on the 27th. of Oct. I have been busy all day getting the bills of small amounts against William Waugh settled up. in the afternoon Van Inwegen brought some work on the Type writer. We worked on it till 11 oclock PM. after which I went down to the Depot to meet Perry Haskins from Blair on the 3.30 AM. Passenger.

Oct. 29. as I expected[,] Mr Haskin's came and brought an undertaker with him. I told them to go right off to bed and I would do the same, which they did, but I went and woke up young Way and he and I went and fixed up the Corpse for inspection. I got to bed about 7 oclock AM.

O V Harris commenced suit against the Pembroke Nursery Company. Mrs Alexander borrowed "Ben[.]" I discovered that my watch was broken after just having gotten it from Kirmse the Jewelery[.]

Mr Mahger gave me some transcripting of testimony to work on. it is a lengthy piece of work.

The Body of Wm Waugh started east this evening per Askins & Pierce.

I put in till 12 oclock Midnight working on the Contest Case.

Oct. 30[.] I broke my artificials last night and had to get Geo Havens to go to Jim Boyd to get them fixed this morning. The weather to day has just be[en] delightfull.

Cleo & I took a drive out to the Claim where upon our arrival we found they had had a small fire which burned up their shanty. We had lunch there and came home by 6 oclock. after supper I started in on my Contest Case again when I was interrupted by Cleo coming after me to see to an drunken man who was bothering her mamma, whom however, Mr. Bert Wilcox managed to quiet before my arrival.

Geo Havens has gone up home to sleep tonight and I am very lonely.

Oct. 31. Fine weather again! I got up early[.] W W Byington put in his time today in moving his safe into the new Bank of Lake & Halley[.]

at 10 oclock the Case of Hawley vs Pembroke Nursery Co came on for trial which after considerable sides having been taken by the Lawyers I finally continued to get proper service on the Deft[.]

Mrs Mears asked to have the loan of "Ben" which I granted. in the afternoon I went over to J. Kass & Co and made out his bills for him[.] after supper I worked on the Contest Case up to the present time 10:50 PM and I must yet write up my docket in the case of to-day and go and get my supper[.]

Nov 1. Fine weather all day again. Early this morning I lost a good job by Atty Hayward not coming around. Bartlett Richards wanted me to do some work for him, but I had to let it go to be on hand for my tril [trial] which was set for 10 oclock.

last night being hallow Eves night the Boys and Girls had a great time getting things in disorder.

I worked on the Contest case today again and got it finished. Yesterday I ordered a numerater to Cost $10.00[.]

Doc Middleton came to town this A.M.

Mrs Alexander sent around for the Horse but I could not let him go. she sent me a nice Box of Cigars per Guy.

Yesterday Dr Waller appointed me to act as his deputy in the capacity of Coroner of Dawes County.

Nov 2. To day the weather has been very nice. I put in a good deal of my time at J. Kass & Co making out his trial balance. Mrs Alexander had dick today. Bob Dorr went hunting today again.

This evening after supper, I went up to the Catholic Fair where I managed to drop some stuff.

The Brick Masons are making things lively on Ricker & Houghtons building.

Nov 3. Fine weather again all day. this morning the Case of O. V. Harris vs Pembroke Nursery Co came on and I rendered Judgment by default.

Maher came in the office and I helped him write out a deciscion of the local Land Office on the Blaisdale vs. Gerecke[.] After Supper I attended the Catholic Fair and enjoyed myself very much[.]

during the afternoon to day I got up a Subscription paper for one Thomas Caim, a poor man and headed it with $1.00. I got him of [off] for his home in a rejoicing manner[.]

Willie Mead came down from Crawford and I invited him to Sleep with me.

I made a pretty good horse trade for Mr Josselyn to day by getting him a horse to keep all winter for nothing or the use of him for his board.

Nov 4. fine weather all day. I worked at Kass & Co. on the trial Balance Book a great deal of the day. had to move my horses to Dr Davidsons and Mrs OLinn's Barn for hay till I can buy some.

helped to get out the Democrat. Von Harris, Dave Keenan and Cooper & Bailey came down from Whitney this evening to celebrate the Catholic Fair. they got pretty noisey.

Nov 5th[.] To-day has been a fine one again. Politics are beginning to loom up in great Shape and the republicans are beginning to awaken to the fact that they will have to work at the coming election if they succeed in getting any of the County Officers elected.

I worked on Kass & Co books but could not get out a correct trial Balance[,] notwithstanding I found our $154.12 to be corrected. In the evening I attended the Catholic Fair in company with Maher from the land office and we had a nice time. Mr and Mrs Alexander were there with Guy and I had a pleasant time. Jake Kass took the gold headed Cane. Mrs. susie OHanlon took the silver tea set and I took the Hat for being the most popular man in the City[.]

After the cane had been voted away, the main St Gang (I among them) all came down to Carters and had a drink. Tommy Carter had a racket with Billy and Billy fired him out bodily, and when we came from the rink Tommy came in pretty full[.] I went to bed.

Nov 6th[.] today has been a most pleasant one all through.

I had a social Chat with Mrs Jossellyn in regards to keeping company with her Daughter Cleona, with motives and views of marriage. what answer I will get, remains to be seen until after I have seen Mr Josselyn, who will be in the City Tomorrow.

After Dinner I wrote a letter to Hon John A McShane in favor of Frank M Van Horn who is desirous of getting a position as Postal Clerk or Rout Agent on the F E M R.R. I also copied his petition to the Department.

after supper I called on Mr and Mrs Alexander and learned for the first time that Chadron will soon lose a nice family as they intend moving to Omaha next week. After coming home I got Willie Mead to help me write out "posters" for Election, upon which we worked till 11 oclock.

Nov 7[.] To day has been very nice weather till about 8 oclock P.M. when it started to get cold and stormy with signs of wind[.] I have been working all day in getting out posters for the Democrats. Willie Mead helped me a great deal. Harbaugh went down to Craig[.] Tip Morton and Pattison went out to the Table.

Everybody is on the look out for a representative to go to the different Polling places. Willie Mead is loaded down with Posters which he will take to Crawford with him to morrow. the Democrat got out a poster detrimental to Republicans and ordered them circulated early tomorrow morning[.] I had to ride clear to Chadron Creek this afternoon to overtake them and give them Kass and Fairchild posters[.]

After finishing the poster business this evening I made out a tally list for myself[.] tomorrow after the Polls are closed when I expect to keep count with the Clerks to see that no Republican money shall count any Democrat out nor that any Democratic money shall buy a Democrat in. I want fair play.

Nov 8th. The weather opened up nice and everything looked good for election[.] the Polls opened with J. A. Wilson, C. H. Lutz, G. A. Eckles as Judges and Chas W Allen and Old Mr Palmer as Clerks of Election. I stayed by the Polls all day and not even went to dinner[.] after they were closed I went to supper and then went right back to See the votes counted, where I stayed till the morning of the 9th inst.

Nov 9. Early this morning found the Judges and Clerks of Election, Chas. Man, J D Pattisson, Jas Dahlman and myself, together with occasional straglers in the office of L. A. Brower where we were counting out slowly but surely the votes Cast at yesterdays election and at 8.20 oclock A.M. we finished at which time the vote of Chadron stood as follows. [Space left blank].

Nov 10. Fine weather all day. I got a good load of Hay again today. I lost my saddle by having to leave it with Frank Albright. I had quite a time rustling around today. every one is anxious to know the returns from outside precincts, but they are hard to get. up till 6 oclock this evening things look sure for Dahlman but at 10 oclock another precinct was heard from which went enough for Clark to put him in the lead by 7 majority. Mr Carty came to me about Willie Mead and the Barber Chair[.] I went to the telegraph office with him[.] I bought a ticket to the Breakmans Ball. After I came from the Depot I attended the meeting of Citizens at the Court House where the people were assembled by call to take an action in a matter wherein to consult with the B. & M. R. R. officials at Omaha and Lincoln with regards to finding out what inducements if any that Road wanted and how much in order to bring their R.R. to Chadron. Messrs. Glover, Putnam, Richards and Hood were unanimously selected after which the Question of waterworks was proposed to which Richards replyed that certain parties would put in $50,000 or $60,000 waterworks providing nothing definite was done between now and Spring by the present City

Council. a Committee was appointed to negotiate with the Party. Mr F. M. Dorrington next proposed the advisability of Chadron making an effort to get the Pine Ridge Agency Supply Depot moved from Rushville to this place. A committee of 3 was thereupon appointed to consult with the County Commissioners about condemning the Government Road.

Nov. 11. Fine weather all day. Several civil suits on hand and at 1 oclock the case of State of Neb vs John W. [name missing] charged with assult [assault] with intent to kill came up for hearing before me. I discharged the defendandt and dismissed complaint[.] we were very busy today getting out the Democrat. Politics seems to be booming yet and Geo Clark does not want to give up.

Nov 12. Fine weather and still the excitement of election has not abandoned. I recd a letter from Mrs Haskins asking for some Clothes belonging and worn by her Bro Wm Waugh at the time of his death.

I answered it right away. Mr Carty came down from Crawford last night where he went to collect the money for a barber chair which he sold to Willie Mead.

Jim Greenwood came to Town. he reports having been to California and all over the west.

I wrote some letters to McShane in favor of F M. Van Horn for postal clerk.

Charlie Nebo came to town yesterday[.] I told him to take "Ben" out to the Ranch.

Nov 13. The weather to day has been a little raw. Charlie Nebo came up to the office this A.M. while Jim Greenwood was in. I loaned Charlie Nebo my plug Hat and we all went to Carter's and had a drink. Jim Greenwood said that Andy Wheat was working for the Murphy Out [Outfit] who give the 79 Brand and are ranging in Montana & British America.

I had Nebo take Ben out to Ben Tibbetts. Geo Havens Slept with me last night.

Jim Greenwood came around and stayed in the office with me quite a while. Homer Hyde borrowed my plug hat to go out walking.

Nov 14.   Fine weather again all day.   this morning I went out to Charley Allens place to have a mortgage acknowledged. When I got home I went up to the Court House to watch the proceeding of the returning board Messrs Sayrs, Fisher and Tucker. by 3 oclock this afternoon the Count was completed as follows [words missing.]

Nov 15.   Today opened up fair and continued so all day. Bob Dorr got back from a Hunt. M. G. Redman of Buffalo, Wyo arrived from Bloomington[,] Ill. with a fine bunch of Blooded and high grade Norman Mares[.] I branded my little Colt with a bar on the inside of the right hind leg.

All Crawford seems to be in the city just now waiting for Court to set.

Mike Ryan and Chas Joraelman came in the Office early this morning to have a pension affidavit made out.

B. C. Hill worked all day getting out the Court Calender.   Dr Gillespie was in Town today with his Daughter Temperance.

Last Monday or Saturday the Whitney times printing press was set up on Egan St. in Judge Cooks building[.]

Nov 16. District Court commenced this morning. Everybody was eager for the fray. Many people in town from the country. I was busy all day trying to drum it into the City Attys head about tending to cases which have been appealed to the District Court, but it seems no use[.]

I wrote a letter to Uncle Louis in Colton[,] California in answer to one I recd from him yesterday. I got a Blank Case for C. A. Burlew from Glover and sent it to him at Hemingford, C.O.D.

The City Council should have met this evening but failed to connect.

Nov 17. To day has been a fine day all through. District Court has been grinding right along and at 2 P.M. commenced on the celebrated Fries House burning case. Jim Tuckers Brother is here from Valentine. This morning I answered a letter of Thos Mullen.

The Democrat came out too late to make a distribution this evening.

Nov 18. To day was a rather windy one and disagreeable. I had lunch up at Dahlmans & Simmons Butcher Shop.

Kirmse got back from Douglas with his girl.

The Fries House Burning case is in progress in the Court.

I had a long Conflab with the County Commissioners relative to my bills.

I got up a petition to the Post Master Generel protesting against the removal of the Post Office from its present place.

Nov 19. I finished up the business of writing up the protest against moving the Post Office. I met Mr robis and told him to take his bed spring off my bed. he did so and I ordered a new set on trial from Wilson. I moved the Colt back up to the old stable. it commenced to eat oats like a good fellow today, for the first time.

About 4 oclock this afternoon one of Ole Putnams fine dappled gray Carriage horses droped dead while standing in the livery stable.

Nov 20. To day the weather has been fine[.] I went to Church in the morning[.] in the evening I called on Mr and Mrs Carter to see the children for the last time before going to Oregon where they expect to spend the winter. I also worked on the protest petition to the Postmaster Genral protesting against the removal of the Post Office of this City from its present location.

Billy Magle came to town today.

After supper I went into Tom Coffeys and played billiards till Geo Havens came after me.

Nov 21.   Fine weather today again and every builder in town is busy building as fast as he possibly can.   I gave the Post Office protest petition to W. H. Carter who in turn gave it to Ben Loewenthal and he took it around and in doing so stirred up a fight among the Business men in the West end that will be factional for a long time to come.   during the forenoon W. H. Carter came and had me acknowledge some assignments in favor of Richard Bros.

After supper I went down to the depot with Jake Kass to bid goodbye to Billy Carter and his family, after which I came up to Mrs Josselyns and there heard great news from Mrs Josselyn[.]

Nov 22.   The weather to day started out cold and snowy and Kept so all day.   the Bankers at Norfolk remitted their account to me which allowed me to straighten up a little.   in the evening I worked on J. Kass & Co. Books.

the Jury in the Case of State vs Fries brought in a verdict of "not guilty."

Nov 23.   To day has been a mediocre one for weather. I copied the Court Docket for the Democrat. W. H. Westover wrote me a letter asking me to hand a Subpoena to Clark.   in the evening I helped to get the Democrat out. little Hamm sold 5 copies on the street. I gave my ticket to the Firemens Ball at the rink to W. G. Pardoe.   after supper I worked at J. Kass & Co. posting up the Books, and while there Jim Greenwood and Wm Hunter came in.   they afterwards came over to my Office where we met Billy Nagle, but we managed to shake Nagle pretty soon[,] after which we took in the town with a paint brush.

I left Jim and Hunter at about 12 oclock and went up to the skating rink to take a look at the "Ball" and found quite an assembly there enjoying themselves very much. The Ladies Guild had charge of the Supper department[.] I met Geo Havens there and we both came home after having eaten Oysters at the new Chop house on Egan St. and making a call on Mrs Josselyn.

Nov 24. I got up pretty early and after knocking around town I got a rig from Hatch and proceeded to go to C. D. Sayrs for Dinner as per an invitation, and where I had a very pleasant time. I returned to town about 4 oclock[.] After supper I played billiards with Coffey and Kass and then went up to the Methodist Church to patronize them in their seeming effort to get out of debt. I subscribed my name for $1.00 per month for the support of their minister. after that I went over to the skating rink and then adjourned to Coffeys where in company with Coffey & Kass I played Billiards and High five till 2 A.M. Geo Havens slept up home.

Nov 25[.] The weather opened and closed with snow to day. I recd a letter from Gillman and Doering of Hemingford and answered it right away. Brien paid up his office rent to Nov. 5th. Geo Havens has been sick ever since the evening of the 23rd inst with a swollen nose and to day he has been confined to the house all day. I went up and Called on him and also attended to the Colt.

After supper I went and posted J. Kass & Co. Books and then went over to Carters and had a settlement with Tony about the amount due me from Carter on the County Claims business, and after much figuring we made my credits in the business amount to $21.20. I came home and invited Bob Dorr to sleep with me.

Nov 26. The weather to day has been very cold. Rose Kass came home night before last. this afternoon I made out some bills for J. Kass & Co. I also paid a visit to Geo Havens to see how he was getting along, and found him improving rapidly. this evening about 6 oclock, Bert Josselyn came in from the Ranch having left there about 4.30 PM to day, and when he got here his fingers were almost frooze. the Doctor Harris was called and I was summoned to appear before the patient and done all I could from experience to releive the little fellow, and by 11 oclock we had managed to make him pretty comfortable.

Nov 27. Very cold all day but clear[.] I went up to see Geo Havens and took dinner with him. after dinner I went over to see Hank Simmons Baby. I turned the colt out in Trumans barn. after supper I went over to Tom Coffeys and played pool.

Nov 28. This morning it was very cold. Mrs Josselyn sent Bert Smith and Ace Johnston out to their ranch to take word to Mr Josselyn about Bert having frooze his fingers. Geo Havens came down as I was getting up this morning and averred his intentions of going to School, although his swollen face is not much better than it was yesterday!

I almost forgot to attend to my pet Colt. Geo and I went up in the dark and put it away. Geo said he was going to sleep with me but he changed his mind afterwards.

I have been working all day on Kass & Co Books.

Nov 29[.] To day has been a moderate one[.] there were a great many people from the Country in Town today. I put in nearly all my time at Kass & Co. making out bills.

Baker, Von Harris and Pete Cooper of Whitney came down this eve. Cooper and Baker are going to get married and I am going up as an invited guest.

I got my shoes mended today by Mr Hancock for $2.00.

Mrs Josselyn again sent Ace Johnson and Bert smith to their claim. it now appears that Bert Josselyn may not loose any of his fingers at all.

There was a rumor around town today that Bert Wilcox was going to have all his furniture taken away from him. I seen Geo Havens and asked him to come and stay with me regular again, but he refused saying it was too cold to run up home every morning, so I went right away and made arraingments with Conger to sleep with me, which he is going to do for a temporary test to see how we get along together as bed mates.

Tim Higgins baby died this morning and as I was going to the Post Office I met G. E. Myers going down to sell them a coffin!

After supper I got Van Horn to Shave me before going to his home, I being so lucky as to just catch him in the shop after having closed.

Nov 30. I was invited yesterday to go up to Whitney this morning with Cooper, Baker and Van Harris to witness the double marriage of the two Former Gentlemen. We left on the morning train and got to Whitney at 9 oclock A.M. I whiled away the time as best I could till Supper time and then went to the Church to witness the ceremony, which was performed at 7.45 P.M. after which all were invited to attend the Banquet and then came the dancing which was kept up all night and untill way late in the morning[.] Thort of Crawford slept with me. I enjoyed myself very much while in Whitney and shall not forget it for a long time[.]

Dec 1. All day to day has been a long and lonesome one to me on account of being in so small a place as Whitney. Von Harris promised to take me to Chadron this A.M. but was prevented from doing so on account of his hay men not knowing how to bale hay which required Von's presence in the country all day. We came to Chadron on the evening train.

I brought a large hunk of the wedding cake home. When I got here I found there had been a change of Venue taken from Wilson to me in a Replevin Case, the Parties to the suit being Herman Brockway and John Jackson. I told them that being as they had waited all day for me I would accomodate them and hear the case after supper. I helped get out the Democrat and got supper and then started in with the Replevin Case which lasted till 11:30 P.M. I did not render Judgment right off but told the Parties I would sleep over it. I went and got an Oyster stew and went to bed right off.

Dec 2[.] The weather today has been pleasant. I forgot to mention that P O Hanlon forgot last Wednesday to tell his son John to take care of my Colt during my absence and it was left tied up with no attention during my stay in Whitney[.] To day I worked on the Cash Book of J Kass & Co. I also received a letter from Mrs Haskins with a $35.00 check enclosed to pay the expenses of William Waugh who shot himself here some time ago. I also got a Saucy letter from Waughs brother James in Richmond[,] Ill.

Mart Morrisey hauled my machine and stove up to my wood shed. The Democrats of Chadron held a meeting in the Land Office this evening to choose a member from Dawes County for a position on the State Central Committee, which resulted in the name of Chas. W. Allen for that position.

Dec 3rd. The weather to day started out cold and raw. I worked on Kasses books and got the Cash book balanced by Noon. I came to the office and got an appeal case off on the Typewriter for Mr Carter (J. W.) and then Mr Houghton came after me to marry a couple from Sioux Co. I ordered the Marshall to round up the sporting fraternity.

After supper a Soldier came in and wanted me to go to the Chadron House and Marry him, which I done forthwith[.] Geo Havens promised to come and sleep with me tonight but I guess he went home as it is now 11.30 P.M. and he is still missing[.]

Dec 4. Geo Havens slept with me last night. I was unable to get out of the House all day on account of my left stump hurting me. Ace Johnson brought me my breakfast and Mr Josselyn my dinner[.] towards night the weather got more settled and I was able to go to Josselyns for supper[.] I worked on the Kass books all day and of course failed to make a trial balance[.]

Dec 5. To day the weather has been very pleasant. Mike Ryan came in from the Table this[word missing]. I have been very busy all day at different Jobs and principally on the Kass books—wrote a letter of introduction for Van Horn to My Brother and John McShane.

Dec 6. Jake Kass kept me busy all day.

the weather thawed all day. I told Breen to get himself another office as I could not stand his being around.

Pete Christensen came back and commenced work for me. Geo Havens came around today.

Dec 7. Geo & I got up early.

The weather has been splendid all day. I took the Colt "Minnie" over to Birdsalls stable to let it run around and found it to be a trotter. Jake Kass and Dorrington had a little row over the Fire Cisterns. I worked on the Kass books nearly all day. As I was setting down to supper, Cameron came after me to get out papers against Chas Gordon, the dude Barber.

After supper I finished the legal business and went over to Kasses and found Jake had gone home a little tired. I was called into Richards Bank to acknowledge the signing of Articles for the First National Bank of Chadron by the directors, after which I came home and went to bed.

Dec. 8. The weather opened up fine this morning. Geo & I got up at 6 oclock. I worked on the Books at Kass again and commenced on the Democrat at 3 P.M. when the Town list got out I took Kass horse and wagon and exercised my colt.

Dec. 9. Geo & I woke up late this morning[.] I was unable to get up right away as my stumps hurt me but by 9 o'clock I got up.

I worked on the Kass books again and got all posted up to date but last months accounts do not balance by 50 cents which we will find on Sunday[.]

I got Joe Poissant to make me a oats tank out of a round piece of Smoke Stack and which is the o.k. thing for my Colt.

Just before supper I took Birdsalls horse and exercised the Colt. I also made a pleasant call on the Board of County Commissioners where I had quite a long and nice talk with County Atty. Ballard.

Dec 10. pretty fair weather all day again till about 4 oclock P.M. when it commenced getting very cold[.] I finished balancing the [books] today. Geo did not sleep with me last night. after supper I went up to the rink and put on the Skates and played in the band for fun. there were a great many people up there[.] I called on Mrs Simmons baby a little in the fore part of the evening.

Dec. 11. The weather today has been very pleasant. I got up rather late. In the afternoon Geo and I got a buggy and went out ridding and we led the Colt behind the buggy. after supper we stayed in the office and wrote up books.

Dec 12. To day has been a very nice day. I put in a great deal of my time fixing up my Stable for the Colt. I had Ace Johnson and Henry Miller at work all day. C W Burlew came up from Hemingford this evening.

Dec 13[.] last night it rained a good deal and this morning there was considerable snow on the Ground. Gene Carr came in from the East. The Corner Stone of the New Court House was laid to day by the Masons Fraternity. At 2.30 P.M. quite a concourse of people witnessed the ceremony which was very impressive indeed[.] the Baptist Church gave a Festival at the skating rink this Evening. Chris Fleming introduced himself in my office this evening with the intention of learning to be an Orator. I guess he will succeed. Miss Brockway bid goodbye to Chadron on the evening of the 13th of Dec.

Dec 14. This morning a little more snow appeared on the Ground making Sleighing much better[.] I received a letter from Bro Geo[.] I wrote up the Corner Stone article for the Democrat. Mrs Leach came in and got out Garnishee papers against W. A. Harrington, who died in Douglas from an overdose of laudum administered by himself. Not much business going on today. Fred Poll got back from Oelrichs where he has been putting up machinery for the Anglo American Cattle Co.

Dec 15[.] Fine weather aqain. I helped get out the Democrat. Mrs Leach commenced a Suit for board bill against W. A. Harrington[.] after supper I attended the Congl Church to hear Revr Scott of Omaha deliver a lecture. before going John Maher and I dropped in on the Episcopal Church supper and patronized the Gang. Maher took down the lecture in short hand. after church we came home and droped in at the Church again for coffee & cakes[.] when I got home I found the clock stopped and Geo asleep. I went down to Tom Coffeys to get the time and there met Al Powell from Oelrichs[.]

Dec 16. Nice weather again. I took the "Colt" out for exercise. all Chadron seems worked up over the Ballard & Allen fight in the newspapers. I wrote some letters to day for Selden. This evening Geo went to the Literary. I issued some more Garnishee papers in favor of Mrs Leach[.]

Dec 17. To day the weather has been very nice[.] Ed Cameron actually got a man to clean off the crossings. I have been busy all day working on a Contest Case for sweet, and copying the marriage record and addressing the Invitation for the Knights of Phythias. after supper, Tom Madden came in the Office and plead guilty to assault and Battery upon Petterson the Brick man and No sooner was he gone than in came Petterson to have him arrested, but I stopped the proceeding after which I went to J Kass[.]

this afternoon I took Chas Jerallman up to my stable to look at my Colt.

Dec[.] 18. To day has been pretty pleasant[.] I stayed in the house nearly all day till 3 oclock P.M. when I got Kass & Co horese [horse] and took the colt out for exercise but it would not lead so I had to take it back again. after supper I played Billiards at Coffeys, after which Geo & I had Oysters at Josselyns[.]

Dec 19. This morning it started out to be a nice day but all of a sudden at 7. A.M. it started to Storm and by 9 oclock 4 inches of snow had fallen. the Case of Leach vs Harrington came up for trial, and was continued, also the case of Walker vs. H. F. Clough & Co came up for trial upon which judgment by Default was rendered in favor of the Plff. for the full amount claimed[.] In the afternoon at 2 P.M. I started by Request of C. F. Yates and went out to M. B. Kelloggs place on White river and had a proper deed signed. I took Henry Miller along. Jake Kass and I went up to the Oregon Glover Restaurant and had a full Stew each, after which we put in a little time looking at presents. W. L. Handy came down from Whitney, also W. E. Alexander from Crawford. Bob Dorr met an old School Mate Mr C. R. Traxler while at the R. R. Eating House. Mr. T. remained in Chadron all day, after which he left for his place of business in Hastings.

J. W. Boone came down from Crawford this evening to get the marriage lisence for W. D. Edgar who in all probability will have the knot tied tomorrow.

Dec 20. The weather started in bitter cold this morning and continued so all day[.] I put in all day in work on my Checks for the Hat at [and] Coat Room for the 23rd and also got Mrs Josselyn to go up to the Skating rink and get her business arraigned. I got a nice present for Cleona and a nice neck Scarf for Geo Havens. Geo came home with me and got me to buy him a pop corn popper so he might pop some corn.

Dec 21. To day has been very cold again[.] I rustled around about the new well bucket and done Chores in general. I made out some small Bills for Kass.

Dec 22. I got the skating rink Hat room in order to-day. Johnny Hanlon helped me. I have been busy all day doing up odd chores to be in readiness for tomorrow. In the evening Geo Havens and I went up Town to look at some christmas cards. last night the City Council held a meeting at which F. M. Dorrington was set down.

Dec 23. To day has been a fine one right through. I went up to the Congl Church and heard the School children giving their Closing exercises after which I came down to the rink with Geo Havens and commenced getting things ready for the Knights of Phythias Ball, and by 8 oclock I was seated on my high chair ready to take Coats and Hats on deposit[.] the Masquerade went along nicely enough, only the order to unmask was given too soon and many who otherwise would have enjoyed themselves were forced to submit and lost all for which they especially came[.]

Mrs Josselyn had Charged of the supper, but could not do justice to so large a crowd. Johnny OHanlon and Geo Havens helped me in the coat room. We all left the rink at about 2 oclock A.M. The, the Chadron Democrat commenced moving in their new Quarters in the basement of the Eckles Building.

Dec 24[.] I slept till 10 30 AM.. I have been doing all kinds of straightening up getting thing[s] out of Confusion over the ball[.] the Democrat Office has been moving all day. this afternoon J F Tucker swore out a warrant against M. Ballard charging him with criminal liable. I issued the warrant and delivered the same to Ed Cameron who being afraid to serve it got Davis to do the job, who finally arrested Ballard and upon coming into court he gave his necessary recognizance to apper for examination before me in the

Penal sum of one hundred dollars with Peter J Breen as his surety which was approved by me[.]

After getting through with that job I sent Cleona Jossellyn and then I went to the Methodist Church to see the Christmas tree unloaded to the little ones[.] Geo Havens went along and of course got the Box I sent him[.]

We both adjourned to the skating rink and from there home[.] to day I got my new Suit from Selden the Tailor.

Dec 25. Merry Merry Christmas to all. I faild to send Lenoras little ones any presents on account of being too busy[.] I took my Christmas Dinner with George Havens at his home and I enjoyed the day very much. after dinner I called to see Mr and Mrs Simmons baby. I took supper at Josselyns and then came home in the Office and wrote a letter to Billy Carter. Geo Havens took a Bath.

Dec 26. To day has been another Holliday[.] J Kass Keept open through mistake but closed at 12 oclock. Nothing of importance has happened all day.

Dec 27. The Tree-Masons [Freemasons?] laid the Cor[ner] stone of the school house today. Birdsall, G Clark and I went up in a Sleigh, it was very cold. After supper I went up to the Rink and took charge of the Coat Room for the Masonic Ball and Banquet. It was a very cold night but the Rink was exceptionally warm and a large attendance was on hand. the supper was as fine a one as I would want to set up too.

Dec 28. To day the weather has been a little more moderate.

at 9. A.M. the Case of the State vs Ballard was called up and upon motion of the Defendant, the case was dismissed for want of prosecution[—]motion sustained.

Dec 29. Cold and bleak weather[.] Kass & Co are busy taking invoice. I bought a load of Hay for the Colt yesterday and took the colt out for exercise.

O H Wilson and Saulsburry came and asked me to seell [sell] pools for them on the 26 hour walking match at the Rink tonight, commencing at 9 oclock P.M. between Salsburry, Blaizdell and Ness, which I done but only sold about [$]20.00 worth. I came home about 3 Oclock A.M. Geo Havens came with me.

Dec 30. My right leg is paining me considerably. I have been knocking about a great deal today[,] principally waiting for the "Democrat" to go to press which finally occurred at 4 P.M. after supper I went up to the Rink and started to sell pools on a 1 mile race between Saulsburry and one named Helmer, but after about $25.00 of pools had been sold they had to be declared off because Saulsburry would not run. after that we got up some local sport by having 3 Boxing matches by local weights which caused much sport & fun[.]

Dec 31. I am going to pass the last day of 1887 in the House. My right stump has pained me so much in the past week that I am unable to put on the Artificial one today, so I had J Kass bring me over his invoice book and I will amuse my self in the office to day.

It is bitter cold today and has been so all day. Pete Christensen brought me my Breakfast and Bert Josselyn kept me supplied the remainder of the day. Ed Cameron the City Marshall was in this Evening to see about the Girls paying their fines, which would go to show that he is getting pretty hard up. Geo Havens came home from the skating rink rather late. John Maher was in the office this evening and we had quite a time with Short Hand reporting.

Chapter VI:
1888 (Diary)

January 1st[,] 1888[.] To day 5 years ago I was an able bodied man and able to cope with the world in almost any capacity but now I am all crippled up and not being able to use my artificials I must remain indoors and have my meals carried to me just as though I were sick in bed, and yet how can I repine for when I think back I cannot help saying to myself how lucky I have been in being permitted to live at all—[.]

I hope the comming year may be a more prosperous one for me and that at i[t]s close, if God lets me live I may be enabled to have a little more comfort around me. I have had a great deal of Company to day but I would much rather not have had any as I was busy work[ing] on J Kass & Co's invoice book. Bartlett Richards brought over Typewriting which I done for him right off. Bert Josselyn carried my meals to me to day. Just about suppertime Mrs White and Mrs Campbell came in the Office to see about not paying any fines.

Bert and Geo Played at the new game some time after which Bert went home.

Jan 2. To day the weather moderated a good deal. I cleaned out the office myself—I got Boyd to fix my leg, but he did not make a good job of it. In the afternoon I went out sleighing with the Land Office

Clerk John Maher. we went out to the Hills to see the School Children Coasting. Lake & Halley moved in the New Bank to day. George Clark came in the Office this morning to get his fee bills in all his cases on my civil Docket. Nick Janis came to Town to day. Old man Burns was in my Office to day to have a Mortgage drawn from Himself and wife to Elbert G Mead.

R. E. W. Spargur handed me a letter to him from Mary A. Woodard (Red Jacket) in which she asked for assistance from the county, so I got some articles from T. H. Glover and gave them to Spargur who took them out to her. after supper I went over to J Kass & Co and worked on the Cash books.

Jan 3. To day everything thawed out fine. Kass & Co. put on runners on his wagon so the snow all melted. I worked on the Cash book for Kass all day. Towards evening some farmers came to me to have a petition of assistance drawn up which I done.

after supper I went down to Coffeys. Geo Havens came in and I went home with him[.] he cried a good deal about not getting to bed earlier. I finally made everything all right with him[.] Henry Miller took sick again a few days ago with lung fever[.]

Jan 4th[.] today has been a little Changable. Judd Hathaway made an assignment in favor for his Creditors[.] it caused considerable excitment as it was altogether unexpected by anyone. I called to see Henry Miller and found him doing well under the treatment of Dr Harris[.]

The City Council met or tried to meet tonight, but failed to get a quorum, so everything went by. Atty Fisher and James F Tucker came in my Office and filed an affidavit and undertaking for an order of attachment against Judd Hathaway. The City Mayor and Council had quite a talk with the City Clerk on the subject of drawing up the water bond. Chris Fleming came around to see me. Geo Havens will sleep at his own home tonight[.]

Jan 5. Bob Dorr took a certificate of witnesship to Judd Hathaway signature of yesterday up to the County Clerks office and filed it with the assignment. I called on the County Commissioners to see about arrangments for the poor. I also work[ed] on the Kass books. after dinner I acknowledged a mortgage for D. Burns and then helped to get out the "Democrat[.]"

Jan 6. to day has been a cold one right along[.] I worked on Kass & Co invoice books[.] Geo Havens went to work for little Ike Gottstein. Ed Cameron was in to Mrs Josselyns to day and was feeling very bad, he having just got up out of bed from a bilious fever. a perfect hurricane is raging just now[.] Geo Havens and I had to plug up the air holes in the room. I painted the Blackboard for Chris Fleming—[.]

Jan 7. To day the weather has moderated considerable. I went over in the "Democrat Office" and picked out myself a file of the Democrat Paper from its first issue[,] June 27th, 1885 to the present date with the exception of a few copies.

I worked on the Kass invoice book all afternoon. Mr Doran from Oelrichs called on me and made an appointment to see me on a very important matter so I set 9 oclock this evening.— The City Council were to have met tonight but faild to get a quorum—[.] at 9:40 P.M. Mr Doran came along and after going to Carters saloon with him he informed me that his mission was to get the fine of Mrs White refunded, which she had paid into the Police Court for the month of January for being a common low down prostitute[.] I laughed him in the face and told him in plain words to mind his own business. Geo Havens feasted on apples and pop corn after he came from the Rink. I went up to the Colt today.

Jan 8th[.] today the weather has been Cleare but rather cold—[.] I got up at 10 'oclock A.M. I took Dinner with Geo Havens at his home and had turkey for Sunday dinner. I stayed in the office all evening. Chris

Fleming, Van Horn and Geo Carson called in during the evening[.]

I attended the Colt to day myself.

Jan 9th[.] The attachment suit of Tucker vs. Hathaway consumed most of the day. I adjourned the case to Consult Atty Bartow about certain law points raised in the case. James Tucker left for Valentine this evening. Geo Havens came home early this evening. James Dahlman came in the Office this evening and had a long talk with me. Chris Fleming called. the County Commissioners refused to allow Ben Snells bills for digging a grave for a pauper last May. I calld on the Land Office clerk, John Maher. I reced a letter from Harry Young containing Christmas Cards, etc.

Jan[.] 10th. To day the weather moderated considerable[.]   the case of Tucker vs Hathaway was again called untill 3 Oclock when I adjourned to await the arrival of James Dahlman from Crawford. I took my Colt out for exercise[.] after supper I issued a warrant for the arrest of Miss Ollie, she being in default of her fine for December. John Maher was in the office this evening[.] Chris Fleming returned my book of historical dates. I made out a report to the County Commissioners of all Criminal Fines collect and paid by myself to the County Treasurer.

the wind of politic investigation is rising very strong at present and there seems to be a hurricane brewing in the direction of ex County Judge Byington.

Jan 11. Fine weather this morning. sun shining in Full blast. Miss Ingersoll had a runaway yesterday while out ridding in her carriage[,] she being thrown to the ground[,] badly cut on the left side of her head directly above her left temple.

the Iron Colums of Ricker Houghton Eckles & Houghton Building are being now put into their positions. Sheriff dahlman returned from Crawford last night. he was in my office this morning and requested that he be not made a party in the Tucker vs Hathaway attachment suit. I made arrangments with John Maher last night that two nights each week he Should call on me to give lessons in short-hand[,] they being Monday and Wednesday.

Miss Ollie Bailey made up her mind to try and get out of Jail, so she had Patsy and Nellie Aaron rustle around for her and by 6 oclock this [word missing].

I done some writing for Frank Van Horn and Chas Allen preparatory to Van Horn going to Rushville. I got out the list for the Democrat. towards evening the weather got very windy and is now blowing very hard. Charles Wilson came in the Office about 8 oclock to read up on points in the Statutes.

Jan 12. to day has been a stormy one. it started to blow early this morning and it kept it up all day.

I called on C. F. Yates and tried to Collect my bill for going to white river but I failed.

I helped to get out the Democrat today[.] this evening Chris Fleming came over and I gave him his first writing lesson.

Jan. 13. To day has been a bitter cold one. Themometer at 20 below all day. I decided the attachment Case in Tucker vs Hathaway. this evening Geo and I went up to the Rink to run the Coat room for the leap year party. the rink was very cold and not comfortable and the attendance in consequence very slim, especially was it so on account of a great many of the middle classes not having been invited by the upper teens. this afternoon I got All Smith's Brother to go up and help me attend to my Colt.

Geo & I came home from the rink at 2 oclock.

Jan 14. To day I took up my dockets to the County Commissioners and showed them the amount of all fines with which they seemed very much please[d]. I got a new Criminal Docket from the County Clerk[.] Mrs Josselyn came over to look at a stove I have on hand, with a view of trading for it, but it did not suit. Geo Havens came home and went to bed very early. Mr

W. A. Selden was in the office all evening and we had a long talk together about every thing.

Jake Kass had a row with one of Bob Dicksons men to day and smashed him in the Jaw.

Jan 15. To day the weather has been very cold indeed, but clear. I got up at about 9 A.M. and missed breakfast. I waited till 3 oclock when I went to dinner with Frank M. Van Horn by special invitation.

Dr Harris and W. A. Birdsall left today for Grand Lake to amputate the feet of S. A Wooden who got frooze some time ago.

Jim Dahlman and Hank Simmons had one of their horses get sick on them while out driving. they had to unhitch him and let him at McIntyres. Old Doc Richardson attended the horse and is doing pretty well with him!

No train from the East yet and everything between here and Emmett is snow bound. Fred Poll is again on a big drunk.

Jan 16. The weather opened up a little bit freeer than for the past few days.

Dr Jackson called on me and reported Mrs Mary A Woodward as being in a very bad condition and entirely without means of support, & sick, whereupon I went and looked the matter up and finding the same to be true I ordered Mrs. Smith to care for her and instructed Dr. Jackson to render her what medical aid might be necessary which was accordingly done.

In the evening I again went up to see the patient to find out what clothing if any she needed and brought Mrs. Smith down town and furnished her with clothes to the amount of $6.40.

Today I had considerable trouble with Mrs. O'Linn in as much as she is always interfering with some one elses business when no possible good to herself can result therefrom. After supper I posted up J. Kass & Co. Books till 8 PM, when I came home where John Maher was waiting to give me my Short Hand lessons. Geo. & I retired about 10 o'clock. Chess Firbrache came back from the East.

Jan. 17th. The weather opened up pretty Cold. Ed Cameron, the city marshall, has now gone to work for Tony Barnard as Barkeeper. A Glass Blower came to town yesterday and opened up for afternoon and evening exhibition, but he shut up shop very early the first night, and I guess he had very little trade. Chadron appears to have very little time for Glass Blowing anyway.

A. J. Richardson returned from Omaha and reported having seen M. O. Maul. Mrs. Woodward asked to be allowed a can of Oysters which has been recommended By the Dr. and I ordered them accordingly and some crackers. I also instructed Mrs. Smith to keep track of everything that was sent to Mrs. Woodward. Mr. Selden came in and told me about Mrs. O'Linn having been to see him and wanted to know all about the purchasing by him of the Sloggey property whereupon I told him I would leave on the evening train for Hay Springs to see Col. McCann myself provided I can get an answer by telegraph that he is there.

Jan. 18th. I returned from Hay Springs on this morning train armed with the necessary authority from McCann for the disposal of his property. I went to see Red Jacket and find out how she was getting along. I found her making great trouble for Mrs. Smith and the latter says she will keep her no more so I went and seen the County Atty. and find out what he says in the matter. Upon hearing the the facts in the case, I got him to assure me that a warrant would be issued for her arrest tomorrow morning. I received a very nice letter from my niece, Cassie Vandersloot in York, York Co.

The city council were to meet tonight but failed to make their appearance so Geo. and I went to bed early.

Jan 19. Very Cold weather all day. I seen Ballard and had him have an order of arrest issued for Mary A

Woodward. I went and got Charlie Wilson and took Danleys sleigh and hauled her down to the Jail. she made quite a kick, but it was no use. I made her go along. Mr Simms came to me and reported a man by the name of [name missing] as being in need of assistance and very poor and unable to be up out of bed—after looking into the case [I] found its merits were good and accordingly ordered Dr Miller to take Charge of him. I also sent my own stove around for the patient and made an agreement with Mrs. Leach at [$]5.00 per week for him and the city was to furnish the fuel. I seen Messrs. Ginn and Blakeny about coal.

I ordered Mr Parkes to make me a blank or envelope case and gave him an order on Hood for the same. The weather is very cold. Col McCann came up from Hay springs and he and Fisher finally Consented to Lease the Sloggy property to Mr Selden at [amount missing] per month for.

The colored man, Millard Miles had his preliminary examination before the County Judge upon a charge of murder. Old Judge Cook appeared as his Atty but he was too drunk to be of any service to his client. The Defendant was bound over to the District Court.

News arrived in Chadron today that Frank Aken died in Douglas 2 days ago, and the [that] Chris Voss wife and two children had frooze to death down in Box Butte County.

Jan. 20th—The weather cleared up a little but started to storm towards the afternoon. I went to see the Citys patient today and found him in no good condition. I made arrangements with Gene Fields to take care of him and board him for $6.00 per week, but then Gene has not come around yet, so I cannot say what I will do in the matter, but one thing is sure, I must have the man moved from Mrs. Leaches as he is getting no decent treatment for his money.

Harry Shelley sent around for some money on account which I let him have. A. H. Henry, an agent for Photographs of Scenes in Dakota, Wyoming and Colorado, was in the office and sold me some Scenes and also the right of Dawes County, so I set young [name missing] to selling them. I wrote a letter to W. H. McCann about the property of Sloggey.

Martin Morrisey filed a contest on Earnest Bross Claim yesterday.

This evening Chas. Allen drew the glass pipe at the Glass blowing exhibition. P. O. Hanlon gave me a bill of [$]24.00 to Collect against Geo Livingstone, whereupon George Livingstone gave me an order on F. C. Poll, but it was not accepted.

Jan. 21. The weather today has been much milder than usual. I went up to the County Clerks office and rendered a transcript of my Docket in a civil case of F. H. Fall vs. John W. Cox, then I took a list of warrants remaining in the Clerks office. after dinner I bought a load of wood and went up to see Mrs Smith. when I came back I found George Fredericks (Colored) in my office to have pension papers attended to. I fixed him out when Dr Miller and J. A. Macomber came in and made an earnest appeal for assistance from the County for Wm Jones who they represented dying and having 6 small children who are almost starving and had no clothes to wear.

I forthwith dropped all proceedings and engaged a team to take myself and the County Physician out. I also ordered some provisions and clothes and put them in the Sleigh. But the County Physician thought it best for the Dr to go who had attended the case before the application had been made to the county for assistance, so I went and got Dr Miller. We left some quilts at Glovers for Macomber and Martin to bring out with them.

We arrived at Mr Jones and found him very low with Pneumonia Fever, the fever being very high. after administering unto the poor sick man all that lay in our power to do and finding out the actual necessities of the children the Dr & I departed for home. After supper I went up to T. H. Glovers and bought 4 pair of shoes for the Jones children paying $4.25 in cash on them and having the balance $2.00 charged to the County. The [$]4.25 which I paid for the shoes being money that was handed to me by Mr Macomber as having come from donaters at his special request.

While I was buying the shoes Mr. Glover informed me of another case, a Mrs Crawford living between Chadron Creek & White River[.] Mrs Glover and Mrs Mears went out to see her and found her in bed (where it is reported she has lain for the past 6 months) she was apparently numb, unable to speak and when asked if she wanted something to eat, she nodded her head in the affirmative and tears came to her eyes. Her husband bear[s] a hard name for cruelty and this seems to be too much for any human being to stand without trying to render this woman some relief[.] I have seen Mr W. C. Brown and got the use of his sleigh for tomorrow. J Kass has offered the use of his horses and Mr & Mrs Glover have promised to go along[.] I seen Dr Harris about going, but he seems very reticent about going. the facts in the case being that he has been paid ahead or in other words is sure of his money as he has the Contract for the County for Doctoring the sick.

I purchased a Slop bucket from J. Kass for Tom Simms, the City Pauper.

I called on Red Jacket to see how she was getting along. I also went up to see Mrs Smith about making arraingments to have her keep Mrs Crawford in case we are obliged to keep her and move her into the City so she can have the proper attention. Pete Christensen failed to carry in wood to day, Make up the Bed and Carry water so I will dock him 25 cts.

the Great walking match came of[f] this evening at the rink. Salsbury seeing he could not beat 5 men in

5 miles, go as you please, threw up the spongue before the first man got through with him.

The City Council met in special session this evening. John Maher was in the Office this evening.

I also ordered some Whiskey and alcohol and extract of Beef from W. G. Burk.

Jan 22[.] This morning I got up at 7. oclock feeling very tired. I got breakfast and got the Horses hitched up to Browns Sleigh. After having consulted in Company with T. H. Glover with County Atty Ballard as to the advisability of going out to Mrs Crawford and bringing her into town for treatment, I started to see Mr Jones again and find out if he was alive and if so to get some beef tea into him. I took Mrs Montgomery along, also Geo Havens and All Smith, but we were met on the Bordeaux by Mr Macomber who informed us of Mr Jones death. I turned around and came to town, notified the County Atty of the facts, asked him what he thought about the idea of a post mortem being held over the body and said that Dr Miller had informed me to the effect that he did not think the bullet which is said to have remained in Mr Jones arm and which a Mr Stricklund is said to have fired some time last Summer, could be any cause or have any bearing upon the Case in the event of his (Jones) death. The County Atty said the Physician should certainly know. I called upon Dr Miller who informed that the man died from Natural Causes, the same being Pneumonia Fever and to that effect he would make a Certificate of death. I thereupon informed the County undertaker who forthwith dispatched a man and guide out for the Corpse.

After dinner Mr and Mrs T. H. Glover, Mrs Mears, Chas Wilson and Myself started out to visit the Sick bed of Mrs Crawford who has been sick for over 8 months, with No Doctor to tend to her for 4 months. this case seems to have been recognized by almost every person in the neighborhood as one pointing towards cruelty from her husband, and in order to make sure of a

Successful issue in the case, I took the deputy Sheriff along as there had been some representations made that her husband was cross and cranky and would allow no one to do anything for her.

Upon our arrival there we found him at home and was as pleasent as any man could be. he had his wife setting up in a rocking chair propped up with pillows with her feet up to the stove. She was sitting in a wooden bottom Rocking Chair, I think it was wooden bottom and am sure it was a rocking Chair. I asked her if she wanted to eat and she shook her head in the affirmative in a manner indicating ravenous hunger, and Showing an egerness for something to eat. her cords of speech were entirely silent and her only means of communication were to shake her head in the negative or affirmative. I started to make her some beef tea (I had the extract ready in my pocket) whereupon Mr Crawford suggested that she had just had a large meal and that she never seemed satisfied, that he could not see why she should eat so much and not improve[.] He wanted to know what kind of beef extract I had. he thought it would do her no good, and spoke as if he thought we might try, but it would do her no good. He again repeated that she had all she wanted to eat, and that he could prove it by a neighbor who was at that time in the house, and whose name was Miller. I however got the children to warm some water for me and having made some tea, I and Mrs. Mears proceeded to administer it to her. Oh that I may never see such a sight again! that poor woman opened her mouth more like a beast of prey who has not tasted blood for weeks and finally gets into some flocks of innocents, than like a human being, and yet her husband previously averred she had eaten a hearty meal. How could such be the case? For the only thing visible to eat in the House was a sack of Flour in the cupboard and a small lard can filled with either apples or peaches were boiling on the stove. I do not pretend to be the Judge in this case as I will leave that to the Creator, but I concluded from the Moment of giving that woman some Nourishment which she swallowed in so ravenous a manner that she was not getting the proper treatment of a Sick human being, that Her Husband had property and could do better for her than he was doing and I must find out why he was so dormant in acting. He had told me that Dr had said that all the medicine in the world would not cure her.

I asked him when the Dr had been there last, to which he replied "Well, quit[e] a long time ago[.]" I asked him if he wanted a Doctor? If he was able to have his wife doctored? If not, if he wanted aid? That we had come out there to look the matter up. That I stood ready to offer him assistance in the Name of the County if he would accept it. I told him his wife could never get well by keeping her in the condition she was then in. I reprimanded him for false modesty and pride. I called up his manhood and reminded him that the eyes of the community at large throughout Dawes County were looking in the direction of his house ever wondering why his wife could not get well. He cried and turned away and I seen plainly that I had touched a sympathetic chord in his heart. His reply to these questions were summed up briefly with the remark that he had already spent a great deal of money trying to doctor her and she was no better, but his poor wife sobbed aloud and moaned. No doubt it is a good thing probably that she could no speak at that moment. I have seen some hard trials and pittyful circumstance in which a Stranger can be placed but this case is I think with out an exception and seemed rather on the order of Romance wherein the Heroine is Slowly poisoned by the Hero, or perhaps it might be Cited with that of the "Two Orphans" when the old hag pinches the Blind Girls arms and makes her say she is treated nice to the passers by. Mr Glover and Mrs Mears then made the bed and I asked the patient if she wanted a Doctor? if she wanted to be cured? to which she again shook her head in her pleading affirmative manner[.] We then laid her down on the bed and I request[ed] Mr Crawford to come outside, and there in the presence of T. H. Glover and the Deputy Sheriff I again read the riot act to him and asked him if he would consent to have his wife moved where a good woman nurse could attend her and wether he would pay for her treatment if I got the people to wait on him. He said in reply as near as I can remember the following to wit "I do not want to ask the County for aid. I have property and will pay my debts if they will give me a show. You can take her to Chadron and I will pay the bill as soon as I am able. I expect to prove up soon. I have some [number missing] head of cattle but do not want to sell them. You can take her if she wants to go, but I think you had better wait a few days and see if she will be able to stand the trip. I do not think that she will be able to stand the trip.["] I however after a few moments consultation within myself resolved that this woman must be doctored and cared for and feeling fully convinced myself that her husband either could not or would not do it, I concluded to have her moved immediately as it could not be possible that at that time of year finer weather could be desired to favor the circumstances. Mr Glover and I removed the Seats on the sleigh after which I told Mrs Glover and Mrs Mears my determination which of course was sustained by every one present. I went to the bed Side of Mrs Crawford and asked her if she would go to a place where we could have some good lady take care of her to which she nodded her head yes and seemed glad to get to go. I then left Mrs Glover and Mrs Mears to dress her and fix her comfortable for the trip[.] The Deputy Sheriff, F. H. Glover and My Self got the Sleigh, in which we had all gone out in ready and it was not long before we had Mrs Crawford all snugly packed and were on our road to Chadron where I had previously made arraingments with Mrs Thersia Smith to take care of her in case she would have to be taken in. We arrived in Chadron at about 6 oclock and soon we had the patient laying easy in a bed in Mrs Smiths house. I left her there in the care of good hands and proceeded to put away my team, afterwhich I went for my Supper at Mrs Josselyns where I was again interrupted by the undertakers coming in from Mr Jones with the Corpse. after telling them where to Find Judge Morris I finished my supper and went to Dr Millers and took him up to see the patient which we had brought it [in]. The Dr Sounded her chest and having made up his mind acted accordingly and left medicine & instructions with Mrs Smith. the patient Seemed to be resting easy and appeared quite happy. I neglected to Mention the fact that when we concluded to take Mrs Crawford into the sleigh I got Mr Crawford to hitch up his team to take Mrs Glover and Mrs Mears in which he done.

I came home and started to go to bed but thinking about some important instructions which Mrs Smith should have so I started up and told her. I came home very late and felt very tired[.]

Jan 23. The weather to day has been pretty pleasant.

Mrs Smith came to my Office and I went up with her to Glovers and ordered some underclothes for Mrs Crawford. I got a team and had the bed of Tom Dixon moved to Mrs Smith.

I got a mattrass and spring from Wm Wilson for Mrs Crawford. I also sent up a stove for her. While I was at Wilsons getting the Mattress & Spring, the City Marshall came after me to try a case of Reckless ridding throuqh the streets. I fined the prisoner [$]5.00 and costs. Mrs Glover and Mrs Mears have expressed their determination to go for Mrs. Crawfords baby tomorrow[.] I went up to Mrs Crawfords after supper.

Frank Aikens body arrived from Douglas this evening and it is now in the Davidson building. the K of P's are sitting up with it and will use my office pretty much all night. I called on the Commissioners and reported Dr Harris as not wanting to go to see the poor.

Jan 24. this morning it was very warm, but towards 9 oclock it commenced to rain then hail and finally snow.

I called on the Commissioners again but they were to[o] busy so I could transact no business about the poor[.] they told me to come in about 2 hours. I called to see Mrs Crawford and found her a hundred percent better. She had been moved into Mrs Smiths front room and seemed very happy and contented. I learned that Mrs Glover and Mrs Mears had gone out for the baby. they got into town about 12 oclock. Frank Aken was buried today with Pythian Honors, from the Episcopal Church. Mr Staunton of Douglas preached a pointed and eloquent funeral service, one that should not be forgotten by all who were so fortunate as to have heard it.

After the funeral Service, I got Mrs Glover and Mrs Mears to go to Mrs Jones House with me and see if we could get one of Mr Jones little Girls for Mrs Mears to take on probation and probably adopt[.] We got a good conveyance and returned with the little Girl about 7 oclock P.M. all o.k. The Poor business has been pretty good this week. I met Mr Crawford in Town today and he seemed pretty well pleased to have his wife cured. he said he would again call on me the last of this week. I was told this evening by Mrs Josselyn that certain parties had been in town and had made the threat that I had better look out that I would surely get shot as Snake Creek Tom (alias Parker) had it in for me and would shoot me sooner or later and that they would not want to be in my boots. I took dinner at Mrs Hoods today.

Jan 25. To day every thing thawed. I called on Mrs Crawford and then on Mrs Mears to see how she liked her new ward. Mr Henry the Scene man from the hills was in but I could not spend much time with him[.]

Wright of Custer was in the City. I went to see the Citys patient. I offered Jim Hartzell a chance at my photographs. I hired Pete Christensen over again. I called on the City Patient, Mr Simms, and Drew up a paper of donation for his benefit.

Jan 26[.] Fine weather. News from Washington to the effect of Mrs Woodwards final proof having been accepted arrived here today. Mr Martin brought in the little Jones boy and took him up to see his sister with Mrs Mears. I bought him a little Cap. W. A. Selden moved into his new quarters in the Eckles Block. Patsy came in the office and wanted to get out papers on Kingsburry. P O Hanlon came in to see about a lawsuit. John T. Jackson was in from the table to see about his logs which Herman Brockway is moving away. I took the Colt out for exercise to day.

Maher, Ballard, Parks, Van Lehr and Chris Fleming were in the office after supper.

I took supper with J Kass and Fred Poll. We had Jack Rabbit and I am feeling very bad over it as I ate too much.

Jan 27. Fine weather all day. I made out my bills against the county and filed them. the case of August Schmoldt was settled to day. Mr George Crawford came in to see his wife to day. he seemed glad to see her so well taken care of and expressed him self as well pleased with her condition. I went up with him to see her. Jake Kass got sick today. this evening I gave Chris Fleming a writing lesson. he appears to be getting on Finely.

Jan 28. To day the weather has thawed out considerably. I worked on the Kass books again. In the afternoon I went up to see Mrs Crawford. I got some potatoes and Rudebages from Mr J Clark and took them to her.

Mr Parks came down town and wanted another 1/2 board. I went to Finney and Williams and got it for him and hauled it to his house myself with J Kass & Co wagon.

M. Ballard had warrants issued at the Instance of a Complaining witness for the Larsh Bros., Fred Danielson, John Katen, O. L. Sloggey and others upon a charge as near as I can find out of gambling or Highway Robbery.

Jan 29. To day has been pleasent again. I recd a letter from Harry Young enclosing an order for a note of his on Keys and Soder. I also got one from Uncle Thomas. I called to see Mrs Crawford and found her getting along quite well. after supper I went up to the skating Rink to he[a]r Dr Mallroy preach a sermon on Temperance. All the Churches in Town were closed for the purpose of hearing him, and consequently the Rink was crowded. I enjoyed the sermon very much and think it had a good effect. I trust it may be a lasting effect to those who so much need the benefits of strict temperance.

Jan 30. This morning business commenced early and continued till 4 P.M. A[.] T. Drew commenced a Garnishment action against Vincent Cronant, which was settled forthwith upon the Plff becoming aware of the facts[.] the case of State vs O. L. Sloggey Et. al charged with keeping a gambling House and Grand Larceny was continued till March 1st[,] 1888, and the Defendants required to enter into a recognizance for their appearance which was accordingly done[.] Mrs Reese came to see me about Mrs Crawford and I found upon investigation she had been to Mrs Crawford and agitated her considerable. I ordered Mrs [Smith] to allow no one to come in there anymore and carry on that way[.] W. A. Seldens Safe came to day and it is here in the Office now[.] the weather has been exceptionally fine all day.

Jan 31[.] Fine weather again all day. Mr Crawford came in to see his wife. He complained about Mrs Reese having been to see his wife at Mrs Smith and having agitated her greatly. I called at Mrs Smiths and told her never again to let any one do the like. I also called on Dr Miller and informed him of the reports concerning Mrs Reeses talkativeness, etc. I wrote Mrs Reese a letter forbidding her the house where Mrs Crawford is at present, under penalty of being prosecuted for disturbing the Peace and quiet.

Thos Glover commenced a Garnishment action this A.M. against J. M. Striker for $25 25/100[.] the goods at the Post office were commenced to be auctioned of[f] today. W. A. Seldan moved into the Sloggy property on King St. Quite a number of parties are going around with a petition for a subscription for a lady at Stuart who has had her hands and feet amputated. E. N. Jossely spoke to me about getting an affidavit up in the shape of an application for an amendment to his homstead Entry No.

Mr Parks was in to see me, also Selden.

Feb 1. Nice weather again. the case of Mary A Powell vs G D. Merryman came up for trial before me. Judgment for Plff was ordered. Auction sale has been going on today at the P. Office.

I done a small job for Van Inwegin[.] severall of the witnesses in the Lynch case from Antelope Co. came in the office to day to have their Bills made out. Chris Fleming took a note from Rosa & Thompson for $100.00 and sold it to the Chadron Banking Co for $90.00[.]

The City Council were to meet this evening but no one ever came around.

Feb 2. Rainy all day. Foggy and not clear. Cold and disagreeable[.] I went to see the City pauper and find out what the reason was that he does not seem to get well. I had a talk with Dr Miller about him.

I called on Mayor Hughes and had a general talk about the Marshalship, the outcome of which was that he appointed C. W. Wilson as special Marshall pending the meeting of the Council in consequence of the present City Marshall being engaged at Bar keeping, and the City is without an active Marshall.

Parks finished my Blank Case And I have not yet completed getting my papers arrainged therein. C C Hughes called on me this evening and we had a very nice Chat together on the probable outcome of the City Election this spring. J Kass was confined to his bed all day. I worked on the Kass books today.

Feb. 3[.] This morning there was a little snow on the ground and it looked as if it was going to be winter again but towards noon the sun came out and thawed the snow.

Ricker & Houghton commenced suit against Burr Shelton for Squire T Harney & Son upon a Whiskey account in 1884.

I took up oats for the colt today and got my Blank case fixed up a little. Geo Havens came around after supper and he and I went up to the methodist Church together to hear Dr Mallory who is at present conducting and has been for the past 3 weeks, a series of revival meetings which can not and are not failing in an accomplishment which is the only possible way in my judgement for a human being to come within the reach of the Holy Ghost and be acceptable unto God.

Though not standing altogether on so iron clad a platform as Dr Mallory and Others, I nevertheless heartly agree with his sincere co-workers that religion is good and beneficial and Godly, but I do not believe in repetition.

Feb 4[.] To day has been a pretty cold one. Gottstein & Brown moved into the old Selden stand on Second St. the Editor of the Advocate called on me and had a long talk on Religion but I do not think he left any wiser. Mr Crawford came in to see his wife. Mrs Smith seems to be very much dissatisfied with keeping Mrs Crawford as she claims she is making to much trouble for her. Mrs Crawford seems to be also anxious to go home. I called on Mrs Wilson to see about procuring Mrs Crawford another place, but Mrs Wilson could only refer me to Mrs Messenger.

I stayed in the office all night.

Feb 5th[.] This morning I got up late as I felt rather bad on account of setting up late and writing so much last night. I went over to see Fannie Powers about certain affidavits she wanted to make. Thos Madden was in the office a good part of the day. I did not go to church to day. I came home after supper and put in my time fixing up my civil docket.

Feb 6[.] This morning Burley Hill woke me up. I made out all Bills against the County for Paupers and gave them to their owners. Mrs Leach got her warrant today and took it to the Mayor to sign[.] I gave her one of my own to have him sign also and return to me.

Chas Wilson came in the Office and reconsidered his resignation and concluded to act as Marshal under instructions of the Mayor[.] I called to see Mrs Crawford and handed Mrs Smith her County Claim to sign for keeping care of "Red Jacket[.]" I made up the files of the Democrat. Bert Josselyn[,] Henry Miller, and Al Smith helped me. Al Smith handed me the key to my stable and said he could not attend the colt anymore. I called on Mr and Mrs Dr Miller and had a nice social chat. Mrs Miller presented me with one of Coltons large size Portfolio Files and Scrap books[.] it is indeed a very neat and handsome present which I hope I may always cherish and preserve never once forgetting the givers thereof.

I came home early and met Mr Peterson the Brick man who handed me an account book of his for me to add up. I bought a load of wood for [$]2.25 and gave an Order on Burr Shelton for goods for $1.70[.]

Feb 7. To day I worked on J Kass & Co books. Clem Davis came to me and made a strong talk for work from me on papers out of my Court. I gave him to understand just what was what[.] Mr Crawford came in to see his wife[;] he called on me and handed me a letter which Mrs Crawford[s] Mother had written to Mrs Smith and myself.

Mr Crawford appears to be very willing to try and raise money with which to help pay the present bills as being incurred for his wifes benefit[.] This morning Geo Clark notified me of his Election to the Vice Presidency of the Prohibitionists of Chadron. Tony Barnard is laying very sick at the Rail Road House with Mountain fever.

Ricker dismissed the suit against Shelton and commenced a new action on account of improper service of Summons[.] Geo Havens came in the office this evening and I managed to get him to tell me the reasons of his not coming around here any more which I soon explained away. Mr D. E Havens came in to see about a Claim which he wants amended. Chris Fleming came around this evening for writing lessons.

Feb 8th[.] I had the county atty Ballard go up to the County Commissioners with me to day and have him explain himself upon the subject of Mrs Crawford. the Commissioners finally issued an order to the sheriff commanding him to summon Mr Crawford and Justice Danley of 49 precinct to appear before them.

Van Horn went around to see all the Chadron Subscribers to the Miss Shattuck fund and find out if they would assent to the fund being turned over to Mrs Crawford on account of the sudden death of Miss Shattuck. all of them consented except a few.

Mrs Knapp called to see me relating to taking charge of Mrs Crawford. I went up to see Mrs Crawford and tell her of the proposed plan of changing her patient to which she greatly objected. Mr S. G. Canfield and Carpenter of Whitney made a flying visit to the Magic City to View the Court House, School House, B & M Depot and transfer Headquarters[.]

George Havens came over this evening and will remain with me again. I wrote a long letter to Miss Royce and sent her pamphlets of D. W. Kolbe & Son. it is snowing quite hard again[.] W. H. Carter returned from California this morning. Chas Jerralman of the table was in town today. Ben Arnold met me today and introduced me to an old time freighter and trader on the Niobrara River in 1878 & 9[.]

Feb[.] 9. Crawford came in today and went before the County Commissioners who told him they would give him till next monday to get his wife to Omaha into a hospital[.] I went up to see Mrs Crawford and found Mrs Smith rather mad because she could not go. I called on Chris Fleming to see if he wanted to loan Crawford any money, but he is afraid of his ghost. I came home very tired and went to bed early.

Feb 10[.] Nice day all day. I fell down by the Gold Bar this morning and almost broke my back. Mr Danielson helped me up.— Doc Middleton came to town from below on land business. Crawford came to town and made a loan on his Cattle & Team for $100.00 at 6 per cent for 30 days, after which I went to see Mr Wells and negotiate for a half rate fare for the out fit. I have now concluded to have Mrs Smith accompany Mrs Crawford to Omaha. I wrote a letter to the Mother Superior at St Joseph Hospital in Omaha, stating the case as fully as I could.

I seen Dr Waller about his bill against Crawford for treating his wife. I tried to get a dress for Mrs Crawford from Mrs Barber[,] the custodian of the ladies aid society box but she was not at home. on my way home I called at Mrs Carters and found the Children had measels. I did not stay long. on my way homeward from there I made an outside call on Mrs Simmons baby—[.] I called on Mrs Mears to see about a change of girls[.] I wrote a letter to Wm Jones at Glen Rock[,] Wyo Territory telling him about the present condition of his half brothers and sisters since his fathers death.

the case of Squire T Harney & Son vs Burr Shelton came on for hearing and the Defendant made special apperance and objected to the jurisdiction of the Court in the case on account of the Defendant not having been served proper. the Defendant moved the

Court to dismiss this case without prejudice to future action, which I done and upon suit having been brought new, I issued summons myself and gave them to C J Davis for service[.]

Feb 11. To day I have been very busy getting things ready to get Mrs Crawford away to Omaha. I had a horse nearly all day. I got Dr Waller['s] claim settled up by a 60 days note. the Rail Road Co gave me good rates for Mrs Crawford and Nurse. Mr Crawfords Brother was in and helped to get Mrs Crawford on board the Cars[.] I went up to see Mrs Barber and had her give me a dress for Mrs Crawford. I got Miss Fleming to come and try to alter it but it would not fit so we had to take her the best I could. The City Council met this evening and done more business in one hour and half than ever before at any previous meeting. the City Atty was present and as usual made an ass of himself[.]

Feb 12[.] I worked on the Kass Books a little[.] in the afternoon I called on Mrs Shelley to see their baby.— All the Saloons Closed and kept Closed all day. In the evening I called on Geo Havens at the news store and asked him to go to Church with me, but he refused so I went alone.

Feb 13. I received a letter from J. W. Dysart stating that Mrs Crawford could not get into the St Josephs Hospital at present so I telegraphed at once to the Mother Superior to find out what has been done about the case. Parks was in the office. I handed an Execution to Sheriff Dahlman against John Root.

Feb 14[.] To day I stayed in the House a good deal. Mr Crawford came in to see how things were getting along[.] Fannie Powers & Pearl came in the office to file a complaint but they weakened when I required them to put up costs. The County Commissioners returned my Files of the democrat. Parks came in to see my again. I worked on the Kass books. Fred Poll is drinking like a fish again[.] Geo Havens and I missed going to the Skating rink. Geo has a bad cold and is making preperations to make himself a hot lemonade.xxxx

Geo and I just went down to Danielsons and had a mess of oysters.

Feb 15. To day has been a pleasant one again. Jimmy OHanlon came up in the office and wrote on the Typewriter. the City Council tried to meet to night but failed for want of a quorum, and thereupon adjourned to Monday evening next at 9 Oclock. I went up to the skating Rink to see the entertainment given by the Ladies Aid society of the Cong'l Church. while there I met Maher, Staley and Cook. we all had supper together.

Feb 16[.] Fine weather all day. Geo Havens has had a cold for the past 2 days and does not seem as getting much better. the Case of Havey & Sons vs Burr Shelton came up to day and a change of Venue was taken to O. H. Wilson. I acknowledged a Real Estate deed for OHanlon today. I was instructed by Dr Miller this afternoon that Mrs Smith had returned from Omaha yesterday morning so I went up to see her and find out why she had not reported before now. I worked on the Chadron Democrat till 6. P.M. Ricker & Houghton commenced suit against C F Yates before me.

Feb 17[.] I have been pretty busy all day. Mr Crawford came in from the country to day. I settled up with Mrs Smith and got a receipt for it. Casady got a Typewriter[.] the saloon men have all been raising hell about the Liquor Lisence. F Mechler has refused to pay up and the Mayor has given him till Nine Oclock in the morning to come to the centre.

Mr and Mrs Fred Wafful returned from Omaha. Mrs Dr Davidson & Son were in the City to day.

Fredericks the jeweler was in to see me about his partner the tailor having locked him out—[.] I sent him to ballard.

I have been drawing up Ordinances relative to disturbing the peace.

John Katen arrested "Old Missou" this afternoon and brought him up to jail[.] he will come up for trial tomorrow morning[.]

Feb 18. Missouri was brought into court this A.M. he plead guilty and paid [$]5.00 & costs[.]

Ira Longcore paid me a check for $25.00 in the case of Glover vs Striker.

Fredericks the jeweler and the old Tailor had a split up to day. Tom Madden let me ride his horse to day.

I settled up with Mrs Leach on the City pauper business.

G. A. Eckles started to commence suit before me for $200 and only offered 50 bonds. I kicked the case out of court.

Spargur & Fisher commenced suit against Rudulph Mann on accounts. John W Rank & John Root called in the Office this morning to overhaul me about having issued notice to Rank about costs. Rank was going to eat me raw. I did not fine him for Contempt but should have do so.

Fred Mechler tried to run a bluff on the City authorities, but the Marshall would not stand it. I called the City Atty in to look at some ordinances I had drawn up but he is to dumb to appreciate any good works.

Feb. 19. To day has been a fine day all through[.] I got up rather late on account of my wash not having been brought down from Mrs Smith. Geo Havens finally went and got it for me. John Ditto & Dan Vance called on me. I got a new pair pants from Selden.

Fred Poll is again drinking and I guess Kass will soon split up the business. I called on Mr and Mrs Simmons to day. After supper Geo & I came right home.

While I was going to supper, I seen a crowd in the restraunt next to Ginn & Blakeny and found Dr Lewis there, taken with a severe attack of heart disease[.]

Feb 20. To day the weather has been very nice. I worked on getting up ordinances all day. Jimmy OHanlon read for me. F.M. Mead got me to copy them. the Council met this evening and passed several ordinances. there was quite an attendence on the part of the prohibitionists. Messrs Wagoner[,] Chase, Van Lehen and [name missing] being present.

after Council I got Dorr to sign the Ordinances and then took them up to Hughes to sign them and have all ready to be set up tomorrow[.]

Feb 21. Court commenced to day. nothing however was done more than calling of the Docket and arranging times for the trial of certain cases.

This afternoon the Case of Chas Spottswood vs C F Yates was called and upon Defendant failing to appear, judgment was rendered by default for Plff accordingly before me.

Dr Gillespie came in to get me to speak to Hughes for a pass for him to go East on.

after supper I went up to Boyds to see about the Dog Tax and Tags from which place I went up to the Methodist Church festival where I met Messrs Maher, Cook and Ward, and spent a very pleasent evening at the Martha Washington Party.

Mr Cook and I returned home together. Geo Havens had preceeded me and I found him snuggly ensconed in my arm chair reading the news[.] It snowed a little toward 10 Oclock.

Feb 22. Clear weather again[;] the snow all disappeared to day. The sidewalks are being pushed as fast as possible. I have been in the Office all day not being able to wear my legs on account of a bad sore on my left stump[.] Geo H. got his checks ready for the Coat room to night[.] Bert Jossely brought me my breakfast[.] Jimmy OHanlon came up with a lot of soupe for my dinner.

last night at about the hour of 9 oclock Billy Wilson commenced to move the post office fixtures to

the new Brick Block on the Cor[ner of] 2nd and
Morehead Sts and this morning everybody was
surprised of the fact.

Master Elmer Hamm was in to see if I would give
him stable room but he failed. Mr Parks was in to see
me and I ordered him to make me a case to keep the
files of the "Democrat[,]" Journal and Advocate in.

Mrs Dunn was in to see me about a stray Cow
which she claimed to be taking care off and that Mrs
Base brown kept coming and turning the cow loose[.]
Notwithstanding she has no claim on said cow. A
Bartow came in and got me to write of some instructions
to the jury for Iowa Parties in the Clough case. little
Elmer Hamm got my supper for me. Geo went up to the
rink to attend the Coat room. about 8 Oclock the gang
over at Jim Owens having got old Gene Fields drunk,
put him up on a box and made a bonfire for him to
make a speech by. quite a crowd is at present listening
to his hara[n]gue[.]

Feb 23[.] The weather opened out fine this A.M.
Burley Hill came in the office to get "Copy" for the
democrat.

after dinner I sent over and had Burley Hill come
over for me to carry me over to the Democrat Office and
while there young Boyd came with my artificials all
fixed up.

after supper, I went up town a little and the
Council tried to have a meeting but were unable to get
a quorum. I went over to Carters and played some
games of pool.

Feb 24. To day has been a fine one[.] I went up
in Court and heard some testimony, and then went
down to Birdsalls stable to see Mr Wooden who had his
legs Cut off. John Katen resigned as night watch last
night.

My left leg is fast giving out and I guess I must
soon remain in the House.

Herman Brockway was in today to see about settling up his suit against Jackson.

the 2nd Case of Sandwich Mfg Co vs. Rudolphus Mann was continued to March 23rd[.] E Ricker Brought suit against F. Mechler for Ferdinand Westheimer & Sons of St Joe MO. after supper Atty Fisher came in the Office and had me copy some charges of the Court to the Jury in the Herbert Clough Case. C. D. Sayrs took supper with me at the Chadron house. Charley Wilson brought Joe Bush around to be sworn in as Night watchman.

Feb 25. Clear towards morning, but about noon it commenced snowing. the Cloug law suit went to the jury this afternoon. E. E. Bonnell was in town but I could not get to see him. Fisher came around early this morning to have some matters settled in the Charge of the Court to the jury. News is running around now that Affidavits will be sent in to the general Post office Department detremental to Billy Wilson—[.]

I went to see Teddy ONeal about making an affidavit about a letter of his which had lain in the Office since last but he seemed to be afraid to do anything.

Feb 26. I stayed in the House nearly all day. Judge Kinkaid came in early this morning to see how the jury were getting along. Mr Steens[,] Handy, Clay and myself and Cap Sweet all had dinner together at the Chadron House, after which we enjoyed a nice bottle of California wine. After Supper I went to Church with the Official reporter Mr Merrick. we attended the Congregational Church and while there James Cavanaugh interrupted the meeting by singing out some slang. Master Elmer Hamm has commenced to stay with me. he appears to be a bright boy and always willing to get around and do something[.]

Feb 27. The City attorney came in this morning and filed a complaint against James Cavanaugh for drunk and disorderly conduct last night and disturbing the District Court this morning[.] I gave him one dollar and costs with a good repremanding and Jimmie darlent will doo soo noo moore.

the Case of State vs Stockdale was tried today and the jury were only out 15 minutes to return a verdict of acquittal. Sayrs appeared for the defense[.] Fannie OLinn made her maiden essay this afternoon in Court.

Pete OHanlon commenced garnishee process against C. H. Watkins for board bill before me this morning. Depty County Clerk A. G. Shears came in the office this evening.

Feb 28. To day it stormed a little but cleared off towards noon.

Dr Gillespie came in and reported a case of sending obscene matter through the mails to one of his daughters. I referred him to W. S. Commissioners[.]

I copied District Court Journal for the Democrat to day. the Case of James English vs. Sanford C West was argued before the Judge to day and decided in favor of the Defendant, West.

2 Cases came up in Police Court for Drunk and disorderly Conduct which were disposed of in a hurry.

Feb 29. To day it Snowed nearly all day. I got out the summons agains[t] C H Watkins and gave it to OHanlon to send down to "Cody[.]" Loui Nathan closed out his business and Mrs Olinn has rented his store room.

Mar. 1. Cold and wintery all day. everybody in town is getting woke up to the fact they have to get a license for their dogs. The City Marshall is making things Hot for them. I have been busy a great part of the day making out licenses for the Citizens[.] After supper John Berry and James Dahlman came in to have a warrant for one Jake Rubbell for Felony.

Mar 2. The weather was clear and just a little bit Cold all day. an advertising agent came along and got the Council into a Job of advertising[.] I sent to the Journal for some more envelopes. in the afternoon I done some writing for Selden[.] L. C. Quigley came in and swore out a warrant against W. W. Gallup for renting his house to prostitutes. I issued a warrant for his arrest and delivered the same to Chas Wilson Depty Shriff.

the dog license is making every one come to the Centre for license[.]

Mar 3[.] To day has been a busy one again for the Marshall as he has made things interesting for the Dogs. the Case of State vs W. W. Gallup was called up in the my Court to day. the Deft plead guilty as charged. I fined him one dollar and Costs[.] Mr Fowler came over to see me and acknowledge some papers before me. W. W. Byington was around to see me and looked over my two dockets.

Mar 4. To day I did not go out much as I was unable to get my washing in time. So I Stayed in the Office all day and primed my desk and file case. Mr Shears Called on me during the afternoon. After supper Earl Hamm and I went up to Church.

Mar 5. C. H. Watkins came in and waived service of summons and special apperance and made an affidavit to the effect of his Marriage to a Mrs Haskens at Sturgis[,] Dak.

Tom Coffey has leased the room formerly occupied by the Post Office[.] after supper Mr Cook the Co expert Called on me and then I went up to the Fireman meeting at the Engine House where arraingments were made for a Ball on the 21st of March.

Mar 6. Fine day again. I got Mr Selden to give me some of his book accounts and we worked on it nearly all day. I also wrote out some letters for Charlie Allen for the K of P.'s and a petition to the Honorable Geo Manny penny asking for the restoration to his rights of H. C. Clifford. John Larsh is on a general drunk and round up and I guess he will get in trouble before morning. Jake Kass was in to see me this Evening[.]

Mar 7. To day I have been more or less Busy working over W A Seldens Book[.] Tom Madden and I took a ride behind his famous race horse. I Called on the Journal office to see about some land and lots. the Council held a meeting in my office this evening and allowed all my bills after which I went down to Carters.

the City Marshall came and made his head quarters on my bed and will no doubt sleep with me tonight.

Mar 8. To day has been a little Cold all day[.] there was quite a lively case of adultry before Justice O H Wilson[.]

Chas Allen left for Omaha this evening to attend the State Democrat Convention at Omaha.

The firm of C H King & Co was dissolved last week and J L Paul & Co take their place[.]

Mar 9. To day has been a pretty pleasent one although it started out this morning with a cold bleak Snow[.] I fell down by the Gun store this morning while going to the Post Office but did not hurt myself much. The City Council were to meet this evening but could get no quorum. Mike Ryan came in from the Table[.] I drew a draft on Mr Whittemore of Long Pine.

Mar 10[.] To day has been nice weather again. I worked on the Selden books all day and finally got Jim Paul to help me.

Mayor Hughes called to see me this Evening and we had quite a chat about politices[.]

I did not get time to attend the Young Men Republican Club which was organized this evening. Mr Shears came in to the office and reported the proceedings to me.

Mar 11. Sunday and a nice day right along. I stayed in the office a good deal of the day. in the afternoon I went up to see Mrs Simmons bably [baby] and after supper I went up to the Chapin house and got John Maher to go to the Methodist Church with me to hear Joe Critchfield speak. We done so and regretted not having gone up there.

Mar 12. To day has been nice and pleasant one. I got out Wm Kisers transcript for the District Court. Lute North was in town today. I went down to see Mr Hughes but found him gone to Long pine. I ordered some books and stationary from Chicago to day.

In the afternoon I helped Selden get his invoice out of new goods. after supper I went up to hear Joe Critchfield lecture which I enjoyed very much. I came home and took the money in the Taylor stwp[.] and put it in the safe.

Mar 13[.] Fine weather all day. I posted up on Kass & Co books. I went down to see Mayor Hughes about having an Interview printed. I recd a letter from Will Ruby of York[,] Penna. I got Selden to send and get some cuts for a tailor shop—[.] Politics is commencing to stir about on City elections and every body is anxious to know what the other is going to do. Tom Coffey opened up his saloon yesterday in great Blast. the prohibitionists seem to be loosing ground.

All the Brick Masons on the Court house quit work to day as J. V. Consaul and O H Placy came to Town.

Mar 14[.] Fine weather again. Mr Strouse[,] Editor of the Alliance Express came up from there and in the afternoon I took him over the Town and down to Bob Dicksons Saw Mill. I used J Kass & Co team to do it with.

this afternoon I and Chas Allen had a talk with A J Richardson who complained very hard against the present managment of the present Post Master Wilson of this place.

after a little while I called on Bisbee and Smith to get some advertising locals and there met Billy Wilson[.] his conversation pointed all the time to Allen, and nothing but Allen seemed to be in his head. I however kept from saying anything one way or the other.

The cases of Sandwich Mfg Co vs. Rudlophus Mann were continued to day in my Court to April 23—1888, by stipulation of Attys on both sides. E. S. Ricker commenced another suit before me against C. F. Yates for Chas C Spottswood.

Mip Ricker & Houghton commenced to clean up in front of their building and are getting railings put around the Basement enterances to their building on Main Street.

Mar 15. to day has been pleasant again. politics are stiring. the Democrat office got a railing put around the basement step. Selden got excited and blowed in $1.50 window money. the advocate paper has come out with a great boom against me. Tom Madden is standing back to see which side of the fence he shall get on. James Tucker is in Town under arrest[.] Old Wilson is getting the report around that I do not want the office of Police Judge[.]

Mar 16. today the Case of State vs O L Sloggy & others was called and the County Attorney asked the case to be continued to April 12 which was done. I went to the rink to the flag sociable[.]

Mar 17. St Patricks day in the mornin, and all day long. in the afternoon I took my Colt for exercise and while out I was called to my Office to make out warrants for Henry Stephen & his son who were charged with disturbing the peace[.] I continued the case to Monday Mar 19 and ordered the defendants to give bonds in the sum of $100.00 a piece which they done.

The political field for the Coming City Convention for City Officers seems to be in considerable turmoil since the past 24 hours. at that time Carley was sure of getting A C Putnam nominated for Mayor but within the last few hours he has concluded that the Hughes element are too strong for him and he has announced himself as drawing out Putnam and going for the City Treasurership himself, but this is right in the face of having told Carter that he (Carley) would fight Hughes first, last and always, and yet he wants Carter and all Carters strength to support him for Treasurer. How could such a thing Come to pass? I[t] is now the universal opinion on the streets that C C Hughes will be Mayor[,] L. J. F. Iaeger[,] Police Judge, J. Kass[,] Councilman from the 1st Ward[,] leaving Tom Glover and Jim Dahlman to name the 2nd Councilman to go for the 2nd Ward[.]

Tom Glover as Councilman in the 3rd Ward and either A W Crites or J. L. Paul in the 1st Ward[,] A. G. Fisher for City Clerk, A. A. Record for Treasurer and P. M. Pritchard City Engineer[.] I cannot say that I am going to have a walk away as the prohibitionists are all going to go against me in a body and all of Egan and West Second Street will be against me because I am a Main Street Man[.] however I shall let them know that I am alive and the Coyotes cannot say that I was tame game.

Mar 18. Sunday all day and still politics seems to be going right along[.] I called on Mayor Hughes during the afternoon after having first consulted with Tom Glover[.] Hughes seemed perfectly satisfied with the ticket I placed before him[.]

Mar. 19. Fine weather again all day and City Politics in full Blast[.] the Brick Bank gang are very uneasy and Carley the leader has at last decided that two tickets must go in the field as he will receive or make no concessions for the Peoples' ticket. J W Smith has been discarded by the Republican gang of which he was a full blown member but because he did not believe in a political issue and wanted to pick men that were acceptable unto a majority of the people they kicked him out. this evening the Republican forces held a meeting in the Court House and I am told they resolved one and all to vote the straight republican ticket no matter what becomes of the waterworks issue.

Mar 20[.] Snowed during the later Part of the day but in spite of all the advocates of the peoples

Convention stood staunch and true for a meeting tonight[.] the case of Spottswood vs Yates went by default today. I attended the hearing of the case of State vs Posphisal charged with Cutting one Henry Stephens with intent to kill[.] the defendant was bound over to the District Court[.] after supper I commenced getting things ready to attend the Peoples Convention at the Rink and adjourned thither where by 9 O'clock all the principal business men of Chadron were congregated[.] A. W. Crites was choosen Chairman by a unanimous vote. the following Parties were nominated without a particle of opposition excepting the office of City Clerk for which position J W Smith and A G Fisher were Cand[id]ates and upon a vote of the House J W Smith was Choosen. C C Hughes for Mayor, A A Record for Treasurer, J W Smith for Clerk[,] L J F Iaeger[,] Police Judge, J. L. Paul for Councilman from the 1st Ward, Kass & Hood from the second ward and T. H. Glover from the 3rd Ward.

P. M. Pritchard[,] City Engineer[.]

Thos Glover and Wm Wilson were renominated for the school board. the convention thereupon adjourned to Carters salon to meet the incoming gravel trains drawn by Engineer Fowler of one leged fame.

Mar 21. Snowed last night. Willie Mead slept with me. I thought I was going to have the measels this morning[.] I however felt all right after having been up a while: The Case of Samuel Westhiemer vs Florian Mechler came up and was continued for 30 days upon affidavit[.] Geo Haven came around and got the Checks to get the hat and Coat room in order.

after supper I went up to attend the firemans ball. we had a nice time[.] Geo Havens slept with me.

Mar 22[.] today has been a fine one again. Col W. H. McCann was in the city and returned right back again to Hay springs[.] today I helped get the Democrat out afterwhich I took my colt out for exercise[.] I had quite a time with the horse I was ridding as my saddle turned with me. Hon[.] W. H. Westover came up from Rushville to day. Joe Ford is getting ready to put in a barber shop in the old Coffey Saloon.

Willie Mead has just come in and will sleep with me.

Mar 23[.] To day has been pleasent again all day[.] I recd a package from the Lincoln State Journal. in the afternoon I wrote on the Typewriter for Spargur & Fisher and also Mary Powell and while thus engaged Mr Chas Pearson of Crawford came in to see about Getting one of Mrs Jones little step Children. I droped all my work and went right out in the Country with Mr Pearson to Mrs Jones who we found hard at work plowing. We soon made the desired arraingments to take a 10 year old lad of[f] her hands as she seemed anxious to get rid of the little chap.

Upon our arrival in Chadron and after supper I took the youth to a barber shop while his future father went and bought him some clothes. I scrubbed him from head to foot and having got him all dressed I took him up to the skating rink where the Chadron Public School Children were giving an entertainment and also to see his sister Nellie who is going to school and being cared for by good Mrs D. Y. Mears[.]

the 2 Children seemed glad to see each other once more, but the lateness of the evening prevented them being together much. I however promised to bring the lad up to bid his sister good by in the morning early as Mr Pearson starts at 9 A.M. for his home near Crawford.

The Dawes County Journal came out this evening with a long rigmarole of stuff against me tending to dishonor my character as much as possible[.]

Mar 24. the weather started out nice but towards evening it commenced getting cold and rained a little[.] I recd a bill of books from the Skeen Stuart stationary Co for Seldens benefit[.]

the day has been greatly occupied by local politicians. I had a long talk with I. N. Harbaugh and found out some reasons for certain parties kicking against me.

Adrew J. Richardson came in from the Country to day and made an affidavit against the Present Post Master[,] Wm A Wilson, relative to handling and delivering the mails. C W Dresser came in the office in the interests of a Garnishee suit against Larry Costello, who is now working on the Chicago and Northwestern Rail Road Company. 10[:]30 P.M. it is snowing hard[.]

Mar 25th[.] to day I stayed in the office all day & evening. it snowed right along all day. Henry Miller came in and made my bed for me. I took the Scientific American over for Cleona Josselyn to look at. Henry went over after supper to get them. I borrowed a lamp from Mrs Kass this evening. I wrote a communication for the Chadron Democrat regarding certain statements in the advocate about my self, also a card to C J Davis explaining myself for his benefit on the coming election[.]

Mar 26. stormed all day. I had Hughes sign some warrants for myself and Mrs Leach on the poor fund. Henry Miller commenced staying in my office this week[.] he appears to be anxious to learn some thing[.]

Ole Hughes came to see me about dinner time and He and Allen and myself had a long conflab about the coming Election issue. Geo Havens commenced working for D Y Mears Bakery. I wrote a letter to Tom.

Mar 27. Clear weather almost all day, but the snow commenced melting towards afternoon. J Kass went up to Crawford for a few days[.]

Tony Whitfield came down from Douglas to day. the Crawford City Officers were all in attendance upon Judge Powers Court to witness a Case of Habes Corpus argued by W H H Westover and who succeeded in getting his client released. C. D. Sayrs represented the State but notwithstanding any arguments that Sayrs might have put up as it was plainly visable that Powers was going to turn him loose anyway. Geo Havens came along towards evening but did not stay any length of time.

Marshall Mahoney came up from Carters with me and we had a long talk.

Mar 28. to day the weather has been very changable and towards evening it snowed a little during the day[.] I sold a [$]30.00 Claim to Tom Moore and bought a [$]27.00 warrant from Dr Miller for $17.55 which I turned again again for $22.95 and loaned Chas Allen $15[.]00[.] Judge James A Wilson came down on Main Street to-day and informed me that he was going to do all in his power to help me to get elected. I have as yet failed to swallow the dose and will wait to see if anything is done in furtherance of that kind of a promise before declaring myself. Mr Barnett the feed man buried his wife from the Episcopal Church on Main St to-day. quite a concourse were gathered in the Church.

Mar 29. To day has been another eventful one all along the political front[.] the line has surely drawn itself to a solid front for Hughes and Bear and the Peoples Ticket[.] this afternoon quite an interesting gang awaited the arrival of the Democrat and so soon as it was published the Journal was satisfied.

Dr Jackson attended the case of Mrs Bakers Child and reported the case to me as deserving aid from the City[.] I looked the matter up and found it deserving charity and acted accordingly—[.] Dell Annis came up from Rushville today.

during the day I had Snyders dray haul my stove from Mrs. Leaches Hotel to Mrs Bakers house[.]

Mar 30. Nice weather again, but politics are booming and everybody is looking out for the Dawes County Journal boodlers to come out But the Journal cannot come out as they had to waite for the Democrat to come out, so as to have something to write about. the advocate came out however regulur as usual, but shot away from the political nock and left every body alone.

I had a long talk with Atty Harbaugh about Hughes being qualified for may[or] and during the conversation I seen that Mr Harbaugh was anxious to become the next City Atty, a matter well worth the consideration of the next Council, as Mr Harbaugh is a man all the way through and not in the least afraid to speak up and above board.

Mar 31. Well, today the Dawes County Journal came out and with it came the certain collapse of all future hope of the Republican party so far as City government of Chadron can be spoken of. the Editor of the Journal shows his great love for me in flowing words of Vulgarity and brings himself fully before the people as a first class blackguard. After supper I got John Maher to go up with me to attend the Republican Ratification meeting at the Court House where we found a small crowd of republicans and a good many who have already identified themselves in favor of the peoples ticket[.] a great many sore heads were however there and appeared to lead the entire meeting through all its transaction. Not much business of importance was transacted nevertheless and in spite of the fact that Bartow, Dorrington[,] Clark[,] Davis[,] Messenger & Cook done most of the howling[.]

after the meeting adjourned[,] Maher & I went up to the M. E. Church to attend an Egg festival where we met Geo Havens.

After that left out we came home and Maher and I transcribed his short Hand notes of the Republican Ratification meeting on [the] Typewriter after which Geo & I went to bed[.]

April 1. april fools day and many are the children I fooled too. Geo and I got up rather late.

I worked around the office all forenoon and in the afternoon I called on Mrs Simmons and while there Mrs Danielson[,] Miss Weber and Mrs Paxton came, whereupon I left and called on Mayor Hughes where I met Hon[.] A W Crites of the Land office[.]   before starting out on the aforesaid visits I turned my office over to J W Smith and John Maher for them to write up articles in reply to Egans last paper for a special edition of the Democrat which will come out on the morning of the day of Election[.]

After supper Geo & I went up to the Congl Church to witness Easter service of the Sunday School[.] After coming home Maher came in and translated a speech of J W Smith which he composed in my office this afternoon.

April 2[.] Every thing is commencing to boom for election.   I sent up and got some more muslin for playcards to help down the Republican ticket[.]   I also took Dr Jackson down to see Mrs Donoughe again and got Mrs Paxton to go and see what she needed, but while Mrs Paxton told me she also informed me that Mrs Donoughe was a queer woman[.]   Oppertunity Hank came down from Crawford this evening and the Marshall run him in forthwith.   About 9 Oclock this evening the Democrat commenced running off an Extra Edition for the benefit of having the last say at the polls tomorrow.   I have Geo Haven, Henry Miller[,] De Forrest Richards and Guy and Charlie Goodnough engaged to carry the extra about town early tomorrow morning.

April 3.   To day the weather has been fine right through till towards 8 Oclock P.M. when a high wind storm set in and raged all night in great fury as if in keeping with the Republican Party whom the People Slaughtered promiscuosly at the polls to day.

I got up pretty early and got all my streamers out on the streets and on teams.

We then organized in the first ward and got the polls opened by 9 Oclock P.M. [A.M.]   Geo Clark, A. Bartow and F O Messenger figured promiscuosly in trying to organize the first ward polls, but notwithstanding that they succeeded in getting a man on the board as judge who was to have been one of the Challenge Committee for the Republican party. Nevertheless the peoples ticket received a goodly proportion of Judges and Clrks[.] Geo Clark was the head man to Challenge, while I stayed along side to see that it was Carried out right on the part of the peoples ticket. about noon, however[,] Bartows knees weakened and Geo Clark commenced to want to walk around, but the peoples ticket kept coming in slowly but surely—. the Judges in the First ward were, G. A. Eckles, John Knoll and Daniel Burns. the Clerks being Mr Fraley and Geo Clay. All the wards by 4 Oclock looked very Blue for the Republicans and a good many of them were wont to get on a bender. All day however passed of[f] smoothly and not a drunken man showed up.

James Cavanaugh came out of Jail to day and got Jimmy OHanlon to go his security for his fine and Cost. the Polls closed at 7. Oclock P.M. and soon the Count Showed for a certainty in favor of the Peoples ticket as follows.

THE PEOPLE WIN.
Water Works and Good Gov-
ernment Insured
THE VOTE BY WARDS.

The election last Tuesday passed off pleasantly. There was considerable excitement, but mostly of a friendly nature. The polls opened at 9 o'clock a.m., and were closed at 7 p.m. The total number of votes cast were 427, most of which were cast for the people's ticket. The "only true republicans" had their straight ticket in the field, and every effort possible was made on their part to elect it, but it was so exceedingly "straight" that it bursted and scattered its sweetness on the desert air, and the people's ticket won all the way through with the exception of one councilman from the third ward, who was beaten by four votes—merely an accident. The following is the vote cast:

FIRST WARD.

For Mayor—
C. C. Hughes...131
A. G. Putnam.. 40
For Councilman—
J. L. Paul...123
F. M. Mead... 42
For Treasurer—
A. A. Record...117
W. C. Brown... 53
For Clerk—
J. W. Smith..104
A. G. Fisher.. 65
For Engineer—
P. M. Pritchard...117
J. W. Boyd... 54
For Police Judge—
L. J. F. Iaeger..131
O. H. Wilson... 38
For Water Bonds...170

SECOND WARD.

For Mayor—
C. C. Hughes... 79
A. C. Putnam.. 48
For Councilmen—
J. Kass... 75
Robt. Hood... 77
P. J. Breen... 49
J. P. Cook.. 41
For Treasurer—
A. A. Record... 90
W. C. Brown... 37

For Clerk—
J. W. Smith.. 81
A. G. Fisher.. 47
For Engineer—
P. M. Pritchard.. 78
J. W. Boyd... 47
For Police Judge—
L. J. F. Iaeger.. 83
O. H. Wilson.. 42
For Water Bonds..123

THIRD WARD.

For Mayor—
C. C. Hughes... 62
A. C. Putnam.. 63
For Councilman—
T. H. Glover... 56
D. Y. Mears... 60
For Treasurer—
A. A. Record.. 72
W. C. Brown... 53
For Clerk—
J. W. Smith... 62
A. G. Fisher.. 58
For Engineer—
P. M. Pritchard... 58
J. W. Boyd.. 66
For Police Judge—
L. J. F. Iaeger... 60
O. H. Wilson.. 61
For Water Bonds..121

MAJORITIES.

C. C. Hughes...121
J. L. Paul.. 81
J. Kass... 26
Robt. Hood.. 36
D. Y. Mears... 4

A. A. Record...136
J. W. Smith.. 77
P. M. Pritchard.. 86
L. J. F. Iaeger..133

SCHOOL DIRECTORS.

T. H. Glover and William Wilson were elected school directors, but by what majority we are unable to learn until the official count of the votes is made.

The republican ticket was beaten in this city Tuesday by a majority of nearly a hundred and fifty, fully half as much of a majority as the republican ticket had in the county last fall. Now will the men and paper who dubbed the people's ticket a democratic ticket and denounced the republicans who names appeared on it as not belonging to their party, call it a democratic victory?

The people's ticket won. The two men that the Journal made its fight against—namely: Mayor Hughes and Police Judge Iaeger—especially came off with flying colors, and in the Third Ward, the great republican "strong-hold," the republican candidate for mayor had only one majority, and their candidate for councilman from that Ward was elected by barely four majority. Charley Elliott was the "challenge committee" for the people in that Ward, and he deserves much credit for the manner in which he attended to business.

It now devolves on the Journal to furnish an affidavit setting forth in unmistakable terms the fact that there was a republican ticket in the field Tuesday, as the majority of our citizens—those who authorized the "red-eyed" handbills and either attended or co-operated with the people's convention—refuse to believe it. It will be remembered that THE DEMOCRAT branded the republican movement as a case of mistaken identity between Dawes county and Chadron. A few sanguine gentlemen—who were troubled with a disease that just at present is quite prevalent among republicans, i.e. overwrought enthusiasm—thought that because they elected county commissioners last fall they could do anything, and following this line they were going to "sweep Chadron as sleek as the sidewalks on Bordeaux street." All the little incidents above mentioned "linger 'round the memory still," but what are the prognostications of a common democratic paper compared with the brilliant foresight of some of the republican leaders of this city!

We wish to make a note of the fact that the recently elected police judge, L. J. F. Iaeger, the "pet candidate," holds office for two years.

No incident of any consequence occurred here on election day, except the pulverizing of the republican ticket for the second time in the history of the city.

A CARD

I hereby desire to tender my thanks to the Dawes County Journal for the able manner in which it assisted me to secure the office of police judge, not only by a handsome majority but by running ahead of my ticket. I am the cowboy who followed the "cattle" into green pastures. L. J. F. IAEGER.[1]

---

[1]*The Chadron Democrat*, April 3, 1888(?).

April 4th. to day I put in going around and treating people and seeing all the cronies. I went all over Town. everybody is feeling rejoiced at the defeat of the Brick Bank Ring. I tried to get a meeting of the Council, but it was no go as Carley would not come[.]

April 5. The Democrat came out late tonight so we could not get it into the post office[.] I have been very busy all day sending off "Extra" Democrat Papers. Dr Lease came to Town. the Brick Bank Gang are a sore crowd. Another attempt to have a meeting of the Council met with utter failure on account of Carleys absence[.] John Maher came and had me help him take testimony of[f] on the Typewriter[.]

April 6. Fine weather all day. Bob Dorr left to go on a few days hunting trip. Chas Mann came in to the office toward noon and while in an alarm of fire was started which proved to be A Weber & Son's Hay barn in the rear of their store on Main Street—[.] the fire department soon put the flames out which would have proved disasterous to Coffey and Carters saloons had the engine been 5 minutes later in getting started. A Weber had D. Burns arrested after dinner but the affair proving to be a long seried volum[e] of family troubles & broils[,] I therefore paid very little heed to the same. Miss Florence Wilson came around this afternoon and requested my services at the Rink tonight to keep order during her Musical entertainment of her Music Scholars[,] so at 7[:]30 I hied myself up to the skating rink after a great effort as I hurt my knee this afternoon during the fire. I was well pleased with the entertainment and after eating a large dose of Ice Cream I returned home to find that the City Council had not met during my absence[.]

April 7. Fine day again[.] I had some words with Wilbur about the fine of D Burns. everything in town is moving off nicely since the election. The City Council endeavored to meet this evening but owing to the absence of Bob Dorr the Clerk[,] they could accomplish nothing whereupon they adjourned to Monday evening—[.]

Apr 8. I went to Church in the morning and stayed for Sunday School. Took Dinner at the Chapin House after which I made a call on Mrs Carters Family and from there I went to Mr & Mrs Simmons to see the baby and while there I played Crocequet with Geo[.]

Apr 9. fine day again. I commenced to whop up some of the Council up about getting the Election returns Ca[n]vassed[,] also made out some bills for Selden and collected some. John Maher came up to the Office this evening and gave me a lesson in short hand. the Case of Spottswood vs Yates was continued to April 13th at one oclock.

Apr 10th. Fine day again—[.] the 2nd Case of Spottswood vs. Yates came on for hearing and was continued to April 13th at one oclock P.M. I wrote a letter to John A McShane for Charley Allen.

I again called on the Mayor to impress on him the necessity of having the City Ballots canvassed according to law in the absence of an ordinance relative thereto in order to protect the validity of the history of the bonds which were voted for waterworks[.] R. M. Stanton came in the office and had a long talk with me relative to City Gover[n]ments.

Apr 11. fine day again. I worked a little on J Kass & Co books. done a good deal of rustling around looking after the City Atty to find out what he was doing relative to the history of the water bonds.

Bob Dorr has still failed to turn up.— last night quite a Cutting affray occurred in Carters in which Fred Danielson accidentally cut himself in the leg while trying to make a bad mans play—[.] D. H. Hoage came up from Antelope to day and had me make out his Bill against Dawes County for witness fees.— I took Cullivaie up to the stable to see my pony. Smith & Ecackler were in the office this evening[.]

Apr 12. Fine weather all day. I wrote to Brother Charles in Portland[,] Ore. Changed my mattrass and helped on the Democrat—[.] Maher and his people were in the office this evening studying Short hand. a few days ago quite a cutting affray took place at Carters in which Fred Danielson got the worst of it.

W H Carter went down to his Ranch a few days ago to take his family there for a short trip[.] the case of State vs O L Sloggey and State vs Fred Danielson & Others came up today and upon Failure of the County Atty to appear to prosecute, and the prosecution witness being absent I dismissed the case at cost of the State of Nebraska[.]

Apr 13. nice day again[.] I went up to the County Clerks office and read the minutes of the County Commissioners proceedings and found that my bond was missing[.]

Geo Haven brought home some old style walnuts which he and I ate in the office. I tried the case of Spottswood vs Yates to day and after long arguments of Counsel I decided the Case in favor of Yates, the Defendant.

I sent word to Mr Bartow in the evening to come and long [look] at my docket to see if the judgment complied with the facts of the case as presented—which he did!

Apr 14. Nice day again. I have been very busy to day working on a Case of Appeal to the Supreme Court of Hiram G McMillan vs DeForrest Richards on Contest of Election for the office of County Treasurer.

Thomas Madden had me transact some business for him[.] After supper I made out my report of the Police Court for the past year, after which I went and got some old socks and had them sewed up to wear.—

L Barnett was buried to day from the episcopal Church[,] his wife having died some 2 weeks ago and it is very evident that he has simply worried himself to death.

Ed Cameron called me to the Land Office this afternoon to identify the signatures of Timothy, Charles and Martin Morrissy. I identified the former in person and by my Dockets the 2nd[.] I was unable to swear to but Identified his signature by my Docket. The 3rd party I was unable to identify.— Quite an excitement took place on bordeaux st this evening after supper in the shape of a foot race in which it seems one of the runners refused to go when tapped off by the starter.

Apr 15. Nice weather till about 2 P.M. when a high wind came up and is still blowing hard. The Base Ballists played this afternoon[.] I went out to see them but did not stay long on account of the wind.

I attended Church at the Congtn'l Church and went to lunch with Rev Powell where I was introduced to Miss Bryant[.] I went from there and called on Mr and Mrs Burly C Hill and from there called on Mr D. E. Havens to see about plowing some lots for me.

Apr 16. The weather today has been stormy more or less all day. I went to see Mayor Hughes in the afternoon. Charlies Oregon friend called on me. I got him to take my Colt down to Dressers pasture where I turned it loose. This evening at the Chadron house quite an altercation took place between a Colored Gambler (C.C.) and J H Culivan which ended in the Colored man having to leave the table at which Culivan was sitting and to which the Colored man undertook to set down to. the City Council tried to have a special meeting tonight but failing to have a quorum they adjourned. Robt Hood the Councilman from the 2nd for the short term, Qualified.—

Apr 17. Nice day again. I worked all day nearly for Fisher on sundry accounts with the typewriter.— Larry Costellos sister came in and paid the [words missing]

Apr 18. Nice weather[.] I turned my colt into Dressers Lot by the Rail Road. This evening just a little before supper quite an exciting foot race took place on

Bordeaux St. between a colored man and W C Browns Butcher in which the latter got beat.

The Council met this evening and passed an ordinance fixing the salaries for the next Council[.] during the passage of this ordinance there was a great scheme let out by F B Carley whose sole ambition seemed to be to leave the City Council for the coming year in as bad a condition as it could be possible for him to do[,] without, as he thinks, anyone getting on or tumbling to his scheme, but his actions are always plainer than words and consequently he always has, and it is very evident always will be set down upon by any good thinking Citizen—who cannot help seeing Carleys ever one rule of Rule or Ruin policy sticking out in all his features while arguing upon any point of public trust[.]

Apr 19. Fine weather again all day. Early this morning I went down to the Douglas train and got a poor woman on the train for Douglass who claims to have a son working in Douglass[,] Wyo. I made her take a sealed letter for the Conductor and not having a ticket I knew he would not put her off. I asked the assistance of the Council but was refused rather buffly[.] The Democrat came out today again and kept me busy nearly all day.

the Council undertook to meet this evening but no quorum being present they adjourned.

Apr 20. Chas Wilson swore out a warrant for Oppertunity Hank on Vagrancy. I suspended Judgment till tomorrow evening. Johny Higgins and Tony Bernard had a set too early this AM. and Higgins appears to have got the worst of it—no arrests were made[.]

Fred Poll is at present very sick and staying at the Chadron House, He having had the Jim Jams pretty bad. Johny Katen and Julius Haler are in attendance on him.

quite an accident occurred down the line of the F.E. & M.V.R.R.—a freight train in which was some car loads of Horses caught fire and 8 head of fine animals were burned to a crisp before any help could be procured.

Charley Elliott came in the office and raised hell about the Marshall having ordered Opportunity Hank out of Town but if he thinks he is going to run the office of Police Judge he is off his nuttshell.

The Council tried to have a meeting this evening but failed to get a quorum, so they adjourned to [date missing] every April after they adjourned. I had a long talk with Mayor Hughes regarding matters in general for the best of all concerned.

Geo Havens did not stay here this evening so I went down to Carters a little while.

Apr 21. Nice day again. I helped Vickery to make some Bases for the Chadron Base Ball Club. After dinner I went to Mr Webers funeral at the Catholic Church and then over to C J Davis barn to see the horses that were burnt in the late rail Road wreck near Valentine. The animals were a pitiful sight to behold. A horse Race for $800.00 was the next thing on the Programme, which took till 7 oclock—Bert Smith was thrown from Sperlings Mare. he was considerably bruised about the head Geo. Livingston lent me his horse to get my Colt out of Dressers pasture, which I and Geo Havens are going to take out to A. C. Fowlers on the Table tomorrow. After supper I made out Mr Seldens Reports as Treasurer of Long Pine, Neb. Mayor Hughes sent up work to see fisher. Geo was just taking a bath and Mr Selden is in the office—as soon as he leaves I will also take a bath and go to sleep too.

Apr 23 Yesterday Geo and I started for Fowlers at 7 AM. with the Colt leading behind the Buggy, but after getting beyond Chadron Creek a few miles the Gentle Colt refused to lead any further so we let [left] it at I. I. Clemins place and made the trip to Fowlers anyway, where we arrived by 12[:]45 P.M. having gone by way of Harry Deans up the Dead Horse.

After Dinner Mr Fowler invited Geo & I to go to his Homestead 2 miles South of his place which we done. This evening Geo and I went to the Opera House.

Apr 25. the City Marshall swore out a Complaint this afternoon against O. H. Wilson and Van Lehen charging them with not having paid License last night for the Opera House. I continued the Case till tomorrow morning. The Council met in my office this evening but on account of the absence of J Kass they adjourned till tomorrow morning at 8 oclock AM. It rained a little this afternoon.

Apr 26[.] The Council met this morning and passed an Ordinance for the calling of a bond Election for $35,000.00. During the meeting the Managing committe of the Odd Fellows called on me to see about taking charge of the Hat Room which was soon adjusted.

I helped on the Democrat again and after supper Geo and I went to the Opera House to run the Hat Room, but there we found Van Lehen making a hell of a mess because he found we were going to make a few dollars and D. Y. Mears helped him as much as possible but all to no purpose as the Managing Committee soon quelled such proceeding and showed Van Lehen who was boss.

George went up to the Church for supper and Got me some fine eatables which I ate in the Hat Room. the ball was a success all around[.]

Apr 27. G W Reed called around to the office and handed me a pie of which I spoke very highly to him last night. towards evening it rained a little[.] John Maher came in after supper and Geo came along about the same time with Strawberries and after having a feast we all went to the Opera House to see Damon and Pythias which we enjoyed very much.

[Apr] 28. This morning it was snowing when I got up and continued so all day. it was a damp snow. at 10 AM. the case of Samuel Westhiemer vs Florian

Mechler came on for trial and the Court rendered Judgment for the Plff. the Post Office inspector was here to day and raised merry Hell with Post master Wilson and every body in town is on to the racket that something is going to happen [to] the post office and very naturally take it to be a change of location. Geo & I went to the Opera House to see Foggs Ferry—it rained a little this evening. Jas. A. Wilson died today at 3 P.M.

Apr 29[.] Nice day but rather muddy. I worked on the Selden books the greater part of the day. Not much of anything transpired through the day. I understand that Justice James A Wilson will be taken to Mt Vernon[,] IA. for burial. his death is to be regretted in some ways while it cannot be supposed that he is any the worse off now.

I am indeed sorry I was not permitted to show him the gratitude I owed him for his unceasing labor in my behalf at the last election day in which he spared no pains in doing all in his utmost power that I should be elected in which he was more pleased than myself at my final success.

John Berry was in Town today. Vincent Lloyd came down from Douglas. Cary Smith (alias Lance Smith) came up from Denver. I spoke to Carter about purchasing the Bob Dickson lots on Main St. Jake Kass returned from a jaunt through the Black Hills where he has been on a visit to old time friends.

April 30th. Tony Bernard got out Carters License this AM. W. A. Selden reported having lost a Gold watch yesterday, it having been taken from his office desk yesterday eve. R. S. Hawley came in the office and got a petition for Liquor license.

May lst. Today I have been busy getting the Hat room ready for the ball given by the Conductors[.] the City has been crowded with strangers all day waiting for the festivities to commence. after supper I repaired to the rink where everything was action.

May 2. this morning at 4[:]30 AM. the last dance closed the ball. Geo & I came home and Geo went straight to getting out his Newspapers. after going down to Carters and seeing all the boys I came home and went to bed about 7 oclock and got up about 11[:]30 AM.

quite a little racket occurred last night at the rink between the night watch man and Chas Elliott. the latter abused the night watch considerably—and seems to make it a great point always to abuse an officer of the law.

Apr [May] 3. To day Mr Chas Pearson came down from Crawford and brought the Jones Boy (Charley) with him and asked me to take him back as he could do nothing with him. Charley seemed much surprised at the affair and said he did not want to go home to his Step Mother. he cried very much. I took him over to Mr Selden and got him to Consent to keep him a few days to see what can be done with him for obedience[.]

I had the stove removed from the office and cleaned the office out by giving it a regular annual Scrubbing[.] the City Council met this evening and after having allowed some bills and commented on the liquor license question and Occupation tax, they confirmed the Nominations of the Mayor by appointing Charles L Wilson as Marshall and A. G. Fisher for City Atty. In the appointment of City Atty. quite a speech was made by Mr Smith the New City Clerk in Favor of Major Powers for City Atty. than whom non[e] other he claimed could fill the important office so well. The Mayor listened attentively to the Oratorical debate and upon its close, he politely informed the Clerk that without any disrespect to him or his seeming favorable speech, he nevertheless could not nominate him. quite a lull ensued in the Council which was finally broken by the suggestion of Mr Mears Councilman from the 3rd Ward that he thought the Mayor should have a preference in appointments. this was the general opinion of the Council which was followed by the confirmation of the Mayors choice.

Apr [May] 4. this morning I took Charley Jones up to Miss Bryants School and gave her instructions as to what treatment to give him. I purchased a slate for him and if the Child can be made anything of, I shall do all in my power to aid him, as I know from experience the wants and trials of an Orphan.

After supper I went up to the Congregational Church to hear Mrs Ann Moore give Elocutionary readings—John Maher and Mr Petterson accompanied me.

May 5[.] The weather started in on a rainy scale and continued so all day. the Republican County Convention was held at the Court House this afternoon. I ordered John Maher to go up and take notes on the case.

The City Council met this evening upon which occasion I fixed up the office adjoining mine on account of there being a stove there, as the weather was rather cold. The Saloon Men were in attendance and Gottstein and Carter were much disappointed at the Council having cut the $1000.00 license down to $500.00 and levying an Occupation Tax of $200.00 on saloons. I filed my bond and was sworn in as Police Judge.

I am in receipt of a great many letters from the East relative to revolver shooting. I also received one from Charles J Page of 82 Davonshire Street[,] Boston.

May 6. Still raining incessantly. about 9 oclock this morning the front Basement wall on the outside of the Sidewalk of Ricker houghton & Eckles building caved in with considerable force and smashed things in general for the the Democrat office. I took up my abode in the office next door to mine and sent word up to John Maher to come down and give me the proceedings of the Republican Convention yesterday, which he done. Charles Allen returned from Omaha yesterday morning.

May 7[.] Nice day today[.] James Cavanaugh commenced putting in the Stone foundation for Ricker & Houghton.

Dr Harris very kindly started to Omaha with R B Danielson whose eye is in a bad condition from an careless oversight of R. S. Hawley, the 2nd street druggist. the action of Harris in this affair is altogether commendable as that of a man, as he is doing all in his power for Mr Danielsons welfare concerning the defect made by Mr Hawley, but it does seem as if a Druggist would, to say the least, after having made a Mistake repair at once to the injured party and try to make amends instead of which I am informed by Mr Danielson that Mr Hawley never came near him untill after several days illness —let it be hoped for the best and that the eyesight of Mr Danielson may be restored[.] John Maher and his Short hand people were in the office this evening[.] Geo carried water and got things all in shape for a bath. Mr T H Glover had a large lot of supplies spoiled by the flooding of his cellar under his store during the recent rain storm.

May 8. Nice weather again. G. A. Eckles is putting a force of Carpenters to work fixing up the front of his building preparitory to putting up his awnings[.] this evening I went to the rink to hear Monte Cristo played. It was a failure[.]

May 9. Nice day all day. I got out Transcripts in the Case of Spottswood vs Yates and have them ready for demand of the attys for Plff.

I bought a canary bird from Mrs Kass for $3.00 and yesterday I put a man to work on Mr Records lot putting in potatoes and lettuse and radishes[.] this morning the man was around and wanted his money[—] $2.00 for work. I wrote a letter to Brother Thomas and my niece Cassie to day.

James Dahlman was in the office today[.]

James Connelly came up to see me about making a bargain to get his house on bordeaux street up on Main St for an office for my self.

May 10. rainy all day. I worked on the Democrat but on account of getting in press late the list did not get out till late—and we did not take it to the Post Office[.] I got my Canary from Mrs Kass. I sent the hair eyed kid to jail.

May ll[.] To day it has been pretty cold[.] I done considerable rustling around. A C. Fowler was in Town and I went up to Hoods lumber yard to see him. I got a nice letter from Cassie this morning.

this afternoon I took Charlie Jones up to the Barber Shop and made him undress and I had him scrubbed from head to foot[.] Mr Selden has notified me to get him another place. I drew a draft in favor of Mr Selden for Jas M. Hays Woolen Mills Company for $200.00. this morning rumor got out that Billy Wilson was going to resign and in order to head any false move off that might possible be made by the Republicans.

Charley Allen had me write a letter to John McShane in regard to certain movements in the event of a change in the Post Masters of this place. Wm. E. Fowler the Engineer was in the Office this Evening.

Geo Havens bought himself a New set of books and is cratching everything to pieces in his endeavor to get things right.

[May] 12. Fine weather. I done a good deal of rustling around to day. Mrs Robt Dickson had her Furniture actioned off today in front of the Bank of Chadron building by Joe Ford.

May 13. Nice weather again! I did not go to Church or Sunday School this morning.

After dinner I repaired to the Base Ball ground to witness a game between the Chadron dudes and a picked nine which resulted in a victory for the Dudes by a score of 21 to 18—both nines done very well and a pick of choice men from them would certainly result favorably in getting up a Yum Yum Club.

After supper I called on Mrs Simmons after which George and I went to the Methodist Church to hear a concert by the sunday school scholars of that denomination which we enjoyed very much.

May 14. fine weather again. I had to get after Charles Jones this morning again, about playing hooky from School, So I called upon Miss Bryant and gave her some New instructions regarding the lad.

May 15[.] Nice weather the fore part of the day. Gottstein started moving a part of the old Gold Bar building to Third Street. in the evening I went up to the Rink to hear King Kennedy the Ventriloquist, but was again disappointed. Judge Kinkaid and Court reporter Merrick came down from Harrison today. Mr. Merrick intends staying in Chadron a few days. Geo Hymer, the "hair eyed Kid" commenced work on the streets today. Mr. Selden started for Long Pine this evening. Early this morning my Canary bird came very near getting killed by a cat[.] I woke up and spoiled the Cats fun.

May 16. It has been raining all day to day. the Case of Davis vs Allen came up for trial, and went by default. I ran across the Cat that tried to kill my Canary yesterday and at once went and got Tony Bernard to kill him, but he Shot high and the Cat escaped. I next got Chas Wilson to hunt for his catship but it was no go.

I recd a letter from M. O. Maul stating some important facts concerning the sickness of Mrs Crawford at Omaha, and in accordance therewith I at once wrote to Dr Paul Grossmann concerning more information.

The City Council met in regular session this evening and transacted a good deal of very important business among which there was a proposition from a Milling Company to put in an electric Light which if at all consumated will be highly beneficial to the City. Mr Robt Hood in his usual Good humor showed his intelligence on Municipal Management. Geo Havens has just got back from Handys where he has been doing the Grand to Miss Handy.

May 17. rained the fore part of the day but towards evening it cleared off[.] Mr Warrack came in to see me in the evening and after fixing up my Office matters He and I went around town a little. Geo Havens did not like it very much.

May 18. Nice weather all day. the Contract for building the Land Office and C. C. Hughes building was let to Grallup Longcor and Noll yesterday and work will be commenced on them immediately[.] I receved a letter from Bro Geo stating of the Death of Uncle Thomas in reading[,] penna. I at once telegraphed to Brother Thomas and wrote to Bro Charley. I called on Thomas Moore to sell my County Claims and upon Jas Connelly to borrow some money to go East with, but received no definate reply.

after dinner Frank Allen came in the Office and made a settlement with C. J Davis.

After supper Geo & I went up to the Skating rink to hear a Chicago revivalist. Selden got back from Long Pine this evening[.]

May 19. I leave for the East tonight to be gone probably two or three months.

July 30[.] I arrived in Chadron right side up with care and found the County Commissioners had appointed F. M. Molyneaux in my place as Justice of the Peace[.] O. H. Wilson turned out and greeted me welcome. I again feel satisfied to be home among my Chadron & Western Friends.

July 31. To day I asked Molyneaux to turn the Office of J. P. back to me, but he refused and is reported to be under the legal wing of ExCounty Judge Byington.

O. H. Wilson returned the Police Docket to me and the office goes all smooth again[.]

Aug 1[.] To day Hon[.] A W Crites and myself made a formal demand on Molyneaux for the J P. Office and he (Molyneaux) wanted time till tomorrow to say what he was going to do in the Matter.

Aug 2. Busy on appeal transcript for Van Inwegew. Molyneaux offers to turn J. P. office back if the County Commissioners will order him to do so. Cooley said they would do so tomorrow[.] got all straightened out at the Post Office to day. last night the Council met and worked on bills. City Clerk Smith as usual was the boss.

Aug 3. Nice weather this afternoon[.] the Fats vs Leans of Chadron plaid a Game of Ball 26 to 27 in favor of the Fats. I had my back shed to the office cleaned out to day. Snell done the work.

After supper I got some minutes off on the Type writer for Maher and then went up to the Court House to attend a Democratic Meeting, but no democratic meeting was to be had. This morning I called upon the County Commissioners to have them issue an order to Molyneaux to turn the office of J. P. over to me, but they asked for time till tomorrow at 9 A.M. and request that Crites Come up to the Court House and enter into a debate with Ballard on the subject.

Quite an attendance was at the ball game to day.

Aug 4. Fine weather today. at 9. A.M. A W Crites and myself went up to the Commis about the J. P. office. It was very plain that Ballard was the main spring in doing all he could to confuse the Commsrs[,] which taken into connection with the Commrs party dislike to me, made it seemingly still more obstinate for me, but the Commer's are beginning to see that I have the sinch and propose to hold it. That the Republicans should seek to vent spite on me in my absence and behind my back is strongly in support of the only thing they have been capable of ever since the commencement of politic in the County. Revenge has been their cry, but strange to say they have ever faild to carry the point.

Aug 5th. Therman Fraley and I returned from the Table Precinct this evening for which place we left Chadron yesterday afternoon to visit A C Fowler and family. upon arriving in Town the report was going around that Herman Kermse and a Brother of John Knoll the stone Contractor had been shot at by some Granger for trespassing on his premises in quest of game.

This morning while we were yet at Fowlers there came a hail storm which while it lasted only a few minutes done little harm in that vicinity, but from the appearance of Clouds further west it must have made considerable destruction.

Aug 6. Fine weather this A.M. Mr Snell fixed up my back shed nicely and has about got things so that not much water can run under my office. Council met.

[Aug] 7. Fair weather. I have still not had a talk with Hughes yet. I have written up Co Atty Ballard and also a card to the General Public.

Fine day. This evening the Band got out and played for the Tariff Debates at the Rink after which all Chadron went up to the Rink to hear the Tariff Question debated on[.]

Aug 10. Damp weather all day[.]

John Maher broke his typewriter. I loaned him mine till he can get his fixed[.] Allen asked me to go to the Japanese party at the M. E. Church this evening[.]

Aug ll[.] Nice weather all day. Joe Ford held Auction on Billy Carters household goods.

"Dad" Haddock and Ed Cameron had to go after Frank Trumble, who was trying to skip from paying a fine and cost in Police Court. "Dad" arrested him and made him come to time.

About 5 Oclock another hard case Showed up by the name of Chas Sublet upon a Charge preferred by M. Gottstein for being drunk and disorderly and Malicious destruction of property. the arrival of the prisoner in Court justified a commital till Monday morning which was done so as to let the defendant have a trial when he was sober.

To day has been a momentous one in the Republican local political rink of the County. I am sorry to say that the Tom Coffey faction of Republicans got left in pretty bad shape and instead thereof Mr A Bartow seems to be the leading candidate now for [words missing.]

Aug 12. Nice weather at 8 A.M. all of Chadrons "bloods" started for Whitney there to witness and some of us to play in a game of Base Ball. We had an elegant time. every body was happy especially for the reason that the Chadron Boys came out ahead 23 to 13—we all arrived home in Chadron by 9 P.M. and some of us were considerably tired.

Aug 13[.] Nice weather today but last night the Lightening cracked so hard as to cause me to reflect and pray as every moment I thought I was going to get it in the neck.

Chas Sublet was brought into court and received a sentence of $25.00 and costs and stand committed in Default.

Dad Haddock has been making considerable [fuss] lately and in fact all day about certain fees in Court[.] he is always ready to get his fees, but slow in doing an officers duty unless actually compelled. It seems very strange that he should act like a demon when only he is on for temporary duty, or for that matter that he should act so at any time.

To day I leased the whole of Kelloggs building for 6 months.

Aug 14. It rained all day nearly. Glover & Turner brought a case from Justice Wilson on a change of Venue. I commenced my sleeping room building today. Parks is doing the work by contract.

Aug 15[.] Rained all day till about 3 P.M. after which I turned the water on my back yard over in Davidsons cellar which had caved in and was no use to any one. the carpenters then commenced to go to work on the building[.] All day the Delegates to the Republican County Convention kept coming into the City from the various precincts and towards evening the City was full of Rampant Republicans.

Aug 16. Clear weather. The Carpenters got to work again on the house. The Republican County Convention met in session and the work of the "Gang" commenced to have its effect[.] About 15 minutes after opening session W. G. Pardoe of Crawford and E W Carpenter of Whitney got it in the neck in great shape. everything was cut and dried by Bartow[,] Egan, Powers, & Carley who run the Convention from first to last notwithstanding there were 7 ballots take for Pardoe. during the most interesting part of the meeting I was called out to take the Bond of Rudolphus Mann who was under arrest by my order for non-payment of debt. Accordingly my fun was spoiled and go I had to.

Aug 17[.] Nice day again. Every body busy rushing things[.] Judge Davis of Blair was in Chadron to day. Pete Cooper came down from Whitney.

after supper I attended meeting of the Chadron Democratic Club which adjourned to a Special Meeting Next Tuesday evening for the purpose of selecting delegates to the State Democratic Convention of Democratic Clubs at Lincoln[,] Neb[.] on the 28th inst.

After the meeting Maher and I went up to the Congregational Church to hear a lecture on prohibition by a lady. She spoke very good and helped the Democratic Cause Considerably[.] The Rapid City Base Ball Club came down this evening and are being boarded at the Rail Road House by our home nine[.]

Aug 18. Fine day. at 1 P.M. the Democratic Primaries came of[f] and were through with in 1/2 an hour.

The game of Base Ball was the principal attraction in the afternoon, and the Grand Stand at the Ground was packed to the utmost. The game was Close up to the 5th inning after which the Rapid City Club took a lead and put [words missing.]

Aug 19th. last night I got very sick having contracted a severe cold a few days ago. Dr Leas attended me and Mrs Josselyn was very kind to me. I have been in the house all day[.]

Aug 20[.] I started out this a.m. but had to go back to bed again. Brower had me do some Typewriting for him concerning his Co-partnership with I. C. Dietrick of Crawford to go into the drug business[.]

The delegates to the Demo Co Convention arrived from the west this evening[.] Hugh OLinn started for Chicago to day with a train load of Cattle.

Aug 27. I got out of bed to day for the first time since the 22nd inst. when the boys all carried me on my mattress to Mrs Millers to be nursed. I came down town this morning but felt very weak so I had to go back again[.] after dinner I came down again and after sleeping at the drug store a little I felt better and Geo Helped me clean up the office[.] it smelled badly, but the Drs got after me and made me go home.

Aug 28. Nice day. Charley Allen[,] Geo Montgomery went to Omaha to go to Lincoln last night[.]

I went down to office this A.M. and heard Case of Ingerlund vs Petersen[.] Motion to dissolve attachment was filed and for answer from Plff. on said Motion[,] I adjourned case to Tue P.M. at 2 P.M. Attys for Pff. came in and said they could not get ready for answer till 3 oclock.

Aug 29. Nice weather today. no business of any account. Bellanger the Grocer failed a few days ago but it is not causing much alarm as the general impression prevails that he has failed with plenty of money.

Aug. 30[.] little windy weather. last night all the switchmen in the Yard got on a bender and the R.R. Co had to put in new men. Mr Sells was in the office to see me this A.M. The Carpenters commenced casing the

House this morning. Geo Havens slept with me last night[.]

Aug 31. Nice day. I felt bad all day. No business of any kind. Von Harris & Cooper were here this evening and I turned somethings over to them[.]

Sept 1[.] I got up late and was unable to eat any dinner. Mrs Josselyn got me some chicken broth for Supper and I ate hearty. today Billy Carter ceased selling any whiskey and the New Proprietor took charge and expects to give a free lunch this evening.

Chas Allen and H. A. Cox arrived from Lincoln this A.M. Allen was very tired and slept nearly all day.

Geo Havens bought a watermelon today[.] Cox & Maher came in and rented 1/2 of my building for the Democratic Headquarters at 9.00 per month.

9[:]30 P.M. The Free Lunch at Carters was a success. all the Rag Tags in Town got filled with fish, onions & Beer.

Sept 2nd[.]   Nice   day.   I   went   to   the Congregational Church this morning[.] They gave the Sacriment to their members. Mrs [Mr] and Mrs McCloud had their younges[t] son baptized.

Sept 3. Nice day. at 9 A.M. the case of Ingerlund vs Peterson came on for trial[.] Plff demanded a jury which was forthwith Impanelled and cause continued to 1 P.M. at which time the case was called and after much fusing in getting the proper talismen, the jury was finaly sworn and trial of cause commenced. The case was adjourned at 5 P.M. till 7. A.M. tomorrow Sept 4th[,] 1888.

After supper I called on Mrs C C Hughes and returned a Glass which she had brought me during my recent sickness[.]

Geo Havens & I went to bed early.

Sept 4. The day opened clear and bright[.] busy all day trying the Ingerlund vs Peterson Case. the jury got the case at 6[:]20 P.M. and were out 4 hours when they brought in a verdict for the Deft.

Sep 5[.] This A.M. the jury delivered their verdict to the Court which was read and the Deft. Atty gave each juror [$].50[.] The Plff by his Atty gave notice of appeal. This evening the Republican delegates to the Representative Convention commenced to flock into the City and things are looking as if they were going to be lively about tomorrow[.]

Sep. 6. Nice day. The Plasterers got done with my house today. I worked on the Demo today and after supper attended the Rep. Legislative Convention at the Court House where it was crowded. it took 140 ballots before the nominations were made[.]

Sep 7. Nice day. at 1.30 P.M. case of State vs. Wheeling upon Assault & Battery was tried before me. I found Deft Guilty who paid his fine and cost and departed. Burly C. Hill is still away to Wahoo with the Malitia Co[.] Quite a number of Gov supply wagons passed through town this A.M.

The New Land Office is Rapidly nearing completion and J. Paul & Co are now cosily located in their new store room owned by C. C. Hughes[.] the excavation of John Nolls building is being pushed rapidly.

Sep. 8. Nice day all day. M. Ballard filed an information before me this A.M. charging one Frank E McCully with assault with intent to Kill. After dinner I went out to the base ball grounds and seen the Crawford Kids beat the Chadron Kids by 28 to 20. This afternoon Mrs Hood commenced a Criminal action against one James Ballou.

The carpenters got done with my house to day and the plasterer finished his part of the contract.

Sep 9. Nice day and very warm. I got up late, and Mrs Miller M.D. invited me to have breakfast after which I came down to the office and bumed around till 12 M. when Frank Van Horn came along and invited me to go to dinner with him so I dressed up and after dinner I went down to the Mail Car with him to see him distribute his mail. Came up town about 6 P.M. went to bed early.

Sep 10th[.] Windy nearly all day. Mr Snell scrubed out the house and I got the painter to work in the afternoon. The Malitia boys came home Yesterday Morning after a very pleasant Picnic at Wahoo. I recd a letter from Geo Kraber.

D. E. Havens filed Motion and affidavit for a continuance[.] Not much business and all the Lawyers getting ready for the District Court.

Sep. 11. Court commenced this A.M. the County Atty being too busing [busy] in the forenoon consequently the Civil docket was called off first. In the afternoon the Criminal docket was called with the State of Nebraska vs Mary Woodard charged with Manslaughter as the first case. the Defendant asked the Court to appoint an attorney for her defense as she said she was dissatisfied with her present attorneys to-wit Spargur & Fisher and suggested that C D Sayrs be appointed which the Court done forthwith and upon Suggestion of County Atty the Case was ordered for trial tomorrow. The last case on the Criminal Docket was State vs Chas Wilson upon a charge of assault with intent to kill. The Co. Atty ordered that it be set for trial and C. D. Sayrs gave notice that he might probably have to ask for a continuance for the Deft. But Wilson came to me and talked about not being satisfied with the work Sayrs was doing and wanted W. H. Westover to take his case, whereupon he called upon Westover and having stated his case was told by that Gentleman to wait till tomorrow morning till he could get to look at the Information[.]

I moved my bed from Mrs Millers house into my new House[.]

New Dentists are in town extracting teeth in a painless manner and much opposition exists between them.

Sep. 12. Windy all day. Court instructed Jury to be present tomorrow A.M. and if Attys were not then ready for Jury trial that he would discharge them and adjourn Court.

Westover got me to copy off some verivications in the Hoffman vs. Tibbells case.

I wrote letters to Sturgis and Page relative to spaying Cattle. this A.M. Red Jacket was discharged to go hence without day [delay] and now the time is only to come when another man falls a victim to her prejudicial malice and hatred as she is a Specific subject and has a mania for killing someone.

Sep 13th. Nice weather. We got the Democrat out early today. Jim Tuckers trial was dismissed virtually today though the Foreman of the Jury before whch his case was tried had been required to sign a verdict of not guilty. The ones who were so anxious to prosecute Tucker are going about like the Curs they really are and thought that because Fisher demand proper service of a Subpoena up[on] him that they would show up and thereby make a great point against Tucker[.] Jas Cavanaugh was up before Police Court this morning again.

Sept 14. Clear weather till afternoon. I bought a wardrobe from Wilson[.] Attend Court nearly all day.

Sep 15[.] Nice day. to day Prop Fosters Case against the School Board upon an action to recover $1,000 came on for trial before the District Court. I was very sick last night and have lost my appetite. Dr Leas gave me some powders[.] Magnus Ingerlund came in the office and offered Solomon Hartzell as one of his sureties on his appeal bond. Geo & I went to bed early. about 10[:]30 P.M. Ingerlund and Molyneaux brought Jerre Hartzell into my bed room for surety on his appeal bond and he signed the bond[.]

Sept 16. Early this A.M. Jerre Hartzell came in my bedroom and complained that not having been fully advised in the premises concerning his signing

Ingerlunds appeal bond, he desired the Court not to accept him as bondsman and he forthwith tore his name from the instrument and laid it back on my table. The Senatorial Convention of Democrats at Rushville nominated H. A. Cox of Chadron for State Senator[.] Pete Magure came down from Crawford last evening. Everybody is out of town today visiting the U. S. Soldier Camp on Bordeaux. about 10 Oclock last night the Jury in the case of Foster vs Chadron School District returned a verdict for $600[.]00 in favor of Plff.

Sep 17. Fine day all through. This A.M. Ballard filed complaint before Wilson against Coons prostitutes at the Soldier encampment. after having brought them into Town and haragued them around in Court for an hour or more and given all the children in Town a chance to gaize on them in their depravity they were finally discharged upon W H Carter standing good for their fines[.]

Fred Rood wrote me a letter this A.M. which I answered right off.

In the Case of Ingerlund vs Peterson I waited all day for the Plff to produce a new bondsman in place of Jerre Hartzell who insisted that he be striken of[f] from the appeal Bond which he signed, but in the absence of no new bondsman having been offered by the Plff. notwithstanding the fact that I notified the Plff. and Plffs. atty to the effect that they must give a new bondsman. I thereupon at 4 P.M. issued an order of a return of the property.

Sep. 21. Nice day[.] Chas Allen spoke to me this afternoon and told me he & Jim Hartzell had bargained for the Base Ball ground during the fair days to wit 26-27 & 28 inst [instant] and asked me if I wanted to take a hand in getting special dancing Indians from Red Cloud Agency to give War Dances to which I of course assented, and notified Jim H. to that effect which was satisfactory to him.

Sep 22. Nice day, but great commotion in Camp among the Radical Managers of the Fair Association who[,] having found out that the Ball Ground is liable to knock off a little money in the Evening after the fair is over with[,] they are now endeavoring to have us give up the job, but it is no use and Charley & I will go to the agency to day yet to engaged special Indians, extra from the ones who are invited to attend the fair, and we Shall also try and get Red Cloud himself to come and make a Speech.

Sep 24th. Allen & I returned from the agency this A.M. I was successful in securing not only Red Cloud himself, but also his personal promise to bring 30 first class dancers for my entertainment to be a seperate concern from the fair association Indians.

After dinner I got out an appeal case for Sweat.

The painters were painting my house when I got back.

Sep 25. Fine day. Jim & I have been busy getting things ready for the Indians. I got Bordman to paint me some signs for the Indian war dances and during the afternoon I drove out to the fair grounds and took some plants out for Snell, after which I drove out to Chas Allens house with Chas. to take some acknowledgments.

Sep 26. Nice day again. Early this A.M. Red Cloud and his band of Warriors filed into town. I took them direct to the Ball Park and ordered them into camp there. But during the day I had considerable trouble in keeping the President of the Fair Association from taking the Indians to the fair grounds[.] the performance commenced at 7 oclock and I had a good house. after the Show I went to Carters and paid off the pools which I sold last evening[.] I got to bed about 3 oclock.

Sep 27[.] Early this A.M. it being fair weather I repaired to the Ball Grounds and gave some of the Indians their share in last nights proceeds in money and for the remainder I purchased Beef, Coffee, & Sugar. In the afternoon I went to the fair[.] At 6 P.M. I gave a street parade with the Indians. The performances at the Grounds commenced at 7 P.M. and I again had a good house[.] about 9 oclock I left the Grounds and went to the Rink to attend the Ball given by the Malitia Co. I also took Spotted Elk along. Geo & I got home at 4 A.M.

Sept 28th. Nice day. I handed Red Cloud the amount due his band out of last evening['s] performance which satisfied him very well. I did not go to the fair today as I was to tired and wished to save myself for the evening. I got Bordman to paint a Transparency for me to carry in the parade this evening and at 7 P.M. I started at the head of the Indians to march through town. We took it by Storm and made a good show[.] the performance commenced at 8 P.M. sharp according to statement on our posters[.] after the performance I settled up with Red Cloud and having bid them all good by I came home more dead than alive.

Many things have happened during the past 3 days of which I have failed to make note of for the reason that I have been too much rushed.

This afternoon I purchased a suit of clothes for Red Cloud and when Spotted Elk found it out he commenced to get sulky and refused to preside over the Dancing at the Grounds.

Sep 29[.] Fine weather again. I have been busy paying off bills contracted for the benefit of the Indian War Dance enterprise. A Movement is on foot for the Republicans to go to Rushville to participate in a Ralley there with Republicans and a Special train has been chartered for the occasion.

I have asked Geo to go along with me.

Sep. 30. Nice day. Geo & I went to Rushville last night and returned at 12.30 this AM. All hands got home safe but some were banged up pretty badly. Major Power, J W Smith and Ed Moran were the principal ones who must now be feeling rather used up.

Oct lst. gay day. Not much business going on.

Oct. 2   Nice day.   I was busy getting money collected for the Benefit of Ben Boyd who is Suffering from a Stroke of paralysis.   I succeeded in getting 27 dollars for him which now makes $129.00 collected.   I also went down to see the agent about getting him a 1/2 rate ticket[.]

Oct. 3.   Clear weather but signs of a change.

While busy at Birdsalls looking after a team I was called upon by Joe Ford who complained of the misconduct of John Taylor. I called on Mayor Hughs. Taylor was arrested and I gave him $10.00 & Costs and 5 days on bread & water.

Martin was arrested and paid his fine this morning.

Oct. 4.   Changable and Cloudy all day[;] light rain in the evening.   I have been busy on the paper and Demo Club lamps and I got the flag pole ready for the Small flag.

Last night I helped John Maher write testimony in the land office and while there I was called to attend a meeting of the City Council for the purpose of presenting some of my bills.

Fred Mead and his family started for Washington Terry. [Territory] last night.

About 12 oclock last night I had quite a time trying to quiet young John Higgins[.] after considerably Jawing he finally went home and the Night Watch & I in Company with Geo Livingston and Larkins went and had oysters.

Miss Boyle came around this forenoon and had some typewriting to do but I was too busy.

Geo Havens and his School Mate are now busy at my desk posting up their Ledgers, for they have just been started at School in Book Keeping. I wrote a letter [to] Aunt Diane and Sol Pitcher.

The City Council went up to view the resiovor. The life of Cleveland and Harrison as portrayed by the genial book agent is being panned out to the Citizens of Chadron.

Oct 5. Cloudy & Cold all day.

I worked on the Demo Club lamps and got 100 fixed on sticks by 3 oclock P.M. and then made arrangments with the Malitiae Co for some Bunting to make a flag with. After Supper the Demo Club held a meeting in my rooms. We made some great resolves and are doing all in the power of the few who meet to make a grand ralley on the 11th inst. to go to rushville, So as to insure a hearty return Compliment from the rushville boys. the Woodmen Society held a meeting in the Court House (old) this evening. every thing is now fixed and if I live tomorrow I can get other things ready for the success of our proposed rushville trip.

Oct. 6.   To day the flag pole arrived.   I immiadeately set to work getting it peeled and in some kind of shape for erection[.]   In the afternoon Tony Smith brought me enough white Bunting to make a Club Flag which I got Mrs. Hopkinson to sew together for me which She completed by 12 oclock P.M.

Oct 7. Geo & I got up late. I was very tried last night. I got Selden to put eyelets in the Flag for me. Park the Carpenter fixed my sleeping room door.

Yesterday Mr Pegg had a public auction at his truck farm.

Agent Jerry Finches having sent in his resignation, Mr. Wells has been appointed in his place and takes Charge tomorrow.

It is very pleasant today.

Oct 8. Cold weather[.] I worked all day getting the Demo Club flag painted and some of the transpariencies struck of[f.]   after supper I got Mrs Limpsaim to Sew the Stars on the flag for me. it took till 11 Oclock. the Post Master (Wilson) was again officially notified to move the post office to Main St, and I guess this time it will come[.] at any rate the Post Office pea nut snap is getting ready to move.

Oct. 9th. Cloudy during forenoon and a little rain, but clear in the afternoon. Busy all day getting the flag pole arrainged and trying to get another pole to splice it to, but finally Chas Allen proposed Nailing the Club flag up against my house to which I objected at first, but upon consideration finding that it would and might cause ill feeling I relented and gave way to Allen.

The Post Office has been on a slow move all day and to night completes the business and tomorrow morning the kickers, Bamboozlers and "Gang" Men will have to redeem some of their well earned treachery from the hands of a few who are not afraid to make a kick at the right time and for some Cause. this forenoon I got Fred Danielson to go to the lower Depot Yards with me to look at some telegraph poles and bridge timbers, upon which Occasion we drove way to Strouskie's outfit (Boliver)[.]

"Ginger" a former Cook on a Cow Ranch in Wyoming and in the Vicinity of where I was frozen is in the City on a proposed drunk. he reports Rafe Rhodes as coming to Chadron. Building is progressing fastly on the Noll and Weber building on Main St.

Mr Crites is also erecting a nice house.

Don Boardman finished painting the Democratic transparencies this A.M. In the afternoon I put a pully in the flag pole[.] Daniel Burns brought suit before O H Wilson against John Noll for Balance of Settlement upon a ditching Contract. I understand that Burns won the case.

Last night John Maher informed me that the Rink could not be had for our proposed Democratic Rally and Speech making on the 12th inst. and consequently we are compelled to make other arrangments[.]

9.40 P.M. Geo. Havens has located himself in my bed room where he proposes to do his Studying in the future[.]

Oct 10th[,] 1888[,] Fair weather. at 10 A.M. I had to try the case of Hirsh vs Havens which was continued till tomorrow at 12 M.

I have been busey all day getting thing[s] ready for tomorrow evenings Rally at Rushville[.] Maher and I figured up after supper and I have been around with another petition for the Cause of Democracy on the 12th inst. here, and I have raised $30.00 toward expenses that cannot be less than $100.00[.] I feel tired out.

Oct 11. Fair weather but it looked a little like Storm and Snow this A.M. I have been busy tacking up the Club flag, getting oil, filling lamps, having Bordman paint more signs, getting the Japaneese lanterns in trim till I am almost worn out. I have also been collecting some on the list and met with only $3.00 so far today and it is now 4 P.M. with [$]66[.]00 more to raise before this time tomorrow.

the Loui Lord Theateratical Co are in Town and Maher, Glover and I are, and have been[,] dickering with them to let us have the Opera house tomorrow evening from 9 P.M. and they are willing but want us to [words missing.]

Oct 12th[.] Nice weather[.] I was busy all day getting things in readyness. Rushville and Gordon Bands Came up on the Flyer. the flag pole was raised today and I had men fix up a fram[e] for the large transpariency. the Loui Lord Theatre Co commenced their show early so as to have the rink in readyness for the Democratic orators. the Torchlight procession was a grand affair and every body was amazed at the turnout. the line of March started promptly at 8.30 P.M. and extended all over the City. 300 people were in line. the two bands (Rushville and Gordon) discoursed good music and our home band looked on in wonder and Silence. After an hour of parading the Rink was reached where the speakers held the Crowd Spell bound by their fluient and flowing Speeches in favor of Democracy[.] Geo and I finally reached home all o.k. after having brought all the paraphanalia from the rink after the speaking.

Oct. 13. Nice and Clear weather. Some Scoundrel cut the haliards of the Rep. Flag pole and let them unreve last night.

J. D. Pattison swore out a warrant against some parties for cutting timber on his land. Co Commissioner Cooley notified me of the approval of all my bills against Dawes Co. I invited Chas Allen and John Maher to go to supper with me at the Congregational Church supper rooms in the old Land Office building after which Allen, Mr Rosencrances and I smoked at Gottsteins and then Geo and I went up to the theartre.

W H. Mcleanne paid me $10[.]00 today by Check.

This afernoon the Republican speechmaking came of[f] at the rink. Mr Caldwell was the Chief Orator on the occasion and oratorically done well & politically he done bad. Hon. D. M. Sells was introduced to open the meeting and done so in an ordinary manner[.]

I made a call on the Temperance Advocate today.

Oct. 14. Sunday! nice weather but I was to busy getting things Ready for next tuesday to go to the agency. George was around all day and cleaned up around the office and Sleeping Room. John Maher was in the office. I had a great time last evening drinking wine with the Boys.

Oct. 15th[.] Fair weather all day. I got up a petition for Frank M. Van Horn to McShane for an extension of time in the Rail way Mail Service for his final examination[.] It is now settled that the Democrats of Chadron are going to have another grand blow out and they all say they are going to Chip in.

I done no business of any importance whatever to day, more than to write to Ben Boyd at the Hot Springs[,] Arkansas in reply to a letter from him asking for money.

this morning Burley Hill and I went down to view the Engine which was wrecked last week up at the node ranch in Wyoming.

Mrs Josselyn was taken sick with Typhoid fever yesterday and consequently a proposed trip to Red Cloud Indian Agency by herself, her Daughter, Mrs Koons and I has been abandoned.

as I was posting up this book, Nigger Taylor came in the office with a couple black trash who desired to be married which I accommodated them in a very short time and then went to bed.

Oct. 16. Nice weather today till towards 4 oclock P.M. when it commenced to blow pretty hard[.] I got some moulding for the House and got a Stove from Christensen and had it set up[.] Von Harris came to town and he and I took supper together. Geo and his School mate are in the room now keeping books. Hank Simmons and I took a ride up to the Court House to day and then went up to see who was living in Tom Dixons house.

Ace Johnson is very sick with the typhoid fever.

Oct. 17. To day has been a nice on[e] and I should have been at the Red Cloud agency but for the sickness of Mrs. Josselyn who was to have gone along in Company with her daughter and Mrs Koons, therefore I set to work and Changed around the things in the office and had the Stove set up. I bought a load of wood to day.

Geo and I went to bed early.

Oct. 18. this morning the wind rose and blew very hard all day making the City dusty.

As I was getting up this morning I came across my overcoat lying outside the house where it had been thrown during last night by some one connected with stealing it at Rushville on the evening of the 11 inst. The Coat is Shot considerably on the left lapple and the Contents of all the pockets were gone save one button. I telegraphed to the Sheriff of Sheridan Co. advising him of finding the Coat.

W. D. Edgar was in to have some [work] done after which Tony Bernard came in for work.

Quite an accident occurred to a family living near Wayside. A small child while playing near a vicious horse was kicked on the head and struck senseless. The family brought the child into the city and Drs. Lewis & Jackson were called to trephine the Skull which while it was successfully accomplished will undoubtedly prove fatal to the child on account of its tender age.

Red Jacket was in the office this AM trying to get a room in which to put the child as she represented that Miss Powell did not want it to be in her house any longer.

Oct. l9th—Cold and Clear. the Water main ditch is being dug today on Main Street between 3rd and 2nd Sts[.] I wrote a letter to the treasurer of the State Democratic Committee of New York for Chas Allen in which he enclosed $20.00 as his Share of donation to the democratic Cause, on acct of being an elector from Nebraska.

Oct. 20th—Fair weather. there were a great many Farmers in town to day. James Cavanaugh was in Police Court this morning charged with Drunk and disorderly conduct. I gave him $25.00 and costs. In the afternoon I got John Ormsbys son to plow my potatoes up. After supper the Dawes Co Journal came out with some remarkable statements about those who the Editor thereof does not like.

during the evening a drunken Farmer drove his team into the water main ditch at the Cor[ner of] 2nd & Main St[.] Julius Hahler helped get them out and was compelled to pull and hauld the driv[e]r of the team around considerably before being able to render any assistance to the <u>dumb</u> animals in the ditch.

Afterwards, the Police arrested the driver and also John Henry (Colored) and locked them up. I ordered the Farmers team to Birdsalls livery stable to be taken care of[.] To day it has be[en] settled that the Democrats of Chadron will have another Grand Rally on the evening of Nov 2nd[,] 1888[,] upon which occasion the Hons[.] Steele of Deadwood and Davis of Lincoln will do the speaking. It is expected a large delegation will be in attendance from Harrison and Rushville[.] After supper I called up to see how Ace Johnson was getting along[.] He has been ill with the typhoid fever for about 3 weeks and is one of the worst patients in the City that the Drs. have on hand. poor boy[,] I guess he is doomed to die[!]

Oct. 21. Nice weather[.] in the afternoon I called on W. H. Markle[,] the breakman who got so badly scalded last Thursday a week ago. he is getting along nicely and has lots of grit and nerve. little Harry Hooker who has been so very sick for the past 4 or 5 weeks is again well enough to be about out doors with his playmates after having had all manner of medicines given him by the Drs. in attendance.

In the evening John Maher came around to the office but as the moon was rather bright he could not perform for me as he wished[.] Geo was a little mad this evening—The cornerstone of the Episcopal church was laid to day[.]

Oct 22. Fair weather[.] the Police Court had some business to day and John Henry was given $10.00 and costs and a Country lad discharged to err no more[.]

Geo Livingston was called upon to make a settlement with P O Hanlon which he done though very reluctantly.

Julius Hahler gave a free lunch in the rendering establishment of John Stetters Butcher Shop to the faithful followers of the Democratic Cause and only Democrats participated[.] This evening at 4.20 oclock Ace Johnson died[.]

Oct 23[.] Fair weather. I called on J B Johnson to see when he was going to bury his son Aca. when I got there I found he was going to bury him this afternoon[.]

I came back and after dinner at 3 PM I attend[ed] the funeral[.] I was much surprised that the School children did not attend[.]

Oct 24. fair weather. the water main on Main Street between 2 & 3 strs was put down to day[.] the men are working hard and cannot hope to get water running before Dec 15th at the earliest.

Dorrington brought an appeal case in the Land Office to me to transcribe, Davis vs Ness[.] Last night at 8 oclock John McHenry and Flora A. Currie were married by G J Powell at Mrs Fowlers residence on North Main St. a youthful chiverai party serenaded the Groom and kept up the racket till a late hour of the night[.]

Oct. 25. It Snowed last night a little but not to Stop any work around town today.

the County Commissioners are all on fire on Township Organization which they and their ring are fighting as hard as possible. they realize that once the Commissionership is wrested from them that their footing on the pockets of innocent Tax payers is gone and forever lost. they are at present Screwing the thumb screws as tight as they can upon the faithful to their cause and are compelling many to keep Silent who should be made of better stuff even though they might advocate a cause for the benefit of all concerned and perhaps fail in having a few paltry Claims allowed by the Commissioners. I am glad to say that I have some bills before the Commissioners for their Consideration and that I need the money pretty badly, but if I am not to be allowed them unless I s[t]ay and fight against Township Organization, then I must allow that my claims are no good, because I favor said organization even though I Shall fail in having said claims allowed.

Chas W Allen informed me to day that Von Harris was going to have E E Egan arrested for Criminal lible[.]

Business was a little brisk to day. Ricker & Houghton brought two suits before me and Ben Snell commenced an action for an account for digging a grave for Benjamine Hemstreet[.]

The Chadron Democrat came out on time to day. Dorrington asked me if I would loan the G.O.P. the Democratic torches upon the evening of Oct 30th when the G.O.Ps will endeavor to have a blow out[.]

Oct. 26. Clear weather but no business going on.

Oct. 27. Nice weather. lots of farmers in town. In the evening I and Charlie Allen, W. L. & Ed Handey had supper together at Old Gene Fields after which we went up to the Court House to attend a called Citizens Meeting for township organization. but in Consequence of an apparent misunderstanding Everybody went up to the Skating rink to hear a Union Labor Party Meeting addressed by I. N. Harbaugh. We therefore adjourned and attended that. It was cold[.]

Oct 28[.] Sunday after getting up I went over to help Cox send out his Circulars, but at dinner time I got very sick and was compelled to go home to bed, being taken with congestion of the liver and pleurisy[.] Dr Harris was called.

Oct 29[.] Still very sick, and I remained in bed all day. a great many friends called during the day to see me. I sent for A W Crites in the evening who drew up a will for me.

Oct 30[.] Still Sick. Dr Harris gave me a severe blister for my Pleurisy[.] In the evening I got up to see that the Demo Club head quars were lighted up properly and to witness the Republican torchlight procession. it was ordinary[.]

Oct 31. I got up this AM feeling some what better and with the determination to refill all the lamps used by the Republicans last night, which I accomplished by 7:30 P.M. but felt very tired[.]

Nov 1. Fair weather. Danielson got his Chairs from me to day[.] I done up my work on the lamps today and finished the oil business. I had the carpenter put in a transome for me in the office[.]

little Elmer Ham helped me[.] Col W R Steele came down from Deadwood this evening and was entertained by the Black Hills Boys in royal style[.]

Nov 2[.] The weather opened up a little windy this AM and it looked a little unfavorable for our Demo Rally tonight but toward 3 oclock P.M. it calmed down and everything went of[f] nice and serene[.] I got the [lamps] all lighted up and by 7 P.M. all the Democrats in town were in line and we started. I in the lead of all[.] the parade was a success not because I in Particular was at its head, but because every body took an active part in it. the speeches at the rink were all good and well put—so much so that Dorrington and Bartow and Gilchrist were unable to stand the fire of the Battery and consequently they went out of the hall.

After the speaking Geo and I came home and went to bed—[.]

Nov 3[.] Early this "AM" I was awoke by the Night Police to make out a warrant for one Thos Holliday who H D Kirmse charged with Petty Larceny[.] I tried him at 1 oclock P.M. and found him guilty and gave him $2.00 and costs—[.]

the Republicans are getting their lamps ready to go to Crawford to give a parade there, and by special invitation John Maher, Geo Havens and many more good Democrats and myself, got on the Special train and accompanied the Republicans. We arrived at Whitney in 27 minutes and there gave a Street parade and those who could got some supper (as we all missed our supper at home)[.] We arrived in Crawford in 32 Minutes more where all hands, (except myself) paraded. the Crawfordites had no torches and were all on the platform to receive a torch—[.] We arrived home at 1.30 Sunday morning—I met my little friend Guy Alexander at Crawford—[.]

During this past week Joe Ford removed his barber shop from Tom Coffeys old place on Cor[ner] Main and 2nd sts. to one of the Buildings owned by Mike

Gottstein on 2nd sts in what used to be a part of the old Gold Bar. Geo Hatch who used to be with Hamm has gone into the room vacated by Ford[.]

Nov 4. Nice day[.] I remained in the House all day. In the afternoon I issued attachment papers for one Geo J Clark against Robt M Marcle[.] Geo Havens and I took a bath this evening[.]

Nov. 5[.] It snowed last night but melted away by evening[.] I fell this morning while going to breakfast and hurt myself considerably. I had some lady callers at the office relative to a cross dog. done some business for severall people[.] When coming from supper I met Tip Morton who told me certain things relative to Old Ballard working the Gamblers to vote for him for County Atty. which I immediately set to work to undo again. the prohibitionists held a rally at the Rink this evening and in their speeches declared out and out for Cleveland and Thurman[.]

Nov 6[.] 12 Oclock Midnight. this morning Election Commenced and all day long I stayed at the polls and remained in the Counting room till a few moments ago. Republican returns from the East have been pouring in all evening giving rep[.] gains all over the East and Republican Majorityes[.] the Republican boys are feeling pretty good. They are spending all their money with Tom Coffey. The counting of the Chadron Precinct is going on very slow and no probability of getting done until tomorrow sometime[.]

Nov 7. Fair weather[.] Everybody on the streets to day has been claiming their respective Candidate elected, Consequently Grover, Harrison, Thurman and Morton must all be elected, but as such can not be, it necessarily follows in the order of things that we must wait till the full and Correct Count can be made, which under any Circumstances cannot be sooner than next Saturday and probably next Monday.

John Maher recd a telegram from J D Calhoun announcing New York as having gone for Harrison and that Cleveland is now beaten in the United States. This is Sad news indeed for poor John, as he seems to see a possible chance of his having to wheel Fisher over the city with a playcard on his back with the following inscription thereon. "I am a damn fool and everyone knows it[.]"

Nov 8[.] Fine weather[.] The Republicans are all feeling gay over the good hopes that Messages are bringing in from the East for the election of Harrison & Morton.

I have not given up anything as yet nor do I propose to until next tuesday.

This evening the Republicans made a grand ratification Parade and speech at the Rink. I gave them the use of all of our tourches with the provision that they were to return them again, but that part of the programe, although promised, was not adhered to and on the contrary they burned most of them and the rest were given to Whitney parties to celebrate with up there[.]

I stayed up till a late hour last night and witnessed some of the very foolish pranks of the Republicans of Chadron. while they were laying out the order of things generaly. There are enough Land Officers, Post Masters and Government employees in Chadron alone to fill all the requisite places that will be liable to be made vacant in the Rep. Administration for the next four years to come[.]

the size of the plank and height at which it Shall be suspended has all been arrainged[.] The only insurmountable obstacle being when and where the execution Shall take place[.]

Nov 9th. Nice warm weather. the Republicans raised Cain last night after every body had gone to bed. the "dead line" was drawn from the Democrat office to the Land Office with all kinds of lettering accompanying it. Crap [crepe] was put over the land office doors by the Republicans and everything done shows just in what manner the fiendish Reps are anticipating some political office for their living[.]

However New York is not counted yet nor are the official returns in from Indiana and should there be such a thing as another 1884 Repeater, I think some of the Republicans had better leave town for a few days to avoid persecution which will certainly be given in retaliation for some of their pranks.

the City Marshal today swore out a warrant against John Traub for Hawking within the City Limits without license. the court fined him whereupon he repaired to Co Atty Ballard for the purpose of having a warrant sworn out against the City of Chadron[.] The Prohibitionists are eager to see the Democratic Party counted in yet, rather than to see the Republican party in power.

My Earnest hope now is that all Democrats will speedily be turned out of office before the Republican President gets a chance to do it.

Nov 10[.] To day The Democrat came out but it was with a black eye. Mr Pegg the great Prohibitionist came on the street this morning and commenced the Soap peddling business and letter paper act, but upon going to the City Clerk for his second days license, he was informed that he would have to put up $10.00 per day which made him very mad and he declared his powers of working at Election and that he would go to the Country to dispose of his goods. County Atty Ballard has filed a complaint against Julius Hahler for selling and giving away Liquor in old 49 precinct on Election day[.] the case has been set for hearing next Wednesday before Judge Powers.

Nov 11. I got up late as I did not sleep good last night.

Geo Havens commenced work for Ike Gottstein again yesterday[.] last night I took down the Democratic Flag and folded it up in the Omaha Herald that gave an Account of the Democratic defeat. I have put the flag away and if I live till 1892 I will not unroll it until it is again to go in use as a Democratic Club Flag.—

All day today I have busied myself in assorting the Files of the Chadron Democrat—[.]

Frank Van Horn has been in the office and seems to think I ought still to intercede in his behalf in order to have him retained in the U. S. Mail service, but the jig is up and I hope he will act upon my advice and quit the Country altogether as the Republicans will surely oust him sooner than he expects and the forelock of time is the best hold for him just now.

Local politics throughout Dawes County are looking bright for the republicans. the only things in their way is each is afraid the other will get a better bone than himself, and they cannot decide which is the best to tackle first. The "Ring" is now again in full blast, notwithstanding the Democrats had it almost bursted but Township Organization having been worked for all it was worth, and the fact of County Atty Ballard having been elected at a time when republicans vote their ticket straight, even a yellar dog is thereon. this is what makes the gang happy and the only thing I can suggest is for the Democrats to look out.

Nov 12[.] Nice clear day. Splendid weather for this time of the year[.] I went up to the County Clerks office and got the last warrant due to W. A. Selden & Co. and also looked after some claims for Billy Carter and Bartlett Richards[.]

Nov 13. Nice day and lots of business all at once.

Isaac Silerstein commenced an attachment and garnishment process against Wm B Corey filing his affidavit against Garnishee upon Ira Longcor and D W Zerbe—[.] After supper I went by previous arrangement to the Rail Road Eating house where I performed a marriage ceremony for Mr Wm R Stannard and Miss Ettie Shorey, after which I repaired home and gave Kleeman a lesson in English, whom I have taken as a student from tonight. I also opened a set of books for

Charles Wilson. Geo and his School Mate are studying hard in the back room.

Aug [Nov] 14. Fine clear weather but a little colder than usual. After breakfast I called on Baker, the Blacksmith to solicit an advertisement for the Democrat, but he having no money to put up in advance I dropped the case.

M Ballard, the County Atty had the case of State of Nebraska vs. Julius Hahler called for trial upon a complaint for selling and giving away whiskey upon Election day[.] It was tried before Judge Powers by a jury composed of three, Tom Moore, W. S. McPheeley and August Grallup.

M. Ballard was assisted by I. N. Harbaugh while C. D. Sayers and A W Crites represented the Defense[.] the examination of witnesses having been gone into and after 6 or 7 witnesses for the state had been sworn and examined the State rested and the Defendant offering no evidence, It was agreed by counsel to submit the case to the jury without argument, who made out a verdict forthwith without leaving their seats that the defendant Julius Hahler was not guilty as charged in the complaint.

Lew Hartzell while making a coupling in the R.R. Yds this afternoon had 2 fingers on his right hand crushed so badly as to necessitate a complete amputation of the middle finger and some patching to be done to the index finger.

I called on him after supper[.]

Geo Havens is now working hard on his books. Chas Wilson was in the office a little this evening and I Showed him how to post books[.]

Nov 15[.] The day opened up with a nice dry, slow falling Snow storm. No wind stirring and every thing pointed toward a deep snow, but towards dinner time it slacked up.

After breakfast I went to see Ole Olson whose daughter died last Saturday for the purpose of publishing the death to day. W H Marcle called at the office and paid the debt of his brother Robt. which was sued before me[.] the Democrat came out this afternoon and of course I helped.— Allen got several Tickets from his brother in Wichita[,] Kas. for a Trip of the Jim Blain RR to Salt River which created quite a stir among the local "publicans[.]"

Having received an invitation to attend a Surprise party at Mrs Fowlers on North Main St to night I must of course get ready to go as John Maher is also going and both of us not having any girls we will make [words missing.]

Nov. 16th—Fair & Cold. I got up a little late on account of having been to the surprise party last night from which I returned about 1:30 AM this day. I have done very little business today[.] this afternoon I done some typewriting for Chas Allen relative to some order that he intends inaugerating as a means of perpetuating and bringing out the honest vote of every American Citizen upon the Question of Tariff reform, and the ultimate down fall and eradication of the Famous national Banking System as it is now being practiced and was put into existence by the Republican party who claim to be the Champions, Friend and benefactors of the poor, weak and down trodden laborer, but instead thereof they are ever and anon. Striving and in many cases they succeed in beguiling and misleading and blindfolding the workman so that he knows not for a certainty what party he really does belong to.

My class of Germans did not come around this evening[.]

Nov 17[.] Fair day. Joe Branner and I called on Lew Hartzell to see how he was getting along with his Crippled hand, and found him doing quite nicely. on our return Joe informed me of his (Joe) proposed marriage tonight and asked me to perform the Job. Having got shaved and had supper, I proceeded on my way up to Mrs J M Davis Boarding house to perform the

Marriage Ceremony for Joe as it was Miss Jennie B. Davis whom he was going to marry. Only two witnesses were present, the brides mother and the servant.

Joe was keeping the affair very silent for the Gang were on to his racket and if they could have got on to his racket they would have made things hot for him[.] So soon as the ceremony was over they proceeded by the darkest and most lonesome route to the depot and there took the train for Kennedy[,] Neb[.] their future home[.]

Nov 20[.] Since posting last I have been unable to raise my head on account of sickness. last Saturday when upon my return from the wedding I seated myself at the office desk and having written about an hour I started to go to bed and upon rising up I found I was stiff as a stick and cold as ice and felt as if a Couple of Saw logs had rolled over me[.] on Sunday I sent for the Dr. and on Sunday night I was no better and my throat almost killed me with pain[.] on Monday morning I got up (by force) and tried 2 cases in the Police Court, but had to go back to bed again[.] In the afternoon the Dr gave me a gargle for my throat which relieved me straight. Slept well last night, and though I'm not well today, I feel able enough to be in the office and attend to a little business. Daniel Burns came in today and paid up the costs in a case against one John Waters and as plaintiff in the case asked to have said case dismissed at his own costs, which was done. Bordman brought my sign over today while I was at dinner[.] John Maher came in the office and informed me per my black board that the future House of Representatives would be Democratic and the senate Republican[.]

Sol. V. Pitcher came up from Rushville this evening in order to celebrated with some of the defeated Democrats[.] We had a little wine in the office between Sol, John Maher and myself after which we went down town a little to see how everybody was feeling.

Nov 21[.] Nice day and at 9 o'clock AM Mr W F Bisbee was married to Miss Florence Glover at the Baptist Church. Owing to a Suit being on hand in my Court at that time I was unable to attend the wedding, but I have heard enough to know that it was a very pretty wedding. Rumor has it that Mrs O'Linn has been to the Eastern part of this state in the interests of the B & M R.R. Co. to whom she is reported to have sold he[r] White River Farm in order to make a rival City for Chadron[.]

A Webber Jr arrived from Omaha yesterday having with him his newly wedded wife. the boys (School) are now Seranading him with tin cans and wire[.]

Davidson the Baggage Master has also spliced himself this evening and Frank Vickory is expected back from Deadwood tonight whither he went to marry Miss Jennie Clark[.] both are from here.

The report is also out that J. W. Willis and Miss Alice Dortou will be married to night at some private and Secure place so none can get on to them.

I have been rather busy today Scoring up old debts and finding out who I owed and what the exact amounts were.

10:40 P.M. Vickory and Lady arriv[ed] on the down train this evening, but Vick stoutly denies being married, although the Boys Cow Belled him in great fashion. John Maher and Wilson the telegraph operator with their gang of dude toughs were out in full blast and "put" one of their number for the first time.

Nov. 22[.] Nice weather. after breakfast I went up to call on W. F. Bisbee and his new bride. The[y] were stopping with the brides parents and received me very kindly. after spending half an hour or so I came away with a full list of all presents etc. last night Geo Havens had a bad time of it he having been out yesterday a little too soon, and took a sort of relapse. To day was paper day and of course that kept me busy. I got my four tin signs from Bordman today and Nailed them up on the Land Office steps and brought one over to the office and hung it up. I issued an Execution in the Ingerlund vs. Peterson Case and delivered it to Jas Dahlman. I had a Police Court Case this morning[.] After supper I gave F Kleeman a lesson in English[.]

Charlie Willetts from Harrison came down this evening. F. M. Van Horn came in the office this evening and showed me a present he had purchased for his little girl Rose for her birthday present.

It is now a settled question that P B Danielson will not run the new Hotel. Mr A Webber, Jr. was on the streets to day with his new wife. It is also a settled fact that it was a mistake last night about Frank Vickory being married. W. A. McGinley from Running Water[,] Sioux Cou. came down from Harrison this eve.

Nov 23[.] Fine day. J. F. Wright of Custer City[,] D.T. [Dakota Territory] was in the office to day and asked to have me make out an affidavit to the effect that on or about the month of March 1887 he came in my office on Second St and had one W J Sogan acknowledge a Quit Claim deed in his favor. As I remembered the Circumstance quite well I done so and after that he got me to make out an indemnification bond from himself and two bondsmen, to wit[:] W. P. Conely and T. A. Coffey, to the Western Town Lot Company for $500.00 for the purpose of getting a Warranty deed from said Company. Geo Havens came down town today and is feeling much better again[.] Quite a Sensation occurred up at the Chadron Public School yesterday[.] It appears that Clifford Larch and a little girl named Ella Boomer misbehaved before the school and Prof Denton expelled them and now the School Board is investigating the case[.] Rumor has it also that Mr. R. E. W. Spargur and Mrs Woodard have come to a separation over a settlement in the Cash Clothing Store. the Brick Masons commenced work on Pete Nelsons New House across the street (Main) south of the Webber building[.] The weather for building purposes is just grand.

Nov. 24th—Fine weather again[.] today being Saturday a great many Farmers were in Town. I bought two loads of wood and had young Chet Sampson and little Joe Ford to put it into the Shed. I also bought a little wisp and looking glass for Rose Van Horns birthdays. Geo Havens has now entirely recovered from his late sickness.

This morning my books—3 Vols Century, 3 Vols Scribners and 1 Vol Scientific American, came up from Lincoln State Journal. I wrote the Democratic list today. After supper Charles Davis came in the office and filed a complaint against Mose Levi for assault and Battery and fighting. I issued the warrant but no arrest was made for the reason that they could not find Mose.

Nov 25[.] Nice weather till after 6 o'clock when it commenced to blow a wind storm. I stayed in the Office all day and read. Geo Havens opened up a private Set of books for himself. John Maher and the boy were in the office to day.

Mr Whitney[,] the Western Town Lot Co man was in the City today. The Officers have as yet been unable to apprehend the party who struck Charlie Davis last night over the head with a shovel[.] Mr Charde from Niobrara passed through the city this evening having arrived on a early train from Wyoming. Geo and I are now going to take a good bath.

Nov. 26[.] Not much business. Pat Hayes was in the office this morning and nailed up my sign which Don Bordman painted for me. Dan McKinzie, the Stone Cutter on the Webber building got the 2 large pillars into position today[.] Work on the Nelson building is going on slowly.

I done a small job of work on the Typewriter for Dorrington today. Mrs Leach was in the office to day to see about what was being done in the Cory Attachment suit[.] She also informed me of having put an attachment suit upon the celebrated 8 footed horse at Birdsalls livery stable.

Nov. 27th[.] —Nice day but colder than yesterday. I made a call on Young at the Depot Hotel to find out about Mose Levi's fight last Saturday[.] Work is going on as fast as is possible by Dan McKensies men who are getting out stone for the Webber building as fast as possible. Von Harris was tried to day before County Judge Powers and as was expected he was bound over for the District Court in $500.00 bonds[.] I bought 2 ducks[,] 2 qts cranberries and some celery which I sent up to Mrs. D. E. Havens to have cooked for dinner on Thanksgiving[.]

Nov. 28[.] Nice weather. the City Marshall arrested Geo Red early this morning charged with Drunk and disorderly and malicious injury. the Court fined him [$]5 & Costs[.] Not much other business going on to day. I wrote some notices for Chas Wilson to parties in the City about stacking Hay and straw in the Fire limits[.]

After supper I got a ticket from Thomas Coffey for the Brakemens Ball at the Rink[.] I went up and stayed till after the Grand March and came home and went to bed[.] After having been in bed about an hour the Night Police brought in John Taylor and Geo Redd who had been fighting again[.] I ordered them to appear in Court on Friday morning[.]

Nov. 29[.] Splendid weather[.] John Jackson moved in from the Table into Dr Davidson's house where he will live during the winter in order to let his boy attend School. I went up to Havens and had my duck dinner which I enjoyed very much. D. W. Sperling called to see Ordinance No 24 relative to Stacking Hay & Straw within the fire limits. I got a pan to stand the office lamps in on account of it leaking so much. F J Houghton came in and told me all about a fight in Oelrichs last Friday in which Col Wilgoski was one of the principals and wherein the Col got much the worst of it. Geo and I went down to Carters Saloon to shake 2 chances on a cake, and Geo came near winning it[.]

Nov. 30[.] Splendid weather still and the stone cutters on the Nelson, Webber, and Noll buildings are cutting as fast as they can throw the hammer and handle the chisel[.]

Mrs Simmons sent in a note in answer to mine of last week in which I asked about some Centurys Magazines. I forthwith got in a buggy and drove out there but could not find the books I wanted[.] After supper, John Maher, Mr Kael and myself attended the social Concert at the Methodist Church. We had a splendid time there and were treated splendidly by the Church people[.]

After the entertainment, Mr Kael and I came down town and after having played a few games of billiards, we separated to go home to bed[.]

Dec. 1[.] To day has been as fine and pleasant a day as any one might wish for in summer. the Stone Cutters, builders and waterwork men are surely being blessed with good weather[.] All day long, the Cry of the Collector has been going over town and many a one is grumbling at the ill luck of getting in any money.

Nigger Taylor has definitely given it out that he will marry which is only being done to get ahead of the City Marshal who has given him notice to leave town. No business of any sort has been going on today. There were lots of farmers in the City today and there seemed to be plenty of trading in the Stores, but legal business was dull. John Larsh was on the streets this afternoon looking as cool and Cheap as a cucumber after having lost all his money during last week trying to break the Club rooms adjoining Strainskys place.

Clem Davis hired the room adjoining my office yesterday for an auction room, but he faild to come around today and use it.

I rec'd. a bill of some Marriage Certificates sent to me from Chicago, but the Certificates have not yet arrived.

Frank Allen came in the office today and paid $5.00 on account on Clem Davis note against himself. I handed the money to Clem in the presence of Atty. Fisher.

I ordered Smith to discontinue my Puck and Jude at the Post office. C. D. Sayers was drunk again today and towards evening came to me and asked me for a Democrat. I told him to go and get one, but he was too drunk and lazy. he went home without one.

Dec 2nd[.] —Got up late. Stayed in the office a greater part of the time and read Geo Kennaus letters on Russians Political exiles in Siberia. In the evening, A. G. Shears, D. W. Sperling, F. M. Molyneau, T. B. Keil, John G. Maher and Selden, the Editor of the Prohibition Northwestern Advocate, droped in to the office and we all had a chat on the National parties and the good and bad effect of the Tariff Issue, Why we belonged to the parties we vote with, etc. It was cold and chilly today.

Dec 3. Notwithstanding it look[ed] yesterday as if snow would surely fall today[,] It is a fine summer day and the brick and stone masons are throwing themselves for all they are worth on the Webber, Nelson and Noll buildings[.] County Treasurer, L. A. Brower, moved his office up into the Court House this morning which almost completes the list of County officers that will be Entitled to offices in the New Court House, all of whom so far as I can learn are now located there.

this afternoon I went up and visited the Court House tenants[.] they are all pleased with their new quarters with the exception of a general lack of furniture which to the visitor is noticeable all over the building[.] John Nelson came to town today from the Agency. there seems to be a movement on foot by some of the Citizens to get the present Night Watch discharged from duty for the reason that he is, as is Claimed, not doing

Dawes County Courthouse in Chadron, Nebraska,
built in 1888

his duty, from the fact that notwithstanding numerous petty larcenies occurring nightly, there are never any arrests made.

After Supper I and Fred Molyneaux played a game of Billiards with Van Inwegin & Cutright in which Fred and I came out victorious[.]

Dec 4[.]   This morning was a finer day than yesterday. I got up early[.]   I rec'd a letter from Cousins, Nora Iaeger and Mamie Le Van both of which I answered right off.

Dec 5[.]   Fine weather again all day[.]   The Stone Cutters are busy knocking things around.   today there have been several busy bodies running all over the town getting Petitions signed against John Katen the present night watch to present to the Council this evening with a view of getting Katen Discharged, but the Council very wisely concluded to appoint a committee to investigate Mr Katens Case in view of no direct charge of misconduct having been set out in the Complaint or petitions[.] Old John Y. Nelson was in the city to day but he failed to call on me[.]

Dec 6[.] Fine weather and Dan McKenzie is happy. Hank Clifford, Charlie Nebo and Indian Agent Galligher came in from the Agency. Doc Middleton came up from Gordon. Old Hank Clifford and I had a long talk about making up an outfit to join the Wild West Combination to go to Europe next spring. Hank has found a full grown Indian that died years ago in perfect a state of preservation, the same as an Egyptian Mummy. He says he can get control of it for $2000.00, but I told him it was too much. Geo and his School mate took charge of the office so I went down to Stranskys and played billiards. I settled up in full with Mrs Josselyn[.]

Dec 7[.] Fine day again. Hank Clifford and Doc Middleton came in the office early. Doc was very sleepy so I put him to bed in my room after which Hank and I talked over the Indian Mummy business and I took him around to show him the 8 footed horse that has been here in hock ever since the last County Fair[.] Hank was much pleased with the animal as a piece of curiosity[.]

I finally wrote to ["Buffalo Bill"] Cody concerning some proposed wild west business. In the afternoon the owner of the 8 footed horse called upon Hank and myself and offered the animal for sale to us for $5000.00. I offered him $275.00[,] quite a difference, but as I originally only valued the animal at $1000.00, I thought I had as much right to go below that figure as far as he went above it.

We came to no bargain but later on I offered him the interest on $5000.00 at 12% per annum as a rental of the animal for two years upon which offer I am afraid he will take me up—[.] I got some lumber and had the walk from my office to my bedroom raised level with the door of the latter apartment for my more easy access thereto.

Ben Loewenthal had a set of Garnishee papers out of my Court served upon one James Duffy and upon the Depty Sheriff undertaking to serve the paper upon the Garnishee the said G. refused to accept them without his fees first being tendered which he demanded. Upon reflection however the Garnishee concluded to accept service but not until he had interviewed me—[.] Mat Baroch commenced an action in my Court against Branch & Co to day—[.] John Noll swore out a warrant against one Phil H Helmer for removing mortgaged property out of the County in which it was mortgaged. I issued a warrant but the officer has as yet failed to find him—[.] I was unable to attend the Concert given by the Ladies of the Congregational Church.

Dec. 8. Fine weather again and Still no snow. the weather in fact now is better than anytime during the summer. No business of any kind going to day.

Ben Loewenthal came into Court and asked to have his Garnishee against Duffy dismissed which the Court granted at once. Geo Havens bought himself a desk at Auction this afternoon and put it back in my room.

After Supper Geo & I went up to the Skating Rink. I did not stay long but came down to Ben Loewenthals opening of his New Clothing Store, after which F. B. Carley and I played a few games of billiards.

Dec 9[.] Sunday Fine weather still. every body in Town was out ridding today. Kass & Co. are busy putting on tin rooffing.

I stayed in the office all day and read.

Dec 10. Nice day again but towards evening it looked like snow. Miss Boyle came in the office and asked me to fix her Typewriter. I went up to her house but was unable to do any good. I sent up for the Typewriter and had it brought to my office where after an hours work I succeeded in remedying it. Mrs. Dr Davidson came in the office for her money for the stove I sold for her a days ago and as I had used the money I went out and collected enough to make the payment.

J. G. Maher came in the office and wrote a Summons for Spargur & Fisher on my Typewriter.

Birdsall Bros are ditching for water connections on Egan St[.] Lyon & Boyd are doing the same[.] Fred Poll put the cornice on Webber Bros. building into place to day. Wm Bailey, the Typo on the Democrat quit work last Saturday and has gone for a short vacation.

Dec 11. Fine weather again and still no snow. John Nelson and Nick Janis came to Town to day and John and I had a long talk about Wild West Matters. I fixed Miss Boyles Typewriter last evening and took it home this afernoon.

Dahlman & Simmons commenced an action on account in my Court. I moved my Typewriter from the bed room into the office this morning.

I received a letter from Frank Drexel, also one from Hank Clifford, the later one being in relation to the dried up Indian found quite recently in the bad lands.

I remained indoors pretty much all day. Maher, Perrin and Wilson were in the Office after supper. Geo posted up his private book this evening[.] It looks very much as if it were going to snow tonight.

Dec 12[.] Geo & I got up at 6[:]30[.] No snow and the day opened up as bright and fair as could be expected in July[.] The Case of Barock vs Branch & Co came on for hearing and was continued for 40 days. business seems to be getting duller and duller every day.

After supper I went down to Carters and played a few games of billiards[.] Tom Coffey had a little trouble with Jas Duffy about a settlement of a bill.

I came home very late.

Dec 13. Pleasant weather and work on the different buildings around town is being pushed right along[.] Jerry fincher came up from Omaha on a Special this morning.

I had a talk with him about some lots[.] A. L. Dorrington handed me an Arizona (W. Yuma) paper in which there appeared a notice concerning Cousin Louis Iaeger Jr having taken up a Minning Claim in the Castle Dome district of that Terry [Territory]. James Cavanaugh boarded the "flier" this morning and left Chadron, but the loss was only temporary as John Henry arrived in town with his "trunk" very shortly after Jimiacos departure. the democrat came out to day. I spoke to John Mead to day relative to getting some work to do out side of my Office work to keep me busy, but received no encouragement whatever.

Dec 14. Fine weather. I got up early. business has been very quiet today.

Dec 15[.] last night it rained a little but the weather has been splendid all day. this morning the Case of Dahlman & Simmons vs. John Anderson came up for trial and resulted in judgment for the Pltff.

After supper I played billiards with Tom Doud.

Dec 16. I got up late this morning. It has been a splendid day and I am Sorry I did not engage a team to go out to fowlers.

I Stayed in the office all day.

After Supper I went to Church with Joe Ford. Geo and Bailey had the office. last week Corey left the Town.

Dec 17. this morning at 8 oclock it commenced to snow and looked as if winter was going to set in in dead earnest, but towards 12 oclock it cleared off and with the exception of a little mud on the streets caused by melted snow, it was as fine weather as ever.

business has been pretty dull to day. I called on A. W. Crites this morning and by special request he came around to the office this evening upon some legal business. I put him and a client in the back room and left the Office in Charge of Geo.

I have been making up a list of Missing Copies of Jude and Puck today and have written to those publishers for the Same, it being my intention to have them bound into book form.

Dec 18. Fine weather all day. Henry Maden called on me per instructions of a postal from myself concerning a debt of his to one Warren J. Burtis of Cedar Rapids[,] Ia.

I have been in the Office all day doing nothing but writing letters and studying what to do.

Spotted Elk came over from the Agency today and called on me for a pair of pants which I promised him during our recent County fair. I took the Gentleman up to Silversteins but could not get him fitted, so I got Ben Loewenthal to fit him out. I wrote a letter to John A. McShane for C W Allen. Geo Havens got mad at me for staying out a little late last night and has declared himself that he will never Sleep with me any more but I am going to get him back again if possible.

I went up to the skating rink to see the District Skule played by our local talent. it was very good—[.] after the play I went with Tommy Doud to Stranskys and played a few games of billiards during which time I was called to visit Red Jacket at Fannie Powers who was said to be dieing, but I found her simply in one of her fits of ill temper of which she has been so characteristic of late. I however sent for Dr Miller and had him give her some medicine afterwhich I and Godsall went to bed in my room.

Dec 19. Fine weather again. Chas Wilson the City Marshall made a raid on the houses of prostitution today—[.] there has been no business to day to mention.

After Supper I went up to the Skating Rink again to see the District Skule but was called to Police Court before the play commenced. I however got through with Court in time to get back to the Rink before the performance commenced.

After it was over, I played billiards with Tommy Doud and as usual got the worst of it.

The Marshall arrested Theo Wagner for disturbing the Peace. Larkens came home and slept with me.

Dec 20. Splendid weather again. This A.M. I received a nice letter and Newspaper from Uncle William. the case of State vs Wagner was tried this morning and Deft fined $1.00 and costs.

Dec 21[.] It has been fine weather all day again. This afternoon John Maher and I went up to the Public School to witness the Closing exercises in Prof Dentons Room which was very interesting and showed some successful work on the part of Prof Denton. Geo Havens returned and has again taken up with me as my room mate.

Dr Jackson returned from Iowa this morning.

Dec 22. Splendid weather yet and the town has been thronged with Farmers all day. P B Danielson Auctioned off some of his Hotel furniture but am sorry to say he could not realize anitty to speak of.

W. A. Seldens wife died this morning from Child birth. the child is alive and doing well. Charlie Allen went to Rushville this morning.

Luke Otis was in the Office this afternoon and asked me to make out a Certified fee bill and balance of Judgment unpaid in the case of Luke Otis vs H H McChesney. W A Selden came and asked me to attend to an Overcoat Raffle for him, whereupon I immediately wrote several postal Cards to holders of tickets, notifying them of the postponement of the Raffle to Dec 31st. 1888 at 8. P.M.

Mrs. A. C. Fowler of Table precinct visited Chadron today. I stayed in the Office all evening. The K of P's will take charge of Mrs W. A. Seldens funeral which is to take place next Monday at 9.30 from the Baptist Church.

Dec 23. Fine weather all day till about 7. P.M. when all signs and indications pointed towards a change in the weather. I bought a bagatelle board for a

Christmas present for John and Ollie Fowler on the Table precinct.

I remained in the Office all day almost. in the afternoon Jas Dahlman, Mat Baroch, Chas Allen, D. W. Sperling, Geo Clay, Editor Sheldon, Jim Boyds Brother and H. P. Simmons were in the office and we all got arguing over the probable removal of the Post Office here under the Republican rule and finally the Conversation turned into direct politics which lasted till 6.20 P.M. and then only ended at my suggestion that I was hungry. After supper I returned to the office after having played one game of billiards with Tommy Doud and wrote a long letter to Uncle William. Charlie Allen came over after awhile. Geo Returned from Church and we retired about 9.30 P.M.

Dec 24. This morning there was considerable snow on the ground. Geo. & I got up early. after breakfast I attended Mrs Seldens Funeral after which [I] purchased some Christmas presents at Myers & Boone and went to the Office to make them. John Maher left for Columbus yesterday evening to spend the hollidays.

I got Maud Danielson to write on some of the presents their address. After supper Dan McKinzie and I went up to the Baptist Church to see the little ones get their presents from the Christmas tree. after a short stay we went to the Congregational Church and there witnessed a merry gathering of Children to greet a real live Santa Claus in the person of Mr. J M Pritchard. He created a great deal of fun among the little ones and while in the church was very nervous for fear someone might run away with his fine team of Elk and Rein Deer which he drove from his Cristal Palace. Before the services were over however, Dan & I adjourned to the Skating rink where the K of P's were giving a Grand Ball and Concert. after paying [$]1.00 apiece and having got seated in a warm place in the Gallery, we were well rewarded by the touching Chords of the Niobrara Military Band in their concert performances.

But when dancing commenced which was preceeded by an unique Grand March at 930 P.M. Dan and I concluded it was time for us to sneak and Sneak we did[.] I retired immediately upon my return to the Office, Geo being busy helping Mrs Josselyn sell meal tickets at the ball.

Dec 25[.] Christmas with 1 inch of Snow—[.]

little Ray Fowler died last night and I trust his Christmas may be in heaven.

After breakfast I and Dan came up to the post Office and I bought a little piano for little Annie O'Hanlon. By invitation I took dinner at the Rail Road Eating House with Mr Young, afterwhich I came up town and read in my Office, during which F O Messenger came in and we had a social chat on the future office holders in Dawes County.

After Supper Geo & I went up to see the Christmas Cantata at the Methodist Church.

The Entertainment as Executed by "Santa Claus" and "his Boys" together with the Sunday School is deserving of great Credit upon the Superintendent and teachers and decries the fact that there is nothing like perserverance. Geo and I went to bed early—[.]

Dec 26. Cold but Clear—[.] I got up a list for the Raffle of W. A. Seldens [$]90.00 Overcoat which is to come of[f] at Joe Fords Barber Shop on the 31 inst. at 8 oclock, P.M.

I have been in the Office all day Clubbing at one thing or other. I received a letter this morning containing a Christmas book with a short note but no name signed to the note—it is from York[,] Pa[.] but I cannot recognize the hand writing and must therefore remain in the dark.

I sent for 5 copies of back numbers of Scribners Magazine to day. Ray Fowlers body was shipped to Ainsworth[,] Neb[.] this A.M.

Dec 27. Clear and cold all day. the Democrat did not come out today as they were unable to get up the ordinances into type. I got Seldens mourning cards printed and brought them over to the office. Dr. A. L. Jackson came in the office with Allen D. Sperling to have me write out an application on the typewriter for the appointment of Jackson on the Board of Pension Examiners to fill the vacancy caused by the resignation of Dr O O. Harris.

The case of Asa M. Lovelace vs Moses Young was called up in my Court today and Continued for Service by publication 40 days. W. P. Conely was in the Office today and instructed me to look after the purchase of lost [lots] 12 & 13 in Block 12 which I forthwith done.

In the evening Allen and Fisher came in the office and fooled around[.] Also Bailey came and wrote on the Typewriter awhile. F. J. Houghton Filed bill of particulars in case of Rascellus K. Cameron vs. Frederick Hafner—after which Geo called me in the back room to eat pop corn. I went to bed early.

Dec 28. Fine weather and thawing all day. the Democrat came out to day. the waterwork men are working hard to complete their work while this good weather lasts—I spoke to C D Sayrs and after a few words told him he could stand his book case in my office but not to make it his headquarters.

Doc Middleton came up from Gordon today and expects to return this evening. Eugene Myers was down from Crawford yesterday and today looking over the City. I promised Doc to go to Gordon with him but it is impossible for me to be gone from town at this present time. After supper Mike Gottstein came in the office and asked me to give him an order for 2 County Claims I have on file which he represented had been allowed. they were respectively for [$]14.00 & [$]11.65[.] I gave them to Mike on account of my note which he holds against me upon his agreeing to cancel and deliver up said note for $75[.]00 more if made in the next 60 days. there was an entertainment at the Rink tonight but I did not go[.]

Dec 29. Fine Clear weather again all day. Geo Havens informed me this A.M. that he had Seen Billy Wilson in a rather precarious condition being taken home in a carriage from a certain Gambling House. if this be so I am sorry to know it—[.] I have had very little business today in fact none—[.]

Pete Nelson was in the office asking me all about the proper dimensions requisite for a Stage for a Hall which he is now erecting[.] John Maher came back from Columbus day before yesterday and brought a sone [son] too along. Sam Hamm the Barber has sold out his barber shop to Hatch and Billy Mead who are to take charge and possession Jan 1st[,] 1889. The Parties who were to rent the South half of my building backed out and have taken Mrs Davidsons building instead[.]

The water commissioners are hard to work this good weather.

Dan McKinzie got the 4 Stone Columns Set into position to day[.] There is a Dance to following the skating programme at the Rink this evening on which Occasion the party who gave the entertainment last night will furnish the music for the dancers upon an Organette[.] Geo Havens is up there and upon his return will have lots to say[.]

Dec 30. Nice weather all day[,] Clear and medium warm. I remained in the office almost all day and had a good deal of company. during the day it leaked out that Billy Wilson had made an assignment for preferred creditors in which Bartlett Richards figured a Chief Mogul—yesterday[.] I wrote several letters to day—[.]

Charles Allen was in the office a good deal today and we discussed the pros and cons of the outlook for the next City election. There are at present several factions kicking against the Council just in order that they may keep their hands in. Mr J. W. Smith the present City Clerk is making quite an unusual and uncalled for commotion against the City Council and if he is not careful will have a Mountain of trouble on his Shoulder[.] Mrs C. C. a colored lady has started up a restraunt in the Dr Davidson building next door to my Office but I fear it will soon play out.

Dec 31. Nice weather again and every Carpenter and Stone Cutter have been throwing themselves at their work with a good will.

At 12[:]30 the case of Cameron vs Hafner came on for tri[a]l and upon motion for Continuans was adjourned to Jan 30th[,] 1888 [1889] at One Oclock P.M.

I have been busy a good deal today in trying to sell chances on the [$]90.00 Over Coat belonging to Selden.

Charlie Allen got me to Typewrite a letter to Lieut Col Alex at Fremot [Fremont,] Neb. advising him of Allen's resignation as Capt. of Chadron Div[.] No 27, Regt. W. R. of K. P.— Tom Coffey won the overcoat[.]

The failure of Wm Wilson is now verified all over town[.]

Chapter VII:
1889 (Diary)

Jan 1[,] 1889. Happy New Year has been the go all day. everybody has been celebrating more or less. I treated up at Coffeys and then came down to Mike Gottstens where all the Rail Road Boys were turning things.

Mrs Geo A. Van Inwegen died this A.M. at 8.30 oclock from child birth[.]

This mornings mail brought me a fine Christmas Gift in the Shape of a Registered package from Leonora & the children containing 3 silk hdkfs [handkerchiefs] and a 2 dollar Bill.

McLaughlin, Pat Hayes and I took dinner at the Rail Road Hotel[,] Mc & I being guests of Pat.

In the afternoon everybody was interested in looking at the Eclipse of the Sun.

After Supper McNeallon raffled off his horse and two saddles—[.] J. W. Smith won it—[.] I had a chance in it but as usual I came out 2nd best.

Charlie Allen was called to the bedside of one of his children who is lying at the point of death at Pine Ridge[.]

Jan 2[.] To day has been perfectly delightfull[.] I went out to the water works and Pump house with D. Y. Mears[.]

I settled up with Smith & Gottstein for the Chadron Democrat. In the Evening I participated by special invitation in a Banquet at Danielsons given by Von Harris—the County Commissioner from the 3rd district—[.] County Commr Burger took his Seat today.

Jan 3[.] Fine weather and McKinzie is hurrying his stone work on the P B Nelson "Opera Block[.]"

the Democrat did not get out on time to day, an unusual occurrence. The Council held and adjourned a meeting this evening. John Henry the Negro was released today by the City Marshall. This Morning at 10[:]30 I attend the funeral of Mrs George A Van Inwegen, who died so sorrowfully in Childbed on the 1st inst [instant]—[.] after the funeral Tom Doud Sr and I had a long chat in my Office over frontier life—[.] after dinner I called on Miss E. Boyle for particulars of Mrs Van Inwegens early life and it was not till after 12 Oclock Midnight that I finished writing a biography of her life and got things ready for the paper, after which Maher, Wilson and I went over to Mrs E. N. Josselyn and after eating Oysters I came home and retired—[.]

To day I recd a letter from Buffalo Bill[.]

Jan 4. Fine weather again and every body happy except the water main Contractor and Water Commissioner D. Y. Mears and John Noll who in consequence of the water having been turned on and the pipe on Second Street leaking to some extent are busy trying to remedy the same[.] C. D. Sayrs commenced several Civil Actions before me to day with William Belanger as Plaintiff in each case.

The Zezi man was on the Street today and found lots of Suckers[.] The Democrat came out today. Bessie OLinn gave her 13th Birthday today and invited here [her] friends from all quarters of the City. Geo Havens was there of Course.

After Supper I called on Mayor Hughes and chatted on the outlook of the political issue for the coming City elections[.]

Jan 5th[.] Fine weather all day and a great Many Farmers in the City.

Last night or I should say this morning about 1 oclock, a fire broke out in Wm Rutters paint Shop in the Rear of L. C. Quigleys Livery Stable on King St. and before the the Fire Department could reach the Scene[,] the Shop (which was a small one) was almost entirely consumed by the flames.

The Special Election for a Contract with the F. E. & M. V. RR Co. It was carried by [number missing] to 16 against[.] To day the Council tested the water works System but no good test was had as several bursts in the pipes occurred.

M. OHanlon Commenced a garnishee process against Richard Furgerson.

In the Police Court today the case of State vs Theo Wagner was tried. the Defendant was fined One Dollar and Costs and went to Jail in default but Fannie Powers was unable to have her baby lay in Jail so about 8. oclock this evening she paid his fine and all went Serene—[.]

Mayor Hughes called in a few moments to see how everybody was getting along.

Jan. 6. Splendid weather again all day[.] No Snow this winter yet to speak off and this kind of weather is altogether unaccountable[.] I stayed in the office all day and Closed up my Ledger A. and transferred accounts to Ledger "B[.]" Geo carried water in this evening and we had a good bath in the evening[.] during the early part of the evening the office was called upon by the usual gang of Sunday politicians[.]

Dec [Jan.] 7. This morning showed up Cloudy and Cold, altogether opposite from yesterday.

The Public Schools of Chadron opened to day again[.] at about 9 oclock it commenced to Snow and continued to snow hard till 12[:]30 PM after which it commenced to thaw again.

P. O. Hanlon came into my court and had his Garnishee suit against Ferguson[.] Montgomery came in and paid [$]2.00 on acct. on Belangers Accts which I have for collection. after Supper I went up to the Engine house to be in attendance upon a meeting of the City Council, but no meeting was had, however we had some fine Sparring by some of the local weights. I have been working all day opening the New Ledger.

Dec [Jan.] 8. Fine day. Clear and cold. Dan McKenzie is working hard on the Nelson Building[.] Business rather dull.

after supper I went up to attend a meeting of the City Council, but no meeting. This evening about 8 Oclock a cutting affray occurred between some colored people of questionable repute who got into a quarrel over a Jealous play. No arrest have yet been made[.] John Maher and I wrote out a letter on the typewriter for Geo A Van Inwegin to the Receiver of the local land Office at this place.

Jan 9. Fine day again. The marshal filed a complaint against W. T. Overby charging him committing an assault upon one Mattie Anderson with intent to kill & murder.

I committed the accused in default of $500.00 bonds for his preliminary examination pending the attendance of necessary witnesses who are at present in Crawford, among whom is the party upon who the assault is said to have been made, they having made their escape on the mornings train for Crawford.

After Supper I attend a meeting of the City Council at which the Resignation of John Katen was read and approved and W. P. Hartzell appointed in his Stead.

Hon Westover and the Sheriff of Sheridan Co were in the City last night.

I came home late[.]

Jan 10[.] To day has been a fine one but not much business going on[.] The Firm of D. Silverstein failed a few days ago and they are at present on the outside of the business[.] The Depty Sheriff arrived from Crawford this evening and brough[t] a witness for the examination tomorrow morning.

The City Marshall arrested two Tommies this afternoon and not having time to try them I continued the Case till tomorrow and made the "dear ones" give bonds for their appearance.

Jan 11th[.] Fine weather again all day. This morning I tried the assault with intent to Murder Case and after having heard all the evidence in the case I bound the Defendant William T. Overby over to the District Court in the sum of $1,000 and not being able to give bonds, I committed him to Jail. I also required the principal witness[,] Mattie Anderson and John Taylor to give recognizance for their appearance in the District Court to testify against the accused in the sum of $300.00 and not being able to give said bail I also committed them.

In the afternoon I called up the two Police Court Cases of State vs. May Hamilton and Little Maud. They concluded to plead guilty to the charge laid against them and also begged for mercy from the Court whereupon I fined them $1.00 & costs—[.] during the day I have made arraingments with Rev Read to see Mrs C C. Hughes relative to getting her to adopt the little boy of Mr W. A. Selden which was born about a month ago[.]

Jan 12. Fine day again and Dan McKenzie has been getting in his fine lick on the Nelson building. The Dr for the County[,] A. L. Jackson issued an order to the Jailor & Sheriff today certifying that the witness Mattie Anderson, now in Jail in default of Bonds for her appearance before the District Court to testify against William T. Overby who Stabbed her, is Sick and unable to be in jail. Dr Jackson I understand succeeded in getting the City authorities to Rent Charley Allens

392

building for a hospital where Sadie Carter is now lying sick with Pheunomona.

C. D. Sayrs commenced action against Joseph Maiden for Walter E. Derrick for $120.00 for keeping Jos Maidens boy. Henry Miller brought me a load of wood to day.

Geo & I Scrubbed out the Sleeping room this morning.

The Sheriff was down to see me about bonds for Taylor.

G. W. Dunn came into Court today and undertook to bulldose but could not make it stick. he finally came to terms and paid some of his honest debts.

The County Commissioners wrote me a letter (per Shears) appraising me of the important fact that they had rejected another one of my bills which was for [$]4.25[.]

Geo Havens went to the Skating Rink after Supper.

It has been rumored around town that Mike Ellmore, a grading contractor on the B. & M. RR was lynched a few days ago for having killed a laborer on the grade.

Jan 13[.] Sunday and a fine day. I stayed in the office all day. after Supper the Marshall and I in company with McKenzie and Tom went to see Mattie Anderson who was stabbed a few days ago and is not expected to get over it.

Jan 14. Stormy and Cold. at about 10 A.M. it commenced snowing and continued so all day at a slow gait.— at 8.30 I recd a message from Denver telling me of Brother Thomas' death. I at once wired to have him embalmed and also wired Jefferson Snyder for $500.00 of his money with which to take him home.

There were two Cases in Police Court this morning. one for Drunk & Disorderly which I discharged and one for Carrying Concealed weapons which upon trial found & proved the Deft guilty. I imposed a light sentence upon him but the deft acted very surley and cross over it—[.]

I telegraphed again to Denver asking how Brother Tom was fixed financially and the cause of his death.

Old man Montgomery came in and settled the balance of his bill with Belanger.

G W Dunn also came like a man and paid his bills in Justice Court[.] Belanger brought over some more bills to be sued on.

I seen W L Casady and told him about turning over to me the house of J. T. Wright on Egan St and I also seen Mr Wagner about the other property.—

Mrs C. C. Hughes has taken Mr. Seldens Baby and will no doubt adopt it[.] The Scab Stone Cutters are holding a meeting with a view to getting Tom Collins out of Jail.

Dan McKenzie worked all day on the Nelson building and hopes to be done in a few more days now.

D. Y. Mears was in the office this A.M. telling what kind of bad boys lived in his part of the town.

Bob Reeds oldest Girl gave birth to an illigitimate child this morning—after supper I attended a proposed meeting of the Firemen at the Engine House but no quorum being present we dispersed.

The inaugrators of a Public Library met at the Rink this evening. The Base Ball association held a meeting of stockholders in A. L. Dorringtons office.

Mike Boland is now trying to get the Mayor to pardon Tom Collins[.]   9.55 P.M.   10[:]30 P.M. the Mayor in Company with Mike Boland called upon me but were unable to effect any release in favor of Collins, the Mayor having got a complete understanding of the case refused to interfere in the matter.

Jan 15. Cold and clear weather. I done a little Business but not much to speak of as I have been waiting all day for a message from Mr Snyder relative to going after my brother Thos in Denver and at 3.40 P.M. a message came to me from Mr Snyder stating that he could not telegraph money nearer than Omaha or Lincoln and for me to bring Brother Thomas Body to Hamburg.—

Thomas Collins finally concluded to pay his fine and costs—and demanded a fee bill afterwards[.]

Jan 16. Stormy and high wind all day. I received notification that $200.00 was put to my credit in First Natl Bank at Omaha which I immediately had exchanged to Bank of Chadron. I will leave tonight for Denver[.]

Jan 17. In Fremont[,] Neb. where I arrived at 3 P.M. today, I stopped at the Eno House. after registering I went out and bought a new block hat and shipped my white hat to Omaha in care [of] Drexel & Maul. on my road I met Alex Kennedy with whom I used to work in Wyoming and we had a long time of talk together.

I leave for Denver this evening at 9.30[.]

Jan 18. On the train bound for Denver where I arrived at 5 P.M. I put up at the Windsor and immediately called upon the undertakers Wolly & Rollins on Laramer St. and learned that Bro Thomas had been buried on the 15th inst. [instant]. they gave me very unsatisfactory accounts as to why they did not embalm the body as I had requested them to do by telegraph[.] I next called upon Geo. Hilbert[,] Bro Thomas partner, but was unable to learn anything definate about Thomas business. I called at Dr Buttons office and found him in but the information received from him was not Satisfactory. after leaving the Drs office myself and Charlie Davis (my attending Messenger boy) went to the Opera to hear the Boston ideals in "Mignon[,]" after which I found out from Geo Hilbert as to the whereabouts of a Charles Ott who was reported to be working in a Gambling house on Curtis Street and known as the "Capitol[,]" thence I sent my messenger who returned to the Hotel whither I had preceeded him with the information that Mr Ott was not at his post but that he had left word for him to call on me and also received a card from the Proprietors of the Capitol giving Charlie Otts new place of business which was 1725 Laramer St. I made my messenger boy sleep with me in Room 117.

Jan. 19[.] I called at the City Detective's office[,] Charlie Lintons place, and got him to hunt up Mrs J. M. Casserley who is reported to have attended Brother Thomas during his illness.

I procured a buggy all day to get around with.

I called on Atty[.] Early in Simms block who I was given to understand was Mrs Casserleys lawyer.

I then called on Dr Button again to get some facts concerning the possibility of poison having been given Bro Thomas[.] I put very little faith in the rumor of death having been caused by poison as seems to be believed by some who claim to know Mrs Casserley. Next I drove back to the City Detectives office and found they had located Mrs Casserley to be living in the same House in which Brother Thomas died (Charles Block) though in another room, 66. Bro died in 54.

I put the Horse up for Dinner and at 2 oclock drove up to Charles Blk. in company with my Messenger who I left to mind the horse while I went up to see Mrs Casserley who was living on the 2nd story in Room 66. I found a Mr Richards there who I was told was the male attendant upon my Bro.

I learned from Both that Tom died very suddenly from Bronchal Pneumonia as previously stated to me by Dr Button, and that only $187.00 in money had been found upon his cloths, that he had some old (very old & worn out to use Mrs Casserleys words) cloths which she had given to Mr Richards to give to some poor people and that Bro Thomas had only and old suit left which he was wearing at the time of his death and that she had given his best suit to the undertaker to dress Brother Thomas in for burial.

According to her story Brother Thomas had nothing left except 1 ordinary business suit and the $187.00 above mentioned. he had left no word nor any writing at all. She however admitted having 2 gold watches and a Stud which Tom had in Bail for $150.00 but Claimed the right of property in them first because she had guaranteed to pay all bills incurred on Toms account during his late illness and Second, because she thought if there was any money left after settling said claims, it should go to her for her extreme trouble and care of him, to which I raised no objection and departed for the time.

After which I drove out to see W. H. Yankee on the Boulavard bet [between] Highland and Diamond Aves but found he was in Aspen[,] Col[.]

After supper I called at 1725 Laramer St to see Charlie Ott, but he was not there yet so I left word for him to call on me at the Windsor Hotel which he did about 6[:]30 P.M.

At 7.30 I called again at Detective Lintons office but found him cold and reluctant and altogether unwilling to do in [any] work in trying to find out from Mrs Casserley as to what money She had belonging to Tom from which I inferred after a carefull consideration that he had been well fixed by Mrs Casserley to keep his mouth shut and balk me as much as possible. I returned to 1725 Laramer St where I met Chas Ott again and also several old time Omaha Boys[,] all of whom I was glad to see and was especially benefited thereby for the amount of news derived pertaining to Bro Thos effects[.] I retired at about 12. P.M.

Jan 20[.] Sunday[.] Red Mulkey and Sullivan and Billie Orliff and Chas Ott were callers on me at the Hotel. Chas Ott promised to call again at 6 P.M. to go with me to see Mrs Casserley and tell her how many suits of cloths Tom had and explain certain matters relative to a Diamond ring which she claimed Tom told her Charlie had stolen out of his vest pocket.

Red Sullivan took supper with me at the Hotel after which I felt very bad and laid down and when Charlie Ott came I postponed the visit till tomorrow[.]

Jan 21[.] Nice day all of which it has been since my arrival in Denver.

I received a telegram late last evening from Snyder asking if Bro Thomas had a wife and children. To which I answered early this morning thus[:] no wife, no children, no will, no property. Cannot move body without more money. Send $350.00[.]

after breakfast I went up to see Mrs C. again and she then offered me Toms Trunk and 5 suits of cloths etc. which she positively knew I was aware of her having by reason of having been to Leadville and seen Richards wear one suit.

During the afternoon to wit 2[:]30 I received a message from Snyder saying that if the body could be forwarded he would send the money as telegraphed for. I therefore ordered Rodgers the City Coroner to get the required permit and exhume the body at once, and after supper I went up to get a first look at poor Thomas. I found him to look as natural as could be but having in a sort of way formed an idea of a probable poisoning act, I felt like having the corpse opened and the Stomach examined to which end I called upon Mip Lowe & Von Shultz, expert chemists for the purpose of ascertaining their price for such work. I found that it would require $500.00 for a chemical analysis and a doubt being in my mind and reasoning that the analysis in either event could be of no benefit to poor Bro. and not knowing where to get the money, I ordered the undertaker to proceed with his process of embalming.

Billy Orliff and I with an express man went to Mrs Casserley for Bro's trunk and effects[.]

Jan 22. Nice day and I have hunted all over town and worn my self out trying to find some clue leading to Bros. money. No Bank in Denver claims to have anything on deposit in his name, Nor are any registered bonds in his name any place to be found. I called at the Undertakers to see Bro Thomas body embalmed. Billie Orliff & I called on a Lady who claimed to know

Something about Brother Thomas relations with Mrs Casserley while on 1732 Lawrence st., but I found her account rather meagre and of little import.

After dinner I sent word to Mrs Casserley that I had taken Thomas body up and would take it East for burial.

I wrote a great many letters today and felt very sick.

I went to bed at 10 PM.

Jan 23[.] I made Mrs Casserley give up Bro Thomas watch chain, locket and Diamond Ring. I purchased my necessary tickets for Harrisburg and got things ready to start this evening on my Journey. I found out this morning that Mrs Casserley knew where Thomas over Coat was and refused to give it up on the strength and ground that she thought she had already given up enough to me. After a great deal of trouble with the newspaper reporters I finally got started at 7[:]50 PM on the Chicago Express.

Jan 24. Arrived at Omaha at 3 P.M. where John Drexel and his Bro Herman met me at the Depot with my letters. I had to change sleepers in Omaha, but I went forward to be in the express Car with the Corpse so as to be ready and tend to the Changing of the Corpse all of which at my special Solicitation was done very nicely.

Left Council Bluffs for Chicago at 6[:]30 PM. and I went to bed early.

Jan 25[.] Arrived at Chicago at 12 M. and had the Corpse transferred to the Pittsburgh & Ft Wayne Depot at once by special wagon. I left to go up to Sherman House to Meet some parties.

After Dinner I went straight to the Depot and got my Sleeping Car ticket to Harrisburg and at 3[:]15 the Train started. we took Supper at Ft Wayne and Breakfast at Pittsburgh, where I also had quite a time with the Baggage men about handling the Corpse so roughly.

Jan 26[.]   The Passenger left Pittsburgh in 2 sections. Bros remains going on the 1st Sec. and my sleeper on the 2nd Sec.   this was not to my taste and when both trains met in Altoona I changed and got on the 1st Sec. and arrived on the same train with the Corpse at Harrisburg at 3.20 P.M. I had another tussel in getting the Corpse changed from the Penn Depot to the Reading Depot. But I accomplished it however and at 4 Oclock the train started for reading where we arrived at 6 Sharp.   here I was met by Mr Snyder and having changed the Corpse for the last time I finally boarded the Hamburg train and arrived there at 6[:]30 P.M. where Bro George met me with the undertaker.

Jan. 27. Cold and a little Snowy. Sister Leonora came up from Reading. she has been feeling very badly of late.

Jan. 28.   A little Snowy this morning[.]   The funeral took place at 1.30 P.M. there were not too many people present at the House. the Church Choir sang at the house and a short prayer was offered after which we all took a farewell look at poor Brother Thomas and then proceeded to the Church where he was laid besides his poor parents—who have gone before him 27 years ago[.] He was aged 35 years 2 mos & 13 days.   After the services at the grave which seemed to almost break my heart we adjourned to the Church where a Sermon in English was rendered by Dr Miller and one in German by Dr Holst. After the Services the Ministers and Pall bearers were invited to take Dinner with the relatives at Aunt Louisa's House from whence the funeral had been conducted.

Mr and Mrs Snyder & Cousin Nora left for reading on the evening train.

Jan 29[.] Nice day[.] Aunt Amanda, Bro Geo and I left Hamburg. Geo & I for Reading and Aunt A. for Phila[.]

Geo and I had some business about Toms money and at about 3 P.M Geo left for Phila[.] I remained and stoped with Mr Snyder.

Jan 30. Nice weather again[.] I went over some accounts with Mr Snyder up at Uncle Thos House.

at 2 oclock I took the train for Lyons to visit Cousin Lizzie Knittle. I stayed with them[.]

Jan 31. Nice day again this morning[.] I got up early took the train for Shamrock and there got a man to take me out to my Aunt Diana for [$].50. I telegraphed to Alburtis to have a buggy come for me at 4 P.M. Aunt Diana was glad to see me but disappointed that I should not stay a week with her. the buggy came as ordered and at 7 P.M. I was again in Reading. I took supper at Aunt Marys where I also met Cousin Mamie Kendig from Phila.

After supper I went down to Snyders and seen Sister Lenora[.] Mr & Mrs S. went to an invitation party and Lenora & I called at Mrs Davis but found her out of the City.

Feb 1[.] Lenora went up to Aunt Diana's and I started this evening at 6 P.M. for Phila where I arrived at 8.40[.] I put up at Greens[.]

Feb 2[.] I called on Uncle William after having first taken a nice bath at the Conintental Hotel. I found Uncle but he had an engagement at 11 A.M. so I named 3 P.M. as a good hour and I then went to Kolbe & Son for my artificials which I had sent there for repairs over 2 years ago.

at 5[:]15 I called on and found Uncle William, I had supper with him after which he accompanied me to the Reading Depot at 9th & Green where I was to go to Langhorn. I arrived at Langhorn at 7 P.M. and found Aunt Amanda's buggy waiting for me to take me to the house where I found Mr Norris in loving attendance upon Cousin Nuisance—.

Feb 3. Sunday, it has been a little Chilly to day. I went through the famous "henery" with Loui who seemed to be a little out of humor all day.

[Feb.] 4[.] Mr Norris left for the City very early this morning. Loui & I left Langhorn at 10 oclock at the 9th & Green St Depot[.] I left him to pay a visit to Mrs Street[,] 3036 Frankford Avenue[,] where I took dinner and left again for down Town in Company with Willie Street her son, who went to the 9th & Green St Depot for my Valise and again met me at Kolbes[,] 1207 Arch Street[,] where I left my repaired limbs to be sent to York and put on my old ones again So as to enable me to get around more easily.

We then called on Dr Barber, 129 South 7th street[,] after which we went to Wanamakers to see something for Geo Havens, but not knowing what to buy for him I concluded to wait.

We next went to 9th & Race Sts where I purchased a Harpphone for $4.56 afterwhich Willie Street went home and I to the Washington Hotel to be with Uncle William. After supper I went up to "Greens" to meet Dr Barber and go to the theatre with him, but not showing up at the appointed time, I returned to the Hotel and had a long talk with Uncle William.

Feb 5[.] Uncle gave me $5.00 and accompanied me to the Broad Street Depot of the Penna. R.R. from where I started for Reading—where I arrived at 10.15 A.M. and went Straight to Aunt Marys[,] 228 N 5th st, where I expressed a bundle to myself at York and wrote a letter to Lenora and at 12 M I left for Tamaqua where I arrived at 1.10 P.M. and was met by Aunt Emma[.] it started to rain about 10.30 A.M. I was please[d] to see Cousin Mamie and Dr Ramsey for the first time since their marriage. It seems almost impossible to realize that Aunt Emma should be a Grand Mother.

Feb 6[.] last evening toward night it Snowed and after supper Mr. Ramsy got out his Sleigh bells and had Aunt Emma and Cousin Mamie help clean them and this morning he gave me a nice sleigh ride and took me down to the barber Shop. I have decided to remain in Tamaqua till Saturday[.]

Feb 7. Nice weather. at 1.30 Aunt Louisa and Cousin Mamie Levan came up from Hamburg. Mr. Murdock Came over from Mucha Chunk to see Cousin Mamie and we all had a very enjoyable time[.]

Feb. 8[.] Nice weather. Mr Murdock left early this A.M. and returned again from his position to spend the evening with Cousin Mamie, but Dr Ramsy & I got them interested in a game of Cards and we playd till a late hour. Mr Murdock refused to go to bed for fear of oversleeping himself. Dr Ramsey made a flying visit to Phila but returned again last evening. Turkey Dinner was the order of the day and I enjoyed myself very much[.]

Feb 9[.] Nice day again. at 4.20 P.M. Aunt Louisa, Cousin Mamie and I left Tamaqua for Hamburg. we were accompanied by Mr Murdock who will spend a few days at Hamburg in his endeavor to recover from a very severe stroke of Lovesickness[.]

Feb 10[.] Aunt Louisa and I drove up to St Johns Church to hear Dr Riely preach in German. in the evening we again attended the Methodist Church in Company with Mary Smith[.]

Feb 11[.] It tried to snow a little to day but I fear it will back down. I went up to the telegraph office to send for a pair of gloves for Mamie. on my way home I had a severe fall on my way home. This evening I received news from Chadron of the death of M. Ballard[.] Reveds[.] Kerr and Hackenburg called on Aunt Louisa after supper. Mr Murdock has not been feeling well since his recent arrival here owing to continual attacks of asthma to which he is subject to[.]

Feb 12. Yesterday it Snowed a little but not enough to make any Sleighing. Annie Kemp having arrived from a weeks visit to Wilmington and elsewhere called at Aunt Louisas' and the out shot of her Call was that she and I went out in the Country for a turkey for Aunt Louisa.

After Supper Aunt Louisa was taken very sick with a headache[.]

Feb 13[.] Still in Hamburg and having lots of fun with Alex & Mamie[.]

Feb 14[.] got letters from the West telling of Ballards death. we all had a Jolly time playing parchesea[.]

Feb 15[.] Still at Hamburg. I was going to start for York but Mamie insisted on my staying till tomorrow.

Feb 16[.] left Hamburg this AM. for York, via Columbia & Reading. I stopped at Reading with Mr Snyder for a little while to get a due bill cashed and left on the 12 oclock train for York via Columbia.

arrived at York at 4.15 P.M. it was raining very hard. before going to Leonora's I went to the barber shop to get shaved, the Children however were on the alert for me as my baggage had preceeded me.

was welcomed by all. I found some alterations in Course of Construction in John's Store.

Feb 17. Cloudy and damp all day. I went to Church with the family at the reformed Church. Rev. J. O. Miller officiated in the pulpit.

after dinner I attended Sunday School with the family and while there I taught a class.

after Sunday School I called on the Misses Bresslers and went to evening Church with them at the Bever Street Methodist of which they are strict members[.] I telegraphed to T. J. Pickett at Washington D.C. asking him to Come up and see me and take dinner at Bresslers with me.

Feb 18. Cloudy and damp all day. I called on Robt. F. Polack, John Kiel, D. G. Fry & Co. and then after dinner I called on cousins Mary Vandersloot and Annie Myers, taking supper at the latter place after which Annie walked home with me. Mr John Keil's father called on me after supper as did also William Ruby. I made an appointment with Mr Keil for 2 P.M. tomorrow and for Wednesday afternoon with William Ruby where I am to take Supper[.] My Dinner to morrow will be at the Misses Bresslers.

Mr Charles Shultz and Souders were in the Store this evening and I had a long chat with them on Western political incidents. tomorrow is to be a City Election at which I trust to learn something of benefit to myself.

Feb 19. I took a walk up George Street and passed by the old King st School house and then Called on Misses Cassie and sarah Conneley and got to Bresslers for Dinner where I enjoyed myself very much, afterwhich I called on Mr James Kell[,] Cor[ner] Market & Centre Square[.] after having talked to him about uncle Dave Mears and receiving a Cordial & pressing invitation to call on Mr Kell's mother[,] 122 N George street[,] (Aunt Peggy) or Margretta, I next paid Brany Pentz the Photographer a visit when after talking over old times, I also had my pictures taken and ordered one dozen. I was told to come in tomorrow and see the proofs.

Feb. 20[.] Nice day as has been all along. having called on Pentz to see the proofs, and having seen Phil & Walter Sparks and Charlie Knohn, I took a walk, after which I got Augustus Polack to take me out to Frystown to see Rev Mr Shellmoyer and get him to come in and look over the German books I brought from Hamburg, which formerly belonged to Grandfather Iaeger[.] he promised to come at 1 PM which he did and by 2[:]30 PM we were done, after which having bid all good bye I paid my engaged visit to Wm Rubys in Bevedere where I arrived and was welcomed at 4 P.M. the 2 Motter boys and Sammy Ruby were also invited and together with Mr and Mrs Ruby and little Elsie, we spent a very pleasent evening together.

during my absence this afternoon John and Lenora were guests at Mr and Mrs Souders as a couple at a party or Special Supper in Honor of Johns old acquaintances.

Feb 21[.] Nice weather again. I called on Pentz to see my proofs again. Charlie Mears and Belle Schall were Married this evening at the Episcopal Church on Beaver Street. Lotta Vandersloot and her Sister Mary gave a Surprise party to Katie Wilt in honor of her 16th birthday. All the young folks gathered at Leonoras house before going.

after supper I called at 122 N. George St upon Mr Kells Mother where I also Met Mr Kells whole family and his sister[.] they were all getting ready to go to the Episcopal Church to see the wedding of Mears & Schall. But old Aunt Peggy, as she was called, and the children remained, the former being unable to go out and talked about their Nephew and Cousin Dave[.] the Children remembered Mr Mears in 1876 when sitting in a certain red lined chair in the parlor by the window and pulling out a big faced silver watch and a lot of 20 dollar gold pieces and some Rocky Mountain Specimens.

Feb 22. Nice day aqain[.] I remained in the House till 1 P.M. when William Ruby called and took me out to show me to [two] Fire Companies and their workings. We returned at 3 oclock and I bade him good by.—

Mr and Mrs Polack & Children, Mr & Mrs Ed Myers & Walter, Mr & Mrs Smyser & Daughter were guests at Dinner today with Sister Leonora and all enjoyed themselves very much. after Supper the Young folks and acquaintances of Lotta & Mary Vandersloot all had a lively time dancing in the parlor after which I adjourned to the National for recreation in a game of Billiards, but I ran foul of two fine musicians and gave them a Job to come along and play for me at Sisters in the Hallway. I shall never forget the Countenances of the guests when the first chords of the music reached their ears, for it was an unprogrammed affair.

Feb 23. I bid good by to all York and left on the 3 P.M. train for Washington where I arrived at 6 P.M. and met Bro Geo who was glad to see me[.]

Feb 28[.] I have been unable to post my diary for the past 5 days for the reason of being to tired and worn out. I have been to the National Museium, Smithsonian Institute[,] Pension Office and Police Head Quarters[.] perfect freedom of the Pension office was accorded me on account of Bro Geo and it was there I met my old Omaha Friend[,] Capt Smith[.] To day Geo, Chickering and myself visited the Houses of Congress and Senate in the Capitol and purchased tickets at the Peace Monument for visiting the Parade after which we looked up quarters for Dr Ramsey and his crowd. I paid for their seats and made a Deposit of $10.00 for their room.

Mar 1[.] I met W. H. McNutt this afternoon at the National Hotel and in Company with Mr Faught of Deadwood we went around Town.

I went to the Treasury Building and was furnished a guide—then I went to the White House in company with Genl[.] Black & Col[.] Judson whence I finally Shook hands with a man who had the backbone to say what he meant on the tariff question (Cleveland)[.]

I also met Cody and Buck Taylor. after supper I went to the National Theatre to hear Emma Abbott in [words missing.]

Mar 2[.] Rained towards night. I met John Burke of the Wild West Co at the National. Buffalo Bill and Buck Taylor came driving along the avenue, and Burke left me and went with them. I and Geo started out to the Washington Monument but Geo got hot because I was kidding him and he went back. So I went alone but could not stand long enough for my turn to go up on the elevator so I came away[.] I took supper early and came home to bed.

Mar 3[.] I went howling all over town in Company with Geo trying to hunt Dr Ramsey & his party. finally I sent a messenger to 453 C St and found they would be in at 5 P.M. and I found them there then[.] after supper we went out to see the elephant[.]

Mar 4[.] rained all day[.] we all got wet at the peace monument.

Dr Ransey and his party all went home. this evening I went to the National Theatre and then to the Inaugeral Ball.

Mar 5[.] Nice clear weather. I got my ticket for Chicago over the B & O. I called on Jack Pickett. Geo and I went home early.

Mar 6. Nice day. Geo Signed $675.00 over to me. I went to the B & O. and Geo went along.

Mar 7. arrived in Chicago at 12.30 P.M. Sammy Gillette met me there. Went to the Theatre to see "Jim the Penman[.]" I also met Mr Brobrook who invited me to call on his Son Fred.

Mar 8. Nice day again[.] I called on Fred Brabrook and made arrangments to meet him at Sherman House at 6[:]30 P.M. when we both went to see Jake Schaefer the Champion billiard man give an exhibition game at his Saloon on Randolph St[.]

Mr Dickenson, Mrs Gilletts Bro. called on me in behalf of his sister whom he wants appointed teacher in one of the public Schools in Dawes Co.

Mar 9. Nice day again. I got ready to go on the 5[:]30 train for Mo[.] Valley and forgot to get my trunk checked at the depot.

Mar 10. Nice day. left Mo[.] Valley for Chadron at 9.25 A.M. I told the Baggage Master about my trunk and had him write to Chicago about it[.]

Mar 11. Arrived at Chadron at 2.55 A.M. and was met by W P Hartzell and George Havens. I found Chadron all O.K. and my heart is once more at rest.—

Mar 12. fine day. I put in 2 or 3 hours calling on old time friends and the remainder of the day I put in getting my office in shape for business.

After supper I called to see Mr D. Y. Mears and on my way I stoped in to see Mr & Mrs Fraley and their baby.

Mr Mears was not at home. The Congregational Church gave an Entertainment at the Rink this evening. Geo & I remained at home. Mr Kiel of Omaha called to see me.

Mar 13. Nice weather all day. a case of Christensen vs. Thiested & Owens came before me on Change of Venue from O. H. Wilsons Court. After Supper I went to the Rink and attended the Congregational Church entertainment. I had my little cane broke this evening at OHanlons[.] George was sick and slept at home.

Mar 14[.] Nice day again. I got my trunk from Chicago today and Geo was tickled with the New Autoharp. I issued a warrant for John King charged with assault with intent to Kill and delivered the same [to] F. O. Messenger.

Mar 15. nice weather again[.] I gave Selden some cloths to alter for me of Bro Thomas'.

C. J. Davis is trying hard to find out who is going to be nominated for Mayor. No doubt he wants the News for the Journal. A. C. Fowler & wife were in the office today.

Mar 16. Saturday and a nice day. The Advocate failed to get back at Allen. the coming City Election is the topic now.

Frank Stuart and Arthur Armstrong came to town from Ft Scott. Ira Longcor filed a lien on the New Hotel yesterday. Henry Miller had a horse fall on him this morning while out ridding. Ches Ferbrache got me to write out a petition applying for appointment in the R. P. O. [Railroad Postal Office] service between Chadron & Casper.

The case of Powell vs M D Miller was dismissed by Mutual Consent. I recd a letter from Cousin Loui relative to his appointment as Collector of Customs at

Ft Yuma. last night Mrs Theresa Smith came to me to help her collect $2[.]50 from a woman for whom she had done washing for. I had it collected by the night watch. Dr A J Gillespie came down from Oelrichs yesterday to be a witness in the Land Office today in behalf of his Bro—[.] John Maher left for Lincoln last evening.

Mar 17. Sunday. I called on Mr & Mrs Havens and also on T. H. Glover. I went out to buggy ridding with Mort Morrissy[.]

Mar 18. I went up in the land office and Done some work for Atkinson parties. I had to take my typewriter up as Mahers machine was all worn out.— C. C. Hughes was in to see me.

Mar 19. Plenty of Police Court business[:] 3 drunks and 1 for carrying concealed weapons. O. H. Wilson came in the office to day to look at the Autoharp. C. W. Allen got a New Suit (Coat & Vest[)]. Mort Eberly an old time Texas Cow Man is paying Chadron a visit.

George Havens is writing a Composition on the Dancing devils in water.

I put on the Kolbe repaired legs to day[.] They feel rather Cumbersome yet.

This evening after supper it rained a little, otherwise it has been a pleasent day.

Yesterday Wm Belanger brought me his bills again for collection[.]

Mar 20. Rained all day. I emptied out the Rain water barrel. There is great excitment going on at present over the city election[.] This evening there was a small fight in Tobias' News Stand, also one in Stranskys Saloon between the gamblers[.]

Mar 21[.] Rain & Snow all day. Muddy. Plenty of scheming over who shall be the next Mayor of Chadron. The Cox faction are somewhat in doubt wether or not to bring Cox straight out[.] I see Frank Allen and he promised to square bills with me in a few days. Tony Barnard got out of bed this A.M. A.M. Wright got back from Seattle[,] Washington Terry

[Territory,] this A.M. he brings glowing reports of prosperity throughout that region, but says there are the usual quota of hangers on there as well as elsewhere who never prosper no matter how good or how bad times may be.

Mar 22[.] Nice day again. Tom Glover got out of the house to day.

I called on Mrs Loving and "Doc" [name missing] on business for J. F. Wright[.] The City Election Scheme is now booming and last reports are to the effect that C. C. Hughes will probably accept to run again.

George Stover and Antwin Janis were in Town today.

Mar. 23. Nice day[.] C C Hughes concluded not to run for Mayor again and consequently H. A. Cox will receive the unanimous nomination[.] This evening at the Rink the Citizens Convention nominated the following City Ticket[:] H. A. Cox for Mayor, A. A. Record for Treasurer[,] John Smith for Clerk, J. W. Boyd for Engineer[,] Geo W Parker Councilman for 2 years from 1st Ward, Robt Hood Councilman from 2nd Ward for two years[,] and Jas Dahlman and T. H. Glover from the 3rd Ward, the terms of the last two councilmen to be decided at the Election.

Longcor, Horner and Rosa were nominated for School directors and[,] as two directors were needed[,] Mssrs. Longcor & Horner were unanimously nominated, after which the Editor of the Advocate introduced some resolutions and asked the convention to adopt them which was done.

Said resolutions were as follows[:] Resolved—That it is the sense of this meeting that every honest effort in favor of law and order Should receive the cordial support of all good Citizens.

Resolved[—]That we pledge the nominees of this convention—if elected[—]to an equal and impartial support and enforcement of present Laws. Seconded and carried.

Mar 24. Nice day. I went to church at Congregational Church and attended Sunday School. After supper I went to church.—Rev J G Powell is sick and was not in the pulpit—[.]

Mar 25. Nice weather. John Maher got me to help him write of some evidence in Land Contest Case of W. L. Casady vs. James Higgins. Dahlman brought me some business this A.M.

Mar 26. Nice day again. 2 cases in Police Court put them on the street. C C Hughes had me make out a Quit Claim deed for him[.] Mrs C. C. Hughes was in the office and very much amused with the Autoharp[.] I wrote to Phila for more music for it.

Bro Chas wrote me to day and asked for Bro Thos diamond ring[.] he never answered my questions to him about his clothes nor did he send me his measure as I requested, But simply demanded the diamond ring.

This evening Attorney Spargur and Bartow had a set to in Spargurs office over some Supreme Court business and Spargur after beating Bartow and his fancy hat up, kick him out of his office on to the sidewalk. John G Maher filed a complaint against Spargur and he made voluntary appearance, plead guilty and paid his fine and walked off. Maher & I done some more writing out testimoney in the Casady vs Higgins case.

Early this morning news came by the papers that F. B. Carley had been appointed Post Master of the Chadron Post Office which quite upset Mr D. Y. Mears and all his friends[.]

Mar 27. Nice day again. Mr Mears was in the office this A.M. After dinner I went down to C C Hughes office and got Mr McDill to copy off some Typewriter work in the Land Case of Casady vs Higgins[.] After supper I attended the Lecture of Eli Perkins and like the rest of the audience I was taken in.

Mar 28. Nice day again[.] Very little business in Court. Eli Perkins Lectured again tonight but only 18 or 20 persons attended. This afternoon, Pitmans new buggy team ran away and smashed the buggy into atoms[.] John Maher and I done some more Typewriting in the Casady & Higgins land case. this evening[,] and while so engaged some one cut down my Democratic Flag Pole which afterward proved to be John G Maher and Will Bailey[.] Dr Leas' Mother in Law died this A.M. at 1 oclock. The paper (Demo) came out on time.

Mar 29. Nice weather. The case of Smith vs. Heuston et al. on promisory note came up before me at 8 A.M. and Judgment in favor of Plff. for $11.64 rend[e]red. The news of the Oklahoma opening is Creating some excitment here.

Clem Davis took a gold watch under execution from Mrs Campbell in the case of Smith vs. Heuston.

John Maher & I worked on the Land case of Casady vs Higgins x[.]

To day was closing day of the Chadron Schools and I and Sayrs went up there[.]

Mar 30[.] About 12.15 A.M. quite an Cutting affray occurred in White and Rubslis Saloon[,] Cor[ner] Main and first Streets between some hoo boos. A warrant was sworn out and the examination held at 9. A.M. The Court found no cause for finding Deft guilty and there upon discharged the Deft and dismissed the Cause[.]

The main 'topic' throughout Town now is—will F. B. Carleys appointment as postmaster be confirmed? The Journal came out with its usual sarcasm on the Police Court.

This evening the Night Police swore out a warrant for one McCarty for cruelty to animals, but I discharged him[.] John Maher and I worked on the Testimony case of Casady vs Higgins[.] Fred Poll came in and had me print some Odd Fellows sacred hymns for the funeral of Bowers who will be buried to morrow.

I loaned Ed. L. Godsell my skates this evening. I wrote long letter to Sister Leonora in reply to her. I recd letters from Wright and Middleton[.]

Mar 31[.] Nice day again, although it raind last night, but only enough to lay the dust. I attended Mr Bowers funeral from the Babptist Church and rode out to the Grave Yard with Culavin, Jimmy Ohanlon, Tug Wilson and their friend. the funeral was as large a one as was ever attended in Chadron. In the afternoon I stayed in the Office and played on my Autoharp for the amusement of all comers. I also took it down to the OHanlon House to show to Mrs OHanlon.

I recd a letter from Mami and one from Hank Clifford regarding his proposed Cabnet show of Fossils[.] Last night a great many Rail Roders were in Town and I understand the jail is full of them for tomorrows Court.

Apr 1. Nice day and Hot in the Justice Court[.] Quigley had a hoo boo bound over to the District Court for stealing his watch and two Chains, but he failed to Convict the fence in the case, and I turned him loose. There were also 2 cases in Police Court[—]1 paid his fine and the other went up. Tug Wilson & Maher were in the office to day at dinner making out a final proof of application[.]

Apr. 2[.] Genl. City Election today for Mayor[,] Treasurer, Clerk, Surveyor, 2 Councilmen in 3rd Ward, 2nd [2] in 2nd Ward and one in the 1st ward and 2 School Directors. No opposition was to the Peoples City ticket as per nominations of the City Convention with the exception of Ben Loewenthal who disputed with Smith for the office of City Clerk, notwithstanding that Smith was the regular nominee of the convention where he beat Loewenthal 1 vote and in the face of Ben having made a Motion that Smith be declared the unanimous choice of the Convention after the ballots had been Counted[.]

Therefore when Ben came out in the 1st Ward and all other wards on an Independent or ward ticket he met with some opposition that otherwise and under different Circumstances would not have happened.— The Polls closed. at following is the result[:]

Tuesday's Election.

The city election last Tuesday was as expected a very quiet affair, very few of our citizens taking the trouble to vote for the reason that there was but one ticket in the field. The officers elected, when chosen at the convention, were sufficiently satisfactory to our citizens as to prevent any other ticket from being nominated, which argues well for them and we believe they will serve the best interests of the city at all times. Following is the result of the election:

CANDIDATES	WARD			TOTAL
	1	2	3	
For Mayor—				
H. A. Cox	141	60	102	303
B. F. Pitman	7			7
Mrs. Fannie O'Linn		2		2
Hod Drew		1		1
For Treasurer—				
A. A. Record	146	63	104	313
For Clerk—				
J. W. Smith	56	33	75	164
Benj. Loewenthal	93	31	29	153
For Engineer—				
J. W. Boyd	97		104	247
For Councilmen—		64		
Geo. Parker	140			140
F. C. Poll, 2 yrs.		42		42
H. S. Ballou, 1 yr.		41		41
Boler, 1 yr.		1		1
J.C. Dahlman, 2 yrs			90	90

T. H. Glover, 1 yr.			90	90
Ira Longcor			1	1
No. of votes cast	149	64	104	317

I collected $9.00 from Dr Richardson for Rent due Mr Wright in Custer City and sent Mr Wright the money right away. I also wrote him a letter concerning the price of his lot.

Apr 3. Nice day again[.] the Marshal is having a great many people working out their poll Tax on the City streets and is getting the streets to look in a fine condition. Maher & I finished the Casady & Higgins contest testimony this evening[.] I paid [$]9.00 to the City Treasurer for Police Court Fines for Jan. & March.

[April] 4[.] Nice day again.

I recd. the Autoharp pickers & music and sent the money for them.

Sent [$]75 to square accts. to the Pittsburgh Limb Co[.] Wrote to Bro Geo & Cousin Loui relative to cousin Louis' custom business.

Belanger was in here this A.M. about his bills.—

I got McDill to copy by letter press the remaining testimony in the Casady vs Higgins contest.

The paper (Demo) came out today[.]

The firemen had the hose out and sprinkled the streets and also Julia at [and] Jerry Mahoney. After supper I went to the City Council Meeting and recd orders to make my annual report.

After the meeting I was called down to Pearl Ellis' House to issue a warrant against Nellie Williams for Disturbing the peace and quiet of Pearl Ellis who is laying sick in bed—the case was continued till in the morning[.]

---

[1]Source is unknown but may be one of several Dawes County newspapers.

Apr 5. Windy day—[.] In the Police Court Nellie Williams plead guilty and paid a fine of [$]1.00 & costs. Ben Tibbits Came to town this A.M.

Geo Havens went out hunting this morning with Profs Denton and Pete Barber[.]

I recd a letter from Wright Enclosing his receipt for the [$]8.90 I sent him the other day and also a Warranty Deed from the Town Site Co to him which he wanted me to have recorded here.

After dinner I went up to County Clerks office with Deed. J. L. Pauls wagon took me up—[.]

Charlie Allen started this afternoon for Peck Place over on Craven Creek.

I recd a letter from Aunt Emma[.]

Apr 5[.] Continued. After supper Maher & I went to the Methodist Church to attend a Mock Quaker wedding.

I lent my Autoharp to Wilson to play for the occasion and while up there I played for some of the people.

The performance was postponed and every body sent home with their money refunded.

after coming home, Geo Called our attention to the great prairie fire which has been raging all day South of the City and between here and the running water—[.] Geo and I went up to Bowers and Denmnou's stable and got John Bowers to drive us out towards the fire. We hauled up at Whites place and within 1/2 mile of the fire where we stayed till it passed the house which was only saved by a Scratch. Geo & I had our hands full in taking care of the team while Bowers went and helped fight the fire the best he could and combined the men succeeded in turning the fire away from the House. We then hitched up and started for Chadron again and in passing Wm Birdsalls place found his barn and stack of Millet all on fire with Doc Richardson there to watch the flames from catching on the House. upon resuming the road to town we met Several Citizens going out to see the sight and when we reached the School house we beheld the fire department out and throwing water around the building[,] fool[s] that they were[,] instead of 50 or 100 men having gone out early in the evening and helped fight the fire with gunny sacks. Several fires had been started in Town during our absence in the country and finally C W Allens shanty on the Cor[ner] of King and 2nd sts was successfully burned down by the incendiaries. However immediately upon our arrival from Whites, to the school House, Bowers and Geo got out of the Buggy and I Started and went down to see after the safety of Mrs Simmons whose husband was reported to be away on business. on my way thither I drove into a barbed wire fence with full force and came near getting killed, but after swearing good and hard and scaring the team about half dead, I managed finally to extricate myself and team and resume my trip of Charity and mercy. I found Mr Simmons had luckily returned home and was then out rustling help. on my way I also woke up McIntyre. The wind blew a terrific hurricane and the wonder is that all Chadron did not burn up.

Pete Overby (a colored man) was arrested upon the testimony of one Jones as the man who fired the Allen building but subsequent investigation proved an alibi and he was released by the sheriff.

Apr. 6. Nice day again! the City Marshal arrested M. D. Miller and P. R. Nelson for violation of Ordinance No. 2, both were fined and paid the same though not until a mittimus had been issued for the latter.

I had a wedding this evening at the Chadron House. they had to wait till the Co Judge came back from Whitney, whom they had telegraphed for a license.

Apr. 7. Cloudy day, though not very disagreeable. Maher and I took a ride out through the burt [burnt] district. We stopped at Strainskys and

Sayrs. we came back to town and got my autoharp and went down to Simmons to make a late afternoon call.

Mrs Mears and Miss Scott were there. We took supper with Mrs Simmons. I received my Chambers Encyclopedia to day and made the first payment on them [$]2.00[.]

Apr 8. Nice day again. I sent [$]8.25 to the state Journal and [$]4.90 to the Century Co. I also forward[ed] the Marriage Certificate to Geo. W. Hollibaugh at Nonpareil, Box Butte Co.[,] Neb.

Apr 9. Nice day. Police Court was busy nearly all day. Nellie Smith and Red Jacket were up and the latter went to Jail for 20 days and in Default of paying a fine & Costs.

Apr. 10. A little Cloudy and rainy all day. Today I am 33 years old— I made out my report of Police Court for the past year with some suggestions to the Council relative to building a City Jail.— Sells commenced an action against Dorrington, Geo & I retired to bed very early[.]

Apr 11. still raining and the Farmers as well as everybody else look pleased. T. A. Coffey came back from the Oklahoma District this morning. I was very sick but got better toward noon[.]

Apr 12. To day has been a pleasant one. The Case of Wilhelm Christensen vs Theosted and Owens was tried before me to day and resulted in a judgment in favor of Defendant John Owens as one of the partners.

After supper I went down around and among the Gang and toward midnight got into a fuss with Tommy Carter who hit me over the head unexpectedly with a heavy cane—served me right as I had no business being there at all.

April 13. Nice day again and the roads are drying up fast[.]

Fisher commenced 3 suits before me this A.M.

I recd the back numbers of Judge Vol 14 and Scribners Magazine Vol 4 by mail, also the rubber cylinder for the Typewriter.

Tom White came in and got a Liquor application.

D. Y. Mears had me write out a petition to the Post Master General asking for the appointment of Mr Mears to the Post mastership of Chadron. Mrs Josselyn came in the Office and borrowed [$]6.00 leaving her watch as security.

Geo Havens wants to go out to A. C. Fowlers and I guess I will have to go with him.

I asked sayrs if he & his family Could go but it is impossible and so we must go alone[.]

April 14. We got back from Fowlers at 8. oclock this evening. Geo & I had a very pleasant time out there. We arrived there in the evening but Mr Fowler had gone to Crawford and his family were at home alone, however Mr Fowler returned early in the morning and we managed to put in Sunday in a pretty good shape[.] Geo & little John Fowler went out hunting in the pasture and Mrs Fowler and Mr Johnson who had also came out from Chadron to stay in his Claim a week, went to Church and in so doing took our team & buggy.

while they were gone Geo.[,] John & I done some pistol shooting. Mr Lyons came just as we were getting ready to go home—[.] the wind blew fearful last night and it was a little windy to day[.] towards evening on our way home we stopped at Pattersons.

Apr 15[.] Nice day in the morning. it rained in the evening.

I got my Vol 14 Puck ready for binding and also Vol 30-31-32-36 & 37 "Century" and Vol 4 Scribners—[.]

I Changed cylinders on my typewriter to day. I done some writing for the American Security Company and in the evening done some Typewriter work for Profs Denton.

Von Harris called at the Office during the time I was working for Denton and being unable to entertain him I requested him to call again.

I wrote out several notices to Citizens relative to side walk grads. for the Marshall this AM. Mr Miller came in the office this evening and refunded me my money on my meal ticket—for the reason that Mrs Miller being unwell and to a certain degree a little out of her head, the family will consequently leave for Illinois tomorrow night, Mr Miller remaining here by himself.

Apr. 16. Nice day. Profs Denton was in the office and had me do some writing for him. after supper John Maher & I went to the immitation Quaker Wedding at the Methodist Church.

April 17. Nice day till toward afternoon when it snowed a little and got chilly.

Charley Wilson had me write his report as Street Commissioner for him to be presented to the Council this evening. After supper I attended Council meeting and upon coming home had some fun with Geo who in trying to hide got under bed where I throwed water on him.

Apr. 18. Nice day again. Pete Christensen was in the office and wanted Red Jacket arrested. The Knutzen boys got me to make out a Damage Claim against the County for a road through 13-32-48. I got Browns Copying press to day and commenced to Copy letters and practice Copying right along for Typewriter work.

A. H. Wilson returned the Autoharp[.] I got the keys to Wrights house from Mrs Loving yesterday. we all tried to tie a Theodore Knot on a Halter and failed. yesterday after supper, Johny Holliday came in the Office to see me, Enroute to Deadwood from Chicago[.] he said he was broke. I took him to Mrs Danielsons and got him his supper and after staying in the office with Geo & I, I got John Maher to take him up to the Chapin House for a bed.

I wrote a letter [to] Uncle William and also to Megeath and Skeen Stuart stationary Co of Chicago.

Apr. 19. Nice day. I work hard all day in experimenting with letter press copying from the Typewriter. Johnny Holliday stayed around the office all day. L. G. Sweat had some typewriting done as Atty for L. A. Butler in a contest case of Wojta Strensky vs L. A. Butler.

I made out my report and Transcript of costs of Criminal Cases tried and examined before me as Justice of the Peace to be filed with the Co Commissioners May 1st 1889. Geo & I oiled my artificials and we went to bed early.

Apr 20. Nice day. this morning at 3 oclock Night Police Hartzell woke me up to have a warrant issued for Inmates of a house of prostitution. when Court opened, Harry Wade plead guilty as one of the parties charged. I sentenced him to $5.00 and costs. and sent him over the road in default. Johnny Holliday tried to get off on the Rapid City train this morning but failed[,] being put off at the Junction. he walked back and came in our bed room while I was washing.

The case of Zeri M. Butters vs Fred M. Dorrington was tried before me this afternoon before a Jury and they disagreed after being out 3/4 of an hour whereupon the case was continued to April 26th at 9 oclock AM.

I bought 1/2 doz new chairs today and got some belonging to me from Mrs Josselyn.

Apr. 21. Sunday[.] —I got up late. after dinner called on Mr & Mrs Havens and played on the Autoharp for them. Miss Murphy and Mrs Welsh came over to hear the music, after which I called on Mr & Mrs A. G. Fisher.

After supper Tommy Carter got into a fuss with Fred Ebner the restaurant man and hit him over the head with a Six shooter.

The Marshal swore out a warrant for him before me and captured him in Danielsons lodging house over

Browns butcher shop and in order to get him the officers had to break in a door.

finally, after getting him they let him go by carelessness.

Geo & I went up to the Methodist Church to hear the Easter Celebration by the Sunday School, but I could not rest and had to come down town to see if they had locked Carter up and when Geo & I got to Carters Cor[ner] we met Pete Breen and Tom Doud who informed me of Carters escape. I proceeded to the station and met Chas Wilson who was preparing to go to Omaha to do some business for the R.R. I talked pretty sharp to him about it and then went up stairs to the telegraph office to head Mr Tommy Carter off. the passenger train pulled out for the East in the mean time and after its departure I was informed that Tommy Carter had gone out on it, he having stood on the dark side of the train till it started out. when he boarded it[,] at the instance of Mayor Hughes I telegraphed the Marshall on the Train (Wilson) and addressed it to hay springs in care of the Conductor after which Geo & I retired[.]

Apr 22. Nice day. Terrance OHanlon had quite a time trying to catch Jim Rothwell whom he wanted to whip. the Depty Marshal Hartzell arrested him and he having given bonds for his appearance was set free till tomorrow morning.

Billy Carter gave me a terrible turning over for having telegraphed after his brother Tommy and intimated how he would fix me if I was able bodied. a great many citizens heard him and he done himself no good by his talk.

Apr. 23[.] Nice day. it rained a little early this AM. and during the afternoon The town has been agitated to a certain extent by the expected arrival of the Omaha Board of Trade which hours [however] did not happen as soon as was first given out.

7:30 P.M. The Board of Trade arrived and the Atkinson Band played while the sports unloaded themselves and took supper. hand shaking and introductions was in order till 9 P.M. when they pulled out for the Wyoming Towns on the main line to be back again tomorrow evening[.]

A subscription list through Town was started by J W Smith & T. J. Cook for the purpose of getting funds with which to banquet the Omahans tomorrow evening[.] I sent John Henry up for a short term in the Jail a few days ago.

Apr 24[.] Nice day. every body got dressed up for the Omaha Board of trade Banquet which is to come off at 10 P.M.

At 3 P.M. the train arrived from the West and having had their dinner a Delegation of Citizens met the Omaha Board of trade with Carriages at the Depot and took them out ridding over the City.

at 9[:]45 P.M. the doors of the Banquet hall were thrown open and 100 citizens & guests participated which finally ended at 11[:]40 when the Board of Trade Train pulled out for Buffalo Gap from where they go by stage to the Hot Springs and thence to Deadwood and through the Black Hills Country in general to return next week on their way home.

Apr 25[.] fine warm weather. I wrote a letter to Wright relative to Mr H. E. Schack having consulted me about his lot No 24 [27?] in Blk. 5 in Chadron about a $900.00 mortgage[.]

Made out New papers in Case of Aultman Miller & Co vs Levi Cornell and mailed them to F. E. Kathan. posted a rent notice on Wright's house. John Noll was around Town for the first time in a long while, he having been very sick.

Apr. 26[.] Nice day again. I wrote to W J Burtis about his note against Maiden. The case of Zeri M. Butters vs Dorrington was submitted to the Court to day upon evidence already in and I rendered a verdict for Defendant. a Herald man was in the office to day and I gave him a song and Dance about why I could not be the Correspondent for the Herald (Omaha) at this place? he said he would present the case to proper parties upon his arrival in Omaha. 2 Burglars broke in 2nd hand store on 2nd street.

During the afternoon 2 acrobatic traveling showmen performed on the Corner of 2nd & Egan st, and they took in many suckers including myself. Atty John P. Arnott of Nonpareil was in the City today. Charlie Nebo came into town this evening and expects to remain all day tomorrow.

Chas Wilson, City Marshal, returned from Omaha.

Dr Lewis was in the office to day and complaining loud against an Occupant of his room over his Drugs store on 2nd st. for being disorderly and maintaining a disreputable reputation. Edward A. Thompson came down from Crawford this evening with C E Ellis (Constable) and commenced Replevin Process on some Horses and a Buggy taken under Execution by Messenger.

Robt Dorr started a suit against T. J. Doud, but after the papers were issued he concluded to waite a few days longer.

Mr and Mrs H. P. Simmons called for their pictures today which I brought away with me from their house during the late prairie fire.

Apr 27[.] Rained a little. I worked of[f] some testimony for John Maher. The old Episcopal Church building, formerly the Chadron Laundry, is at present undergoing renovation preparitory to Miss Lewis, a new photographist, opening up a photographic gallery.

about 7. P.M. City Marshal Wilson brought John & A. E. Rothurd [Rothwell] and Terrance OHanlon before the Police Court which was adjourned for the purpose to the Engine house on 2nd street. the Charge against the Parties was Fighting and upon trial of the Cause the court ordered a new complaint to be filed against John Rothwell for carrying concealed weapons, whereupon the Court found Terrance OHanlon [$]3.00 & Costs, John Rothwell [$]3.00 & costs for fighting [$]10.00 and costs for carrying concealed weapons.

A. E. Rothwell was discharged—considerable excitement was kept up in Police Court till near 10 o'clock P.M.

Apr 28. Rainy and unpleasant. Chas. Wilson & I put up the little stove in the bedroom to day and he and I staying indoors reading all afternoon. John Maher, Bailey & the Night Police also were in during the afternoon.

after supper I attended the regular monthly union temperance meeting at the Baptist Church where I met Geo also. Mr Sheldon addressed the Congregation on Temperance. after Church Geo, Mr Sheldon and I came home. I found the Marshal and Cora Benton awaiting me to have a warrant issued for Tony Bernard for Drunkeness. I finally got rid of her[.]

Apr 29. Nice day again. Cora Benton was up again this A.M. to have a warrant for Tony Bernard but failing to put up security for costs I refused. the Marshal made several arrests among the Coon prostitutes, 2 of whom the Court found guilty of vagrancy. John Rothwell came in Court and paid his fine and costs adjudged against him last Saturday.

The Rail Road baggage room caught fire yesterday evening about 12 oclock and almost proved to be a large conflagration only for the energetic and prompt work of the Chadron Fire Department.

Apr. 30. The weather looked a little Cloudy in the morning but towards 9 oclock cleared off pretty good. J. G. Maher & I went up to the Congregational Church to hear Rev. Read & Powell, Ricker & Baird[.]

after Dinner I attended the exercises at the High School in Prof. Dentons Room, fully 100 visitors were present[.] After supper I attended a Social gathering at Rev G W Reads house at the Baptist Church on

Morehead sts. and had a very pleasent time, having been introduced to a great many whom I knew by sight only. I came home about 10[:]30[.]

May 1[.] This was a nice day again considering that it sleeted and rained towards the later part of last evening.

I had my office Scrubbed out while I was up to the Social last night and the mud is Just right on the outside to be well carried in again.

After Supper I attended the last meeting of the City Council.

A. E. Sheldon & Others filed a remonstrance against the issuing of licenses to B. Gottstein & Co., Wojta Strensky & J. W. Owens but the Council did not act on it for Statuary reasons[.] John Noll was ordered to be notified that from date the City Council would take full charge of the water works and the water commissioner was instructed accordingly to collect water rents and see the water ordinances inforced.

May 2[.] Nice day. The Demo came out on time. Deforrest Richards, J. W. Tucker & Mike Ellmore were in Town today.

Doc Middleton was up from Gordon yesterday and Pre-empted a 160 near that place upon Contestants preference right having expired. I recd the odd numbers of "Century" which I ordered sent to Lincoln. I immediately sent them to Lincoln.

Today at dinner C W Allen, Chas Elliott, J Kass, Fred Poll, W H Carter & myself were specially invited to a feast by Julius Hahler at Stetters Butcher Shop. at 12 M. we were all on hand and guts, marrow and sinews flew before the Crowd. Hancock & Larsh are on a drunk.

Guss Trouth, Clerk for Ben Loewenthal left for Louiville[,] Ky[.] this evening.

After supper I took a peep into the Odd Fellows Hall over Loewenthals clothing store, came home and went to bed early.

May 3. Considerabl wind all day. advocate paper came out in flaming words over the City Councils late proceedings relative to granting licenses to saloons.

I got my report from J. L. Paul and copied it in the letter book. Tony Barnard got 20 letters written off by typewriter.

The case of P. C. Woods vs Riely Robert for obtaining money under false pretens was on examination before Justice O H Wilson this afternoon. the evidence adduced the fact that Defendant agreed to make the Plff a U. S. Detective for $100.00 to which the Plff. agreed but sickening of his bargain undertook to get even. the Plff paid deft $10.00 and gave not[e] for $90.00 secured by a chattel. Defendant did not negotiate the note before maturity and upon trying to foreclose the mortgage he was compelled to release the Chattel for want of an indemnity bond, hence the Plff is now in posession of the Chattels and the Question arises can the Mortgage be foreclosed? I think yes, if a bond can be satisfactorily given.

The Court discharged the Defendant.

Mrs. Bennett came in the office and extended an invitation to me to attend a Social party this evening at the House of Mrs Bradway. I attended and took my autoharp with me and there met a very nice party of ladies and gentlemen. After refreshments had been served, I tumbled to the fact that it was Church Sociable to which we had been invited. Geo was also there he having come with Pete and Delos Barber.

We came home about 10[:]30 P.M. the wind was very high.

april [May] 4th. Nice day. I recd. a check from Bank of Crawford for the Cornell case.

Jim Owens opened his saloon to day. The invincible BaseBall Club went around collecting money for BaseBall suits to day.

this evening John Maher got me to write of[f] some testimony for him but after 4 pages were written he had to go to the skating rink with his red headed girl.—

Old man Noonan paid the balance of $4.00 rent for April on Wrights shack. I wrote to Wright.

I sent Jos Megeatle $1.50 to close accts. I got the files of the Democrat for Vol 4 and brought them over to my office.

Dr romine moved his Chattel mortgaged chest (tool) out of my sleeping room.

Apr [May] 5. Nice day. went to Church in the morning[.] after coming from Church I was met by Mrs Boomer at the Pea nut snap who seemed to be in a violent state of excitement and wanted the Night watch or day police to come with her up to her house.

I told her I would send the marshal as soon as I seen him and at the same time I qot up and started towards Stranskys Corner where I met Bill Bristow one of the Night Police. I pointed Mrs Boomer who was then crossing Main Street towards the Gold Bar Corner out to him and told him that she wanted an officer at her house and that he should go up there and see what the matter was. his reply was that she was hunting him and that he and her had just had a row and that she had shot at and hit him in the shoulder. He further stated that the row was caused by Nellie Boomer coming in his room while he had been washing and Mrs Boomer & her Sister coming in the house shortly afterward. She, Mrs Boomer had proceeded at once to accuse Nellie of having been in his room which Nellie denied[.] she then attacked Bristow with a whip and accused him of having raped Nellie. He took the whip away from her and told her to be quiet and said he had done nothing. She next shot at him with the above result.

After learning these facts, I repaired to go to my dinner but was overtaken in the office by the Night Police and Mrs Boomer & her Sister having learned that the accused could not be tried on Sunday and that the party would not leave town and for her to get an

Attorney to draw up her Complaint properly and that the County Attorney was the proper party to make out such a charged complaint. She & her Sister left after having been fully assured that the accused should not escape, however Mr Boomer arrived from the Claim in the evening who at once proceeded to have a warrant issued before Judge Powers, the Judge having assumed to draw the complaint up himself.

about 4 oclock I drove to C D Sayrs place and had a talk with him about Bristow's case and told him then that I was prejudiced in the case and did not want to have it tried or examined before me for the reason that it was a common talk everywhere that the Girl was on it.

Mr Sayrs consented to come in early tomorrow morning and look the case up.

after I came home, I attended prayer meeting and Church[.]

May 6. Nice day though a little Changeable toward evening.

Sayrs came in early this A.M. as agreed and advised his Client to waive preliminary, give $500.00 bonds for his appearance and make them go into a competent place to try the case.

this was accordingly done and Hank Simmons & Joe Ford went on his bonds.

I wrote out some testimony in a Contest Case of Levi G. Sweat vs Fred Burnham, making two copies one for Bartlett Richards and one for Sweat.

after supper George Havens and Pete Barber brought some strawberrys.

May 7[.] Nice weather. Wm Bristow swore out a search warrant for the House of Hariet Boomer for his personal effects. the Marshal upon presenting and preparing to read the warrant was told he could have the goods without the warrant. Mr Boomer at once proceeded to Molyneaux & Fosters for more law on the subject.

I wrote out some testimony and Interrogatories for Sweat vs Burnham Contest Case.

The old City Council steped down and out this evening. Hood & Kass being the only ones however who went out. The Council now being as follows for the ensuing year. 1 Ward—J. L. Paul, 1 yrs.; Geo. Parker 2 yrs.; 2nd Ward, H.S. Ballow, 1 yr., Fred Poll 2 yrs.; 3rd Ward F. H. Glover 1 yr., Jas. Dahlman 2 yrs.

I was Called upon to swear in the City Clerk who in turn swore in the Council.

After which Mr Boomer presented a communication to the Board asking for the removal, from the police force, of Wm Bristow. The article was table[d]. The M D Miller Family left this evening for the East.

May 8th[.] Fair weather again. C. D. Sayrs bought himself a new suit at Spargur & Fishers.

Bartlett Richards swore out a warrant against one Benton Bible for perjury.

The Governor of Nebraska passed through Chadron this evening on an inspection tour over the Northwestern system with officials. the party stopped over here several hours and were driven through the City by Citizens.

Some one tried to poison Mr Flanders' Stallion last Sunday night (May 5th). at present he is alive and hopes for his recovery are entertained strongly.

May 9. It rained a little early this A.M. Spotted Elk came to Town and brought me a note asking for [$]1.50 I gave it to him. W A Birdsall went around Town this afternoon with a petition for money for the Benefit of Ira Blake who is severely stricken with rheumatism. I donated $2.00 and after supper circulated a petition for the same purpose and got $3.50 more. I came home and went to bed early.

May 10. Cloudy all day. Atty Bane from Ainsworth has rented rooms in Opera Block and expects to remain in Chadron and pursue the practice of Law. Pardoe & Wilgocikie were in the Office this afternoon.

After breakfast I turned over to Robt Reed the money I collected last evening.

Joseph Branner arrived from Dr Wallers Ranch at Kennedy this morning, his wife having preceeded him here two weeks. Joe has severed his engagement with Dr. W. and will go into business himself this summer. I made out a Transcript of Judgment on my Civil Docket in Case of Madden vs Brigham and took it up to District Court Clerk and filed it against Frigham for Madden on the Judgment Docket there. I paid 40¢ for filing.

I came home and Chas Allen & I went in the bedroom and made a fire[.] after a social chat he went away and I fell asleep. I attended a social at Mrs Bennets. It rained hard.

May 12. Sunday and Nice all day. I attended Service in morning at Congregational Church. it rained this evening.

[May] 13[.] Nice day again[.] Doc Middleton came up from Gordon early this AM to see about a certain party filing over his preemption.

Ben Tibbitts came to Town[.] Nick Janis came over from the Agency. Lawyers, witnesses, Clients and Defendants are all swarming into the City to be on hand for the District Court. Atty Westover is in the city wearing a plug hat and eager for the chase.

In Police Court this AM I suspended Judgment against Massett on condition he leave town in 24 hours.

May 14. Nice day. I went up to attend the opening of Court in the New Court room.

The Judge called attention of the Bar to some sort of formal dedication of the Court House by that body and suggested that the bar do something that way. No one responded, all being afraid it might cost a little.

Rumor now has it that John W. Smith is going to open up the New Hotel and is at present selling out by invoice to H. D. Kirmse[.]

the carpenters are working on the Shelving & Fixtures of A. Webers New Grocery Store which will be occupied as soon as finished[.] I ordered some posters printed for a Billiard tournament at J. W. Owens Billiard Parlor and had them distributed. it rained today[.]

May 15[.] It has been rainy and drizzly all day. Court in active session all day granting Divorces and getting ready to try the heavy Criminal Cases. Judge Cook and C. Dana Sayrs had quite a lively time in Court today over a Negro who will come up for trial for murder.

After supper I attend Council Meeting, it being the first meeting where the New Mayor H. A. Cox presided.

After the Council had transacted some business the Mayor made his appointments for the ensuing year as follows:

City Atty—A. G. Fisher
Marshal—Chas. Wilson
Chf Fire Dept.—W. G. Burke
Asst. Chief Fire Dept.—L. A. Lennington
Night Police—W. P. Hartzell
Night Police—Wm Bristow

After which the Council adjourned from the Council room[.] I went to the Congregational Church festival in Rosa & Thompson building where I spent $1.40 for the benefit of the Church and then came home. it has been wet and Damp all day.

May 16. a little wet and rainy all day. District Court in full blast. the case of State vs Wm Bristow was taken up about 9 oclock A.M. W. H. Westover was called into the Case to assist Sayrs. the examination of witnesses on both sides occupied all day and after Supper the arguments of Counsel were put to the Jury.

F. M. Molyneaux opened for the state with a brief talk about what appeared to him as facts—he was followed by Hon[.] W H Westover of Rushville for the Defense with a 3/4 hour speech which woke up every Juror in the box and set them conscientiously thinking. he was followed by his colleague C. D. Sayrs who had conducted the case from the start. he made a speech which went not only to the bottom of every heart of the Jurors but as his eloquent words resounded through the Court room the prevailing silence showed that every word & syllable he was [declaiming] was not only appreciated but being listened to. after an hour hard talking he closed with tremendous applause from the audience.

The Court very promptly & properly repremanded the applauders and showed them wherein they were endangering the County into a probable needless expense by Continuing to applaud any attorney in the future given the Statement that under the present circumstances if the County Atty had been applauded and the Jury were to bring in a verdict of guilty the Court should have considered it his opinion to have set the verdict aside and ordered a new trial.

At Eleven Oclock the Jury retired to their Jury room, and everybody went home to bed.

May 17th[.] Nice day though a little Chilly. I forgott to mention in my yesterday posting that H. A. Cox had John E. Fiant arrested in my Court for obtaining goods under false pretense. he waived a preliminary before me and I put his bonds at $500.00 and sent him to Jail on default.

this morning I made up the transcript and certified it up to the District Court now in session. the Jury in Case of State vs Bristow charged with rape come out unable to agree this afternoon and were discharged by the Court and the Prisoner put under $500.00 bonds for his appearance at the next term.

Tony Bernard had me do some circular work this afternoon.

W. P. Hartzell & Wilson filed several complaints in Police Court against 2 drunks and 2 cases for Carrying concealed weapons. among the later was "Mirsh rate Pete." Night sessions of District Court is now going on and the case of State vs Heath charged with Murder is at bar.

about 6 oclock Rufus Slaughter and W H Westover came in my office for the purpose of the former executing a Chattel Mortgage Note in favor of Westover for $100.00.

Geo Came in the office and Asked permission to attend Court. Roy & I started a Billiard Tournament at Owens Billiard Parlor.

May 19. Sunday. Nice day—[.] I went to Church & Sunday School in the morning and during the afternoon I drew out a Map and Schedule list for the tournament.

May 20[.] Monday it rained a little to day. in District Court the Chadron Democrats vs Dawes County Case came up for argument and the Attys for defense, Pardoe & Sayrs waived a trial by Jury and professed a willingness to have the Case submitted to the Court. the Negro Heath was tried and found guilty of Assault with intent to wound. he will be sentenced at the Close of the term.

This evening Paul & Smith played a Match game of Billiards for the Cue. Geo Havens slept up at Peter Barbers House. Johnny Riggs came up from Rushville & I invited him to Stop over with me, which he did.

Mr Ben Tibbitts is here in attendance upon Court and also Chas Nebo & wife.

May 21[.] Nice day. very hot. I have been in attendance upon District Court nearly all day as a witness in the $5000.[00] Damage Case against Ben Tibbetts by Henry Hoffman who was arrested in 1886 for shooting Tibbitts Horse. A great deal of testimony is being introduced.

I wrote out a petition for L. G. Sweat for subscription to a Cemetery Fund.

Mrs Fred Mead and her Father, John Hollenbeck returned from Washington terry [Territory] to attend Mrs Hollenbeck who is not expected to live.

Young Geo Helm is lying Serously ill with dropsy. last Sunday night some one broke into Mr Helms stable and stole his double set of wagon harness.

Tony Bernard is erecting more billiard tables to compete against Jim Owens. John Larsh is Superintending the work.

At 6.30 P.M. I went up to Cong'l Church for supper after which we attended Court.

May 22. Nice day. the Jury in the Case of Hoffman vs Tibbitts came in at about 10 A.M. and gave a verdict for Defendant which was received with Joyful greeting by Ben & his friends. We all adjourned to Jim Owens saloon and washed our throats.

I was a witness for both sides of a Case in District Court to day as a Public officer in the Case of Sioux City Seed & Nursery Co vs. Fred Truxes et al[.]

Court adjourned at 3[:]30 PM. in order to allow Attys to get ready for the formal Dedication of the Court House by members of the Bar this evening. the Banquet of which occasion will be at the Depot Hotel.

I did not go as it looked like rain. I sent my Autoharp up to Mrs Fraleys.

May 23. Nice day again! it failed to rain last night. All the lawyers are feeling sick today on acct of the racket last night—[.]

it is claimed that there was something put in the ice cream which made all hands sick. 2 cases in Police Court to day. I sent them both up. the paper came out O.K. (Democrat)[.] Mr J. B. Cotton of Wamego is visiting Chas Allen—[.] Dr Carver is reported as being in Town.

May 24. rainy all day. George Havens was taken sick yesterday and consequently stayed at home last night. Mike Welsh was in Police Court this morning for Drunkeness. I sent him up for [$]1.00 & costs. I ordered my legs to day from D. W. Kolbes in Phila.

last night the City Council Met and the Question of rent for the Engine house was brought up. Hank Clifford came to town to day with his fossils. After supper I bought a lot of tickets for "Thumbs Up" lecture but I got sick and had to go to bed. Will Bailey slept with me. Geo has been on his ear for the past few days and has slept home. I purchased a set of Britanic Encyclpdias 24 vols for $144.00 with an agreement to take the Chamberlin set off my hands at $18.00 rebate. The Jury in case of Brennan vs F. E. & M. V. R. R. returned a verdict for Plff. for $258.00.

May 25. the Democrat Jury are still out this 12'M.

The case of Patsey Baum vs. Adam P. Baum for Divorce came on this evening before the Court (Dist) and a decree of Divorce was granted without any alimony and no exclusion charge of the Children were given.

After the divorce case the Court listened to evidence in Case of J. K. O. Sherwood vs Dawes County upon a rehearing for an allowed Claim which the Commissioners subsequently disallowed—[.]

at the conclusion of the taking of evidence in the case, The jury in the Democrat Case brought in verdict in full for the Chadron Democrat—whereupon we all adjourned to J W Owens saloon. Hank Clifford rented the Messenger building from Eckles for the purpose of placing and setting up his fossil Collection. Messrs. Engalls and Rodgers, Radcliff & my self took a stroll up to the Court house this A.M. The two former gentlemen are members of the Western Farm and loan Company and Comparitive strangers here though they seemed highly pleased with the showing of the City.

Mrs Wilbur sold out at auction sale and Joe Ford had quite a hard time getting his Commission out of her. Young George Helm is again able to be out of bed.

Bowes & Demon have bought out Birdsall & Co livery business some two weeks ago.

Mrs Josselyn has been trying hard all day to get money $25.00 to go to tennessee to attend the funeral of her Sister, but it is no go—[.] she came to me to borrow but I had my sand bag chuck full of that kind of pleading. She appeared very much taken down but aristocratic people should manage to hold their feelings high at all times.

I married Frank Conklin to Miss Lizzie Johnson this afternoon at Mrs. Langworthys house.

May 26. Sunday and Clear pleasant all day. Judge Kinkaid, Allen G. Fisher, Mr Radcliff and myself attended Memorial Services at the Rink this forenoon.

County Atty & Mr Radcliff took dinner with me.

The Rink was well filled this morning and the Grand Army took a good part in the service.

Dr Carvers Indian delegation came over from the Agency today and Started for Europe this evening. there was quite a crowd at the depot to see them off. Mrs E A Josselyn started for tennessee this evening to attend the funeral of her sister. I called on Judge M. P. Kinkaid this evening but was interrupted by the District Court Clerk, Shears and a Book Agent.

John Maher wrote out the report for Mr Radcliff this evening on my Typewriter.

Atty C. D. Sayrs came in from the Country late this evening so as to be ready for tomorrow mornings train for Harrison, Neb. Hank Clifford presented the Judge M. P. Kinkaid with 2 nice specimens from the bad lands.

Mrs F. M. Mead intends leaving for Tacoma again.

After supper we all went to the Depot to see the delegation off.

C. Dana Sayrs walked in from his home to be ready for the Harrison train tomorrow morning to attend court.

May 27. Nice day. it rained a little last night. I took the stove down in my bed room. Sayrs Slept with me last night. he got up at 5[:]30 AM. but missed the 7 oclock A.M. train. Sidney Kendall swore out a warrant against Ella Clark for Assault and Battery.—

Mr. G. M. Radcliffe, the Encyclopedia fiend had me do some listing for him.

I called on Mrs Loving to see about a Notice which the Marshal served upon me relative to nusiance existing on Mr J. F. Wrights lot on Morehead St.

Julius Hahler presented me with a neat Diamond willow cane.

Steve Jackson (colored) came in the Office this evening and protested against a certain Notice served on him by the Marshal ordering him to clean up his lot.

John Smith had his crooked finger cut off some time last week.

I wrote a letter to Wright about his waterworks for the Morehead property.

William A Crow commenced an action of Attachment and Garnishment against Mr Wilbur.

Geo Havens came around to the Office this evening.

Domnick Schnell filed motion for continuance in his cases with Aultman, Muller & Co. for 30 days from May 31, 1889.

May 28th. Cloudy and rain during forenoon. C. J. Davis brought Ella Clark into Court. I continued the Cause till June 18th, 1889 at 10 oclock—and took personal recognizance. Tom Madden came in the office this morning & drew a map of the Green River Country in Wyoming for Billy Wilson who expects to imigrate thither to the newly discovered gold fields.

Quite a number of "Boomers" passed through Chadron yesterday. C. D. Sayrs slept with me and this morning he and A. G. Fisher went up to Harrison to attend Court.

Mr Wilbur came in my office to argue his attachment suit against him—and in the afternoon Mr Crow came in and paid the costs and had [word missing].

Steve Jackson made up his mind to clean up his lots—[.] It showered considerable all day and has been generally wet.

I wrote out a Pin Pool tournament for John Larsh[.] Judge Kinkaid & Reporter returned from Sioux County this evening. I had Strawberries for dinner in the Office and Shorty Brown, Mr. D E Havens, J M Peck & Hank Clifford participated.

I wrote out some Grand Army exercises for Clem Davis. after supper I participated in a game of pool at J W. Owens.

this even. 28th, Hank Clifford & I attended the 1st lecture given in Pete Nelsons Opera Block—"Thumbs Up" by Rev. Staunton of Douglas. the audience was a failure as far as attendance went.

May 29. At the Mass Meeting called at the Rink this eve for the purpose of appointing a fourth of July Committee, F M Dorrington got more in his soup than he cared for.

May 30. Decoration day was observed by the people here but not by the weather exactly for it has been blowing all day. The Democrat came out on time.

J W Boyds Bro came back from Wyoming this evening.

John Maher, Fisher and myself attended the Court House where the Grand Army held their services[.] Mr. C. J. Davis as Post Commander filled his position with credit and respect to all. At 12 M and immediately after services the Malitia formed and headed the procession to the cemetery.

Yesterday evening Just before the Mass Meeting at the Rink, Mr F B. Carley met me in Boyds Gun Store and in an informal way suggested to me that the political issue would soon commence again in Dawes Co. he told me after some parrying that the Reps. intended to Nominate Fred McConnel for Sheriff but I think he only said it to hear what I would say upon County Matters.

George Haven, D Soss & Pete Barber came in the Office this evening and upon Geo demanding to have strawberries I sent for some. C W Allen being in the Office at the time he help[ed] us eat them. My Centuarys came from the State Journal together with 1 Vol of Scribners and Vol 14 of Judge.

May 31. Rain a good part of the day. C. D. Sayrs came down from Crawford. he spoke to me about the Continuance case in the case of Aultman Miller & Co vs Daniel Schnell. I called on Cleona Josselyn.

June 1. Nice day again untill toward evening when it rained. I played Pin Pool with Larsh & Sells and wound up the game, but afterward Larsh wound me right back again by winning it all back. After that we all went over to Stranskys and had a hell of a good time till the We Sma hours of Sunday morning.

June 2. Sunday the weather was Clear but the roads heavy. I went to the Catholic Church with Pete Breen and afterwards to the Congregational Church Sunday School and I enjoyed a very instructive lesson.

Geo & I retired very early in the evening.

June 3[.] Very changable all day.

I borrowed $25.00 from G. A. Eckles for one month at 5 per cent and paid him one dollar for getting me the loan. I gave Brother Thos Diamond ring on pledge for Security—

Mr. Rodgers and Mr. [name missing] called on me during the afternoon and I took them up to see Hank Cliffords Fossil Collection.

I acknowledged a deed for Mr. & Mrs C C Hughes, and also a loan application & mortgage for Daniel Burns[.] Atty. Saterlee came down from Crawford.

Ira Ellenwood recd news that his Sister had gone insane[.]

After supper I sent up an affidavit for a marriage license to Judge Powers for William Boise & Bertha Hoffman.

June 4[.] Nice weather all day. I married Mr Wm Boise & Bertha Hoffman this evening at the Pacific House. It rained this afternoon. The water main Bursted on Cox, Shelton & 4th[.] Wilson & I turned it off.

June 5. Nice day again. Very warm. Pete Sweeney came down from Crawford this evening with a Negro who had been one of a company of Negro Soldiers who attempted to shoot the Town of Crawford to pieces yesterday. He reports that John Owens was shot twice but not fatally.

Co Atty Pardoe, City Marshal Wilson and W. D. Edgar & myself took a strawberry slush at J. W. Owens.

during the afternoon I got McLaughlin to paint a "Relief Sign" for the Johnstown sufferers and then I got Van Lehn & Hamilton to drum for me and I drove them all over town and advertised to the Citizens that a meeting would be held at the Rink this evening at 7.30 for the Relief of Johnstown Sufferers—and at that time quite a number were assembled and A Bartow was called to the Chair and C W Allen Secretary. A Committee of 7 were appointed by the Chair who should have full charge of managing the affairs of the Johnstown relief business in Dawes County and following are the said committee: Judge N. P. Cook, C W Allen, Mayor H. A. Cox, F M Dorrington, E. E. Egan, L. A Brower and B. F. Pitman, after which the meeting broke up and the Committee at once adjourned to Judge Cooks office.

Charley Morrisey was married this morning at 8 oclock at the Catholic Church to Miss Lizzie Moran of Cheyene.

I played a match game of billiards with John Smith last night and got beat.

George Havens commenced work for H. D. Kirmse in the Post Office—[.] he quit Tobias yesterday. I wired Snyder for 500 dollars today.

June 6. Very nice day. Hot.

The different soliciting committees for the Johnstown Sufferers have been to work all day. I donated $10.00 to the Cause.

I recd an answer from Snyder saying I could have no money now.

W. D. Edgar is on the sick list. Tip Morton and the Co Commissioners are having a lively time over a road.

Doc Mathews of ONeill was in town today.

I played some pool with him. The water main bursted by the Court House about 9 P.M. No meeting of the City Council tonight.

J. L. Paul & Co are putting in framing for the large display windows of their store to enable them to keep flies off this summer.

June 7. Wet and rainy all day.

the Marshal commenced killing dogs again. I recd a letter from Mary Vandersloot and answered it right off. I also wrote to Denver for Brother Thos. picture[.] the committee on decoration for the Johnstown train is busy painting signs to go on the outside of the Cars.

Hank Clifford is hard at work on his fossils.

Ed Cameron has started out with an outfit to go into the bad lands to hunt fossils.

the Wyoming Boomers from Chadron left here yesterday and will no doubt return soon with their bellies full of adventure. the Soliciting Committee on the Johnstown Sufferers had a meeting this evening.

June 8[.] Clear day. the Marshal had been hunting untagged dogs again.

The case of Donoghue vs Taylor for forcible detention of property was called and Judgment given for Plff. Deft. defaulted. The sheriff by his deputy seized 2 trunks upon a writ of restitution.

Hank Clifford found out today that Steve Jackson (Colored) had a horse belonging to him and he immediately hunted Steve up and they have made a stipulation to the effect that by monday morning next Steve will either give up the horse or pay Hank $20.00 for a good title[.]

Marshal Wilson arrested Elmer Snyder for leading a cow across the side walk. Burr Shelton championed the Defendant and after getting in some high toned Slang was very indignant that his highness or any of his employees should be persecuted by such base Main Street Curs as the Marshal & Police Court. it is raining now again[.]

June 9[.] Lute North was in town today. we went to the Ball game but soon got tired[.]

June 13[.] have been to busy to post up. Weather changeable.

[June] 14[.] Weather still Changeable. Chas F Yates was closed by the Sheriff to day at 11 AM. The Johnstown Sufferer Train left this AM in charge of H. A. Cox[.]

The High School exercises have been going on since yesterday.

Yesterday I sent John Larsh up to Jail and let him out on probation this afternoon to rustle enough money to leave town with[.]

this eve I sent Geo over to get 2 buckets lemonade for my company[.]

Chas Allen went to the agency[.]

There is a book agent in town that can out talk any body in Gods earth[.] Arkansas John visited me.

June 15[.] Nice weather although it started out to rain in the morning. moved a poor woman in Bob Dorr house today[.]

Godsall arrived from Oelrichs this evening whence he had gone to arrest C. F. Yates, but he failed to bring his victim along. M. E. Smith & Co. of Omaha have replevid the goods from Richard Bros and are invoicing now. plenty of business in Justice Court all day.

Pete Knutzen got out a search warrant against Henry Tons and the later punished this Court by employing Molyneaux as his attorney. Sayrs appeared as Knutzens Atty and won the case.

Robert Hood commenced suit before me against Frank Campbell.

Mrs. Melinda Tyree swore out a warrant against one Louis Funkhouser for assault and Battery.

Night police Hartzell & I went down to see the Oelrichs Train come in. on our way up town, Fisher met us and hurried me up to the office where Henry Hall and Amelia Williamson both of Buffalo Gap were waiting to have me marry them.

Not having the license however it was some time before they returned from the Co Judges office[.]

After having fixed them up all O.K. I & Hank Clifford repaired to J W Owens[.]

June 16[.] Sunday and Ball game was the go. Lute North & I went. Jack Welch and I had quite a time betting on innings.

June 17. Plenty of business in Court over the Yates failure[.]

June 18. Nice weather. today the case of State vs Ella Clark charged for assault and battery[.]

A Jury found her guilty and I fined her one dollar and costs[.]

June 19. Nice day. not much business[.]

June 20[.] Nice day. today the case of State vs Louis Funkhouser came on for trial. Charged with assault and battery.

2 Jurys were empanelled[.] the first disagreed standing 3 to 1 for conviction[.]

The 2nd stood 4 to 2 for conviction and finally brought in a verdict for the Defendant. Smith and Ed Robinson opened up their fruit stand on 2nd st[.]

June 21. Nice day. George bought 2 catfish and I took dinner with him up home[.]

June 22. James Cavanaugh was up in Police Court again. I sent him to the Quay in default and the Marshal chained him to the sidewalk in front of Coffeys saloon.

Harry Way gave me a ride this evening behind his little pony[.] George and J W Good had quite a time trading horses[.]

Charlie Allen & Sheldon went over to the Red Cloud Agency to engage Indians for the fourth. Joe Allen is to sleep in my room till they come back[.]

June 23[.] Fine day. I bought Joe Allen a Sunday suit of clothes and he & I went to church & Sunday School before dinner. In the evening I retired early.

June 24[.] James was turned lose today[.]

June 25[.] Rained a little[.] Van Inwegin got back from his Chicago trip a few days ago[.]

June 26[.] Very busy. Yesterday the case of State vs Best. for Assault and Battery was tried by Jury[.] Deft acquitted.

Hank Clifford moved his stuff in the Gold Bar to day[.]

June 27th[.] I simply go back to this date to show that Thomas Paul the great Chadron Drayman was arrested and fined in Police Court for leaving a team of horses unhitched[.] Today I finished a big job of typewriting for John Maher in cases of Butler vs Stranskey and Sweat vs Burnham[.]

June 28. To[o] busy to post up yesterday. It rained to day hard. Western Farm Mortgage Co. commenced suit before me. the several committees for the Fourth of July were to have met at Dorringtons this evening, but outside of Lowenthal[,] Owens, Mrs Pitman, Mrs Dr Koons and Miss Nelly Morgan, no one appeared[;] however the later [latter] part of the Company was as much as might have been desired by myself, I being the only single man there[.]

June 29. the Printers & Court House Employees played ball today. Mr Shears got me to copy some of the papers in the case of Henry Hoffman vs Ben Tibbitts on appeal to the Supreme Court for $5,000 damages.

L. C. Quigley undertook to make a sale of his livery & sundry property to day but was duly stopped and the goods under execution by Sheriff Dahlman upon an old Pierce County Judgment. C. D. Sayrs commenced an action of repleven in the District Court for Quigley.

After supper Hank Clifford, E. L. Godsall, John Maher and myself drove out to Billy Carters place West of town to look at some cattle for the Fourth of July, after which we were invited into the house by Billy who introduced his Family to the company and entertained us in a thorough royal manner as he does and knows how to his friends. After leaving Carters we drove to my office and got the autoharp and went down to Hank Simmons a little while and then came home.

Marshal Chas Wilson is and has been on a little spree since yesterday.

June 29 continued. Tom Saul came around to the office late this evening and complained about Charles Wilson (City Marshal) being drunk where upon Tom and I had quite a forcible argument over his having been arrested & fined a few days[.] Saul left a wiser man concerning his late trouble.

June 30. I went to church and in the afternoon to the Ball game. while there Mayor Cox and I had some conversation about Wilsons spree[.] After the game I had a chat with Godsall & Hartzell about how Charlie was getting on with his spree[.] after supper I took a horse back ride to look out a suitable location for putting the Indians in camp. I think the grounds adjoining the Ball grounds are good enough for the purpose.

July 1[.] About 3 AM Marshal Chas Wilson woke me up to tell me about his having been on a spree. Police Officer Hartzell was with him. Wilson informed me that he was going to quit the Marshalship in accordance with his resolution laid down on the last drunk "that if ever he would get drunk again he would walk out of town." I was rather sick last night and got up early.

About 2 Oclock P.M. Chas Wilson came in the office and formerly [formally] notified me of his intention to quit the marshals office. I have been busy buying provisions for the Indians.

McPheeley jumped me about the Indians getting too much money, and informed me that a separate fund was being raised for the purposes of getting up Horse Race purses.

In the evening I took a pauper down to the OHanlon house but they having no room, I took him over to Henry Stephens who accommodated him[.]

Mayor Cox temporarily appointed W. P. Hartzell Marshal until the first meeting of the Council[.] George Havens treated Charles Wilson & I to Ice Cream.

I changed the furniture around in the room this evening and George & I took a bath[.]

July 2[.] Nice day. About 2 Oclock this morning Wm Bristow arrested D. M. Sells for Assault and Battery upon Van Inwegin. I was woke up and took Sells bond for $500 with B. F. Pitman as surety.

Sells had his right eye cut pretty badly while Van Inwegin is reported to have had his skull fractured. Sayrs and I took strawberries for lunch.

After dinner the case of Turner & Jay vs C. F. Yates and First National Bank came on for hearing upon replevin suit[.] the Court rendered judgment for the Defendant.

July 3. Nice day, busy getting things ready for tomorrow. the Indians came into camp this afternoon and as soon as Jack Red Cloud came I took him over to the Photographers and had his pictures taken. After supper the 4th July Committee met at Dorringtons office[.] Charlie Wilson resigned today and Mayor Cox appointed W. P. Hartzell temporary Marshall, but during the afternoon he insisted on appointing Joe L. Branner to the office. I conceeding to the appointment after considerable argument.

I got the Mayor to appoint Joe immediately so as to give him a show[.]

Charlie Wilson left for Crawford this AM[.]

July 4th[.] Hot day. I was kept busy all day with the Indians, and every thing passed off quietly and satisfactory[.]

I got through with my horse at 7:30 P.M.

During the day I had old Red Cloud and his wifes pictures taken together and then Reds, alone, and then Red, John Maher and I together and then Spotted Elk alone.

About 3 P.M. Mrs Slatterlys team attached to a spring wagon out by the Indian Camp took fright and ran away[.]   the neck yoke in some way became detached from the pole and it ran into the ground stopping the vehicle short and breaking the pole off in the middle.   the team broke the double trees and got away from the driver.

the Indians caught the team. No one was hurt.

After supper I went up to the Rink to see the Bowery Dances but came home soon and went to bed[.]

July 5th[.] Hot day again.

I was busy trying 2 cases of the Western Farm Mortgage Co vs. Metz and Pelren.

Mrs OLinn brought 3 suits in my court against Woodford and Rockwell.

The temporary appointment of Marshall Branner does not seem to meet the approbation of some of the Council who claim they knew nothing about it[.]

July 6. Hottest day for years. Ther [near?] 103 in shade.

The case of State vs D. M. Sells for Assault and Battery was continued to July 13th at 9 A.M.[,] 1889, on account of Dr Jacksons statement that the assaulted party could not leave his room but notwithstanding this

"Billy the Bear," Red Cloud, and John Maher (left to right)

statement about 6 Oclock the patient sallied forth on the street with his plug hat as staunch and brave as ever.

The Indians have about all left town.

this evening after supper the Dorrington Hose Team made a practice run in 37 seconds.

I took the hides of the 3 cows, killed for the Indians, up to John Stetters who offered me 1.50 apiece, but after having unloaded them Julius Hahler offered me 1.50 for the 3. I took twenty five cents and donated the balance to them as the hides were worth $4.50[.]

July 7[.] Cool all day and tried to rain but failed. I stayed in the office all day and marked envelopes and chatted politics[.]

The City Marshal business seems to be working up considerable opposition, among people other than myself who seem to think that the temporary appointment of Joe Branner has something of the George Clark, Burr Shelton, Ed Egan, F B Carley, Birdsall Bros and A Bartow Clique about it, Clothed with a sheeps hide with the wool drawn over Mayor Coxs eyes.

July 8th[.] It rained a little to day[.] I cleared out Sayrs desk for Joe Branner.

The Sullivan and Kelraine fight is causing quite a stir in town[.]

Jake Kass returned from Seattle day before yesterday[.] Geo Stover came over from the Agency.

Hank Clifford commenced packing up his Fossils to day[.] C. C. Hughes came back from Chicago today preparatory to moving away from Chadron[.] P O Hanlon came in the office after supper and got out a set of Attachment and Garnishment papers against C. F. Runkel. Geo Havens and Kirmse had a few words about Geo. not having been at the store last Sunday. To day I put Brother Thomas picture out to photographer to have enlarged and also sent a lot of his pictures east to relatives[.]

July 9. Associated press dispatches give it that Sullivan won the fight in the 72 round.

Gollords 13 year old boy came in the office this A.M. and complained that he was working for Dave Cockrill and that his Father would not let him work unless Cockrill paid his wages to him (his father) which the boy does not seem to want as he says his father uses the money for other purposes than supporting the children. I referred the case to C. W. Allen[.] Young Pete Breen skipped the town for some unknown reason last Sunday evening and it is rumored the Old Man closed his Grocery Store this morning. Mrs Donaway and Kass came to look at a house for rent. Hank Clifford is making arrangements to Sell out a half interest in his Fossil Exhibition, providing Burr Sheltons collection of Indian trinkets can be purchased[.]

July 10[.] Nice day. posted up the books etc. I wrote a letter to J. F. Wright[.] Preacher Powell came in to chat with me. Joe Ford let his white barber go.

Geo Leonard has sold out his restaurant[.]

Tom Saul is working hard on the excavation of the Putman & Myers building. 1 Case in Police Court this AM[;] also old Fredericks bothered the Police Court considerably about wanting Tuttle arrested.

the City Council met this evening, but could do nothing towards making any returns from the County Commissioners so as to allow them apportioning the City funds.

Mrs Richards from Chadron Creek came in to see me about getting one of the Gaylord children[.]

July 12. I have been busy both in Court and elsewhere. I went to work on J. Kass & Co books[.]

July 13[.] It rained very hard last night.

The case of State vs D. M. Sells was continued to July 17th 9 AM. After supper W D Edgar & crowd went down to the Rail Road House and serenaded or tin horned W G Pardoe the County Clerk, after which H S Ballow received a like dose[.]

July 14. Nice day[.] J Kass and Fred Poll went out in the country to put up a binder. I worked on the books a little, but George and I took a ride down to the stock yards to look at some horses from Oregon[.] the Chadron Band gave a private pic nic at Butlers Grove today and consequently the city was pretty well deserted[.]

July 15[.] Hot day. I worked on the Kass books again[.]

A little after supper one Allen a Piano tuner and one Roundtree had quit[e] a fuss at the Chapin House over the formers wife. Allen claiming that Round tree had been using too much liberty with Mrs Allen while he (Allen) had been West.

Allen went and got a Gun 22 Cal but had no cartridges in it.

The Marshall arrested him and the Court dismissed the Case[.]

quite a wind and rain storm sprung up about 7 oclock.

Dr A L Jackson while out driving near the ball Grounds had his buggy upset and was considerably hurt himself though not seriously.

about 2 Oclock this afternoon I went out to Tom Maddens farm with him to acknowledge a transfer of some city property. I enjoyed myself very much out there. Tom treats me splendidly and he has a lady for a wife.

There is at Present going on a considerable and somewhat animated fishing and generaling among local republican weights and politicians for the Position of Register & Receiver of the W. S. Land Office here. Col. W. H. McCann of Hay Springs being foremost for Receiver and Hon Blanchard of Rushville for receiver.

Mayor T. F. Powers is also in the line of aspirants but fate is against him and he must fail—if for nothing else a lack of common sense and decency.

Tom Saul is still working on the Myers & Putnam excavation and is doing good work.

I discharged the County Pauper this morning and gave him a pair of Bro Thos shoes[.]

July 16[.] Very Hot day[.] I received a letter from Chas Wilson this A.M.

have worked on the Kass books all day.

Tom Doud has been considerably worked up over one Johnson a New York dude who it seems played him for a sucker.

during the afternoon Mrs Leach and Hayward called to see what I could do in the matter of getting proper provisions for Mrs Baker, a poor blind woman with a worthless husband who fails to support her and family.

I assured her that I would certainly take steps in that direction[.]

My county pauper whom I discharged tried to walk to Crawford to day but had to come back. I offered him his supper but he refused to eat[.] I then sent him down to Henry Stevens, with orders that he get a bed there, and meet me tomorrow morning at the depot at 6:30 when I will pay his fare to Crawford if it is Gods will that I live till then[.]

After supper I got ready for performing a wedding which was performed at 9:30 for Robt Walker and Mary Plunk.

July 17[.] Nice day. quite a ball game today between Chadron and Evergreen Club. it was play for the Chadron boys.

after the game the Marshal arrested George Leonard for maintaining a Nuisance. I fined him and after Court while I was on the street Leonard cursed and abused me so that I ordered him rearrested and fined for disturbing the peace which by advice of Burr Shelton he appealed, giving Burr as his surety.

The City Council met and adjourned till tomorrow eve[.]

July 18. Fine day. All Chadron was up in arms today over the first game of Ball between the Oneill and Chadron Clubs. Over $500. was put up 2 to 1 on the Oneill Club by their backers[.] Tom Coffey lost over $120.00 alone[.] The Oneill Club won by 4 to 0[.]

In Justice Court the Case of George Leonard vs. Fred Wafful was on trail and the evidence on both sides having been taken at about 2:45 P.M. The Court adjourned till tomorrow morning in order that the Jury could go to the Ball game, for fear of returning any kind of a verdict if held away. The Council met this evening but not much work of importance was accomplished and an adjournment taken to Monday July 22nd[,] 1889[.]

July 19[.] Fine weather again and like yesterday all Chadron was out to witness a second game of Ball between Oneill & Chadron[.] Ira Ellenwood and George Clark Umpired the game. The Chadron Boys won, but of course it was settled about that before the game began[.] After supper the City Marshall again arrested George Leonard for maintaining the nuisance and the Court fined him fifty Dollars and costs to which he gave notice of appeal[.]

After supper I cut down Leonards fine to One Dollar and Costs which he forthwith paid[.]

July 20[.] Nice day again and for the 4th time the City repaired to the Ball grounds to witness the closing game between the Home team and Oneill Club[.] bets went even up and the Chadrons going to bat first. Bettinger made a swipe over the left field fence and scored the plate for the first run for Chadron which seemed to daze the Oneillers and lost them the game[,] Notwithstanding that in the last half of the 9th inning the score stood 4 to 2 in favor of Chadron while the Oneills men had 2 men out and 1 on 2nd base and one man on 3 base with 3 balls called and 2 strikes called[,] which made the Chadron sports feel a little shaky, but the batter was put out on strikes.

Professor Holmes (Catcher for the Chadron Club[)]] had his right hand severely bruised by catching the hot curves of Kid Freeman who was sent for and put in the box by McPhieley[.]

in the 5th inning Tex Eitinger, the pitcher for Oneill kicked on umpire Joe Haslem which finally resulted in one of Oneills own party umpiring the game which he however did fairly in the face of having over $200. bet on Oneill winning[.]

Henry Myers daughter died this morning from the supposed black Measles. Henry Stephens came to me and had me go down to see after the case, but I found undertaker Myers had been there and made the necessary arrangements[.]

July 21[.] Nice weather. I went to morning service at the Congregational Church.

took dinner with Judge Cook, on Egan Street at the New Restaurant[.] I received a letter from Cousin Nora[.]   After supper Bailey & I went up to the Congregational Church to hear Rev Powell preach on Sullivanism and Danielism[.]

July. 22[.] It rained very hard last night.

Today I have been busy on J Kass Co books[.]

the City Council met tonight and after going over a lot of bills they referred them to the finance Committee. after meeting[,] Paul Glover and myself went down to Stranskys.

July 23. Fine day. Geo and I got a rig at Bowers & Demon and went out to Mr. A. C. Fowlers on the table to fetch in my colt. We took Geo's saddle pony along and arrived out there at 6:30 PM. I got unwell after our arrival[,] caused from drinking too much buttermilk.

the case of State vs. D. M. Sells was dismissed to day July 23[.]

July 24[.] Nice day, though it rained a little last night.

We got an early start with the colt and had good luck driving and leading it, Geo doing the leading and I the buggy part[.] on the way, I stopped at Harry Deans claim, where he was then cutting Rye and got some samples of his Rye. Next I stopped at Mike Gillmore and got a sample of his Oats and new potatoes, and Geo & I also took a look at Mikes new well[—] 296 feet deep. it had splendid clear water in it. We arrived home at 1 P.M. and found that there had been a fire at or close to Tom Glovers House[.]

July 25[.] Nice cool weather.

I rented Bennets Stable from F. J. Houghton for $2.00 per month, and immediately put Mr Eddy and Tom Wilson to work fixing it up[.] I also had Tom Saul deliver me some new dirt to rig out the stable[.] We could not get all the carpenter work done on the stable[.]

July 26[.] Nice day again. Mr. Eddy and I finished up the stable by dinner time. I made out transcripts for F. M. Dorrington in the cases of Western Farm Mortgage Co and Scott Metz and Will F Pelren[.]

Daley brought the colt down from Bower & Demons barn & I put it in its new stable[.] J. D. Pattison offered to let me have the loan of a good mare for the rest of the summer[.] I accepted.

Mr. E. E. Record started to make a bitting rig[.]

July 27. Nice day. the sun was under a peculiar cloud nearly all day making things look yellow all over. Mr Stransky brought some company in to see me[.] Mr. D E Lambert[,] special agent of the Interior Dept. called to see C D Sayrs who afterwards brought him in the office and introduced him to me.

Mrs Sayrs & Ettie were in the office a little this afternoon. I applied the bitting rig to the colt, also bought 1500 lbs. hay for $3.75[.]

I typewrote some articles of agreement for C. W. Allen preparitory to his leaving with H. C. Clifford for the East[.]

July 28. Nice day[.] I went out to Mr Sayrs for dinner. he came in with the buggy for me and brought me home about 5 P.M.

Spotted Elk came over from the Agency to see me. I gave him his dinner at Mosiers[.] I was feeling a little bad and went to bed early.

July 29. Nice day again. I got Hank Clifford to talk to Spotted Elk for me concerning my purchasing 2 spotted or pied colts from the Indians if they can be had. I stood good for $1.00 worth of sugar for Spotted Elk, and also gave him a general letter of recommendation to go on a hunt on lance Creek[,] Wyo[.] A. C. Fowler was in town today. last night Stranskys saloon was broken into and $175.00 taken out of a drawer and also $10.00 out of the Money drawer[.]

Aug 1st[.] Since July 29th I have been to busy to do any posting. today Henry Stephens was arrested for whiping his wife[.]

Aug 4[.] since August 1st have been too busy in getting my warrants from the City Clerk[.] Mayor Cox has gone to Fremont, there to accept a probable position at running a passenger train[.]

Aug 5[.] Chas Allen left for the Agency to get Indians[.] I am suffering from Poison Ivey again[.] I bought some nice dress goods for Mr Sayrs at Auction[.]

Aug 6[.] I sent my colt out to McVickers to have it broke to drive[.]

P. B. Nelson was arrested for refusing to remove some condemned nuisances.

Aug 7[.] I got up early and took Bob Ford with me and drove out to McVickers to see him handle the colt the first time[.] It worked so well that we drove it to town double.

After dinner I and Pete Barber drove down to Butlers Park to a Union Sunday School Picnic[.] it was a tame affair, and I just chanced to meet a few boys with whom it was possible to have a good time[.]

Major Powers and McCann are announced in todays papers as the New Land Officers at this place[.]

I am still suffering with Poison Ivey.

P. B. Nelson appeald his case to the District court to day.

It is now 9 P.M. and trying hard to rain[.]

Aug 8th[.] Nice day. I worked on the Kass books nearly all day. Dave Mears showed me around his office and asked me [to] run the Water Commissioners office during his absence to the springs[.] Fred Poll got back from Lusk, as did also Jake Kass yesterday with a new mare.

The Council held a meeting this evening over the proposed funding bonds. I wrote some letters in the bedroom before retiring. I am suffering intensely with poison Ivey.

Aug 9th[.] Chas Allen & Hank Clifford got back from the Agency[.] Jake Kass had his new mare hitched up, but she faild to show up good. the Chadron Base Ballists started out for Rapid, there to play ball. I am getting on very slow with curing the Poison Ivy. I worked at Kass & Co nearly all day[.] Chas Allen & Hank Clifford are packing up preparitory to going to Chicago where they expect to open up their show, and I hope they may make a big winning.

News from Rapid City this evening is to the effect that Chadron got away with the Rapid Club. I retired early—[.]

Aug 10. a little cold last night. pretty nice day till toward 3 oclock PM when it commenced to drizzle and by nine P.M. managed to rain a little. Clifford & Allen shipped their fossils[.] John Smith & Glover started for Chicago this evening.

News from Deadwood is that the Chadron Ball Club got beat today by 29 to 12.

Cora Bentons household goods were auctioned off on Egan St. this P.M. by Messenger[.]

C. F. Yates bed room set which he originally purchased for his lady Employee, Miss Mary Smith, were auctioned off, in front of my office this morning.

Ed Godsall took me down to the depot in Dahlmans buggy to find City Clerk Smith, and get from him my warrant on the City which I immediately sold to Tom Moore. Ed then took me up to the County Treasurers office where I wanted to pay J. F. Wrights Taxes on his Egan St lot.

My poison Ivey is still bothering me, but I am slowly getting it under control.

Aug 11. Sunday. I thought I would stay in the House to day and doctor my poison, but upon going to breakfast I learned that last evening about 6 P.M. there had been a cloud burst up on Chadron Creek and a little boy (Goodenough) had been drownded.

Everybody almost in town went out to the Scene of death[.] I took my colt out for exercise but when I got to Browns I thought that the Dam out at the water works might be washed out so leaving the colt at browns, I put spurs to my horse and arriving at the Engine house, found my prediction more than verified for not only was the dam gone but the water had been all through the engine room for over 13 inches deep and washed every movable thing away down in the brush. I immediately set out for town to employ men to fix things and on my way I met Fred Poll and Pat knowles the Engineer. they proceeded on out and I came on and hired a team and driver and rode around through town and notified people to save as much water as possible[.]

After dinner we all went out and filled up Sacks with dirt[.] I doing the teaming we then bailed out the 2 wells and came home. I was feeling pretty tired, and my poison Oak was very much irritated by heat.

Aug 12. Monday. Nice day. it rained last night. at 7 AM the working gang including myself all started out to the Engine house there to fix up the dam[.] We hauled cinders I doing the driving. at 10 AM we got the dam in and by 11 we had the water high enough to fill up both wells. We got up steam and started pumping at 20 minutes to 1 Oclock P.M. after which we commenced to finish up the odd place, and while thus engaged the team got unruley and getting the better of me, threw me out and under the front wheel of the wagon and which passed over me. Fred Poll and old Bill were right there and grabbing the team they got me lose minus my left foot which having become pinched in between the Single and Double trees was broken short off at the ankle Joint and it being wood faild to hurt me. I got up on the wagon and continued to drive till the close of the day. I had my supper sent to me from Sweetsers.

Aug 13[.] It rained a little last night. this morning at 2 o'clock L E Blaizdell woke me up to get a warrant out for Fields and Oppertunity Hank, but I refused to issue on[e] upon the stated grounds of his. I worked on Jake Kass & Co books. I put on my old legs. in the afternoon Geo & I drove out to the waterworks and up to the reservoir to see how things were going on. Afterwards we took a spin around the Race track where C W Dresser was exercising his colt. It rained along about 8 o'clock. Geo and I retired early. Geo took a bath.

The little 8 yr old boy who was drowned day before yesterday was buried yesterday.

Aug 14[.] It rained considerable last night. Wm Bristow woke me up at 2 A.M. to issue a warrant for a tramp thief. Milo T Stright appeared in Court today and plead not guilty to a charge of selling mortgaged property. he asked for and got a continuance but failing to give bonds I remanded him in the custody of the Sheriff[,] not however until after I had gone way up Chadron Creek for him, and not finding him there, I found upon my return that he had never left town. D Y Mears returned from the springs last evening.

Young Jack Smith went up to Rapid City this morning.

I burned up my old rubbish around the house.

J T. Hickey, of the celebrated Hickey Ward in the early days of Chadron, came back from Colorado last monday. The Republican Political pot seems to be getting hottier every day.

Aug 16[.] Nice day. Yesterday the Deputy Sheriff & I drove up Chadron Creek in search of Milo T. Stright whom I admitted to personal recognizance till during the afternoon. We overtook his wife & children but he was not there.

When we came back he showed up early and the sheriff locked him up. Fred Poll is still on his protracted spree.

I wrote a letter today to C C Hughes relative to the proposed Funding and City Hall bonds at the special suggestion of Councilman Paul & Atty Fisher[.]

In the evening I drove out to Billy Carters and took my colt out to hitch up double but as Billy was not at home I left the Colt there. W P Hartzell went out with me[.] on our way home one of the livery horses broke the Single tree cliet [cleat].

Aug 17. Nice day. I and Patsy drove out to Billy Carters in Stranskys single rig. At Carters we hitched the colt up with Carters pacing gray. everything went lovely. In the afternoon I again hitched up and drove around town, after which I turned the rig over to Carter.

The colt showed signs of having caught distemper out at Carters.

C. D. Sayrs has not been around the office to day.

Mary Powell was in the office putting some bills into my hands for collection[.]

I took supper at the Chadron House, and called to see T. J. Doud who is confined to his room with poison ivey[.]

The Ft Niobrara regulars are camped on the Bordeaux and are on the alert for the Troops from Ft Robinson who are on the look out for the former. when they meet there will be a sham battle. R. E. W. Spargur is having auction sale this evening[.] I bought 3 good woolen shirts averaging 78 cts apiece[.]

Billy Carter was in Town all day trading horses[.]

The Chicago Cattle Shippers have now about all arrived and are ready for business[.]

Aug 18[.] Sunday. Harry Way took me out to the Soldier Camp N. W. of town and his mare came near killing both of us. I played billiards a good deal and stayed up to witness the late game among the "boys[.]" Mrs McGinley had a runaway this afternoon and hurt two of John Larshes children, breaking ones arm and leg. I called to see the Josselyn family after supper[.]

Aug 19. Nice day. I work nearly all day on a plate [plat] of Valentine for Tom Moore[.]

Fred Poll is still on his spree. the Ft Niobrara troops left here this A.M.

today I handed in an order to Sweetser on T. J. Doud for $4.50 worth of merchandise given me by the Democrat Co[.]

The Chadron Base Ball Club left for Oniell tonight.

C. D. Sayrs went down to Hay Springs on business for Dorrington[.]

Aug 20[.] Nice day. Kirmse sneaked out of going to Oniell last night and consequently Geo Havens started with his Gang to the Red Cloud Agency to witness the Big Beef Issue.

The case of State vs Milo Stright for Selling Mortgaged Property was before me for examination today and resulted in the Defendant being discharged. Marshall Branner filed a complaint against Mrs McGinly for fast driving[.]

Aug 21[.] Nice Cool day.

Not much business. I put in about an hour up at Stranskys Barn with my colt bitting it[.]

In the evening I hitched it up in P OHanlons buggy and we took a ride[.]

George and his gang came home from the Agency after having seen all the sights. The G. A. R. are now in Camp out at the fair Grounds[.] News has been received from Robt. H. Martin at Tubtown[,] Wyo[.] to the effect that Daniel McKinzie was sinking very fast with mountain fever on the 15th inst. with no Doctor to attend him. Dr. Lewis has been delegated by the K. P. to go up to him and bring him to Chadron.

Aug 22. McLeod has been having auction all day. I took the colt out to the Race track and had OBrien to hitch it up Single.

In the afternoon I hitched the colt up myself and drove out to the G. A. R. encampment at the fair grounds.

Fred Poll while out ridding last night had J Kass & Cos buggy team run away[.] Fred has his shoulder blade broken.

George Havens quit working for Kirmse today.

the Marshal swore out a warrant against G W Hatch for fast driving[.]

Aug 24[.] Cloudy & Smoky[.] It blew very hard last night.

This morning about 10 o'clock 3 fires broke out Simultaneously in 3 different places. they were all extinguished with the loss of 1 barn however[.] Ben Arnold is here proposing to get up a Company for the purchasing & Selling of Cattle & Stock and taking up land near Eli[,] Cherry Co[,] Neb.

I forgot to post up yesterday. I wrote a letter to Snyder about the settlement of Bro Thos Estate.

Aug 25[.] Sunday. It rained a little this morning but cleared up in the afternoon with a light wind blowing[.] I stayed in the house all day and cleaned up & assorted books and read.

About 4 PM Harry Way & Geo came around and Harry allowed me to use his cart and harness to drive the colt with[.] Afterwards George hitched up his nag and went driving. James Moffitt got his foot hurt badly at the freight depot by a truck falling on it.

Aug 26[.] Nice day. In the afternoon the West Point and Chadron Base Ball Clubs played. Score 10 to

6 in favor of Chadron. Geo Clark umpired and done pretty well. Not much betting on the game.

This morning's Omaha Bee contained a Biographical Sketch of my life and is causing considerable amusement throughout the city[.] In the evening I had a jolly time with old time Black hillers at Jim Owens.

George Havens is as usual a very bad boy and has gone to work for his first love, the old Ike Gottstein stand[.]

I was pretty busy all day[.]

Aug 27. Fine day again. The Chadron Cornet Band got out and played for the Baseball Clubs and marched to the Park. All Chadron shut down to visit the game, which proved to be one of the Rankest of all Rank games and must tend to disorganize the home club. Geo Havens got Harry Ways cart and harness this evening and we intend getting up early tomorrow morning for an early drive.

Cobors (Horse Jockey) has taken up quarters out at the Race Track. The Scotts Bluff Horse Trainer Mr [name missing] is also now located at Birdsalls Barn where he has taken several local horses for training.

Aug 28. Nice warm day, though it blew very hard early this A.M. Geo & I did not get up as early as we had hoped so I had to make my drive myself[.] I went out to the Race track[.]

Good business but not much money.

In the afternoon I hitched up again and afterwards sent Harry ways cart home[.]   Mr J. T. Sampsons and family have returned from Fremont. I made out a bill of sale and mortgage for William V. Hawley[.] After supper a Patent Medicine Man turned himself loose on the public and about 9 Oclock a single horse attached to a buggy ran away tearing things into splinters. Who it belonged to I cannot yet say. Mrs Sharky was in the office this P.M. having a great talk with Sayrs about getting a pension on acct of her dead husband whose death she fails to prove[.]

August 29[.] Nice day.— All Chadron started at 7:30 for Crawford and Ft Robinson to take in the sights of the Encampment and witness a sham battle, but the sham battle failed to materialize[.] We all had a good time. After leaving Crawford for the Ft the train ran into 3 Indian ponies killing them instantly. We returned at 10 PM pretty well tired out.

Aug 30[.] Clear day till 4 PM when a high wind started[.]

I put some more linement on the Colt.

C. D. Sayrs was not in town today[.]

Mrs Theresa Smith came to me and borrowed $5.00 to help her get some things together to go to Crawford to set up a lunch counter[.]

Aug 31. Fair Day. the Marshal arrested some prostitutes[.]

Not much business in the office.

Sept. 1[.] Nice clear day in the morning but towards noon it commenced to blow and get dusty[.]

I went out to Mr Sayrs for dinner where I met Mr & Mrs De Lambert[.] on my way out (I rode Georges pony) I stopped at Stranskys where I also met Mr Ben Davis. We had 2 bottles of soda water. I spent a very pleasant day with Mr Sayrs and had a long and interesting chat with Mr De Lambert about the early days of Cow Punching and about how I got froze on the Laramie Plains. On my way home I again stopped at Mr Stranskys, whose wife had returned from Chadron whither she had repared to visit her grandchild[.]

After partaking a glass of good Beer with mine host and two other Gentlemen (Englishmen from the little Bordeaux) I struck out for home. I must confess I have not been to church for a long time and my main reason is that I am back sliding on account of feeling that I am not wanted among church goers here who consider themselves so much better than myself.

Geo and I retired early but not until Geo had been down to the Depot to see and bid good by to Inez Rosa who left this evening for Neligh to attend School.

Sept 2[.] Nice warm day and notwithstanding that this is a New Holliday (Labor day) the special City Election for the proposition of funding the indebtedness of the City—and building a City Hall, was held and I am sorry to have to record the fact that both propositions failed to carry[.] Some voted against it because they thought bonds meant higher taxes, all of which is verily so. Others voted against it because they were tools of Chronic Kickers and still others voted against it in order to get even as they supposed with some of the Councilmen for imagined wrongs done. The undeniable fact however remains and stands as bold as the noonday sun which is that the City is responsible to innocent parties for the acts of its servants, and if the servants have done wrong it is the loss of the City. provided they fail to recover from the servants in a special action, but that the citizens can repudiate any outstanding indebtedness when such indebtedness shows upon its face as a full value received is mere folly to countenance for a moment.

Therefore like the immortal Boss Tweed of New York, it might be said to the kickers "what are you going to do about [it?] I done it. You undo it[.]" When judgments once rest against the City of Chadron and the Court orders a special levy then "there will be weeping and wailing and gnashing of teeth[.]"

The kick, and it has mainly eminated from the principal Republican Mugwamps here who now are bigoted enough to think that it was Dawes County which elected Harrison[.] I say then again that the "Kick" against City Bonds came from a part of a party who always want to be leaders, although failing to possess that ruby of all instruments, the quality of proposing and management, but on the contrary ever ready to step in with silks and broad cloth and reap the laurels of others who have tolied and struggled a life time for an honest end, only to be defiled and overshadowed by the God of Gods, some one elses wealth to which all humanity bows too irrespective of Color or Creed. Again this "Kick" is only a Symbol or forerunner of what the Dawes County Journal and the supporting Mugwamps of that sheet contemplate accomplishing in the coming County Election this fall. They will have enlightened the public so they think, as to the city business and therefore are entitled to due respect concerning county affairs and consequently all of Uncle Sams dear Republican friends will get a "Pap" spoon.

The "Journal" figures on being on high ground but like the hoggish boy who never had anything at home, thought he could make people think he was raised in wealth and affluence by Calling for nothing but pie and Cake at the first City-Hotel he struck, the boarders got on to the nibsy quick and simply called him a hog, so will it be with Egan, Carley, Bartow, Clark, Sherwood and others who will aim to fly this fall, only to be called fools and hogs.

Geo brought Pete barber home to sleep with us.

Mr Rischer swore out a warrant for John Bowers.

Sept. 3. Cold night. C D Sayrs went to Crawford this A.M.

about 5 days ago Mrs James A Wilson while retiring to bed slipped and fell to the floor breaking both bones near the wrist of her left arm.

I made out two transcripts for C. H. Bane.

the West Point and Chadron Base Ball Clubs played on the Chadron diamond this afternoon. Chadron got left. H. D. Kirmse had his finger hurt pretty badly.

about 4 oclock it commenced to blow from the North in a terrific manner and the probabilities now are that all the soil in British America has changed hands to Nebraska and Texas parties and is at present being transported by King element and his demonic crew.

Sep 4. Clear day but very cool. John Jones on Bordeaux Creek had his hand hurt by a threshing machine. King the Jeweler is putting a New Front in his store on 2nd street.

Sep 5th[.] Clear day and pleasant. C D Sayrs & Wm De Lambert left for Fowlers. Chas Reiche and John Bowers settled their difference at law this morning without coming to trial[.]

After Supper I went up to Jerry Mahoneys where I patronized an Ice Cream party for the benefit of a Library for the Catholic Sunday School. While there Culavin was setting under a Japanese lantern and got his good clothes all daubed with tallow and wax—[.]

little Jessy Danielson is very Sick with measles and so is Mr. Albert Chapin[.]

George Helm is still in bed with the dropsy.

Sept 6th. Nice day again. I have been rustling all day trying to get signers on Main Street to help pay the rent of the Post Office in order to keep it from going on Second St. but I find it hard work.

Geo Havens Uncle Frank died at Council Bluff[s,] Ia. a few days ago.

I hitched up the Colt this afternoon. I drove down to McIntyres with the Colt.

D. Y. Mears received a very welcome registered letter from Valentine this A.M.

The Water works are temporary shut down on account of the bursting of the Crown head.

Sep 7. Fair day again[.] I worked on Kass & Cos[.] Books.

Dave Powers & Billy Whittick bought a new spring wagon from Jake[.] there were two cases in Police Court this morning[.]

Mr McFadden the new banker called to see me about renting Wrights house on Morehead Street[.] I went up and showed it to him. Mr McFadden is moving in his Safe in the Bakery Building on Second St.

The Gy[m]nasium Boys are having a great time acting with their new outfits in their new enterprise of a local Gy[m]nasium Club. The City Council held a special meeting this afternoon and dismissed W P Hartzell and Wm Bristow as Night police and appointed one Ovalease in their stead.

Mayor Cox came back from Fremont yesterday.

I paid J F Wrights taxes today on his Egan St property.

Sep 8[.] Sunday and a nice day[.] I got up late. James Hartzell was drunk to day.

Major Powers received his appointment as Receiver of the Local Land Office of Chadron and consequently the Republicans are all feeling good and hanging around him.

Mrs M OHanlon was taken sick to day. Tony Bernard came down from his Ft Robinson Saloon on Soldier Creek.

Little Guy Alexander called on me this afternoon[.]

Billy Carter and Family visited Mr & Mrs Simmons'[.]

I have about made up my mind that if the business men on Main Street do not feel enough interested in paying the Rent of the Post Office in order to have it remain on Main Street, that there is little use in my bothering any more[.] I entertained some company this afternoon by showing them relics in my room.

Geo Havens and his pal, Pete Barber have gone to church and contemplate taking a bath before retiring[.]

Sep 9th[.] Nice day. Delos Barber started in to tend to my horse & Room at [$]5.00 per month[.]

I had Mr Eddy fix up my Stable again to day.

I done some Typewriting for Dorrington about a rehearing in a certain case, where Robt Reed had filed upon the townsite of Hay Springs[.]   C. D. Sayrs got back from the Table precinct[.]

at a Meeting of the fire department this afternoon it was decided to purchase a hook & ladder truck.

I have been very busy today[.] Stutz Theatre Co performed at the Rink this evening. when the show let out there was a high sand storm raging.

Bob Dorr slept in my room this evening[.]

Sep. 10th[.]   Clear day again.   not much business[.]

Sept. 12.   Fair day[.]   Wm Benham & Thos Madden had a suit to day before me and the case was compromised.   Yesterday C D Sayrs commenced an action against Willis & Grant Belangie for Joseph Pimper.

Brother Thomas Picture and Mothers which I had sent off to be enlarged came to day.   they cost me $25.00[.]

Sept. 13.   rained hard last night.   This A.M. I called on Mrs Elizabeth Jones to collect a note in favor of R. C. Banard, but I got no pay[.]   Tony loaned me [$]20.00 for twenty days.

W Stransky is negotiating to sell out his liquor business[.]   James Hickey and S. M. Christensen have been dickering on a sale of a lot on Morehead St belonging to Hickey but it fell through[.]   Hickey came to me to try and get him someone to buy his property.

I went and seen Ira Ellenwood who promised to help me buy it[.]

Sep 14th[.]   Cold as it has been for the past three days.

Ira Ellenwood faild to come to time as he promised last night[.]   C. Dana Sayrs went up to Whitney this morning to attend a lawsuit[.]   he came back again in the evening. his daughter Mame came in for him and reported their cow very sick from having got in the corn.

2 bears and 4 actors came to town today and amused the populace.

A W Crits completed moving his lawbooks in to the Bank of Chadron. Joe Ford held an auct[i]on on Zeri M Butters team[.]

Sept 15[.] Fair day. went to church—[.] recd a letter from Lenora—[.] answered it, as well also as one to J. J. V. I attended the Y. M. C. A. in afternoon & went to church in the evening[.]

Sept. 16. 2 cases in Police Court today. C. Dana Sayrs lost his cow last Saturday.

I borrowed OHanlons carriage and drove the colt and Geos pony.

after supper Mr Morrow and I got ready to go to the Agency but we concluded to wait till tomorrow.

today I got some provisions for the Peck family and sent them out by Mrs C. J. Davis[,] Mrs Baety and Mrs D Y Mears, who also took them some clothes. the City Council held a special meeting this afternoon to dwell upon the advisability of confessing judgment in favor of the National tube works of Chicago, but the council refused to do so and offered instead to submit a proposition before the people to vote bonds to pay off the outstanding indebtednes of the waterworks, which finaly was accepted by the Agent of the tube works who then also informed the Council that in the event of the proposition for bonds failing to carry, the Tube Company would at once commence proceedings against Chadron in the U. S[.] Court.

Sep. 19. Mr Morrow and I got back from the Pine Ridge last night having seen the Big Beef Issue. we had a nice time going and coming.

last evening Dan McKinzie & Geo Daley arrived from Tubeville[,] Wyo.[,] in care of a committe[e] who went thither to bring them here for medical treatment[,] they having been taken sick over a month ago with Mountain fever. I called on them at the Ohanlon House where J. Gaylord is taking care of them. I recd a letter from Wright this AM[.]

W. Stransky is Still dickering for a sale of his salon[.]

Sept. 20[.] Nice day. —till towards the afternoon when it commenced to blow hard. the case of Stotts vs Stotts was continued to Oct 4th[,] 1889[,] at 9. oclock. A.M. I took the rabbitt & 2 doves down to McKinzie and Daley. we got the paper out today. Just before dinner, I went up in the Land office with Roscalles Cameron to see why the Final Proof Notice of Dick Dwyer should not be published in the Democrat after having been requested so to do by the owner.

Major Powers presented himself in his usual ambiguous manner and interfering with outside business belonging to the Register, informed Mr Cameron that he might make any and as many requests as he might see fit about where his notice should be printed but that he (Powers) would print it and put it in whatever paper he saw fit so to do.

Ben Tibbits & Son and N. Janis are in Town.

Antowine Freeman, Hank Cliffords Son in Law, was in Police Court charged with being drunk—[.] I turned him loose with a good reprimand.

Sept. 23. Skipped a few days again. today it blew a little. Red Cloud and his Indians came over from the Agency. I wrote a letter to Gunther the Chicago Candy Man for Jack Carruthers. I called on Burr Shelton to see if the Dawes County Fair could extend any courtusey to the Indians, but received an evasive reply.

Mrs Theresa Smith opened up a restaurant next door to the Red front. Oppertunity Hank is on his usual spree. James Tuck was up in Police Court this a.m. for drunkeness. I sent him up in default. I made a fire for the first time in my sleeping room stove. I have been working a good deal in getting expressions about making a Call for the County Convention.

Sept 24[.] Harry Hindeman slept with me last night.

R. De Lambert arrived from the East.

I made out a call for the Democratic County Convention on Oct 9th and Primaries on the 7th[.]

The Indians are bothering me considerably for provisions etc which I am unable to give them. I issued warrants for the Roe family.

Miss Powell called to see me late last night about her well, which James Tuck had maliciously ruined while drunk by mistaking it for the back house.

after supper I found out that the Dawes Co fair association would probably admit all the Indians in the fair free.

I invited Red Cloud, Spotted Elk and Frank McMannus the inte[r]preter to take dinner with me tomorrow noon at Sweetsers.

about 8 P.M. I was called as overseer of poor to attend a man taken with the chills & fever[.]

Sept 25. Fair day. The Indians all moved out inside of the Fair Grounds.

Red Cloud, Spotted Elk and Frank McMannus took dinner with me[.]

In the afternoon I moved my Typewriter out to the Fair to help do some marking.

Sept 26. Nice day. I went out to the Fair, but when I got there found that Burr Shelton had made himself officious in order to insult me, and in the face of being told by Putnam that Mr Mann had specially requested me to come out and mark goods.

he (Shelton) insisted it was a lie and that man [Mann] had told him that he did not want me on the grounds and had no use for me and never asked me to come out to assist—[.]

I paid my way in, said no more[.] I shipped my Typewriter into Town and stayed to see the races[.]

After [entry incomplete.]

Sept 27. Nice day. I again attended the Fair and stayed out all day.

Sep 28. Nice day again. I attended the fair again. I buried Joseph Kaddolick[,] a pauper to day.

Sept 29.   Sunday.   I went to Young people meeting and Church.

Came home feeling bad at the stomach.

Sep 30[.]   Nice day[.]   plenty of Police Court business. I called to see Mrs Joseph Kaddolick today.

Oct. 1. It has been very nice day[.] I got A Fafek to go with me to Mrs Kaddolick and having found out her wants, I ordered her some groceries.

I called to see George Helm who has been laying sick with dropsy for the past three months.

Oct 2. Nice day. last night at 8 Oclock, Mr Helm and I started out for Mr Blinn on dry Creek to get him to come in and Dr his son George[,] we having heard that Mr Blinn was a sure cure for cases of Dropsey and as Dr Jackson seems to be at sea their can no harm come of any magnetic treatment. We arrived at Mr Blinns about 11 Oclock and succeeded in getting him to come along with us. We got back to Chadron at 1 A.M. today.

I boiled some water for him but Mr Helm beat me in getting his hot first.

I got to sleep about 2 oclock and Dorrington woke me up to do some work for him.

I got up and first off called to see how George was doing[.] he spoke up freshly and said he was feeling much better showing quite plain that Mr Blinn has done him good. Mr Helm started out to go some where to sell some fruit trees and left Mr Helm in charge of the Boy.

The Republican primaries were held yesterday and the little lambs were compelled to come up and eat the lumps chosen for them by Messs [Messrs.] Bell[,] Wetton & Co.[,] Egan, Carley[,] Bartow and Powers.

This afternoon I done quite a job of writing for E. S. Ricker[.]

Oct 3[.] Nice day. I called in Dr Clary to consult with A S Jackson over Geo Helms case and the consultation resulted in different tactics being adopted[.] In the evening I hired Seymour Miller to commence helping to nurse Geo on account of Mr Blinn having been compelled to leave this afternoon for his home and from thence for the East. the Republican delegates for the County Convention are about all in Town.

Oct 4[.] Nice day. The Rep Convention came off as billed and the pill made by the brick bank Gang has been thrust down their throats. to some it was bitter as gall and in fact more so, but they had to take it all the same. following is the ticket to be up for election by the Rep Party [names missing.]

after the convention I moved Geo Helm down into my room and gave him the free use of everything I had. I got everything he needed and hope I may never be so mean as to neglect the sick and disabled[.]

Oct 5. Fair day and warm. Dr Clary prescribed more medicine for Geo to be taken every 6 hours—in connection with his other medicine. Old Mr Helm does not seem to have much faith in Clarys treatment notwithstanding Geo is decreasing in size every day. I worked on Dorringtons papers for Mrs Fries Land, before the Secretary of the Interior[.]

I went out to Obriens and got him (Geo) some butter milk—[.] I also bought him a rocking chair at Wilsons.

He measured 38 1/2 inches around the stomach across the navel and hips today.

The Republican parties who did not get what they wanted are talking about springing an Independent ticket.

John G. Maher and Wm Wilson are now coming out to be candidates on the [words missing.]

Oct 6. Sunday. I remained home all day and looked after Geo who seems to be getting better.

Oct 7. Nice day. District Court commenced to day.

The Democratic Primaries were had in my office and the following delegates were elected[:]

CHADRON PRECINCT ELECTION.

For Delegates to the Democratic
County Convention.

A. W. Crites.
C. M. Conger.
W. Stransky.
W. L. Casady.
H. E. Drew.
John Macumber.
J. W. Rucker.
J. Kass.
Tom Madden.
Peter O'Hanlon.
Matt Baroch.
Milton Carlton.
E. S. Ricker.
J. G. Stetter.[1]

George Helm is feeling sick this evening on account of having drank too much butter milk. I got Dr Clary to come and see him. we gave him hot water injections after which he felt better.

C. Dana Sayrs is going to sleep with me tonight. It is blowing considerably[.]

Oct 8. Nice day. Court is in session. This A.M. Geo was better and has continued feeling better all day.

---

[1]Handbill, Democratic Party, Chadron, Nebraska, October, 1889, Dawes County Historical Society, Chadron, Nebraska.

Tom Lockett sent me in some butter milk but I sent it right down to Dan McKinzie and Daley—[.]

George Havens went up to Crawford this morning to tell his father to come down to attend court—[.]

There seems to be considerable skirmishing going on now in the ranks of malcontent Republicans who got left in their own convention, as to what kind of a ticket the Democrats are going to put up and after our convention they hope to spring an Independent Ticket[.] Billy Wilson, W. L Casady, and John Maher are aspirants for Co Clerk. the two former though thinking they are the only heavies in their party are nevertheless dead and virtually buried neath public Scandal and ridicule[.]

Oct. 9th. Nice day[.] the Democratic County Convention met at the Rink Opera House and nominated the following ticket for County Officers.

John G. Maher for Clerk, Jas Dahlman for Sheriff, W. C. McCauley for Co Judge, G W Hitchcock for Clerk of the Dist Court, W. H. Carter for Co Commissioner[,] J I Leas for Coroner. I had aspired for the nomination of Clerk of the District Court but through A. V. Harris I was defeated. I however think the Democratic Choise a good one and that the ticket will be elected in part is beyond a question.

Oct 10[.] Nice day. Jake Kass went up to Lusk.

Oct 11. Nice day again[.] I hitched up the Colts and went to McIntyres for butter milk for George, who is now getting along nicely. Old Man Blinn and son left for the East this evening.

I commenced to bandage Georges limbs. D. E. Havens lost his suit against P B Nelson.

My artificial limbs came from Phila[delphia] but being unable to pay for them they are still in the Express office.

Tom Lockett has again been beaten in the District Court upon failing to turn over certain cattle which he had taken to herd[.]

Oct. 12 12th[.] Cloudy and after dinner it rained. Old Mrs Smith called on me this morning for a load of wood[.] I ordered it for her. The Sheriff of Newcastle, Wyo[.] came in the office and swore out a warrant for Geo. L. Cutler for horse stealing. Geo Helm refused to take his kidney medicine this A.M. I drove out to OBriens and got him some Butter Milk[.] Geo Havens was not feeling well today[.] he took Houghtons carriage home for me.

I called to see Old Mrs Smith on my return from OBriens[.]

Oct 13[.] Cloudy day. I staying in the house all day and read and assorted books.

Geo Helm is getting very sassy and dont want to take his medicine anymore.

Dr Clary bound up Geos right leg. after supper Miller again reported that George did not want to take his medicine.

Oct 14[.] Cloudy & Cold. District Court is still in session.

George had another mad spell this A.M. I brought him his dinner, but he would not eat it. So I read the riot act to him—[.] he got in better humor for supper and ate some Oysters and stewed chicken for supper. I hurt my leg this A.M.

I recd a telegram from Bro Geo for $250.00 but was unable to comply with his demand[.]

Oscar Fischer has quit work for Stransky over a week ago[.]

I wrote to J. F. Wright, Sister Leonora[,] Mr James Smith at Council Bluffs[,] Ia[.,] relative to his wife who is a pauper of Dawes County.

Also to Niece Cassie Van Dersloot[,] Cousin Mamie Levan and Uncle Jackson Levan.

Chas Wilson came in from off the road this evening. Henry Tons split up some wood for me.

Oct 15[.] Nice day. I recd a letter from Snyder enclosing his check for $500.00[.] I got the money and immediately set out to get my new legs at the Depot.

I and Jack Cruthers hitched up the two colts to go down to the Stock Yards, but Minnie kicked over the tongue and then there was hell to pay. She finally broke the tongue but before we could get her unhitched she made a terrible mess of everything. I gave up the trip and came to Town.

I paid the Chambers Encyclopedia man $10.00 on acct and also had Mattie (the colored cook at Danielsons) to get herself a new dress at Miss Smiths on acct of doing the extra cooking for Geo Helm.

Tony Bernard got a new cash register drawer for Stranskys bar today, but is yet unable to make it work. I slept bad last night.

I recd a telegram from Geo for $250. I answered that Snyder would not let me have it.

Oct 16. Fair weather[.] I got a good deal of wood today[.]

I was in the court house and copied the docket for the Demo[.] after supper I called to see Dan McKinzie and Geo Daley. I slept in my bedroom on a cot last night but caught cold. Charlie Wilson was in the office a good deal today. Joe Branner and T. J. Doud left night before last for Lincoln with prisoners[.]

I went down to mail a letter to Leonora on the Eastern train and there heard A. L. Wright declare himself as to what kind of work he is going to do against John Maher.

I recd 2 more telegrams from George for [$]250 and one stated that Snyder wanted my order for same. I concluded to answer no more[.]

Oct 17. Fair day. The Democrat came out on time today.

W D Edgar came to me and tried to get me to come out and run against Cooley for County Commissioner, but I advised him of his weakness of brain and He thereupon departed in peace to tell Egan that the scheme would not work. Old Mr Helm was in to see his boy and seemed please[d] with the way he was getting along.—

Dr Clary informed me that he would charge the boy $2.00 a day[.] he change[d] the routine of medicine.

I paid of[f] the Gottstein Chattel today and am once more a free man so far as Chattel Mortgages go.

Yesterday I paid up all my back office rents and am free there, too.

The political situation as to rumor seems to be greatly enlarging in favor of Dahlman and John Maher and from present indications all goes to point towards a certain election of John Maher—for the reason that Handy has concluded not to run independent and thereby John is the gainer of Handy strength which means a solid railroad vote[.]

Oct 18th[.] Fair day. District Court adjourned this evening and the Democrat Publishing Co got a final order to get all Blanks which the county had not used. I steared Hill and Conger over the battle field and with the aid of a Gang we succeeded in getting a considerable lot of blanks calculated to enrich the coffers of the Dawes County Journal—[.]

I had a great time at Stranskys[.]

Oct 19th[.] Nice day again and a great many people were in Town.

Geo Helm walked about the room for the first time this morning[.] Dr Clary is going to get him on his feet sure, I believe.

I wrote a long letter to his sister Mrs Mary Hayes at Cumberland[,] Ohio, Gurnesey Co.[,] for him. After supper the Post Office was formerly moved into the Washington Block on 2nd Street and I presume the Land Office will shortly follow and then the Dawes County Journal will go in the basement so as to have the Republicans all nicely together in one lump.

The Chadron Cornet Band is now playing in honor of the grand event.

Oct 20. Sunday and a nice day. I did not dress up but stayed in the office all day, and wrote a letter to Gunther the Chicago Confectionist and Black over at Pine Ridge Agency.

E E Record has sold out his harness shop to D. Y. Mears[.] The Birdsall Boys and their Gang went out rabbit hunting today.

I received another telegram from Brother Geo asking me for money, but I answered no.

I cannot consent to be thus bulldozed out of my money by telegraphs[.] I feel that if there is anything wrong He can write to me and tell me and then there may possible be a chance to reflect. I have not forgotten the time when he was well heeled and I was without a home and asked him for aid and he asked and told me to go to those who had inherited all.

Oct 21. a little cloudy all day. I had two new suits commenced before me to day by Spargur & Fisher. R. E. W. Spargur has moved his mamoth Clothing house out of the Opera block and gone into the New Washington block next door to the post office.

George Helm is getting along nicely and is now able to sit up in a chair several hours, but his eletarium pills are not acting as usual since having the order refilled[.]

After supper I got Boardman to paint signs for John Maher for County Clerk. We worked till 12 oclock. Boardman slept with me[.]

Oct 22. fair day. Geo Helm has been very sick with vomiting caused from the eletarium pills.

Mrs Leach got her bill to put into the county for taking care of Mrs Martin.

Miller scrubbed out the sleeping room.

After supper I went to the theatre[.] today I received the final release papers from Leonard to be signed[.] I drew on Snyder for $515.91 by sight draft[.]

I seen Crites about calling a precinct caucus. I done so by ordering out posters for tomorrow evening at 7[:]30[.]

Oct 23[.] fair day till towards night when it got somewhat cloudy[.] The Black Hills Nursery has been delivering trees all day. Old Mr Helm has not been near me to see about his son George.

The Precinct Primary came off as was programmed with the following nominations—Assessor, Henry Stephens[;] Justices[,] Chas Morrisey & Myself[;] Constables [names missing;] Road Supervisor[,] J W Smith[;] Judges of Election, Jason Rucker[,] John W Smith[,] F. M. Van Horn[;] Clerks of Election[,] Willis Campbell[,] G F H Babcock.

After the convention treating the crowd by the nomanies was in order and kept up to a late [words missing.]

Oct 24. Nice day[.] the Democrat came out on time as usual.

Geo Helm has been on a pouting spree all day but I gave him a good scolding and he came to his ps & Qus.

Oct 25[.] Nice day but a little cold—[.] Billy Wittige came in to see me about renting Wrights house and informed me that he had come to a stand still with Dave Powers. I got 29 1/2 yds of muslin at 8 1/2¢ from Mrs Smith for John Maher to get signs painted for him. The band plaid in the street after supper—[.]

I went up to the Gy[m]nasium Club[.]

Oct 26. Fair day and plenty of work in Justice Court.

The pay case on the F. E. & M. V. Rail Road came in[.]

There has been hail Columbia poping among Rail Road Conductors, 6 or 7 being bounced for "knocking down[.]"

Dr A. N. Jackson called with Dr Clary to see Geo Helm, but for no consultation, nor upon no suggestion of mine.

I discharged William Bristow to day.

After supper I went up to the Rink but was called away to issue a warrant for Ada Larkins for shooting John Larkins[.]

[Oct] 27[.] Fair day. I put on my new limbs again to day but stayed in the office all day. C W Allen returned from the East this A.M.

Oct 28[.] Fair day. 1 case in Police Court for Drunk and Disorderly discharge and 1 case for discharging fire arms [$]10.00 & Cost[.]

all business on the slack. I took supper at the Catholic fair[.] It started to rain about 10 P.M.

Oct 29. rainy & cold all day. I have got a $18.90 rate for Geo Helm to his sister in Ohio. Chas Helm has promised me that he would try and have money $35.00 for the trip by Wednesday eve or Thursday morning sure.

I attended the Catholic fair after supper and took part in an Entertainment, entitled Checkmated[,] I playing the role of Mr Heath.

Oct 30. Clear day. About 9 A.M. Mrs Bates and Miss Pospisal came in and begged some provisions on the Countys acct for Mrs Joseph Kaddolic. I gave them an order for provisions.— Ed Graves sold out to Joe Baddy[.]

Oct 31. Blind Boone played at the Nelson Opera House. I was too busy to go to the Catholic fair.

After supper I got Boardman to paint Campaign Banners[.] I started out to collect money for Geo Helm to go East with and wound up with $22.00[.]

Nov 1. George Helms ticket arrived this A.M. I got Mahana to give Seymour Miller a pass as far as Mo[.] Valley.

I got George Helm a Suit at Loewenthals and after supper I put him on board the train for the East.

before going to the depot, Geo walked over to Dr Jacksons office and bid him good by[.] I collected more money for Geo. but had to borrow $15[.]00 from Eckles to make all good. I got a bran new mattrass from Harry Way.

Nov 2. Fair day. I done a good deal of electioneering as there was a great many people in Town.

Billy Carters chances for getting elected as County Commissioner now are good. John Maher has a good swing for getting elected.

I signed the papers of release to Jeff Snyder to day and had them sent on.

Nov 3. Clear and cold and some indications for snow.

I was to have gone out to the Bohemian Settlement with Henry Stephens, but I got up too late.

Geo Havens hitched up the Colt with his pony and went out driving—[.]

Chas Wilson and I stayed in the office.—

Chas Allen slept with me last night—[.]

Nov 4. Cold day and tried to snow nearly all the time.

Politics Politics all day long and the clouds begin to darken and look bad for all candidates on both tickets excepting John Maher who is undoubtedly elected right now. I seen John W. Smith and found out from him personally that the game with him was only to see me downed. I am going to have a hard time getting elected and will do all I possibly can, but if I am not I must do the next best possible thing.

Spotted Elk cam over from the Pine Ridge Agency and reported that Red Cloud had met with an accident whereby he had several ribs broken on his right side.

Morrow and John Willis returned from a shooting tour in the Sand Hills.

Tom Madden was in the office and assured me of his hearty support in my behalf.

Hale and Thomson commenced suit against Bendixon, the Shoemaker to day.

Nov 5. Fine day and people were out in full force for Election[.] the fight for John Maher, Jas Dahlman and Billy Carter was fierce and nothing was done but for them.

553 cast their Ballots. I am going to stay up all night to see that I get a fair Count.

The town this evening is all in an uproar over the anticipated result. the popular feeling is all for Maher and Dahlman and Carter[.]

Nov 6. Fine day. I went to bed at 2 P.M. to day a defeated candidate for Justice of the Peace but while I was beaten I am glad to be able to record the fact that Maher, Dahlman and Carter got elected, as far as can be learned at present by a handsome majority[.] Cooley is knocked and Handy is Vindicated and the Republican Ring is no more.

However my enemies are also much pleased over my own defeat and feel that though they have lost the greater part of their game, that they have neverless winged me for a time anyway, but it may be for the best as God knows I have been doing my share of looking after poor people and paying bills out of my own pocket for them.

I got up at 6 P.M. and found things still booming for Carter.

Nov 7. Nice day. The special Election for Funding the indebtedness of Chadron was held to day and carried in favor of the proposition[.] after supper I was called to go to the Chapin House to acknowledge an instrument from Mr & Mrs Brundage to Bartlett Richards.

Nov 8[.] Nice day. I recd a letter from Elmer Hum in Pittsburgh[,] Kas. and one from Aunt Lousai Levan. The Democrat came out all ok today.

Nov 9. Nice day. In the evening I went up to skating rink and took tickets for Ed. Godsall.

Nov 10. Sunday and cold, it snowed last night. This morning Thomas E. Turner was found dead in his bed—[.] George Havens came down and told me about it before I got up.

Nov 12. Thomas E. Turner was buried this afternoon. I went up to the house to take a parting look at him. he looked very natural and unlike a dead man. The Belanger Case was partly settled[.]

Nov 13. Cold and Clear[.]

I received notice from the Bank of Chadron that my $515.95 draft had been honored whereupon I proceeded to draw and pay up bills.

Nov 14. It snowed last night in good shape. W. H. Hayward took me out sleighing. I ordered some wood for Mrs Smith. The Democrat came out late this evening.

George Havens is now tending my Colt and doing the Chores around my office.

Nov 15[.] Clear and cold. D. Y. Mears has decided to qualify for the office of J. P. on January 1st—[.] John Larkins had me fix up a collection against H. D. Kirmse a few days ago and yesterday he placed a protested check of J W Battershall in my hands for process. The Gillespie family were in my office today and got out process. I got McLeod to let Wm Harris[,] a pauper have a pair of boots on the County.

I bought a 6 months note from Hugh Davidson for [$]25[.]00 due March 15[,] 1889 [1890?].

Nov 16. Fair Day. I ordered som green wood from young Welch. Old Welch and Black had quite a quarrel today up by the Post Office.

Joe Ford held auction to day on the James Striker attached stock[.] After Supper I attended the Rink and took tickets, after which Geo and I got Oysters at Owens.

Nov 17. Sunday and Fair all day. I remained in the house all day with a sore on my right leg. I got a letter from Snyder enclosing $10[.]21 as a final balance and also one from Mrs Mary Hayes at Cumberland Ohio.

John Larkins called to see me and kept me company for several hours[.]

Oct [Nov] 18[.] The case of Gillespe vs Stotts et al came on for hearing and was continued to Dec 30th for publication[.]

Fisher (city atty[)] fetched the City funding bonds history $15,000 in for me to transcribe by typewriter[.]

I loaned John Maher [$]200[.]00 and took his note for $220.00.

I also bought 10 shares of Chadron loan and building stock with 7 mos paid up dues. I gave Joe Ford $75.00 for them.

I bought a load of green wood from young welch for [$]3[.]00. Jake Kass has gone up to Rapid to look for a Plumber[.] C J Davis came back from his hunt through the west. The political situation for Messers Carley and Egan is very much on the wane and there is great weeping and wailing and gnashing of teeth for it is quit probable and almost an assured fact that they will no more lead by the nose as many republicans as they have been accustomed to and Mr Carley is not just as safe in his Post Office position as he would like to be.

Dave Mears has been threatened by the Egan faction with their everlasting ire should he fail to qualify on Jan 1st for the office of J. P. in my stead, and consequently no blame can attach to him as he very rightly expects some future favors from those whom have always upheld him even though he in his inner heart revolts against some of their actions[.] Joe Ford goes to Custer tomorrow[.]

Nov 19. J. Kass got back from Rapid last evening.

to day has been very pleasant and the snow has about all melted.

I got some venison from Brown. after breakfast I commenced work on the City bond history[.]

Nov 20[.] Fair till late in the afternoon when it rained[.] I went to the Chalk talk Show last night.

I worked some more on City bonds history. W Stransky interceeded for C H Cook today, so I again ordered him into Henry Stephens care.

Another case came up in Police Court this A.M.

There was quite a disturbance among the Saloons last night caused by the Negros getting "Gay"—[.] I drew out a plan of Insurance book for Jake Kass for the Chadron Loan & Building Assctn.

Nov 21. Fair day. George Dorrington and Miss May Hawley were married this evening at the residence of the brides parents. the boys tin canned the couple and were responded to by the Groom who ordered all hands to go to Fred Ebners and get what they wanted. My right stump has been hurting me considerable of late and I am feeling very bad tonight.

during the day I worked some more on the City bonds history[.] George and Johnny OHanlon were in the office till a late hour.

Nov 22[.] Fair day. I started to remain in bed but had to be carried in the office to examine John Oneil charged with stealing 2750 cigars from William Fleming of Rushville[.] Upon hearing the evidence I bound the man over. My right stump pains me very much and I am unable to put on my artificials so I remained in bed all day[.]

Nov 23[.] Still in bed[.] Conductor Seallors died to day at 4 PM from Colic and inflamation of the bowls.

I remained in bed all day. Ben Snell got out an attachment against Richard Donaway for $15.00[.]

Nov 24[.] Conductor Seallors was buried to day. the Drs held a post mortem over him[.]

George Havens slept with me last night.

After supper I read till 12 oclock and then had to go for water down to Stranskys.

Nov 25th[.] Clear and Cold. I got up to day and walked around. there was a case to day before the Co Judge of State vs Willis and Grant Belanger for stealing cattle. Sayrs and Harbaugh for the Defense and Crites for the prosecution.

The Defendants were acquitted. T. J. Doud was to day Closed up by outside nonresident creditors and Wm H Carter[.] the Keys of the establishments were handed to Wm H Carter, who appears to have 4 or 5 Thousand invested in the business by virtue of mortgage.

Nov 26th. Fair day. heap sick all day, too much tuti Fruiti last night[.] Geo waited on me.

Nov 27. Fair & Cold. I got a nice letter from Leonora.

I got up out of bed and knocked around a little[.]

Nov 28th. Thanksgiving and a magnificent day. John Maher and I were invited to W H Carters for Dinner. Geo Drove us out with Mrs OLinns buckboard and our ponies. he called for us at 3 P.M. Every body seemed to have had a splendid time in Town.

In the evening the Comus Club select dance came off at the Rink[.] I stayed home and wrote a letter to Leonora and read.— I took supper at the Baptiste Church Fair in the Nelson building[.]

Nov 29. Nice day again. Bob Stuart was in Police Court this A.M. for drunkeness. I suspended Judgment a few days.

Ed Godsall invited me to accompany him to the Country to serve some papers on Old man rice & Crowd. I went and had a very pleasant time[.]

Stetter Bros moved into the Old Wilson Furniture Store on Second Street with their Butcher shop.

John Maher and I and Mat Baroch have decided to ask George Harner to accept the nomination for Mayor at our Next City Election.

Nov 30[.] Saturday and Splendid weather[.] Red Jacket and Taxidermist Tuttle had a racket.—

Geo fixed up around the stable and piled fire wood in the shed.

I issued an Execution against J. S. Martin[.]

Ed Murnan was in Police Court but I let him off[.]

Joe got out warrants for the vagrants.

Clem Davis returned from the North Loup Country whither he had been on the Belanger Cattle business.

Mrs Woodard had a smash up at her stable today while hitching up her ponies. Geo Havens and Tom Wilson came to her rescue.

Little Murphy (Frank) fell of a stable roof today while playing "follow the leader" and broke his wrist[.]

Atty Fisher came down from Harrison today.

Dec 1[.] Dreary all day. Chas Allen came over from the Agency and put up with me—with his sorrel horses.

John Larkins called me aside after supper and informed me of a trade he was going to make with W. Stransky tomorrow[.] I went to Church this evening and heard Rev Powell preach a nice sermon.

Dec 2. Nice day. Mrs McGinley was before the police Court today charged with prostitution[.] She was granted a continuance till tomorrow at 2 P.M.

John Larkin and Fields, Carter and Stransky were in the office this A.M. making a $1,700.00 trade whereby Larkins is to have entire control of the Carter Saloon Corner.—

Dec 3. Nice weather. Col. Gallagher came over from the agency. Mrs McGinley was tried to day and acquitted. C. Dana Sayrs appeared for the Deft. a small fire broke out in the rear of Dr Leas drugstore[.] it was put out before any damage was done.

The Hartzell Boys and Tom Coffey had a quitting spell last night and dissolved partnership in business. Mr Murphy came into Police Court and desired to verbaly stand good for Ed Murnuns fine & costs but refused to sign the Docket to that effect and consequently left the mittimus in the hands of the Marshal.

Chas Allen and A. E. Seldon had quite a long conflab in my private office[.]

Sidney Johnson came to the office to get a pipe stem which I took from Frank Brady.

Dec 4. Fair day. Not much business[.] Col Galagher came over from Pine Ridge.

Larkins is making some alterations in his saloon[.]

Geo Havens is trying to sell his pony to E. E. Record.

Mrs Danleys baby died a few days ago[.]

I wrote several letters. J. A. Jennings came in today and had his note extended to Jan 25th[,] 1890[.]

Dec 5[.] Nice fair day[—]rather raw. I filed the Jennings Chattel today. Red Jacket is causing a great deal of trouble[.]

I found out today that D. Y. Mears has filed his bond for Justice and he thereby appears impatient for the time to arrive when he can help to take my living out of my mouth.

Mrs Joe Beattys horse run away today while being feed out at John Macombers. the buggy was hitched to the horse and it was demolished considerably though fortunately no one was in the buggy.

The Democrat did not come out to day.

I wrote to Mrs Mary Hayes at Cumberland[,] Ohio about Geo Helm.

Chas Allen has been buying a great many articles of houshold furnature today.

Geo Havens has sold his horse to Mr Record (E.E.)[.]

Dec 6. Chas Allen left for the Pine Ridge Agency. Fine weather again.

I took sayres buggy and drove the Colt out[.]

Dec 8. I forgot to post yesterday but nothing of importance occured.

We are having fine weather[,] just like summer all the time.

Dec 9.   Fine weather still and very little business[.]   I almost forgot to mention about having attended a Maquerade skate at the Rink last Saturday night on the 7th.

Willis Bros took judgment by default today against A J Richardson.   News came from Fremont today of the loss of Mayor Cox's children all in one night and that they were buried yesterday.

Dec 10[.] Nice day again. Marshal Branner held up Ed Brown and made him settle part of his business there where he paid $4.00 which was all he claimed he had, but promised to pay the rest tomorrow.   I took Sayrs buggy again and exercised the Colt.

I made out a transcript for J Kass & Co and filed it with the Clerk of the Court.

Theo Figgie presented an order for [$]3.60 as witness fees in the Pimper & Belanger case and I honored the same.

I wrote to Uncle William Iaeger, William A Clark[,] F. G. Thearle and Charles Allen.

Dec 11. Nice day again but dull business.

After Supper I attended the Larkin Saloon opening and had a very nice time.

Dec 12[.] Regular summer weather again[.] W H Tobias has sold out his store.   I paid Mr Jones his wi[t]ness fees in the Belanger Case.

This afternoon I was called to try a case over in Justice Wilsons Court between W Christensen and R. B. Balliew[.]

Dec 13[.]   Fair day again[.]   the case of Christensen vs Balliew was closed today in favor of Plff. Judge Spargur returned from N. Y. I and Geo attended a church social at Mrs Bross' house.

Dec 14[.] George sold his pony to E E Record. business dull. I had a wedding this evening at D. J. Fieliys laundry.

Dec 15[.] Sunday and nice day. I stayed in the house nearly all day.

George slept with me last night. In evening I went to church[.]

Dec 16. Nice weather. Not very busy. Bob Stuart in Police Court. I gave him $1[.]00 and cost. sent him up in Default. This evening before going to bed I overhauled the trunks in my room.

Dec 17. Nice day. Delos Barber commenced taking care of my room again and George Havens has gone to work for Smith and Robinson[.]

Peter J. Breen and Dick Dyer have bought out Tom Coffey and purchased the Gold Bar fixtures from Gottstein & Co and will hereafter run a saloon and Gambling den on the Cor[ner] of Egan & 2nd streets. rumor has it that Tom Coffey intends opening up a saloon again in his old stand on Main Street.

Smith & Robinson have now completed having their Restaurant enlarged. H H Morton has gone in the sporting business and taken charge of the gambling rooms over J Owens' saloon.

After supper I proceeded to mark all my collars & cuffs. I got Benny Myers to press them with a hot iron for me.

Dec 18. Fair day—business rather dull[.]

Dec 24. Since posting up last I have been trying to do so much that I have had little time to write.

I have been busy selecting presents for Guy Alexander, Cord and Harry Carter, Norma Simmons, Mary and Etta Sayrs, Earnest and Maud Davis[,] Don Gillette, George & Walter Havens[,] Guy Sawyer and Pearl Glover[.] again all day today Delos Barber and I have been cleaning up and arranging the Hat Room at the Rink for the Conductors ball tomorrow night. After supper I went up to Church to witness the Childrens gladness over Santa Claus[.]

Dec 25[.] Christmas Day and splendid weather reigned all day.

I got W R Corwin to drive me out to Mrs Sayrs to spend Christmas with them. I took Mr & Mrs Sayrs a nice "Carving Set" for Christmas. I had a splendid time. Maud and Earnest Davis were there all day. Mr. Sayrs brought me home. Their dog followed us and we whipped it but it failed to go home.

At 6[:]30 I went to the rink and found Delos has every thing arrainged nicely. Mr Bross called to pay me and bid good by to all.

During the evening the Sociability was somewhat marred by the drunken conduct of W. D. Edgar who persisted in pushing himself where he would only appear rediculous. Dick Dyer and Mrs H. N. Merritt were married today by County Judge Ballard.

Dec 26[.] The Ball broke up about 3 oclock this morning.

I had a case in Justice Court at 10 A.M. which was continued[.]

The Democrat could not come out today. Mr Sayrs commenced stabling his horse in my barn[.]

Dec 27. Still splendid summer weather[.] Mrs Annie Smith, the Pauper, moved out of Tom Dixons house. I gave an old man permission to move into it[.] I was hitching up the Colt this evening when it took fright and ran away with Sayrs buggy. Martin the drayman caught the runnaway on Main Street. No damage was done to the buggy and but slight injury to the harness.

I again hitched her up and Wm Bristow and I drove her[.] Mr Sayrs went to Crawford to help prosecute a case of giving away liquor[.]

Will Gallup and his Brother had quite a row at their House last night over some family matters of a base and rude character.

The Belanger Brothers have finally skipped out of the Country after having mortgaged all of their Sisters Cattle. She is in Chadron now and trying to regain possession of the stock.

I telegraphed Sayrs at Crawford for her and he came down this evening. After supper I checked off for Ben Lowenthal a little[.]

Dec 28[.] Snow and cold. Mr Sayrs started for home about 3 P.M.

Rev Powell came in to see and talk to me.

George Havens started for Newcastle this morning in search of his Father to satisfy his mother who fears he is sick[.]

I received a registered letter from Leonora containing a [$]5[.]00 bill for Christmas.

I remained in the office nearly all day and worked on Ben Loewenthals Petit Ledger—[.] I went to supper with Ben Loewenthal at Smith & Robinson[.] Charles Wilson will stay with me tonight on account of the stormy weather which prevents him going to his home on the Bordeaux[.]

Dec 29[.] Sunday and a nice day[.]

I went to church[.]

1890 Chadron High School senior class (left to right, front): Maud Wier, H. F. Maika, Annie Jeffers, De Loss Barber; (back) Mary Sayres, Annie J. Wright, George J. Havens, Lydia Maika, Ord Jennings

Chapter VIII:
1890 (Diary)

Jan 1st 1890[.] Happy New Year! to all! Chas Conger, Mr. G H. T. Babcock and my self made New Year calls all day.

last night I went up to the Academy where an old year Watch party was held. I had a good time.

Jan 2[.] I worked on Bens books and got them all straightened out.

Jan 3[.] Ben Loewenthal is very sick[.]

Jan 4[.] Snow and splendid sleighing[.]

Jan 9th[.] I turned my J. P. Office over to D. Y. Mears today, and at the same time was employed by Robinson & Smith to go and straighten out their Books which I agreed to do for $10.00[.]

Jan 10[.] N W Smith sold out to Robinson and Robinson has concluded take a months lay off and run his own business[.]

Jan 14[.] George Havens quit working for Robinson in order that he might go to school.

Jan 16. I am slowly finding out that Willie Robinson is holding out on the old man but Robinson is too sick to tell him about it[.]

Jan 17. Masquerade Ball at the Rink[.] Tom Coffey wanted to fight me because he thought I was giving him away at the Ball[.]

Jan 21. Stormy and snowing. George Havens is now staying with me and taking care of the Colt, he having commenced on the 16th inst. Ed Robinson [words missing.]

[Finis]

Chapter IX:
The Final Years
by Dr. Allen Shepherd

The diaries of "Billy the Bear" Iaeger came to a close in 1890, but he continued to live and work in Chadron until his death in 1930.

Iaeger added a new personal dimension in his life when he began courting Temperance Gillespie (1872-1962), daughter of Dr. and Mrs. A. J. Gillespie of nearby Whitney, at the beginning of the 1890s. Neither a difference in age—"Billy the Bear" was thirty-two and Temperance was eighteen—nor Billy's physical handicap seemed to have impeded the match. Temperance was a most beautiful young lady and considered a fine catch. Iaeger was not only enamored with her, but he also was proud that he had won her hand away from an English suitor. Both men had arrived at the Gillespie home—the Englishman in a spanking new livery, and Billy in a mud-spattered rig. The young lady climbed in with "Billy the Bear," who warned his rival: "If I ever catch you around here again, I'll whale the life out of you."[1] The Englishman never came back.

The couple were married on April 12, 1892, by David Y. Mears, justice of the peace and Chadron's first

---

[1] *The Omaha Daily News Magazine*, November 16, 1919.

Temperance Gillespie around the time of her marriage

MARRIAGE · LICENSE.

OFFICE OF THE COUNTY JUDGE.

THE STATE OF NEBRASKA, } ss.
_____ County.

LICENSE is hereby granted to any person authorized to solemnize marriages according to the laws of said State, to join in marriage Mr. _Louis J. Iaeger_ and _Miss Temperance Gillespie_ of the County aforesaid, whose ages, residence, etc., are as follows:

NAMES OF PARTIES	AGE	COLOR	PLACE OF BIRTH	RESIDENCE	FATHER'S NAME	MOTHER'S MAIDEN NAME
Louis J. Iaeger						
Temperance Gillespie						

And the person joining them in marriage is required to make due return of the annexed Certificate to the County Judge of said County within ninety days, of the manner of the parties, time and place of Marriage, and by whom solemnized.

IN TESTIMONY WHEREOF I have hereunto set my hand and affixed the seal of said Court, at my office in _____ in said County, this _____

_____ day of _____

_____, Judge.

CERTIFICATE OF MARRIAGE.

To the County Judge of _____ County, Nebraska:

THIS CERTIFIES That on the _12th_ day of _April_ A.D. 189_2_ at _Chadron_ in said County, according to law and by authority, I duly JOINED IN MARRIAGE Mr. _Louis J. Iaeger_ and Miss _Temperance Gillespie_, and there were present as witnesses _Louis Hartzell_ & _Eben Hartzell_

Given under my hand the _12th_ day of _April_ A.D. 1892.

L. Mews
Justice of the Peace

Marriage license of Temperance Gillespie and "Billy the Bear" Iaeger mayor. The bride's sister Flora and her husband Lewis Hartzell were their attendants, and the ceremony took place at their home. Among the many presents they received were:

> Silver tea spoons, [given by] Mr. Edwin Myres, York, Pa.; silver berry spoon, Mrs. D. W. Kolbe, Philadelphia, Pa.; silver butter knife, T. A. Coffey, Chadron; silver butter dish, Lowenthal Bros.; silver spoon vase, D. C. Middleton; silver desert spoon, T. J. Dowd, Jr.; silver napkin rings, Mrs. D. Y. Mears and Mrs. W. H. Reynolds; silver napkin rings, Mr. and Mrs. F. M. Vanhorn; silver tooth pick case, G. P. Washburn; Table Linen, Dr. C. Bressler and daughter, York, Pa.; Silk umbrella, Lowenthal Bros; Table linen Geo. Havens, Hot Springs, S.D.; Japanese lacquered box, J. D. Bacon and P. T. Barber.[2]

The union was a happy one. Two sons were born to this marriage, Louis John Frederick Iaeger, Jr., on January 1, 1893, and Richard Gillespie Iaeger on June

---

A card in L. J F. Iaeger's confectionery store window Sunday announced the fact that he was "at home with the baby, 9 lbs." Investigation later proved the fact that it was a boy and a democrat and as Billy stood a package of Duke's Mixture on the event, we'll smoke several times on the new boy. Mother and child are doing well.

Birth announcement of Richard Gillespie Iaeger, **Chadron Journal,** *June 21, 1901*

---

[2]*Chadron Journal,* April 15, 1892.

*Photo of Temperance Gillespie given to "Billy the
Bear" before their marriage. Inscription on back reads:
"Look at this three times a day regularly
and that should be sufficient[,] Temperance"*

Richard (left) and Louis Iaeger, Jr., 1901 or 1902

319 Egan Street

16, 1901. "Billy the Bear" and his bride made their home and raised their sons at 319 Egan Street (at the behest of "Fannie" O'Linn, the name was changed to Chadron Avenue in 1922).

When Louis, Jr., returned home from World War I in 1917, this modest home with picket fence was remodeled to accommodate him and his new bride, Hildur Anderson Iaeger, who made their home with Louis's parents.

Professionally, Iaeger began to explore various lines of business to support Temperance and his sons. He was at various times bookkeeper, bookkeeping teacher, stenographer, assistant to the city clerk, city clerk, justice of the peace, clerk of the Dawes County Court, and deputy clerk and clerk of the District Court. Some of these positions became a family monopoly, in fact. Temperance served as her husband's assistant, and after his death in 1930 she was appointed clerk of the District Court. Their son Louis, Jr., was Temperance's assistant. "Billy the Bear" also was

*Dawes County Courthouse staff (ca. 1910): "Billy the Bear"
Iaeger (far left), Harry Coffee (second from left), County Judge Ernest
Slattery (right of fountain) and Vet Canfield (second from right)*

involved in businesses such as a confectionary and pool hall.[3]

In these various lines of work after 1890, Iaeger met and associated with an interesting bevy of people over the years. One of the most colorful was James C. Dahlman, a fellow cowboy and Democrat who served on Chadron's city council, as mayor, as sheriff, and as representative to the Democratic National Convention in 1892. In 1906 Dahlman moved to Omaha to carve out a niche as that city's long-time mayor. Another colorful personality was John Maher, a hoaxer par-excellence who thrived on titilating P. T. Barnum's suckers. This "Paralyzer of the Truth" sponsored such schemes as the "discovery" and public display (for a fee) of the "Petrified Man of the Black Hills." Another of his schemes was the celebrated Chadron to Chicago horse race, begun here on June 13, 1893, in front of the Blaine Hotel. Iaeger was chairman of the committee which planned the race. Despite opposition by Chadronite Mary Smith Hayward and the Humane Society, contestants such as "Doc" Middleton, John Berry and Joe Gillespie spurred themselves and their mounts eastward toward Chicago. The winner was the first to get to "Buffalo Bill's" tent, pitched at the Chicago World's Fair. The declared winner of the $200 first-place prize was Joe Gillespie.[4] Judge Eli S. Ricker, another fellow Democrat (who bolted to the Populists in 1890) and a Iaeger confidant,

---

[3]See the *Rushville Standard*, March 19, 1906; George Watson, Jr., *Prairie Justice: A 100 Year Legal Study of Chadron and Dawes County* (Chadron, Nebraska: B & B Printing, 1985), also surveys Chadron's legal profession.

[4]Byron "Rip" Radcliffe, *The Chadron to Chicago Cowboy Horserace of 1893* (Chadron, Nebraska: B & B Printing, 1984) is an excellent source on this episode. Joe Gillespie's pearl-handled Colt revolver, holster, and quirt are at the Dawes County Historical Society.

became famous less for his politics and subsequent journalistic activities than for his writings about and collection of Plains Indian artifacts. Nor were Iaeger's acquaintances limited to only the white community. Iaeger first met the famous Lakota chief Red Cloud while pursuing rustlers in his early cattle days before he moved to Chadron. They kept in contact as Red Cloud periodically visited Chadron from the Pine Ridge Reservation until his death in 1909.[5]

As is evident from "Billy the Bear's" diaries in the preceding chapters, Iaeger participated enthusiastically in the social life of Chadron and the surrounding area. In name, Chadron had an entire "Opera Block" with the Nelson Opera House as its centerpiece. It is likely that

"Billy the Bear" and friends:
(left to right, seated) "Billy the Bear," Freddy Davis,
Red Cloud and Fred Wilke; (standing) Walks Fast,
Afraid, Dr. Davis and George Fire Thunder

---

[5]*Chadron Times*, July 28, 1905; *Mediator*, June 22, 1907.

Chadron, Nebraska, 1908

he flocked with other Chadronites to the Pace Theatre on Main Street to see such films as D. W. Griffith's "Birth of a Nation," Rudolph Valentino in "The Four Horsemen of the Apocalypse," and Al Jolson in "The Jazz Singer." Like other small towns, Chadron also created a municipal band, emulating the John Philip Sousa craze. Spurred on by Sousa, Iaeger (who played a number of musical instruments himself) formed a band in Chadron, and it played for various civic events. The thirty-six-piece band made at least one trip to Omaha, in 1906, to see its march master's old crony James C. Dahlman. Iaeger always seemed to be where the action was.[6]

While Iaeger lived in Chadron, his state and nation were striving to come to terms with the new

---

[6]For a brief cultural survey, see John Olsen's chapter in Rolland Dewing, et al., *Chadron Centennial History: 1885-1985* (Chadron, Nebraska: Chadron Narrative History Project Committee, 1985), 81-88.

machine age. This technological challenge manifested itself in different ways, but one of the most fundamental was the appearance of the automobile. Chadron's streets were graced with vehicles ranging alphabetically from Buick to Whippet, and "Billy the Bear" was not left out. He travelled around Chadron in a little vehicle supposedly designed by son Richard.

Small-town America was a collection of joiners, and "Billy the Bear" was among them. Before television and movies and with limited outside communication, Americans in the hinterlands joined clubs and societies by the dozens. Different clubs seemed to cater to different professions: The Masonic blue lodge in Chadron, for example, was heavily populated with railroaders from the Chicago and Northwestern, and Rotary catered especially to businessmen. One of Chadron's several fraternal clubs was the Eagles, and

Left: "Billy the Bear" with "Cowboy Jim" Dahlman
in Omaha on a band trip in 1906
Right: "Billy the Bear" in a vehicle he used
around the town of Chadron

one of its most prominent members was "Billy the Bear" Iaeger. He took a prominent leadership role, not just locally but statewide: He served as state treasurer and ran for the state office of Grand Worthy Secretary.[7]

Irrespective of where his intellectual or social diversions took him, in his serious moments Iaeger always returned to politics. Plato said that people are political beings. Quite right. Some are more political than others, however, and "Billy the Bear" fell into that fold. He took his politics passionately, actively identifying himself as a Democrat and strongly supporting the party in both Dawes County and Nebraska. He sensed that the party of Jefferson expressed the interests of the common folk better than the monied aristocracy of the G.O.P. This political prism, somewhat accurate yet also somewhat simplistic, guided Billy as a commandment writ in stone.[8]

Such attitudes were both product and shaper of America's political crucibles. Iaeger's settling in Chadron coincided with one of the most fundamental political upheavals in American history—the emergence of the Farmer's Alliance and the Populists. It was symptomatic of the nation's agricultural depression and of the willingness of normally conservative farmers to search for alternatives outside the traditional two-party system. Iaeger's faith in the Democratic party never wavered, but many Americans lost faith in both the Democrats and the Republicans in the late 1880s and 1890s. Nonetheless, in 1896, Iaeger, a resident of a rural community and good Democrat, likely

---

[7]*Mediator*, June 22, 1907.

[8]For a history of Cornhusker Democrats, see James F. Pedersen and Kenneth D. Wald, *Shall the People Rule? A History of the Democratic Party in Nebraska Politics, 1854-1912* (Lincoln, Nebraska: Jacob North, 1972).

enthusiastically supported both hard-pressed farmers and fusion candidate William Jennings Bryan.[9]

After the turn of the century, "Billy the Bear" probably also favorably inclined toward at least some of the progressive movement's reform program. He seemed continually to be for the "underdog" of society; so the progressives, at least those typified by municipal reformers and anti-trusters, likely received his support.

Richard (left) and Louis Iaeger, Jr., ca. 1914

Iaeger did not participate as a soldier in either the Spanish-American War or World War I in spite of his political activism,

---

[9]As a "favorite son," Bryan took Nebraska's eight electoral votes, but the popular vote was rather evenly matched. Bryan received 115,999 to McKinley's 103,064. In Dawes County, the Republicans received 825 votes, Democrats 26, Democrats & People's Independent 938, and a sprinkling of people voted for the National, Prohibition and Socialist Labor candidates (*Abstracts of Votes Cast: Book B*, Dawes County Courthouse, Chadron, Nebraska).

for obvious reasons. Still, his enthusiasm and support went with fellow Chadronites who served to "make the world safe for democracy" in World War I. Chadron saw Company H of the National Guard organized. This unit eventually made it to Europe as part of the 34th "Sandstorm" Division which arrived in France on October 5, 1918. Iaeger served on the homefront, where he was active in the American Red Cross. His wife Temperance rolled bandages for the Red Cross to send overseas, and both of their sons Louis, Jr., and Richard enlisted. Richard, being under age, was sent home when his indiscretion was discovered. With a German name and heritage, one wonders if "Billy the Bear" suffered from the anti-German hysteria common in Nebraska during the war, since the Dawes County Council of Defense zealously insured that Kaiser Wilhelm got no support locally.[10]

As the Twenties roared to a close—that decade of Coolidge prosperity, Babe Ruth, speakeasies, the Charleston, Al Capone, the Ku Klux Klan, and buying stock on the margin—so did the life of "Billy the Bear" Iaeger. His America, that of rip-roaring Gilded-Age empire-builders, of cowboys and miners, was gone. His health began to fail also. In 1924 Iaeger suffered his first stroke, which left him speechless and paralyzed for a brief time; in 1930 he suffered a second. Unlike the stricken bear on the San Francisco stage, he now could not escape the falling curtain. He died on March 6, 1930, in Chadron. He had lived forty-five of his seventy-four years in the Chadron area and had served as clerk of the district court for the last twenty-two years. All

---

[10]For studies on this episode, see Frederick Luebke, *Bonds of Loyalty: German Americans and World War I* (DeKalb, Illinois: Northern Illinois University Press, 1974); and Robert N. Manley, "Nebraska State Council of Defense," Master's Thesis, Department of History, University of Nebraska at Lincoln, 1959.

DEMOCRATIC CANDIDATE
for Clerk *of* the District Court

VOTE FOR
☒ L. J. F. IAEGER
(Billy, the Bear)

While I am unable to do physical labor, it is acknowledged by all
that I can do this kind of work with credit to the office and myself.   Your vote will give me that opportunity.

Top: "Billy the Bear," 1920
Bottom: "Billy the Bear's" campaign card, 1920

city businesses and all courthouse offices closed during Iaeger's funeral, which was conducted by Rev. E. C. Newland of the Congregational Church. "Billy the Bear" was laid to rest in the town's Greenwood Cemetery.[11]

A decade after her husband's death, Temperance and family moved to southern California. She and Louis, Jr., died there and are buried in Forest Lawn Cemetery in Pasadena, alongside Louis's wife Hildur Anderson Iaeger and daughter Madeline Iaeger Butler. Richard also died in California but was returned to Chadron to be buried beside his father.

---

[11]*Chadron Chronicle*, March 13, 1930.

Bibliography

Books

Andrist, Ralph K. *The Long Death: The Last Days of the Plains Indians*. London: Collier Books, 1969.

_____. *The American Heritage History of the Confident Years, 1865-1916*. New York: American Heritage, 1987.

Athearn, Robert C. *High Country Empire*. New York: McGraw-Hill, 1960.

Atherton, Lewis. *The Cattle Kings*. Lincoln, Nebraska: University of Nebraska Press, 1972.

Aymar, Brandt, ed. *Men at Sea: The Best Sea Stories of All Time*. New York: Dorset Press, 1988.

Bronson, Edgar Beecher. *Reminiscenses of a Ranchman*. Chicago, Illinois: A. C. McClurg & Co., 1911.

Caughey, John Walton. *Hubert Howe Bancroft: Historian of the West*. Berkeley, California: University of California Press, 1946.

Cody, William F. "Buffalo Bill." *The Adventures of Buffalo Bill*. New York: Bonanza, 1904.

Creigh, Dorothy Weyer. *Nebraska, Where Dreams Grow*. Lincoln, Nebraska: Miller & Paine, 1980.

Dewing, Rolland, *et. al. Chadron Centennial History: 1885-1985*. Chadron, Nebraska: Chadron Narrative History Project Committee, 1985.

Dykstra, Robert R. *The Cattle Towns*. New York: Atheneum, 1970.

Fussell, Paul, ed. *The Norton Book of Travel*. New York: W. W. Norton, 1987.

Hutton, Harold. *Doc Middleton: Life and Legend of the Notorious Plains Outlaw*. Chicago, Illinois: Swallow Press, 1974.

Luebke, Frederick. *Bonds of Loyalty: German Americans and World War I*. Dekalb, Illinois: Northern Illinois University Press, 1974.

Manley, Robert N. "Nebraska State Council of Defense." Master's Thesis, Department of History, University of Nebraska at Lincoln, 1959.

Olson, James C. *Red Cloud and the Sioux Problem*. Lincoln, Nebraska: University of Nebraska Press, 1965.

Osgood, Ernest Staples. *The Day of the Cattleman.* Chicago: University of Chicago Press, 1968.

Pedersen, James F., and Kenneth D. Wald. *Shall the People Rule? A History of the Democratic Party in Nebraska Politics, 1854-1912.* Lincoln, Nebraska: Jacob North, 1972.

Radcliffe, Byron "Rip." *The Chadron to Chicago Cowboy Horserace of 1893.* Chadron, Nebraska: B & B Printing, 1984.

Russell, Don. *The Lives and Legends of Buffalo Bill.* Norman, Oklahoma: University of Oklahoma Press, 1960.

Sandoz, Mari. *Old Jules.* Lincoln, Nebraska: University of Nebraska Press, 1962.

Sheldon, Addison E. *Nebraska: The Land and the People.* 3 vols. Chicago, Illinois: The Lewis Publishing Company, 1931.

Shepherd, Allen. *Madrid: A Centennial History.* Astoria, Illinois: K. K. Stevens Publishing Company, 1987.

Stone, Irving. *Men to Match My Mountains.* New York: Berkeley Books, 1983.

Watson, George, Jr. *Prairie Justice: A 100 Year Legal Study of Chadron and Dawes County.* Chadron, Nebraska: B & B Printing, 1985.

Articles

Higgins, Jay (Forest Supervisor). Memorandum, Halsey, Nebraska, March 19, 1924. In E. Steve Cassells and Larry D. Agenbroad (comps.), *Cultural Resource Overview of the Nebraska National Forest.* Longmont, Colorado: Plano Archaeological Consultants, 1981.

"Louis John Frederick Iaeger." In Addison Erwin Sheldon. *Nebraska: the Land and the People.* Vol. 3. Chicago, Illinois: The Lewis Publishing Company, 1931.

"Louis John Frederick Iaeger." In *Compendium of History, Reminiscences, and Biography of Western Nebraska.* Chicago, Illinois: Alden Publishing Company, 1909.

Masefield, John. "Sea Fever." In *Salt-Water Ballads.* New York: Macmillan Company, 1916.

Newspapers

Chadron Chronicle: March 13, 1930.
Chadron Citizen: February 23, 1893.
Chadron Journal: April 15, 1892; June 21, 1901.
Chadron Times: July 28, 1905.
Mediator: June 22, 1907.
Omaha Daily News Magazine: November 16, 1919.
Rushville Standard: March 19, 1906.

Archives

Dawes County Courthouse, Chadron, Nebraska. *Abstracts of Votes Cast: Book B.*
Iaeger, John Frederick William "Billy the Bear." *Diaries.* Dawes County Historical Society, Chadron, Nebraska.
_____. *Scrapbooks and Memorabilia.* Dawes County Historical Society, Chadron, Nebraska.

INDEX

Man of Many Frontiers is full of many individual people's names, and most, but not all, of them, are indexed here. Only where "Billy the Bear" provided both first and last names at some place in his diary did we include a person in the index; moreover, when only a first or last name appeared, we included the page number only when we were certain who was being discussed.

524

Making History is a historical consulting firm in Omaha, Nebraska, that specializes in historical research, writing, lectures, exhibits, and publishing, in addition to the restoration and reprinting of historic and heirloom photographs. If you are interested in preparing a special historical exhibit, if you need the perfect lecturer for an event or fundraiser, or if you have a non-fiction historical manuscript you wish to publish, write or call us at:

Making History

2415 N. 56th Street
Omaha, Nebraska 68104
(402) 551-0747

MAIL ORDER FORM

Please send the following to the address below (PRINT CLEARLY):

Name_____

Organization_____

Street/Box_____

City_____State_____Zip Code_____

QUANTITY	TITLE	TOTAL
_____	Jerry E. Clark, *Nebraska Diamonds: A Brief History of Baseball Major Leaguers from the Cornhusker State* (92pp; ISBN 0-9631699-0-4) $11.50	$_____
_____	Jerry E. Clark, *Anson to Zuber: Iowa Boys in the Major Leagues* (234pp; ISBN 0-9631699-1-2) $20.00	_____
_____	Jerry E. Clark and Martha Ellen Webb, *Alexander the Great: The Story of Grover Cleveland Alexander* (60pp; ISBN 0-9631699-2-0) $10.00	_____
_____	Robert E. Adwers, *Rudder, Stick and Throttle: Research and Reminiscences on Flying in Nebraska* (458pp; ISBN 0-9631699-4-7) $25.00	_____
_____	Dr. Allen Shepherd, Belvadine R. Lecher, Lloy Chamberlin, and Marguerite Radcliffe (eds.), *Man of Many Frontiers: The Diaries of "Billy the Bear" Iaeger* (553pp; ISBN 0-9631699-3-9) $25.00	_____

Subtotal $_____

Nebraska residents add 6.5% sales tax _____

Add $3.00 for first copy; $1.75 each additional (shipping)_____

Total balance enclosed (US funds only) $_____

Please make check or money order payable to *Making History*.

Mail your completed order form and check or money order to:
Making History, 2415 N. 56th Street, Omaha, Nebraska 68104.

Organizational/wholesale discounts available.
Write or call 402-551-0747 for information.

MAIL ORDER FORM

Please send the following to the address below (PRINT CLEARLY):
Name_____
Organization_____
Street/Box_____
City_____State_____Zip Code_____

QUANTITY	TITLE	TOTAL
_____	Jerry E. Clark, *Nebraska Diamonds: A Brief History of Baseball Major Leaguers from the Cornhusker State* (92pp; ISBN 0-9631699-0-4) $11.50	$_____
_____	Jerry E. Clark, *Anson to Zuber: Iowa Boys in the Major Leagues* (234pp; ISBN 0-9631699-1-2) $20.00	_____
_____	Jerry E. Clark and Martha Ellen Webb, *Alexander the Great: The Story of Grover Cleveland Alexander* (60pp; ISBN 0-9631699-2-0) $10.00	_____
_____	Robert E. Adwers, *Rudder, Stick and Throttle: Research and Reminiscences on Flying in Nebraska* (458pp; ISBN 0-9631699-4-7) $25.00	_____
_____	Dr. Allen Shepherd, Belvadine R. Lecher, Lloy Chamberlin, and Marguerite Radcliffe (eds.), *Man of Many Frontiers: The Diaries of "Billy the Bear" Iaeger* (553pp; ISBN 0-9631699-3-9) $25.00	_____

Subtotal $_____

Nebraska residents add 6.5% sales tax _____

Add $3.00 for first copy; $1.75 each additional (shipping)_____

Total balance enclosed (US funds only) $_____
Please make check or money order payable to *Making History.*

Mail your completed order form and check or money order to:
Making History, 2415 N. 56th Street, Omaha, Nebraska 68104.

Organizational/wholesale discounts available.
Write or call 402-551-0747 for information.